Brazilian Portuguese

for dummies®
A Wiley Brand

Brazilian Portuguese

3rd Edition

by Karen Jacobson-Sive

Brazilian Portuguese For Dummies®, 3rd Edition

Published by: **John Wiley & Sons, Inc.**, 111 River Street, Hoboken, NJ 07030-5774, www.wiley.com

Copyright © 2022 by John Wiley & Sons, Inc., Hoboken, New Jersey

Published simultaneously in Canada

For general information on our other products and services, please contact our Customer Care Department within the U.S. at 877-762-2974, outside the U.S. at 317-572-3993, or fax 317-572-4002. For technical support, please visit https://hub.wiley.com/community/support/dummies.

Wiley publishes in a variety of print and electronic formats and by print-on-demand. Some material included with standard print versions of this book may not be included in e-books or in print-on-demand. If this book refers to media such as a CD or DVD that is not included in the version you purchased, you may download this material at http://booksupport.wiley.com. For more information about Wiley products, visit www.wiley.com.

Library of Congress Control Number: 2022939668

ISBN: 978-1-119-89465-0 (pbk); 978-1-119-89467-4 (ebk); 978-1-119-89466-7 (ebk)

SKY10078071_062124

Contents at a Glance

Introduction 1

Part 1: Getting Started with Brazilian Portuguese 7
CHAPTER 1: You Already Know Some Portuguese! 9
CHAPTER 2: The Nitty-Gritty: Basic Portuguese Grammar 25
CHAPTER 3: Oi! Hello! Greetings and Introductions 39
CHAPTER 4: Getting Your Numbers, Times, and Measurements Straight 61
CHAPTER 5: Speaking Portuguese at Home 77

Part 2: Brazilian Portuguese in Action 101
CHAPTER 6: Getting to Know You: Small Talk 103
CHAPTER 7: Dining Out and Going to the Market 121
CHAPTER 8: Shopping 141
CHAPTER 9: Going Out on the Town 157
CHAPTER 10: Using Technology To Keep In Touch 173
CHAPTER 11: Chatting About Business 195
CHAPTER 12: Recreation and the Outdoors 209

Part 3: Brazilian Portuguese on the Go 225
CHAPTER 13: Planning a Trip 227
CHAPTER 14: Money, Money, Money 253
CHAPTER 15: Getting Around: Planes, Buses, Taxis, and More 265
CHAPTER 16: Going to Sporting Events 293
CHAPTER 17: O Carnaval! 309
CHAPTER 18: Socorro! Help! Handling Emergencies 325

Part 4: The Part of Tens 341
CHAPTER 19: Ten Ways to Pick Up Brazilian Portuguese Quickly 343
CHAPTER 20: Ten Common Brazilian Portuguese Slang Words 349
CHAPTER 21: Ten (Plus One) Brazilian Portuguese Terms That Make
            You Sound Fluent 353

Part 5: Appendixes 357
APPENDIX A: Verb Tables 359
APPENDIX B: Portuguese-English Mini-Dictionary 369
APPENDIX C: Answer Key 389

Index 393

Table of Contents

INTRODUCTION 1
    About This Book. 2
    Conventions Used in This Book. 2
    Foolish Assumptions. 4
    How This Book Is Organized 4
        Part 1: Getting Started with Brazilian Portuguese 4
        Part 2: Brazilian Portuguese in Action 4
        Part 3: Brazilian Portuguese on the Go 5
        Part 4: The Part of Tens 5
        Part 5: Appendixes 5
    Icons Used in This Book 5
    Beyond the Book. 6
    Where to Go from Here 6

PART 1: GETTING STARTED WITH BRAZILIAN PORTUGUESE 7

CHAPTER 1: You Already Know Some Portuguese! 9
    Exploring the Roots of Portuguese. 10
    Reciting Your ABCs 11
    Conquering Consonants. 13
        The letter C 13
        The letter D. 14
        The letter G. 14
        The letter H. 15
        The letter J. 15
        The letter L. 15
        The letters M and N. 16
        The letter R. 16
        The letter S 17
        The letter T 17
        The letter W 18
        The letter X 18
    Exercising Your Jowls with Vowels 18
        The letters A and Ã 18
        The letters E and Ê 19
        The letter I. 20
        The letters O and Ô. 20
        The letter U. 20

Differentiating Regional Accents.............................21
    Rio de Janeiro...21
    Interior of São Paulo state................................21
    Northeastern Brazil...21
    Rio Grande do Sul...22
Recognizing the Sound of Portugal's Portuguese.................22

CHAPTER 2: **The Nitty-Gritty: Basic Portuguese Grammar** 25
Agreeing with Nouns and Adjectives 26
Looking at Articles...27
Introducing Pronouns..28
Examining Verbs and Building Simple Sentences............30
Delving into Verb Conjugations..............................31
    Using the -ar verbs..31
    Using the -er and -ir verbs................................34
Making Contractions: It's a Cinch!..........................35
To Me, to You: Indirect Objects 37

CHAPTER 3: **Oi! Hello! Greetings and Introductions** 39
Saying Hello 40
Making Introductions 41
Using First Names, Last Names, and Nicknames —
Brazilian-Style...42
Dividing the World between Formal and Informal..............43
Describing Permanent Qualities: Ser 46
    Using an example..47
    Warming up to ser..48
Describing Temporary Qualities: Estar......................51
    Using an example 52
    Warming up to estar..53
Speaking about Speaking: Falar 53
Saying Goodbye..57

CHAPTER 4: **Getting Your Numbers, Times,
and Measurements Straight**...........................61
Counting to 100 and Beyond...................................62
Ordering Sequences: First, Second, Third...................65
Telling Time 66
Talking about Days of the Week 68
Specifying Times and Dates....................................71
Getting Familiar with the Metric System 72

CHAPTER 5: Speaking Portuguese at Home 77

Seeing What Makes Up a Home 78

Living in the Big City 80

Getting Some Sleep..................82

Waking Up 83

Chatting about Food..................84

    Getting breakfast..................85

    Discussing lunch 86

    Cooking up dinner..................87

Cleaning House 89

Going for a Walk Around the Neighborhood 90

Making a Phone Call 92

    Connecting with the calling verb: Ligar 96

    Dealing with verbal mush..................97

Being a Gracious Guest 99

PART 2: BRAZILIAN PORTUGUESE IN ACTION 101

CHAPTER 6: Getting to Know You: Small Talk 103

Where Are You From?..................103

Figuring Out Family Connections 107

Using Possessives: "My . . ."..................108

Knowing Who, What, and Where 111

Talking in the Past Tense 112

Pulling It Together with Connector Words..................117

Three "Save Me!" Phrases..................118

Sharing Your Contact Information 118

CHAPTER 7: Dining Out and Going to the Market 121

Trying Brazilian Foods..................121

    Sampling the classics 122

    Finding a place to eat 123

    Perusing the menu 124

    Bom apetite! Ordering and enjoying your meal 126

    Satisfying your sweet tooth 128

Buying Drinks..................131

Basking in Brazilian Barbeque..................132

Mastering Eating and Drinking Verbs..................133

Shopping at the Market 135

    Picking up practical items..................136

    Buying produce at an outdoor market..................136

CHAPTER 8: **Shopping** 141
Scoping Out the Shopping Scene 141
Saying What You're Looking For 142
Talking about what you want to buy 142
Naming colors in Portuguese 144
Trying and Trying On: The Verb Experimentar 145
Taking It: The Verb Levar 146
Making Comparisons and Expressing Opinions 148
Exploring Brazilian Treasures 151
Negotiating Price in Outdoor Markets 153

CHAPTER 9: **Going Out on the Town** 157
Talking about Going Out 157
Inviting someone out and being invited. 158
Asking what a place or event is like 159
Taking in Brazil's Musical Culture 160
Using the musical verb: Tocar 161
Using the dancing verb: Dançar 163
Using the singing verb: Cantar. 163
Exploring Art. 164
Going to the Movies 165
Falling in Love — in Portuguese 168

CHAPTER 10: **Using Technology To Keep In Touch** 173
Talking and Texting with a Digital Device. .174
Dealing with verbal mush. 177
Connecting with the calling verb: Ligar 179
Telling Someone to Call You 180
Leaving a Message 181
Making Arrangements over the Phone 183
Texting to Check In 184
Digital Talk Know-How 184
Staying Informed through the Internet 186
Emailing 187
Socializing on Social Media 190
Keeping Your Tablet at Your Fingertips 191
Talking about Feelings Using Words and Emoji 192

CHAPTER 11: **Chatting About Business** 195
Qual a sua profissão? What Do You Do? 196
Applying the doing verb: Fazer 197
Mailing Things the Old-Fashioned Way 201

Placing a Business Call 202
Making Appointments and Conducting Meetings 203
    Expressing profit, loss, revenue, and expenses 204
    Asking about business goals 205
Working from Home 205

CHAPTER 12: **Recreation and the Outdoors** 209
Finding Out What's Really on a Brazilian Beach 210
    Getting outfitted for a day at the beach. 210
    Checking out other beach attractions .212
    Describing beautiful beaches 214
Exploring the Amazon Rainforest 216
Talking about Biodiversity 217
    Considering plant life 218
    Identifying wildlife 218
Asking People What They Like to Do 219

PART 3: BRAZILIAN PORTUGUESE ON THE GO 225
CHAPTER 13: **Planning a Trip** 227
Picking the Best Time for Your Trip 228
Obtaining a Passport and Visa. 232
Researching Public Health Concerns 232
Packing for Your Brazilian Getaway 233
Deciding Where to Go. 234
    The North 235
    The Northeast 235
    The Central-West 236
    The Southeast 237
    The South 238
Talking about Going: The Verb Ir. 241
Going Through Customs. 244
Choosing a Place to Sleep 245
    Making reservations 245
    Checking in and out: Registration 246
    Asking about amenities 247
Getting Possessive. 248

CHAPTER 14: **Money, Money, Money** 253
Introducing Brazilian Reais and Centavos .253
Getting Ahold of Brazilian Currency 254
Using Brazilian Banks and ATMs. 256

Checking Prices and Making Purchases.........................258
    The paying verb: Pagar........................259
    Paying for items and services 260

CHAPTER 15: **Getting Around: Planes, Buses, Taxis, and More** ...265
Making a Plane Reservation...........................266
Taking Buses 270
Traveling by Taxi 271
Using Ride-Hailing Apps..............................274
Renting a Car 275
    Interpreting traffic signs..........................277
    Parking it...277
Talking About Coming and Going 278
    Announcing an arrival.............................278
    Talking about leaving 279
    Discussing the wait 280
Navigating Cityscapes.................................281
    Talking about distance............................283
    Asking for directions 285
    Discussing how to get there.......................287
    Over here, over there 290

CHAPTER 16: **Going to Sporting Events** 293
Getting Hip to Soccer — Brazil's National Pastime...............294
Buying Tickets 295
Finding Your Seat....................................297
Ordering Brazilian Concessions 298
Making Sense of Yelling Fans..........................300
Talking about Sports..................................301
    Using the verb jogar, to play 301
    Considering practice 302
    Expressing preferences 303
    Winning and losing 304
Searching the Place...................................304

CHAPTER 17: **O Carnaval!** 309
Exploring Carnaval in Brazil 310
    Rio's Carnaval....................................311
    Carnaval in Salvador 314
    Carnaval in Recife/Olinda 318
Dancing the Samba! 320

CHAPTER 18: **Socorro! Help! Handling Emergencies**..............325

Stick 'em Up: What to Say (and Do) if You're Robbed...........326

Don't panic!...........327

Asking for and receiving help..........328

Reporting a problem to the police 329

Handling Health Emergencies.....................330

Heading off illnesses with vaccines.....................330

Watching out for tropical illnesses 331

Expressing pandemic-related needs 432

Dealing with your normal illnesses..................333

Handling injuries 334

Talking about your health problem 335

Discussing Legal Problems....................338

PART 4: THE PART OF TENS....................341

CHAPTER 19: **Ten Ways to Pick Up Brazilian Portuguese Quickly** 343

Go to Brazil!....................343

Find Brazilians (Or Other Portuguese Speakers) Near You........344

Date a Brazilian 344

Read the News in Portuguese 345

Check Out Brazilian Websites 345

Listen to Brazilian Music....................346

Watch a Brazilian Movie....................347

Watch Globo....................348

Take a Portuguese Language Class....................348

"Say It Again, João!" 348

CHAPTER 20: **Ten Common Brazilian Portuguese Slang Words**....................349

Brega/Cafona....................349

Cara....................350

Chato....................350

Chique....................350

Esperto....................350

Gato and Gata....................351

Grana....................351

Legal 352

Pinga....................352

Valeu....................352

CHAPTER 21: **Ten (Plus One) Brazilian Portuguese Terms That Make You Sound Fluent** 353

Né? 353
Tá 354
Ah é? 354
Então 354
Sabe? 355
Meio 355
Ou seja 355
Cê Instead of Você 355
A gente 356
Pra 356
Tô 356

PART 5: APPENDIXES 357

APPENDIX A: **Verb Tables** 359

APPENDIX B: **Portuguese-English Mini-Dictionary** 369

APPENDIX C: **Answer Key** 389

INDEX 393

Introduction

Brazil's diversity is immense, whether you consider the Indigenous, African, and European roots of the majority of its inhabitants or whether you put the staggering biodiversity of Brazil's lush landscapes under a microscope. Latin America's most populous and largest nation is also the region's largest economy — and it just happens to be home to friendly people, stunning beaches, and great music.

Need I say more? (I can't stop gushing — did you know that Brazil is in the *Guinness Book of World Records* for having the biggest street carnival in the world, in Salvador, Bahia?). Yes, it's time to learn Brazilian Portuguese.

Business or pleasure — the book in your hands is perfect as a solid crash course for learning Brazilian Portuguese, no matter your motive. I've stocked this book with cultural insights to complement the basics of the language. This third edition even has a chapter for businesspeople who are interested in speaking a bit of Portuguese to enhance their career. I've also updated the book to go over social media vocab, even including slang abbreviations you can use to react to posts online.

Portuguese is the sixth most-spoken language in the world, due in large part to Brazil's huge population that hovers now around 213 million. Be sure to check out Chapter 1 to find out which other countries in the world, including Portugal, speak Portuguese. I point out differences between the Portuguese that's spoken in Brazil and Portugal in Chapter 1, but this book focuses on Brazilian Portuguese.

A bonus to learning Brazilian Portuguese is that it can help you to understand a little French, Spanish, and Italian, too. They're all Romance languages, so many words of these languages sound similar.

The sounds of Brazilian Portuguese can be difficult to make for non-native speakers, but stick with it and have fun. I'm not promising fluency here, but you can find out how to make small talk with a Brazilian, ask for directions in a city, and even make some plans. So go buy yourself some Brazilian music and fill your space with the sounds of Brazil. You'll fall in love with this lyrical language.

About This Book

Here's the good news: This isn't a class you have to drag yourself to or a language book that's weighed down with complicated grammar rules, like so many others you may find in a bookstore or online. It's a reference book for learning to speak Brazilian Portuguese that you can pick up at your leisure. You're the boss. You may choose to leaf through, glancing only at chapters and pages that grab your attention. Or you can read the whole thing from start to finish. (From finish to start is okay, too — no one's looking.)

The first few chapters may be helpful to read first, though, because they offer basic information about pronunciation and point out words that appear throughout the book. Of course, if there's a chapter you just have to read first, it's okay. After all, if you're heading to Brazil for Carnaval or for business, I'm guessing you'll want to flip to those chapters right away.

Just keep in mind that more advanced instruction comes later in the book as your knowledge and ability progresses. However, all chapters contain background, grammar, and dialogues that reflect the information you need to know at a particular level and in the situation of focus.

Conventions Used in This Book

To make the book easy to follow, I've set up a few stylistic rules:

» Portuguese terms are set in **boldface** to make them stand out.

» Pronunciations and definitions, which are shown in parentheses, follow the terms the first time they appear in a section.

» Within the pronunciation, the part of the word that's stressed is shown in *italics*.

» English translations appear in italics.

» Verb conjugations (lists that show you the different forms of a verb) are given in tables in this order: *I, you* (singular), *he/she, we, they,* and *you* (plural). Pronunciations follow in a second column.

Here's an example of a conjugation chart for the word **ser** (seh) (*to be*). Because the subjects always come in the same order, you can see that words in this chart mean *I am, you are, he/she is, we are, they are,* and *you are.*

Conjugation	Pronunciation
eu sou	*eh*-ooh *soh*
você é	voh-*seh eh*
ele/ela é	*eh*-lee/*eh*-la *eh*
nós somos	*nohz soh*-mooz
eles/elas são	*eh*-leez/*eh*-lahz *sah*-ooh
vocês são	voh-*sehz sah*-ooh

In each chapter, you can also find the following sections:

>> **Talkin' the Talk dialogues:** The best (and most fun) way to learn a language is to hear real-life dialogues, so I include little conversations throughout the book. The dialogues come under the heading "Talkin' the Talk" and show you the Portuguese words, how to pronounce them, and their English translations. Most of these conversations exist as audio files you can find online on the website associated with this book (www.dummies.com/go/brazilianportuguesefd3e), so when you see an Audio Online icon, be sure to listen along.

>> **Words to Know blackboards:** Knowing key words and phrases is also important in the quest to speak a new language. I collect important words that appear in the Talkin' the Talk dialogues (and perhaps add a few related terms) and put them in a special blackboard-shaped box that follows the dialogues.

>> **Fun & Games activities:** At the end of each chapter, find an activity designed to help you practice some of the words and concepts featured in that chapter. Don't worry; the exercises cover the essentials of a topic — nothing too difficult. The answers to these exercises are in Appendix C so you can quickly find out whether you got the right answers!

Foolish Assumptions

To write this book, I had to imagine who my readers would be. Yes, you! I think if you've picked up this book, you're probably an open-minded person who enjoys learning. That's excellent. Here are some other things I imagine about you:

>> You're interested in learning enough conversational Brazilian Portuguese to get by in most social situations, not fluency.

>> You don't want to memorize long lists of vocabulary to learn Portuguese.

>> You have little or no experience with the Portuguese language.

>> You're interested in learning about Brazilian culture as well as its language.

The only thing I ask of you is to leave any foolish assumptions behind that might prevent you from getting the most out of this book. For example, it's nonsense that only younger people can learn languages. The desire to learn is all you need. And it doesn't matter how well you did in high school French or German, or whichever language classes you've taken before. This book is designed to take a fresh approach to learning languages, and I won't grade you.

How This Book Is Organized

This book is divided by topic into parts and then into chapters. Chapters are further divided into sections. The following sections tell you what types of information you can find in each part.

Part 1: Getting Started with Brazilian Portuguese

This part covers the basics of Portuguese — how to pronounce words, construct sentences, and so on. I also point out Portuguese words that are so close to English that you already know their meanings.

Part 2: Brazilian Portuguese in Action

Discover everyday words and phrases in Portuguese and practice speaking this language. Instead of focusing on grammar points and philosophizing about why the language is structured the way it is, I jump right in to show you how it works.

This section highlights how to talk to new Brazilian friends and business associates.

Part 3: Brazilian Portuguese on the Go

Here are the tools you need to take your Portuguese on the road, whether you're trying to figure out which part of Brazil you want to visit or talking with a Brazilian about the bus schedule. These chapters are devoted to the traveler in you, the one who checks into hotels, hails a cab, and attends sporting events or Carnaval in Brazil.

Part 4: The Part of Tens

If you're looking for quick advice about Portuguese, this part is for you. Here, you can find ten ways to pick up Portuguese quickly, ten common slang expressions, and ten expressions to help you sound fluent (even if you're faking it).

Part 5: Appendixes

This part of the book is a straightforward reference — conjugation tables for the most common verbs and two mini-dictionaries: one translates common words from English to Portuguese; the other defines Portuguese words in English. Here, too, is where you find answers to the Fun & Games activities.

Icons Used in This Book

Drawings and symbols always liven things up a bit, don't they? Here are some icons that point you to important information:

TIP

This icon shows you where you can find some fascinating tidbits that highlight either a linguistic aspect or give travel tips. Tips can save you time and frustration.

REMEMBER

This handy icon pops up whenever you run across a bit of information that you really should remember after you close the book. These tidbits may tell you something important about the Portuguese language or Brazil in general.

SOUND
NATIVE

When you see this icon, you can find insider pronunciation and vocab tips that go beyond basic Portuguese and can help you impress your Brazilian friends.

CULTURAL WISDOM

These snippets provide insight into Brazilian culture.

AUDIO ONLINE

The online audio files contain conversations between native Brazilians. This icon marks the "Talkin' the Talk" sections that are included online at www.dummies.com/go/brazilianportuguesefd3e and reminds you that you can listen to the dialogue while you read it.

Beyond the Book

In addition to what you're reading right now, this book comes with a free, access-anywhere Cheat Sheet containing tips and techniques for learning Brazilian Portuguese faster. To get this Cheat Sheet, simply go to www.dummies.com and type **Brazilian Portuguese For Dummies Cheat Sheet** in the search box.

Where to Go from Here

When you have a spare moment, pop open the book to find out about Brazil and Brazilian Portuguese. Also, try to complement the information in this book with other activities that enhance your knowledge of Portuguese, such as reading the news in Portuguese or listening to Brazilian music. Have fun! Oh, and **boa sorte** (*boh-ah soh-chee*) (*good luck*)!

1

Getting Started with Brazilian Portuguese

IN THIS PART . . .

See the links between Portuguese and English.

Master the basics of Portuguese grammar.

Say "Hello" — and "Goodbye."

Work with numbers, time, and measurements.

Be a homebody — in Portuguese.

Chapter **1**

You Already Know Some Portuguese!

M uch like English, the Portuguese language comes in several different versions. The accent you hear in Brazil is pretty different from the Portuguese that's spoken in Portugal. In fact, some Brazilian tourists in Portugal say they can't understand a word that's spoken there! The situation is similar to a conversation among English speakers from Texas, South Africa, and Ireland: It would probably sound like they were speaking three different languages. No doubt they'd struggle to understand each other.

Within Brazil, there are also regional differences in the way people speak — just as accents differ in various regions of the United States. Think about the accents of people in Alabama, Minnesota, and New York. So it is in Brazil. People in **São Paulo** (sah-ooh *pah*-ooh-loh), **Rio de Janeiro** (*hee*-ooh dee zhah-*nay*-roh), and the touristy city of **Salvador** (sahl-vah-*doh*) have different twangs to their speech, but it's still pretty easy to understand all of them if you know Portuguese.

Written Portuguese, however, is pretty standard, especially the writing you find in a newspaper or other type of publication. A Brazilian can understand a Portuguese newspaper or read the works of Portugal's Nobel Prize–winning author **José Saramago** (zhoh-*zeh* sah-rah-*mah*-goh), no problem.

The Portuguese in this book is Brazilian Portuguese, as opposed to the Portuguese spoken in Portugal and countries in Africa, including **Cabo Verde** (*kah*-boh *veh*-jee) (*Cape Verde*; islands off northwestern Africa), **Moçambique** (moh-sahm-*bee*-kee) (*Mozambique*; on the coast of southeast Africa), **Guiné-Bissau** (*gwee*-neh bee-*sah*-ooh) (*Guinea Bissau*; in western Africa), **Angola** (ahn-*goh*-lah) (in southwestern Africa), and **São Tomé e Príncipe** (*sah*-ooh toh-*meh* ee *preen*-see-pee) (*Sao Tome and Principe*; islands off western Africa).

Exploring the Roots of Portuguese

The beautiful Portuguese language belongs to a linguistic family known as the Romance languages. Back when the Roman Empire was around, Rome was the center of a wide swath of Europe, northern Africa, and parts of Asia. With Rome's influence came its language — Latin.

The closer a place was to Rome, the more likely it was to absorb Latin into its language. This was the case with Portugal — where the Portuguese language originates — as well as the language of places like France, Spain, and even Romania.

So how did Portuguese get all the way to Brazil? A Portuguese conquistador named **Pedro Álvares Cabral** (*peh*-droh *ahl*-vah-reez kah-*brah*-ooh) landed in modern-day Brazil on April 22, 1500, and is the person credited for having "discovered" Brazil. Many indigenous people were already living in the area, of course, many of whom spoke languages that are part of a linguistic family today called **Tupi-Guarani** (too-*pee* gwah-rah-*nee*).

CULTURAL WISDOM

Brazilian Portuguese uses some **Tupi-Guarani** words, which commonly appear as names of towns in Brazil — **Ubatuba** (*ooh*-bah-*too*-bah), for example, is a pretty beach town in **São Paulo** (*sah*-ooh pah-*ooh*-loh) state. The town is nicknamed **Uba-Chuva** because **chuva** (*shoo*-vah) means *rain* and it rains there a lot! **Tupi-Guarani** words also name native plants and animals. *Armadillo*, for example, is **tatu** (tah-*too*). After you get used to speaking Portuguese, figuring out whether a word is Latin-based or **Tupi-Guarani**-based is pretty easy.

Still other words in Brazilian Portuguese are based on African languages, a result of the vast influence that Africans had on creating modern-day Brazil and its culture.

While the development of the modern-day English language wasn't influenced by **Tupi-Guarani** or African languages, what you may not realize is that it has a lot of Latin influence. Linguists consider English to be a Germanic language, and it technically is. But due to the on-and-off French occupations of the British Isles, many of those French (Latin-based) words rubbed off on English. Some people say as much as 60 to 70 percent of English is Latin-based.

That's great news for you. It means that many Portuguese words have the same root as English words. The *root* of a word is usually the middle of the word — those few sounds that really define the meaning of a word. Some examples of Portuguese words that resemble English words and have the same meaning include **experimento** (eh-speh-ree-*men*-toh) (*experiment*), **presidente** (preh-zee-*dang*-chee) (*president*), **economia** (eh-koh-noh-*mee*-ah) (*economy*), **decisão** (deh-see-*zah*-ooh) (*decision*), **computador** (kom-*poo*-tah-*doh*) (*computer*), **liberdade** (lee-beh-*dah*-jee) (*liberty*), and **banana** (bah-*nah*-nah) (*banana*). And that's only to name a few!

Another benefit: **O português** (ooh poh-too-*gehz*) (*Portuguese*), like all Latin languages, uses the Roman alphabet. Accent marks that you don't find in English appear over some of the vowels, but they add to the charm of Portuguese. Learning Portuguese is much easier for English-speaking people than learning Japanese or Arabic, which use totally different alphabets.

Finally, due to the modern influence of the United States throughout the world — which, in many ways, is much greater than Rome's ancient influence — English words are used in Portuguese, with no adaptation in the way they're written. Examples include **email** (ee-*may*-oh), **shopping** (*shoh*-ping) (in Brazil, **shopping** is a noun that means "shopping mall"), and **show** (shoh) (*show/performance*).

Reciting Your ABCs

A few of the sounds in Brazilian Portuguese can be difficult to imitate at first, because the sounds aren't used in English. But most Brazilians can understand what you're saying, even if you don't say every **palavra** (pah-*lahv*-rah) (*word*) perfectly. Many Brazilians think a foreign **sotaque** (soh-*tah*-kee) (*accent*) is charming, so don't worry about it.

On the upside, the way that phonetic sounds correspond to letters in Brazilian Portuguese is very systematic — much more so than in English. This means that after you get used to the way a letter or combination of letters sounds in Brazilian Portuguese, you can get the hang of the language pretty quickly. There are few surprises in the **pronúncia** (proh-*noon*-see-ah) (*pronunciation*) of this beautiful language.

AUDIO ONLINE

The set of online audio files that accompany this book contains a pronunciation guide to give you a better feel for Portuguese sounds.

At the beginning of this chapter, did you notice that the pronunciation is shown in parentheses after the Portuguese word? That's how this book shares the pronunciation of all new words. The italicized part is where you put the emphasis on the word as you speak it.

Are you ready to discover the basics of **português** (poh-too-*gehz*) (*Portuguese*)? You can start with the alphabet. Practice spelling your name:

- » **a** (ah)
- » **b** (beh)
- » **c** (seh)
- » **d** (deh)
- » **e** (eh)
- » **f** (*eh*-fee)
- » **g** (zheh)
- » **h** (ah-*gah*)
- » **i** (ee)
- » **j** (*zhoh*-tah)
- » **k** (kah)
- » **l** (*eh*-lee)
- » **m** (*eh*-mee)
- » **n** (*eh*-nee)
- » **o** (awe)
- » **p** (peh)
- » **q** (keh)
- » **r** (*eh*-hee)
- » **s** (*eh*-see)
- » **t** (teh)
- » **u** (ooh)
- » **v** (veh)

» **w** (*dah*-bli yoo)

» **x** (sheez)

» **y** (*eep*-see-lohn)

» **z** (zeh)

TIP

When I refer to the sound *zh* as part of a phonetic transcription (the pronunciation guide in parenthesis), think of the *s* sound in the word *treasure*. That's the *zh* sound I'm talking about.

Conquering Consonants

Getting through this book should be a cinch after you go through the basic pronunciation guide in this section. Skipping the guide is okay, too — you can get the gist by listening to the online audio files and reading the pronunciations of words in other chapters aloud. But if you want to get a general idea of how to pronounce words that don't show up in this book, this is a great place to begin. I start with the consonants — you know, all those letters in the alphabet that aren't vowels.

SOUND NATIVE

Here's a fun aspect of Brazilian Portuguese. When a word ends in a consonant — most of these words are foreign (and mostly English) terms that Brazilians have adopted — it's pronounced with an added *ee* sound. Some examples are **club** (*kloo*-bee), **laptop** (lahp-ee-*top*-ee), **hip-hop** (heep-ee-*hoh*-pee), **rap** (*hah*-pee), and **rock** (*hoh*-kee).

That said, most consonants in Brazilian Portuguese have the same sound as in English. I point out the exceptions in the following sections.

Ready? Here we go!

The letter C

A **c** that begins a word usually sounds like a *k*:

» **café** (kah-*feh*) (*coffee*)

» **casa** (*kah*-zah) (*house*)

If the c has a hook–shaped mark under it, like this — ç — it makes an s sound:

>> **França** (*frahn*-sah) (*France*)

>> **serviço** (seh-*vee*-soo) (*service*)

The most common use of this type of **c**, called the **cedilha** (seh-*deel*-yah) (*cedilla*), is when a **c** comes at the end of a word that's followed by –ão. It's the Brazilian equivalent of the English –*tion* ending.

>> **evolução** (eh-voh-loo-*sah*-ooh) (*evolution*)

>> **promoção** (proh-moh-*sah*-ooh) (*sale/discount/sales promotion*)

The letter D

If a word begins with a **d**, the sound is a hard *d*, like in English:

>> **dançar** (dahn-*sah*) (*to dance*)

>> **data** (*dah*-tah) (*date* — as in calendar date)

The word **de** (jee), which means *of*, is an exception.

If the **d** comes in the middle of a word, it can have either a hard *d* sound or a *j* sound — as in the English word *jelly*.

>> **advogado** (ahj-voh-*gah*-doh) (*lawyer*)

>> **estado** (eh-*stah*-doh) (*state* — as in a state in a nation)

>> **liberdade** (lee-beh-*dah*-jee) (*freedom*)

>> **modelo** (moh-*deh*-loo) (*model*)

>> **pedir** (peh-*jee*) (*to ask for*)

The letter G

The **g** in Portuguese usually is a hard *g*, like in the English word *go*:

>> **gato** (*gah*-too) (*cat*)

>> **governo** (goh-*veh*-noo) (*government*)

>> **segundo** (seh-*goon*-doh) (*second*)

But **g** takes a *zh* sound, like the *s* in *treasure*, when followed by an **e** or **i**:

>> **biologia** (bee-oh-loh-*zhee*-ah) (*biology*)

>> **gente** (*zhang*-chee) (*people*)

The letter H

The Brazilian Portuguese **h** is a pretty versatile consonant. If the word begins with an **h**, the letter is silent:

>> **honesto** (oh-*neh*-stoh) (*honest*)

>> **hora** (*oh*-rah) (*hour*)

In the cases of words that contain **lh** or **nh**, the **h** sounds like a *y*:

>> **companhia** (kohm-pahn-*yee*-ah) (*company*)

>> **Espanha** (eh-*spahn*-yah) (*Spain*)

>> **maravilhoso** (mah-rah-veel-*yoh*-zoo) (*marvelous/amazing*)

>> **palhaço** (pahl-*yah*-soh) (*clown*)

The letter J

The **j** in Portuguese always sounds like the *zh* sound an *s* makes in the English word *treasure*:

>> **joelho** (zhoh-*el*-yoh) (*knee*)

>> **Jorge** (*zhoh*-zhee) (*George*)

>> **julho** (*zhool*-yoh) (*July*)

>> **loja** (*loh*-zhah) (*store*)

The letter L

The **l** in Portuguese normally sounds like the *l* in English:

>> **gelo** (*zheh*-loo) (*ice*)

>> **líder** (*lee*-deh) (*leader*)

But if it comes at the end of a word, the l sounds like *ooh:*

- » **mil** (mee-*ooh*) (*one thousand*)
- » **Natal** (nah-*tah*-ooh) (*Christmas*)

The letters M and N

The **m** and **n** in Portuguese generally sound like *m* and *n* in English:

- » **janela** (zhah-*neh*-lah) (*window*)
- » **medo** (*meh*-doo) (*fear*)
- » **mel** (*meh*-ooh) (*honey*)
- » **não** (*nah*-ooh) (*no*)

But at the end of a word, an **m** or **n** takes on an *ng* sound:

- » **cem** (sang) (*one hundred*)
- » **homem** (*oh*-mang) (*man*)

The letter R

If the word begins or ends with an **r**, the **r** sounds like an *h:*

- » **Roberto** (hoh-*beh*-too) (*Robert*)
- » **rosa** (*hoh*-zah) (*pink*)

If *r* comes in the middle of a word, on the accented syllable, it sounds like an even stronger **h**. In the words **porta** and **carta** that follow, use your belly to push air out of your mouth as you say the *h*. It's a breathy *h*, not a guttural sound.

- » **carta** (*kah*-tah) (*letter*)
- » **porta** (*poh*-tah) (*door*)

If a word has two **r**'s (**rr**), they make an *h* sound, as in **burro** (boo-*hoh*) (*dumb*). If the **r** comes at the end of a word, it also makes an *h* sound like in **burro:**

>> **caminhar** (kah-ming-*yah*) (*to walk*)

>> **gostar** (goh-*stah*) (*to like*)

The letter S

The Portuguese **s** is generally pronounced the same as the English *s*, except it often becomes a *z* sound at the end of a word:

>> **dedos** (*deh*-doos) (*fingers*)

>> **olhos** (*ohl*-yooz) (*eyes*)

An **s** between two vowels also makes a *z* sound:

>> **casa** (*kah*-zah) (*house*)

>> **coisa** (*koh*-ee-zah) (*thing*)

The letter T

The **t** in Portuguese has a soft *t* sound in general. In English, you don't use the soft *t* sound very often.

TIP

Say *ta, ta, ta* in a quiet voice, without making a soft 'h' as if you're marking a rhythm. That's the soft *t* of Portuguese.

>> **atuar** (ah-too-*ah*) (*to act*)

>> **motocicleta** (moh-too-see-*kleh*-tah) (*motorcycle*)

>> **Tailândia** (tah-ee-*lahn*-jee-ah) (*Thailand*)

But **t** sounds like *ch* when followed by an **e** or an **i**:

>> **forte** (*foh*-chee) (*strong*)

>> **notícia** (noh-*chee*-see-ah) (*news*)

>> **passaporte** (pah-sah-*poh*-chee) (*passport*)

>> **time** (*chee*-mee) (*team*)

The letter W

The letter **w** doesn't naturally occur in Portuguese, but when it does, it sounds like a *v*. The only places you really see a **w** is in a person's name.

>> **Wanderlei** (*vahn*-deh-lay)

>> **Wanessa** (vah-*neh*-sah)

The letter X

The **x** generally has a *sh* sound in Portuguese:

>> **axé** (ah-*sheh*), a popular Brazilian musical and dance genre

>> **bruxa** (*broo*-shah) (*witch*)

>> **lixo** (*lee*-shoo) (*garbage*)

>> **taxa** (*tah*-shah) (*rate*)

The letter **x** can also have a *ks* sound, as in English: **tóxico** (*tohk*-see-koh) (*toxic*).

And the **x** can also sound like a *z* in some cases, such as **exame** (eh-*zahm*-ee) (*exam*).

Exercising Your Jowls with Vowels

In this section, I go over all five vowels in Portuguese, including the ones with accent marks.

The letters A and Ã

The letter **a** normally has an *ah* sound:

>> **ajuda** (ah-*zhoo*-dah) (*help*)

>> **amigo** (ah-*mee*-goo) (*friend*)

>> **Tatiana** (tah-chee-*ah*-nah), a woman's name

TIP

If the **a** has a squiggly mark, or *til* (*chee*-ooh) (*tilde*), on top of it (**ã**), then the letter makes a nasal sound. Instead of opening your mouth to say *a*, as in the English word *at*, try closing your mouth almost completely while you make the same sound. Do you hear that? It becomes more of an *uh* than an *ah*. Then try to open your mouth (making the same sound) without bringing your lips farther apart. Yes, that's the **ã** sound!

The **ã** is very common in Brazilian Portuguese, but it took me more than a year to say it like a Brazilian. If you're in the same boat, don't sweat it; most Brazilians can understand what a person's trying to say even if the **ã** is pronounced wrong.

The **ã** occasionally comes at the end of a word:

>> **maçã** (mah-*sah*) (*apple*)

>> **Maracanã** (mah-rah-kah-*nah*), a soccer stadium in Rio

TIP

Most often, **ã** is followed by an **o** (**ão**). Together, these letters make an *ah-ooh* sound. But say it fast — *Ow!* — like you've hurt yourself and with the nasal sound you just practiced.

>> **informação** (een-foh-mah-*sah*-ooh) (*information*)

>> **não** (*nah*-ooh) (*no*)

The letters E and Ê

In general, the letter **e** sounds like *eh*, as in *egg* or *ten*:

>> **dedo** (*deh*-doo) (*finger*)

>> **elefante** (eh-leh-*fahn*-chee) (*elephant*)

If it comes at the end of a word, though, **e** usually has an *ee* sound:

>> **boate** (boh-*ah*-chee) (*nightclub*)

>> **dificuldade** (jee-fee-kool-*dah*-jee) (*difficulty*)

If the **e** has a hat on it (**ê**), don't worry; it's still the *eh* sound:

>> **gêmeo** (*zhem*-ee-oh) (*twin*)

>> **três** (trehz) (*three*)

The letter I

The letter **i** has an *ee* sound, pretty much without exception:

>> **inglês** (eeng-*glehz*) (*English*)

>> **livro** (*leev*-roh) (*book*)

The letters O and Ô

The letter **o** by itself has an easy-to-make *oh* sound.

>> **onda** (*ohn*-dah) (*wave*)

>> **ontem** (*ohn*-tang) (*yesterday*)

At the end of a word, though, it usually sounds like *oo*:

>> **Gramado** (grah-*mah*-doo), a city in Rio Grande do Sul state that's famous for its film festival

>> **tudo** (*too*-doo) (*everything/all*)

The **o** also comes with a hat (the circumflex) on it (**ô**), which makes an *oh* sound. The accent mark doesn't change the pronunciation of the letter.

>> **Alô?** (ah-*loh?*) (*Hello?*)

>> **ônibus** (*oh*-nee-boos) (*bus*)

The letter U

The **u** has an *ooh* sound:

>> **ou** (ooh) (*or*)

>> **urso** (*ooh*-soo) (*bear*)

>> **útil** (*ooh*-chee-ooh) (*useful*)

Differentiating Regional Accents

The Portuguese pronunciation I describe in this book works for most of Brazil, and it's certainly understandable to any Brazilian. But there are some minor differences in accent by region. Usually the difference is how people of a region say a certain sound and the intonation or musicality. In this section, I point out a few hallmarks of certain regional accents so you can tell which part of Brazil your conversation partner is from.

Rio de Janeiro

Cariocas (kah-ree-*oh*-kahs), people from the city of **Rio,** are famous for saying *sh* instead of *s.*

Word	Rio Pronunciation	Standard Pronunciation	Meaning
esquina	eh-*shkee*-nah	eh-*skee*-nah	*corner*
mulheres	mool-*yeh*-reesh	mool-*yeh*-reez	*women*

Interior of São Paulo state

People from inland **São Paulo** state (not the city of **São Paulo,** which is close-ish to the coast, compared with the rest of the state) — along with people in rural parts of the bordering state of Minas Gerais — are famous for sounding like Americans speaking bad Portuguese because they pronounce the Portuguese **r** in an accented syllable like a hard English *r* instead of a strong *h.*

Word	Interior of São Paulo Pronunciation	Standard Pronunciation
interior	een-teh-ree-*or*	een-teh-ree-*oh*
porta	*por*-tah	*poh*-tah

Northeastern Brazil

In this part of the country, which includes the big cities of **Natal** and **Fortaleza,** most people (**Bahia** state is an exception) say a hard *d* for **d** instead of *j* as in *jelly.* And their **t** is similar to a snappy English *t* instead of the *ch* sound made in the rest of Brazil.

Word	Northeastern Pronunciation	Standard Pronunciation	Meaning
bom dia	boh-oong *dee*-ah	boh-oong *jee*-ah	*good morning*
forte	*foh*-tee	*foh*-chee	*strong*

Rio Grande do Sul

Gaúchos (gah-*ooh*-shohz), people from **Rio Grande do Sul** state, are known for talking in a sing-song voice that goes up and down a lot. These people live near the borders of Argentina and Uruguay, so their accents sound more Spanish and Italian (many Italian immigrants settled in Argentina/Uruguay, as well as Spaniards) than Brazilian.

Recognizing the Sound of Portugal's Portuguese

The Portuguese tend to use the *sh* sound for the letter **s**, as people from **Rio** do. European Portuguese speakers also often drop the *e* from the end of words; **especialmente** (*especially*) becomes eh-*speh*-see-ah-ooh-*ment* in Portugal. In Brazil you hear eh-*speh*-see-ah-ooh-*men*-chee.

Slang is different in Portugal, too. For example, the Portuguese say **fixe** (feesh) instead of **legal** (lay-*gow*) to say *cool*, as in *That's cool, dude*. See Chapter 20 for more Portuguese slang.

FUN & GAMES

Try to match these Portuguese letters with the sound they generally make in English.

1. **a**   a. *s*

2. **u**   b. *ch*

3. **t**   c. *ooh*

4. **ç**   d. *v*

5. **w**   e. *ah*

See Appendix C for the answer key.

pronouns

» **Understanding verbs in their various forms**

» **Checking out Portuguese contractions**

» **Talking about what happens to you and me**

Chapter **2**

The Nitty-Gritty: Basic Portuguese Grammar

ck. Grammar. Remember that word from high school? Most people teach grammar as if words were complicated math symbols to be arranged just so. I think learning a language should be more about exploring fun cultural stuff. So I'm putting my foot down. In this chapter, grammar isn't presented as a set of rules to memorize. Instead, I describe Portuguese sentence-building by showing you how to assemble your ideas in everyday situations. (If you're disappointed about this because you really want to do some math, maybe you can get your fix in Chapter 4, where I show you how to say numbers in Portuguese.)

Figuring out how to categorize types of words and knowing where they go in a sentence is like putting together a puzzle. And here's some good news: Portuguese and English use the same pieces! When I say "pieces," I'm talking about categories of words that are used to construct sentences — parts of speech. Don't worry if you don't know what that means, we'll do a little review!

Agreeing with Nouns and Adjectives

Just like in English, nouns in Portuguese are a main feature of speech — the most important pieces of the puzzle. They're used to name people, places, and things, such as **casa** (*kah*-zah) (*house*), **amigo** (ah-*mee*-goo) (*friend*), **Maria** (mah-*ree*-ah), (*the name of a woman*), **caneta** (kah-*neh*-tah) (*pen*), and **Brasil** (brah-*zee*-ooh) (*Brazil*).

Portuguese nouns come in two types: masculine and feminine. Masculine nouns usually end in **-o,** and feminine nouns usually end in **-a.** If a noun ends in a different letter, you can look up the word's gender in a Portuguese-English dictionary. To an English speaker, assigning a gender to a door, a key, a chair, and other things may seem unfamiliar; but many non-English languages include this gender coding.

The gender of a noun is important because related adjectives need to match the noun they're describing. In other words, every time you describe a noun with an adjective in Portuguese — such as **bonita** (boo-*nee*-tah) (*pretty*) or **simpático** (seem-*pah*-chee-koo) (*nice*) — you change the last letter of the adjective to make it either masculine or feminine, depending on what or who you're describing. Like nouns, masculine adjectives normally end in **-o,** and feminine adjectives end in **-a.**

REMEMBER

In Portuguese, the adjective normally comes *after* the noun. This word order is opposite of the English construction, where you first say the adjective and then the noun (*red dress*, for example, or *beautiful sunset*). The noun-adjective switcharoo is one of the few differences in word order between Portuguese and English.

So here's how nouns and adjectives get paired off in Portuguese. In the first two examples, notice that the ending of **lindo** (*leen*-doo) (*good-looking*) changes, depending on the gender of the noun it follows. In the other examples, see how the adjective (the second word) changes its ending to match the ending of the noun before it:

>> **homem lindo** (*oh*-mang *leen*-doo) (*good-looking/handsome man*)

>> **mulher linda** (mool-*yeh leen*-dah) (*good-looking/beautiful woman*)

>> **quarto limpo** (*kwah*-too *leem*-poo) (*clean room*)

>> **casa suja** (*kah*-zah *soo*-zhah) (*dirty house*)

>> **comida gostosa** (koh-*mee*-dah goh-*stoh*-zah) (*delicious food*)

Some adjectives are neutral and stay the same for both masculine and feminine nouns. These adjectives often end in -e rather than -o or -a. Adjectives in this group include **grande** (*grahn*-jee) (*big*) and **inteligente** (een-*teh*-lee-*zhang*-chee) (*intelligent*):

> **Ela é muito inteligente.** (*eh*-lah *eh* moh-*ee*-toh een-*teh*-lee-*zhang*-chee.) (*She is very intelligent.*)

> **Ele é muito inteligente.** (*eh*-lee *eh* moh-*ee*-toh een-*teh*-lee-*zhang*-chee.) (*He is very intelligent.*)

If a noun is plural, just add an **-s** to the end of the noun (just as you do in English) and add an **-s** to the end of the adjective too: **cachorros pequenos** (kah-*shoh*-hooz peh-*keh*-nooz) (*small dogs*).

When you're talking about a group of men and women, if there's just one male in the group, then you refer to the whole group using masculine pronouns and adjectives. For example, use **eles** (*eh*-lees) (*them*, masculine) to talk about a group of three women and one man. Say **Eles são simpáticos** (*eh*-lees *sah*-ooh seem-*pah*-chee-koos) to mean *They are nice*, whether you're referring to a group of five guys, or a woman and a man. Use the plural, feminine form **elas** (*eh*-lahs) (*them*, feminine), only when all members of the group are female. In that case, you'd say **Elas são simpáticas** (*eh*-lahs *sah*-ooh seem-*pah*-chee-kahs) (*They are nice – a group of females*).

Looking at Articles

As with Portuguese nouns and adjectives, the gender game is also at play when it comes to articles — words like *the, a, an,* and *some*. Now's the time to *ooh* and *ah* over grammar; **o** (ooh) means *the* for masculine nouns, and **a** (ah) means *the* for feminine nouns.

In the following phrases, see how the first and last letters match:

>> **o homem lindo** (ooh *oh*-mang *leen*-doo) (*the handsome man*)

>> **a mulher linda** (ah mool-*yeh leen*-dah) (*the beautiful woman*)

>> **o quarto limpo** (ooh *kwah*-too *leem*-poo) (*the clean room*)

>> **a casa suja** (ah *kah*-zah *soo*-zhah) (*the dirty house*)

SOUND NATIVE

Brazilians use the word *the* in front of nouns much more often than people do in English. Whereas you say *Books are fun*, they say **Os livros são divertidos** (oohz *leev*-rooz sah-ooh jee-veh-*chee*-dooz) (Literally: *The books are fun*). *Brazil is big* in Portuguese is **O Brasil é grande** (ooh brah-*zee*-ooh *eh grahn*-jee) (Literally: *The Brazil is big*).

If a noun is plural and masculine, use **os** (ooz); use **as** (ahz) if the noun is plural and feminine:

>> **os barcos grandes** (ooz *bah*-kooz *grahn*-jeez) (*the big boats*)

>> **as flores amarelas** (ahz *floh*-reez ah-mah-*reh*-lahz) (*the yellow flowers*)

To say *a*, as in *a hat* or *a table*, say **um** (oong) for masculine nouns and **uma** (*ooh*-mah) for feminine nouns:

>> **um banheiro** (oong bahn-*yay*-roh) (*a bathroom*)

>> **um livro** (oong *leev*-roh) (*a book*)

>> **uma mesa** (*ooh*-mah *meh*-zah) (*a table*)

>> **uma pessoa** (*ooh*-mah peh-*soh*-ah) (*a person*)

To say *some*, use **uns** (oonz) if the noun's masculine or **umas** (*ooh*-mahz) if it's feminine:

>> **uns sapatos** (oonz sah-*pah*-tooz) (*some shoes*)

>> **umas garotas** (*ooh*-mahz gah-*roh*-tahz) (*some girls*)

>> **umas praias** (*ooh*-mahz *prah*-ee-ahz) (*some beaches*)

REMEMBER

When you make the plural of a word ending in **-m**, such as **um**, the **m** always changes to an **n**: **Um homem** (oong oh-*mang*) (*a man*) becomes **uns homens** (oonz oh-*mangz*) (*some men*).

Introducing Pronouns

You use pronouns to refer to people when you don't say their names. Here's the way Brazilians do it:

>> **eu** (*eh*-ooh) (*I*)

>> **você** (voh-*seh*) (*you* — singular)

- » **ele** (*eh*-lee) (*he/him*)
- » **ela** (*eh*-lah) (*she/her*)
- » **nós** (nohz) (*we/us*)
- » **eles** (*eh*-leez) (*they/them* — all males or males and females)
- » **elas** (*eh*-lahz) (*they/them* — all females)
- » **vocês** (voh-*sehz*) (*you* — plural)

Brazilians don't have an equivalent of the English word *it*. Because things are either masculine or feminine in Portuguese, Brazilians refer generally to this type of noun as **ele/ela/eles/elas.** You don't hear this too often, because Brazilians tend to use the name of what they're talking about. But **a mala** (ah *mah*-lah) (*the suitcase*) can become **ela** (Literally: *she*) if both speakers understand the context. **Eu perdi ela** (*eh*-ooh peh-*jee eh*-lah) (*I lost it*) can mean *I lost the suitcase.*

SOUND NATIVE

If you're talking to a person who's a lot older than you or to an important person, like your boss or a politician, instead of using **você,** use **o senhor** (ooh seen-*yoh*) (Literally: *the gentleman*) or **a senhora** (ah seen-*yoh*-rah) (Literally: *the lady*) to show respect.

NEUTRAL PRONOUNS

If you're non-binary, you can say, **Eu sou não binário** (*eh*-ooh *soh nah*-ooh bee-*nah*-ree-ooh) (I'm non-binary). If you want to ask someone what their pronouns are, say **Quais pronomes você prefere?** (*kwah*-ees proh-*noh*-mees voh-*seh* preh-*feh*-ree?) (What are your preferred pronouns?) In English, the common way to refer to a non-binary person is *them.* In Brazilian Portuguese, as of press time, there was no widely accepted non-binary pronoun. People have come up with different neutral pronoun possibilities, such as **ile** (*ee*-leh) and **elu** (*eh*-loo). The lack of accepted neutral pronoun terms in no way reflects on Brazilian society — there are plenty of opinions out there and support of gender equity awareness in general. But the concept of a neutral pronoun is far trickier in Portuguese, because the grammar is trickier. You have to change every adjective to match the pronoun. Instead of **o/a** endings reflecting a masculine or feminine pronoun, some Brazilians want adjectives to take on an **-e** ending to go with a neutral pronoun. Instead of **alto** (*ah*-ooh-toh) (*tall* – male) and **alta** (*ah*-ooh-tah) (*tall* – female) some Brazilians are now saying **alte** (*ah*-ooh-teh) (tall, non-binary person). Nouns such as **filho/a** (*feel*-yoh/yah) (*son/daughter*) are transforming into **filhe** (*feel*-yeh) (neutral expression of child). I'm personally fascinated to follow this movement in Brazil and find out what becomes common parlance to refer to non-binary people in Brazil. This is real evolution of language, in real time! It's always a good idea to be respectful of others. Stay tuned.

Here are some sentences using pronouns:

Eu falo português. (*eh*-ooh *fah*-loh poh-too-*gez*.) (*I speak Portuguese.*)

Você escreve. (voh-*seh* ehs-*kreh*-vee.) (*You write.*)

A senhora é brasileira? (ah seen-*yoh*-rah eh brah-zee-*lay*-rah?) (*Are you Brazilian? — to an older woman*)

As is the case in Spanish, speakers of Portuguese don't always use subject pronouns in cases where everyone involved already knows who's being referred to.

Examining Verbs and Building Simple Sentences

To really make a sentence come alive, you need verbs. Along with nouns, verbs make up the main parts of a sentence. Verbs can link describing words to what they describe. The most basic linking-verb words in Portuguese are **é** (eh) (*is*) and **são** (sah-ooh) (*are*).

The following sentences simply use nouns, verbs, and adjectives in the same order you'd use them in English:

A casa é bonita. (ah *kah*-zah eh boo-*nee*-tah.) (*The house is pretty.*)

O amigo é simpático. (ooh ah-*mee*-goo eh seem-*pah*-chee-koo.) (*The friend is nice.*)

As rosas são vermelhas. (ahz *hoh*-zahz sah-ooh veh-*mel*-yahz.) (*The roses are red.*)

All you need to create a sentence are a noun and a verb. When the person, place, or thing is doing something, a verb signals the action. Action verbs include **estuda** (eh-*stoo*-dah) (*studies*), **vai** (*vah*-ee) (*goes*), and **canta** (*kahn*-tah) (*sings*). Here are some complete sentences:

Os amigos falam. (oohz ah-*mee*-gooz *fah*-lah-ooh.) (*The friends talk.*)

O gato dorme. (ooh *gah*-too *doh*-mee.) (*The cat sleeps.*)

A mãe cozinha. (ah *mah*-ee koh-*zeen*-yah.) (*The mom cooks.*)

When you want to ask a question in Portuguese, you don't have to change the order of the words. Just say the same thing, but raise the pitch of your voice at the end of the sentence, as you do in English.

A casa é bonita? (ah *kah*-zah *eh* boo-*nee*-tah?) (*Is the house pretty?*)

As rosas são vermelhas? (ahz *hoh*-zahz *sah*-ooh veh-*mel*-yahz?) (*Are roses red?*)

The verb can change a bit depending on who's doing the action. The next section tells you how to know which verb form to use.

Delving into Verb Conjugations

Conjugation is basically a matter of matching a verb to a subject. Portuguese verbs mostly come in three varieties: they end in **-ar**, **-er**, or **-ir**. The **-ar** ending is your best friend; with a few exceptions, **-ar** verbs tend to be conjugated the same way, all the time. The **-ir** and **-er** verbs can be a little trickier. General rules for their conjugation exist, but not all verbs ending in **-ir** or **-er** follow the rules. Appendix B lists verb conjugations, including some of the rule-breakers.

To conjugate a verb, just snip off the ending (**-ar**, **-er**, or **-ir**) and add a new one, depending on who's doing the action. The following sections explain which endings to use.

TIP

If the noun is not a person but rather a thing or place, first check out whether it's singular or plural. If it's singular, use the **ele/ela** (*he/she*) conjugation; if it's plural, use the **eles/elas** (*they*) conjugation.

Sometimes, you don't have to conjugate the verb at all. This often happens when you'd use an *-ing* ending in English:

Dançar é divertido. (dahn-*sah eh* jee-veh-*chee*-doo.) (*Dancing is fun.*)

Falar português não é difícil. (fah-*lah* poh-too-*gez nah*-ooh *eh* jee-*fee*-see-ooh.) (*Speaking Portuguese is not hard.*)

Using the -ar verbs

To use a verb that ends in **-ar**, replace the **-ar** with one of the new verb endings: **-o**, **-a**, **-amos**, or **-am**; the correct ending depends on the subject of the sentence. Table 2-1 shows you how the endings match up with the pronouns.

TABLE 2-1

Verb Endings to Use with -ar Verbs

English Pronoun	Portuguese Pronoun	Verb Ending
I	eu	-o
you	você	-a
he/she	ele/ela	-a
we	nós	-amos
they	eles/elas	-am
you (plural)	vocês	-am

Take, for example, the verb **falar** (fah–*lah*) (*to talk/speak*). First remove the **-ar** ending. You now have **fal**, which is the *root* or *stem* of the word. Now just add the proper verb endings.

Conjugation	Pronunciation
eu falo	*eh*-ooh *fah*-loo
você fala	voh-*seh fah*-lah
ele/ela fala	*eh*-lee/*eh*-lah *fah*-lah
nós falamos	nohz fah-*lah*-mooz
eles/elas falam	*eh*-leez/*eh*-lahz *fah*-lah-ooh
vocês falam	voh-*sehz fah*-lah-ooh

Now consider the **-ar** verbs **adorar** (ah-doh-*rah*) (*to love [something]*), **fechar** (feh-*shah*) (*to close*), and **começar** (koh-meh-*sah*) (*to begin*). Some of the nouns in the following examples are not people, but they're all singular like the English word *it*, so you use the **ele/ela** conjugation:

> **Ela adora viajar.** (*eh*-lah ah-*doh*-rah vee-ah-*zhah*.) (*She loves to travel.*)

> **A loja fecha cedo hoje.** (ah *loh*-zhah *feh*-shah *seh*-doo *oh*-zhee.) (*The store closes early today.*)

> **O concerto começa agora.** (ooh kohn-*seh*-too koh-*meh*-sah ah-*goh*-rah.) (*The concert begins now.*)

Talkin' the Talk

AUDIO ONLINE

Vitor (*vee*-toh) and **Danilo** (dah-*nee*-loo) have just met at the gym. The two guys chat about the physical activities they like to do besides lifting weights.

Danilo: **Que tipo de esporte você gosta?**

kee chee-poh jee eh-*spoh*-chee voh-*seh goh*-stah?

What type of sport do you like?

Vitor: **Eu caminho muito.**

eh-ooh kah-*meen*-yoh moh-*ee*-toh.

I walk a lot.

Danilo: **Você não joga futebol?**

voh-*seh* nah-ooh *zhoh*-gah foo-chee-*bah*-ooh?

You don't play soccer?

Vitor: **Só às vezes.**

soh ahz *veh*-zeez.

Only sometimes.

WORDS TO KNOW		
que	kee	what
tipo	chee-poo	type
esporte	eh-spoh-chee	sport
gosta	goh-stah	you like
caminho	kah-meen-yoh	I walk
muito	moh-ee-toh	a lot
e	ee	and
não	nah-ooh	no/not

joga	zhoh-gah	play
futebol	foo-chee-bah-ooh	soccer
só	soh	only
às vezes	ahz veh-zeez	sometimes

Using the -er and -ir verbs

Conjugating regular **-er** and **-ir** verbs isn't difficult. For most **-er** and **-ir** verbs, just replace the **-er** or **-ir** with **-o**, **-e**, **-emos/-imos**, or **-em**. Table 2-2 shows you which endings to use.

TABLE 2-2   Verb Endings to Use with Regular -er and -ir Verbs

English Pronoun	Portuguese Pronoun	Verb Ending
I	**eu**	**-o**
you	**você**	**-e**
he/she	**ele/ela**	**-e**
we	**nós**	**-emos** (for **-er** verbs), **-imos** (for **-ir** verbs)
they	**eles/elas**	**-em**
you (plural)	**vocês**	**-em**

A simple **-er** verb you can practice is **comer** (koh–*meh*) (*to eat*). Remove the **-er** ending and add the new endings to the stem.

Conjugation	Pronunciation
eu como	*eh*-ooh *koh*-moo
você come	voh-*seh koh*-mee
ele/ela come	*eh*-lee/*eh*-lah *koh*-mee
nós comemos	nohz koh-*meh*-mooz
eles/elas comem	*eh*-leez/*eh*-lahz *koh*-mang
vocês comem	voh-*sehz koh*-mang

Many **-er** and **-ir** verbs have special endings. With verbs that end in **-zer**, for example, like **fazer** (fah-*zeh*) (*to do*) and **trazer** (trah-*zeh*) (*to bring*), you remove **-zer** to get the stem; the verbs then take the following endings: **-ço/-go, -z, -z, -zemos,** and **-zem**. The last two endings are similar to the **-er** verb endings (for *we* and *they*).

Here are some examples, using the *I* and *you* forms:

> **Eu faço muitas coisas.** (*eh*-ooh *fah*-soo moh-*ee*-tahz *koy*-zahz.) (*I do many things.*)

> **Você traz um presente.** (voh-*seh trah*-eez oong preh-*zang*-chee.) (*You bring a present.*)

Making Contractions: It's a Cinch!

When you make contractions in English — such as *can't* and *don't* — you use an apostrophe to show that a letter is missing. Brazilians, too, combine words to make them shorter or easier to pronounce, but Portuguese doesn't use apostrophes. And in Portuguese, contractions aren't a less formal way to say something. The new word made from combining two words is the only way to express the concept.

Specifically, Brazilians combine prepositions including *in, on, of, through,* with *the* (known in grammar books as an 'article'). Even though this might sound confusing, the reason Brazilians talk this way is to make speaking easier! And more fun, too, in my opinion. This section helps you recognize how and when Brazilians combine two words into one word.

Take a look at what happens in Portuguese when you combine **em** and **o**. These examples are for singular, masculine nouns. **Em** (ang) means *in/on,* and **o** (oh) means *the*. But **em o** (*in the*) doesn't exist in Portuguese. Brazilians use **no** (noo) instead:

> » **no banheiro** (noo bahn-*yay*-roh) (*in the bathroom*)

> » **no quarto** (noo *kwah*-too) (*in the bedroom*)

> » **no telhado** (noo tel-*yah*-doo) (*on the roof*)

Take a look at what happens with feminine and plural nouns. Instead of **no**, you now have **na** (feminine and singular), **nos** (masculine and plural), and **nas** (feminine and plural):

>> **na mesa** (nah *meh*-zah) (*on the table*)

>> **na cozinha** (nah koh-*zing*-yah) (*in the kitchen*)

>> **na rua** (nah *hoo*-ah) (*on the street*)

>> **nos livros** (nooz *leev*-rooz) (*in books*)

>> **nas praias** (nahz *prah*-ee-ahz) (*on beaches*)

This blending of two words to make a single word also happens when Brazilians combine **o** with **de** (deh) (*of*) and **por** (poh) (*through/on/around*). For example, when you want to say *of the*, you combine **de** and **o** to form **do/da/dos/das**. To say *through/on/around the*, use **pelo/pela/pelos/pelas**.

TIP

If you're confused about which form to use, just remember that **o** goes with masculine nouns, **a** goes with feminine, and **s** makes words plural.

Here are some examples:

>> **dos pais** (dooz *pah*-eez) (*of the parents*)

>> **das professoras** (dahz proh-feh-*soh*-rahz) (*of the teachers*)

>> **pelo telefone** (*peh*-loo teh-leh-*foh*-nee) (*on the phone*)

>> **pelas ruas** (*peh*-lahz *hooh*-ahz) (*through the streets*)

Brazilians also use contractions specifically to say *of him*, *of her*, or *of them*. (See Chapter 6 for more on how to use contractions with possessive terms, including *his*, *her*, or *their*.)

>> **dela** (*deh*-lah) (*of her*)

>> **dele** (*deh*-lee) (*of him*)

>> **delas** (*deh*-lahz) (*of them* — females)

>> **deles** (*deh*-leez) (*of them* — males or males and females)

Here are some examples of sentences using contractions:

Gosto de viagar pelo mundo. (*goh*-stoo jee vee-ah-*zhah* peh-loo *moon*-doh.) (*I like to travel around the world.*)

Ele mora no Brasil. (*eh*-lee *moh*-rah noo brah-*zee*-ooh.) (*He lives in Brazil.*)

Nos Estados Unidos, há cinquenta estados. (nooz eh-*stah*-dooz ooh-*nee*-dooz, ah sing-*kwen*-tah eh-*stah*-dooz.) (*In the United States, there are 50 states.*)

As chaves estão em cima da mesa. (ahz *shah*-veez eh-*stah*-ooh ang *see*-mah dah *meh*-zah.) (*The keys are on the table.*)

To Me, to You: Indirect Objects

One of my favorite aspects of Portuguese grammar is *me* and *you* being on the receiving end. In grammar books, these words are called *indirect objects*; the words *me* and *you* are in the sentence, but they're not the ones doing the action.

Te (teh) means *you*, and **me** (meh) means *me*. (That one's easy to remember.) Put these indirect objects right before the verb. Take a look at some examples:

Eu te dou dinheiro. (*eh*-ooh chee *doh* jing-*yay*-roh.) (*I give you money.*)

Me diga o seu nome. (mee *jee*-gah ooh *seh*-ooh *noh*-mee.) (*Tell me your name.*)

In the first sentence, **eu** is the subject. In the second sentence, the subject isn't even stated. You can tell that the verb **diga** is in the **você/ele/ela** form. If someone looks at you and says, **Me diga o seu nome,** it's no mystery that they're asking *you*, not *him* or *her* or some other person. Brazilians leave out the subject of the sentence sometimes when it's obvious who they're talking about. Just like in English, you can drop the *you* at the beginning of a sentence when you're asking or telling someone to do something.

SOUND NATIVE

Brazilians love to use the formula **me** plus a verb:

Me faz um recibo, por favor? (mee *fah*-eez oong heh-*see*-boo, poh fah-*voh?*) (*Can you write a receipt for me, please?*)

Me traz água, por favor. (mee *trah*-eez *ah*-gwah, poh fah-*voh.*) (*Bring me water, please.*)

Me explica isso. (mee eh-*splee*-kah *ee*-sooh.) (*Explain this to me.*)

Me leva até a rodoviária? (mee *leh*-vah ah-*teh* ah hoh-doh-vee-*ah*-ree-ah?) (*Can you take me to the bus station?*)

Me dá o seu passaporte, por favor. (mee *dah* ooh seh-ooh pah-sah-*poh*-chee, poh fah-*voh.*) (*Give me your passport, please.*)

FUN & GAMES

Carolina (kah-roh-*lee*-nah) and **Maurício** (mah-ooh-*ree*-see-ooh) are husband and wife. Match each adjective given below with him or her. Keep in mind that some adjectives can be used with both of them.

1 inteligente

2 simpático

3 tranquila

4 linda

5 alto

6 jovem

7 médico

8 organizado

Answers are in Appendix C.

IN THIS CHAPTER

» **Beginning a conversation**

» **Introducing yourself and friends**

» **Conversing in formal versus informal situations**

» **Understanding the verbs "to be" and "to speak"**

» **Parting ways**

Chapter 3

Oi! Hello! Greetings and Introductions

S aying hello and goodbye are the nuts and bolts of any **língua** (*ling*-gwah) (*language*). If you visit Brazil or meet a Brazilian friend or colleague, take the opportunity to **praticar** (prah-chee-*kah*) (*practice*) these basic **palavras** (pah-*lah*-vrahz) (*words*). Walking in and out of **lojas** (*loh*-zhahz) (*shops*), **restaurantes** (heh-stah-oo-*rahn*-cheez) (*restaurants*), and **hotéis** (oh-*tay*-eez) (*hotels*), you may hear **Tudo bom?** (too-doh *boh*-oong?) (*How are you?*) and **Tchau!** (*chah*-ooh!) (*Bye!* — from the Italian word *ciao*, which also means bye).

After exchanging a greeting, the **próximo passo** (*proh*-see-moh *pah*-soh) (*next step*) is introducing yourself to people and introducing the people you're with. You'll want to tell people your **nome** (*noh*-mee) (*name*) and maybe even your **apelido** (ah-peh-*lee*-doh) (*nickname*).

Your **conversa** (kohn-*veh*-sah) (*conversation*) may then involve explaining what you do for work and maybe what you like to do in your spare time. You can use common description techniques to talk about someone else, too. For example, what is your **amigo** (ah-*mee*-goo) (male *friend*) like **fisicamente** (*fee*-zee-kah-men-chee) (*physically*) — **alto** (*ah*-ooh-toh) (*tall*) or **baixo** (bah-ee-shoh) (*short*)? Is he **legal** (lay-*gow*) (*nice*) or **tímido** (*chee*-mee-doh) (*shy*)?

Finally, you may want to talk about how you're doing or how someone else is doing in a particular **momento** (moh-*men*-toh) (*moment*). Are you **cansado** (kahn-*sah*-doo) (*tired*)? **Feliz** (feh-*lees*) (*happy*)? How about this one: Are you **pronto** (*prohn*-toh) (*ready*) to learn some basic Portuguese?

Saying Hello

Knowing how to say hello is the bare necessity of using any language. After you communicate a friendly greeting, the scene is set for social interaction — the fun part! What comes after the hello is unpredictable, and that's the beauty of **a vida** (*ah vee*-dah) (*life*).

Here are the most common ways of saying *hello* in Brazil:

>> **Oi.** (*oh*-ee.) (*Hi.*)

>> **Olá.** (oh-*lah*.) (*Hello.*)

If you're walking into a shop, restaurant, or hotel, it's more common to use *Good morning* or *Good afternoon* — just like in English:

>> **Bom dia.** (*boh*-oong *jee*-ah.) (*Good morning.*)

>> **Boa tarde.** (*boh*-ah *tah*-jee.) (*Good afternoon/Good evening.*)

>> **Boa noite.** (*boh*-ah *noh*-ee-chee.) (*Good evening/Good night.*)

TIP

You may be wondering when to use each of these phrases. It's simple: Use **bom dia** until **meio dia** (*may*-oh *jee*-ah) (*noon*), and use **boa tarde** from noon until dark, usually about 6 or 7 p.m. In the early evening and night, use **boa noite**.

Another way of greeting someone is to ask, "How are you?" Check out the two ways of saying this:

>> **Tudo bem?** (*too*-doh *bang*?) (*How are you?* Literally: *Everything well?*)

>> **Tudo bom?** (*too*-doh *boh*-oong?) (*How are you?* Literally: *Everything good?*)

Here's how you answer:

>> **Tudo bem.** (*too*-doh *bang*.) (*I'm good.* Literally: *Everything well.*)

>> **Tudo bom.** (*too*-doh *boh*-oong.) (*I'm good.* Literally: *Everything good.*)

SOUND NATIVE

What's the difference between **Tudo bem** and **Tudo bom**, you ask? Here's the big answer: Nothing! They mean the same thing. If someone asks you, **Tudo bem?** you can answer either **Tudo bem!** or **Tudo bom!** Or try **Tudo ótimo!** (*too*-doh *ah-chee-moh!*) (*Everything is great!*). When responding, it's polite to ask the person how they're doing, too. Say, **E você?** (*eeh* voh-*seh?*) (*And you?*).

People commonly combine some of these phrases, like **Olá, tudo bom?** (oh-*lah*, too-doh *boh*-oong?) (*Hello, how are you?*) or **Oi, tudo bem?** (*oh*-ee, too-doh *bang?*) (*Hi, how are you?*).

Making Introductions

Introducing yourself is as easy as **torta de morango** (*toh*-tah jee moh-*rahng*-goh) (*strawberry pie*). Here are two different ways to do it:

>> **Meu nome é . . .** (*meh*-ooh *noh*-mee eh . . .) (*My name is . . .*)

>> **Eu sou . . .** (*eh*-ooh soh . . .) (*I'm . . .*)

To ask someone their name, say **Qual é seu nome?** (*kwah*-ooh *eh* seh-ooh *noh*-mee?) (*What's your name?*).

After someone asks you for your name, you can answer and then say **E o seu?** (ee ooh *seh*-ooh?) (*And yours?*).

If you want to **apresentar** (ah-preh-zen-*tah*) (*introduce*) a person who's with you, use one of the following phrases:

>> **Este é meu amigo . . .** (*es*-chee *eh* meu-ooh ah-*mee*-goo . . .) (*This is my friend . . . [name of man]*)

>> **Esta é minha amiga . . .** (*eh*-stah *eh* meen-yah ah-*mee*-gah . . .) (*This is friend . . . [name of woman]*)

>> **Estes são meus amigos . . .** (*es*-jeez sah-ooh meh-ooz ah-*mee*-gooz . . .) (*These are my friends . . . [names of multiple people or men]*)

>> **Estas são minhas amigas . . .** (*eh*-stahz sah-ooh meen-yus ah-*mee*-guz . . .) (*These are my friends . . . [names of women]*)

Flip to Chapter 6 to find out how to refer to specific family members — such as *mother, brother, cousin,* and *uncle* — in Portuguese.

Using First Names, Last Names, and Nicknames — Brazilian-Style

In Portuguese, *first names* are **nomes** (*noh*-meez) (Literally: *names*), and last names are **sobrenomes** (*soh*-bree *noh*-meez) (*surnames*).

When someone says **Qual é seu nome?** (*kwah*-ooh *eh* seh-ooh *noh*-mee?) (What is your name?), they want to know your first name. If they say **Qual é seu nome completo?** (*kwah*-ooh *eh* seh-ooh *noh*-mee kohm-*pleh*-too?) (*What's your full name?* Literally: *What's your complete name?*), then they're asking for both your **nome** and **sobrenome**.

CULTURAL WISDOM

Many Brazilians use two last names — one from their dad's family and one from their mom's. The longer the name, the more likely it is that the person is from a **família rica** (fah-*mee*-lee-ah *hee*-kah) (*rich family*) that enjoys preserving **tradição** (trah-dee-*sah*-ooh) (*tradition*).

If a person's name includes two last names, then the mom's last name goes before the dad's. Some people even have two first names and two last names. Check out this mouthful: **Henrique Alfredo Gonçalves de Almeida** (ang-*hee*-kee ah-ooh-*freh*-doh gohn-*sah*-ooh-veez jee ah-ooh-*may*-dah).

Sometimes names come with a **de** (jee) (*of*) or **da** (*dah*) (*of* [before a name ending in -*a*]), as in **Vinicius de Moraes** (vee-*nee*-see-oohz jee moh-*rah*-eez), one of the composers of the famous song "Girl from Ipanema" (1964).

Do you know what the Brazilian version of *Smith* is? The most common last name in Brazil is **da Silva** (dah *see*-ooh-vah). In fact, there are way more **da Silvas** in Brazil than there are *Smiths* in English-speaking countries.

CULTURAL WISDOM

A former **presidente** (preh-zee-*dang*-chee) (*president*) of Brazil has a very unusual name. It's **Luiz Inácio Lula da Silva** (loo-*eez* ee-*nah*-see-oh *loo*-lah dah *see*-ooh-vah) (served 2003–2010). He has two first names, but the third name, **Lula**, is an **apelido** (ah-peh-*lee*-doh) (*nickname*) for **Luiz**. It's like saying John Scott Johnny Smith. It's not common in the United States for a nickname to be part of a full name like this; but in Brazil, especially for the rich and famous, an **apelido** is often legally added to the full name for marketing reasons and to avoid lawsuits.

Brazilians have an obsession with **apelidos** (ah-peh-*lee*-dooz) (*nicknames*) and using first names only in the case of celebrities. The former President Lula has always been known in Brazil simply as "Lula." The president who served right before Lula, **Fernando Henrique Cardoso** (feh-*nahn*-doh ang-*hee*-kee kah-*doh*-zoo) was simply called **Fernando Henrique**. No one — not even on news shows — refers to these leaders as **Presidente da Silva** or **Presidente Cardoso.** If people want to be formal, they say **Presidente Lula** (preh-zee-*dang*-chee *loo*-lah), which is like saying *President Barack* when referring to former U.S. President Barack Obama.

Only recently, I learned that the real name of Brazil's most famous soccer star of all time, **Pelé** (peh-*leh*) (his career spanned 1956–1977) is actually **Edson Arantes do Nascimento** (*eh*-jee-soh-oong ah-*rahn*-cheez doo nah-see-*men*-toh). I discovered that in the United States, after I moved back after spending three years in Brazil! In Brazil I heard him referred to only as **Pelé** — never by his real name.

Brazilians also prefer to stick to **nomes** in general. I have friends who say they don't even know many of their friends' **sobrenomes,** even after knowing them for a long time.

Dividing the World between Formal and Informal

One way to think about people is to divide them into two categories: those you call Mr. or Mrs. and those you call by their first names.

Brazilians use the terms **Senhor** (seen-*yoh*) (*Mr.*) and **Senhora** (seen-*yoh*-rah) (*Mrs.*) pretty much just like you use *Mr.* and *Mrs.* in English. When you're talking to your elderly **vizinho** (vee-*zeen*-yoh) (*neighbor*), he's **Senhor** so-and-so. When a **casal** (kah-*zah*-oo) (*couple*) walks into a real estate agency, for example, they're addressed as **Senhor e Senhora** (seen-*yoh* ee seen-*yoh*-rah) (*Mr. and Mrs.*) so-and-so.

Brazilians often use **o/a** (ooh/ah) (*the*) before saying Mr. or Mrs. It's like saying "the Mr. Oliveira." Here are some examples:

> **o Senhor Wilfredo Oliveira** (ooh seen-*yoh* veel-*freh*-doh oh-lee-*vay*-rah) (*Mr. Oliveira*)

> **o Senhor Luciano da Silva** (ooh seen-*yoh* loo-see-*ah*-noh dah *see*-ooh-vah) (*Mr. da Silva*)

> **a Senhora Mônica Tavares** (ah seen-*yoh*-rah *moh*-nee-kah tah-*vah*-reez) (*Mrs. Tavares*)

> **a Senhora Fernanda Gimenes** (ah seen-*yoh*-rah feh-*nahn*-dah zhee-*men*-ez) (*Mrs. Gimenes*)

CULTURAL WISDOM

Another thing to note is that in Brazil, it's common for people in the service industry to use **Senhor** and **Senhora** for young people — even teenagers. There's the term **senhorita** (sen-yoh-*ree*-tah) (*Miss*), but it's very old-fashioned. And it's normal for people to say **Senhor David** or **Senhora Luciana** — using the first name instead of the last name.

I'm called **Senhora Karen** (seen-*yoh*-rah *kahr*-eeng), whether I'm at the **cabelereiro** (kah-beh-leh-*ray*-roh) (*hairdresser's*), talking to an **agente de viagens** (ah-*jehn*-chee jee vee-*ah*-jehnz) (*travel agent*), or at my favorite **padaria** (pah-dah-*ree*-ah) (*bakery*). At first, I wondered whether people thought I was middle-aged (I lived in Brazil from ages 25–28), but then I noticed the same treatment for teenagers. Whew — it was nice to know that the word **Senhora** wasn't a reflection of how old I looked!

Of course, when two people know each other reasonably well, the formal titles drop off and people just call each other by their first names.

Imagine you're a man talking to a hotel concierge. They treat you with respect because it's their job to serve you. They may ask you the following questions:

> **O senhor mora aqui?** (ooh seen-*yoh moh*-rah ah-*kee?*) (*Do you live here?*)
>
> **O senhor está cansado?** (ooh seen-*yoh* eh-*stah* kahn-*sah*-doo?) (*Are you tired?*)
>
> **O senhor é brasileiro?** (ooh seen-*yoh* eh brah-zee-*lay*-roh?) (*Are you Brazilian?*)
>
> **O senhor gosta do restaurante?** (ooh seen-*yoh goh*-stah doo heh-stah-oo-*rahn*-chee?) (*Do you like the restaurant?*)

And here are some more typical questions that the concierge may ask a guest. Can you tell that, in these examples, the guest is a woman?

> **A senhora gosta de dançar?** (ah seen-*yoh*-rah *goh*-stah jee dahn-*sah?*) (*Do you like to dance?*)
>
> **A senhora é americana?** (ah seen-*yoh*-rah eh ah-meh-ree-*kah*-nah?) (*Are you American?*)
>
> **A senhora vai para a praia?** (ah seen-*yoh*-rah vah-ee pah-rah ah *prah*-ee-ah?) (*Are you going to the beach?*)
>
> **A senhora está de férias?** (ah seen-*yoh*-rah eh-*stah* jee *feh*-ree-ahz?) (*Are you on vacation?*)

Now imagine that the speaker who's asking you all these questions is your new neighbor — a Brazilian. All the **o senhors** and **a senhoras** become **você** (voh-*seh*) (*you* [informal]). **Você** is what you call people when it's appropriate to be casual. The neighbor might ask you, **Você gosta do bairro?** (voh-seh *goh*-stah doo bah-ee-hoh?) (*Do you like the neighborhood?*)

Talkin' the Talk

AUDIO ONLINE

Tatiana (*tah*-chee-*ah*-nah) is a tourist in her 70s, deep in the Amazon, getting settled at her jungle lodge. She's meeting her tour guide, **Lucas** (*loo*-kahs), for the first time. He's a young guy. Notice how **Tatiana** calls **Lucas você** and he calls her **Senhora**. **Caipirinha** (kah-ee-pee-*ring*-yah), by the way, is Brazil's national drink; it's made from **cachaça** (kah-*chah*-sah) (sugarcane liquor, lime, and sugar.)

Tatiana:	**Olá, você é o guia?**
	oh-*lah*, voh-*seh* eh ooh *gee*-ah?
	Hello, are you the guide?
Lucas:	**Olá. Sim, sou.**
	oh-*lah*. sing, *soh*.
	Hello. Yes, I am.
Tatiana:	**Qual é seu nome?**
	kwah-ooh *eh seh*-ooh *noh*-mee?
	What's your name?
Lucas:	**Lucas. E o nome da Senhora?**
	loo-kahs. ee ooh *noh*-mee dah seen-*yoh*-rah?
	Lucas. And your name?
Tatiana:	**Tatiana.**
	tah-chee-*ah*-nah.
	Tatiana.
Lucas:	**A senhora é de onde?**
	ah seen-*yoh*-rah eh jee *ohn*-jee?
	Where are you from?
Tatiana:	**Sou do Rio. E você, é daqui?**
	soh doo *hee*-ooh. ee voh-*seh*, eh dah-*kee*?
	I'm from Rio. And you, are you from here?
Lucas:	**Sim, sou. A senhora quer uma caipirinha?**
	sing, *soh*. ah seen-*yoh*-rah *keh* ooh-mah kah-ee-pee-*ring*-yah?
	Yes, I am. Would you like a caipirinha?
Tatiana:	**Eu quero! Obrigada!**
	eh-ooh *keh*-roo! oh-bree-*gah*-dah!
	Yes! (Literally: I want!) Thanks!

CULTURAL WISDOM

If you vacation in Brazil, many people you come into contact with will be people in the tourism industry who will call you **o Senhor** or **a Senhora**. Make sure to **lembrar** (lehm-*brah*) (*remember*) to use **o Senhor** or **a Senhora** rather than **você**, especially if you meet **um idoso** (oong ee-*doh*-zoo) (*an elderly person*). It's nice to show respect.

WORDS TO KNOW

guia	<u>gee</u>-ah	guide
daqui	dah-<u>kee</u>	from here
quer	keh	want
uma caipirinha	<u>ooh</u>-mah kah-ee-pee-<u>ring</u>-yah	a caipirinha (Brazilian national drink)

Describing Permanent Qualities: Ser

The verb **ser** (sehr) (*to be*) is the way to describe someone or something. Use this verb when you want to communicate the equivalent of *is* or *are* in Portuguese.

Brazilians use **ser** for permanent qualities of a thing or person. I'm talking about qualities of places and people that don't change much: *New York is an island. New York is a big city. New York is pretty. She is married. He is from California. He is smart and nice.* The verb **estar** (eh-*stahr*) (*to be*) is also used to mean *is* and *are*, but only in situations where the quality being described is temporary, such as being sleepy. I cover the ins and outs of **estar** in the section "Describing Temporary Qualities: Estar" later in this chapter.

Say you're talking about your friend Ana, who has a rich husband. When you're thinking about whether to use **ser** or **estar** to say the husband *is* rich, don't worry yourself over questions like *What if Ana's husband goes bankrupt tomorrow?* or *What if Ana gets divorced tomorrow?* Use the decade rule: If the quality you're talking about seems like it will last another ten years, then use **ser**.

If you make a mistake, don't sweat it. That's how you learn. Plus, Brazilians are nice. They won't laugh at you.

Using an example

To clarify how to use the verb **ser**, I'm going to use the **exemplo** (eh-*zem*-ploh) (*example*) of **Gisele Bündchen** (zhee-*zeh*-lee *boon*-chang), Brazil's most famous fashion **modelo** (moh-*deh*-loh) (*model*) — one of the most famous supermodels of all time in the world. If you don't know what she looks like, do an online search for her name and then come back to this text.

Did you do it? Okay. What are **Gisele's** permanent qualities? These are qualities about her that last for **um longo período** (oong *lohn*-goo peh-*ree*-ooh-doh) (*a long time*) — at least a decade or so. When talking about these qualities, use the verb **ser**. When conjugated for *she*, the verb **ser** is **é** (eh).

Ela é (eh-lah *eh*) (*She is*)

>> **alta** (*ah*-ooh-tah) (*tall*)

>> **bonita** (boo-*nee*-tah) (*pretty*)

>> **uma modelo** (*ooh*-mah moh-*deh*-loh) (*a model*)

>> **rica** (*hee*-kah) (*rich*)

>> **do Rio Grande do Sul** (doo *hee*-ooh *grahn*-jee doo *soo*) (*from Rio Grande do Sul state*)

I talked about what she looks like (physical characteristics), what her profession is, and where she's from. These are a few things that probably won't **mudar** (moo-*dah*) (*change*) about **Gisele** for another **dez anos** (dez *ah*-nohz) (*ten years*). She certainly won't get **baixa ou feia** (*bah*-ee-shah ooh *fay*-ah) (*short or unattractive*) any time **logo** (*loh*-goo) (*soon*).

The verb **ser** is the one most often used in Portuguese. It's an irregular verb (look at Chapter 2 for a quick lesson on verbs), but it's the easiest irregular verb there is in Portuguese. Check it out in the following table.

Conjugation	Pronunciation
eu sou	*eh*-ooh *soh*
você é	voh-seh *eh*
ele/ela é	*eh*-lee/*eh*-lah *eh*
nós somos	nohz *soh*-mooz
eles/elas são	*eh*-leez/*eh*-lahz *sah*-ooh
vocês são	voh-*sehz sah*-ooh

Warming up to ser

Entendeu? (en-ten-*deh*-ooh?) (*Did you get it?*). **Ser** is just the plain old *is* and *are* and *am*. How basic is that?

Now that you know the verb **ser**, you can say a ton of things:

Eu sou homem. (*eh*-ooh *soh oh*-mang.) (*I am a man.*)

Eu sou da Califórnia. (*eh*-ooh *soh* dah kah-lee-*foh*-nee-ah.) (*I am from California.*)

Ele é muito alto. (eh-lee *eh* moo-*ee*-toh *ah*-ooh-toh.) (*He is very tall.*)

Nós somos amigos. (nohz *soh*-mooz ah-*mee*-gooz.) (*We are friends.*)

Elas são simpáticas. (eh-lahz *sah*-ooh seem-*pah*-chee-kahz.) (*Those women are nice.*)

Ela é jovem. (eh-lah *eh* zhoh-vang.) (*She is young.*)

Nós somos da Austrália. (nohz *soh*-mooz dah ah-ooh-*strah*-lee-ah.) (*We are from Australia.*)

Eles são inteligentes. (eh-leez *sah*-ooh een-teh-lee-*zhang*-cheez.) (*They are smart.*)

SOUND NATIVE

Gente boa (*zhang*-chee *boh*-ah) is a very common phrase in Brazil. It's used to describe people who are laid-back and down-to-earth. It literally means *good people*, but you can use it to describe one person or a group of people. Here are a couple phrases you can use to win Brazilian friends:

Você é gente boa. (voh-*seh* eh *zhang*-chee *boh*-ah.) (*You're a really cool person.*)

Os seus amigos são muito gente boa. (oohz *say*-oohz ah-*mee*-gooz *sah*-ooh moo-*ee*-toh *zhang*-chee *boh*-ah.) (*Your friends are really great.*)

As you can see, **ser** goes perfectly with descriptions of things and people. Take a look at Table 3-1 to check out some basic adjectives you can use with **ser**. These words are sure to come in handy.

TABLE 3-1   ## Adjectives Describing Permanent States

Adjective	Pronunciation	Translation
alto	*ah*-ooh-toh	*tall*
baixo	*bah*-ee-shoh	*short* (height)
caro	*kah*-roh	*expensive*
barato	bah-*rah*-toh	*cheap*

Adjective	Pronunciation	Translation
bom	*boh*-oong	*good*
mau	*mah*-ooh	*bad*
curto	*kooh*-toh	*short* (length)
comprido	kohm-*pree*-doh	*long*
pequeno	peh-*keh*-noh	*small*
grande	*grahn*-jee	*big*
fácil	*fah*-see-ooh	*easy*
difícil	jee-*fee*-see-ooh	*difficult*
divertido	jee-veh-*chee*-doo	*fun*
chato	*shah*-toh	*boring/annoying*
gordo	*goh*-doh	*fat*
magro	*mah*-groh	*thin*
jovem	*zhoh*-vang	*young*
velho	*vehl*-yoh	*old*

Talkin' the Talk

AUDIO ONLINE

You're at a charming cafe in the old part of Rio and overhear the following conversation between **Marco** (*mah*-koh) and **Ana** (*ah*-nah). Note all the uses of **ser** to describe New York.

Marco: **E como é Nova Iorque?**

ee *koh*-moh *eh noh*-vah *yoh*-kee?

And what's New York like?

Ana: **É muito grande. Também é muito bonita.**

eh moh-*ee* toh *grahn*-jee. tahm-*bang* eh moh-*ee*-toh boo-*nee*-tah.

It's really big. It's also really pretty.

Marco:	**É uma ilha, né?**
	eh ooh-mah *eel*-yah, neh?
	It's an island, right?
Ana:	**Manhattan é uma ilha.**
	Mahn-*hah*-tahn *eh* ooh-mah *eel*-yah.
	Manhattan is an island.
Marco:	**E foi lá para visitar a sua irmã, né?**
	ee *foh*-ee *lah* pah-rah vee-see-*tah* ah soo-ah ee-*mah*, neh?
	And you went to visit your sister, right?
Ana:	**É. Ela é muito legal.**
	eh. eh-lah *eh* moh-ee-toh lay-*gow*.
	Yeah. She's really cool.
Marco:	**Ela é casada?**
	eh-lah *eh* kah-*zah*-dah?
	Is she married?
Ana:	**É. O marido dela é de Nova Iorque.**
	eh. ooh mah-*ree*-doh *deh*-lah *eh* jee noh-vah *yoh*-kee.
	Yeah. Her husband is from New York.
Marco:	**Como ele é?**
	koh-moh eh-lee *eh?*
	What is he like?
Ana:	**É rico e simpático!**
	eh *hee*-koo ee seem-*pah*-chee-koh!
	He's rich and nice!

• •

WORDS TO KNOW

Como é. . .?	koh-moh <u>eh</u>. . .?	What is . . . like?
Nova Iorque	noh-vah <u>yoh</u>-kee	New York
muito	moh-<u>ee</u>-toh	really/very
grande	<u>grahn</u>-jee	big
também	tahm-<u>bang</u>	too/also
ilha	<u>eel</u>-yah	island
foi	<u>foh</u>-ee	you went
para	<u>pah</u>-rah	in order to
visitar	vee-zee-<u>tah</u>	to visit
irmã	ee-<u>mah</u>	sister
legal	lay-<u>gow</u>	cool
casada	kah-<u>zah</u>-dah	married
marido	mah-<u>ree</u>-doh	husband

SOUND NATIVE

If you want to sound a little more casual when speaking Portuguese, use **né** at the end of a sentence to mean *Right?* Né is the contraction of **não é** (*nah*-ooh *eh*) (Literally: *isn't it*), though Brazilians also use **não é** in place of **né**. Also, use **É** (*eh*) to affirm a question someone just asked you – use É when you would respond, "Yeah." These words aren't necessary for you to learn, but they're fun, and Brazilians use them all the time!

Describing Temporary Qualities: Estar

Use the verb **estar** (eh-*stahr*) (*to be*) to describe the temporary qualities of a thing or person. Is the state of the person or thing likely to change in a few minutes? In a few days or weeks? In a few years? If so, then use **estar**. In terms of people, **estar** is used most often to describe mood or physical state or location.

Estar enables you to convey that you're **nervoso** (neh-*voh*-zoo) (*nervous*) about something, or you're **doente** (doh-*en*-chee) (*sick*) — right now. Tomorrow you may be *happy* and *not sick*. If you use **ser** with these adjectives, you're saying that you'll be *nervous* or *sick* for many years. Hopefully that isn't the case!

But don't worry too much about this. If you mix up the verbs, Brazilians will still understand what you're saying.

Using an example

Consider the model **Gisele Bünchen** (zhee-*zeh*-lee *boon*-chang) again. To describe some of her *temporary qualities,* use the verb **estar**. If it helps, you can think about temporary qualities as someone's *state of being,* which often changes from minute to minute or from one day to the next.

When conjugated for *she,* the verb **estar** is **está** (eh-*stah*).

Imagine **Gisele** is on a photo shoot and having a bad day. **Ela está** (eh-lah eh-*stah*) (*She is*):

>> **com fome** (koh-oong *foh*-mee) (*hungry*)

>> **com sapatos vermelhos** (koh-oong sah-*pah*-tooz veh-*mel*-yooz) (*wearing red shoes*)

>> **em Roma** (ang *hoh*-mah) (*in Rome*)

>> **triste** (*trees*-chee) (*sad*)

These phrases describe her emotions and daily physical needs, temporary aspects of her appearance, and her physical location. All of these aspects are things that will change soon about **Gisele**.

Tomorrow, **Gisele** will go back to the United States, where she lives, and she will probably change her **sapatos vermelhos**.

REMEMBER

Estar is for qualities of a person, place, or thing that are temporary. Both **ser** and **estar** are used to say *am, is,* and *are.* To find out the different forms of **estar**, take a look at the following table.

Conjugation	Pronunciation
eu estou	*eh*-ooh eh-*stoh*
você está	voh-*seh* eh-*stah*
ele/ela está	*eh*-lee/*eh*-lah eh-*stah*
nós estamos	nohz eh-*stah*-mohz
eles/elas estão	*eh*-leez/*eh*-lahz eh-*stah*-ooh
vocês estão	voh-*sehz* eh-*stah*-ooh

Warming up to estar

Here are some common phrases that use **estar**:

Ela está de férias. (*eh*-lah eh-*stah* jee *feh*-ree-uz.) (*She is on vacation.*)

Nós estamos com fome. (nohz eh-*stah*-mohz koh-oong *foh*-mee.) (*We are hungry.*)

Eu estou triste. (*eh*-ooh eh-*stoh trees*-chee.) (*I am sad.*)

Ela está no carro. (*eh*-lah eh-*stah* noh *kah*-hoh.) (*She is in the car.*)

Eu estou em casa. (*eh*-ooh eh-*stoh* ang *kah*-zah.) (*I am at home.*)

Eles estão no Brasil. (*eh*-leez eh-*stah*-ooh noo brah-*zee*-ooh.) (*They are in Brazil.*)

Again, with **estar**, you're talking about people's emotional states, their physical states, and where they're located.

Speaking about Speaking: Falar

Now onto a really easy, fun verb: **falar** (fah–*lah*) (*to speak/to talk*). Talking is, after all, how to really learn a language! This book is a good primer for learning Brazilian Portuguese, but you can catch on much more quickly if you can spend some time in Brazil or find a Brazilian where you live who will **falar** with you. Luckily, Brazilians love to **falar**, so they're the perfect conversation partners.

To discover the different forms of **falar**, take a look at the following verb conjugations:

Conjugation	Pronunciation
eu falo	*eh*-ooh *fah*-loh
você fala	voh-*seh fah*-lah
ele/ela fala	*eh*-lee/*eh*-lah *fah*-lah
nós falamos	*nohz* fah-*lah*-mohz
eles/elas falam	eh-leez/*eh*-lahz *fah*-lah-ooh
vocês falam	voh-*sehz fah*-lah-ooh

Falar is the **verbo perfeito** (*veh*-boh peh-*fay*-toh) (*perfect verb*) to use to talk about speaking Portuguese — or any language at all. Browse through Table 3-2 to find out how to say the names of other languages.

TABLE 3-2   ## Some of the World's Major Languages

Language	Pronunciation	Translation
inglês	eeng-*glehz*	English
português	poh-too-*gez*	Portuguese
português de Portugal	poh-too-*gez* jee poh-too-*gah*-ooh	Portuguese from Portugal
português do Brasil	poh-too-*gez* doo brah-*zee*-ooh	Brazilian Portuguese
espanhol	eh-spahn-*yoh*-ooh	Spanish
russo	*hoo*-soh	Russian
chinês	shee-*nez*	Chinese
francês	frahn-*sez*	French
italiano	ee-tah-lee-*ah*-noh	Italian
alemão	ah-leh-*mah*-ooh	German
árabe	*ah*-rah-bee	Arabic
hebraico	eh-*brah*-ee-koh	Hebrew

And hey, did you notice that Brazilians don't capitalize the **primeira letra** (pree-*may*-rah *let*-rah) (*first letter*) of names of languages in Portuguese? This convention is different from English, where you **sempre** (*sem*-pree) (*always*) capitalize the first letter of **línguas estrangeiras** (*ling*-gwahz eh-strahn-*jay*-rahz) (*foreign languages*).

Here are some easy ways to use **falar:**

> **Eu falo inglês.** (*eh*-ooh *fah*-loh eeng-*glehz*.) (*I speak English.*)
>
> **Eu gostaria de falar chinês.** (*eh*-ooh goh-stah-*ree*-ah jee fah-*lah* shee-*nehz*.) (*I would like to speak Chinese.*)
>
> **Você fala muito rápido!** (voh-seh *fah*-lah moh-*ee*-toh *hah*-pee-doh!) (*You talk really fast!*)

Na reunião, nós falamos durante cinco horas! (*nah* hay-*ooh*-nee-*ah*-ooh, nohz fah-*lah*-mohz doo-*rahn*-chee *sing*-koh oh-ruz!) (*During the meeting, we talked for five hours!*)

Elas falam muito bem. (eh-lahz *fah*-lah-ooh moh-*ee*-toh *bang*.) (*They speak really well.*)

Você fala quantas línguas? (voh-seh *fah*-lah *kwahn*-tuz *ling*-gwuz?) (*How many languages do you speak?*)

TIP

I bet this will be one of your favorite phrases of the whole book: **Como se diz. . .?** (*koh*–moo see *jeez*. . .?) (*How do you say. . .?*). This great phrase got me out of many linguistic jams.

Talkin' the Talk

AUDIO ONLINE

Maria Lucia (mah-*ree*-ah loo-*see*-ah) is in a café in the Ironbound section of Newark, New Jersey, which is home to large Portuguese and Brazilian populations. A waiter mistakes her for a non-Portuguese speaker; she's actually Brazilian. Notice how the waiter uses **a senhora** when speaking to the customer (a formal way of saying *you*,), and the customer uses the informal **você** to refer to the waiter (who is young – it's okay to address a stranger informally if they are under 30, say).

Waiter:	**A senhora fala português?**
	ah seen-*yoh*-rah *fah*-lah poh-too-*gez*?
	Do you speak Portuguese?
Maria Lucia:	**Sou brasileira. Você fala quantas línguas?**
	soh brah-zee-*lay*-rah. voh-*seh* fah-lah *kwahn*-tuz *ling*-gwuz?
	I'm Brazilian. How many languages do you speak?
Waiter:	**Eu falo inglês e francês — e português, é claro!**
	eh-ooh *fah*-loh eeng-*glehz* ee frahn-*sez* — ee poh-too-*gez*, eh *klah*-roh!
	I speak English and French — and Portuguese, of course!
Maria Lucia:	**É difícil falar francês?**
	eh jee-*fee*-see-ooh fah-*lah* frahn-*sez*?
	Is it hard to speak French?

Waiter:	**Não, é fácil.**
	nah-ooh, eh fah-see-ooh.
	No, it's easy.
Maria Lucia:	**E é difícil falar inglês?**
	ee eh jee-fee-see-ooh fah-lah eeng-glez?
	And is it hard to speak English?
Waiter:	**Inglês é mais difícil para mim.**
	eeng-glez eh mah-eez jee-fee-see-ooh pah-rah ming.
	English is harder for me.
Maria Lucia:	**Bom, eu só falo português!**
	boh-oong, eh-ooh soh fah-loh poh-too-gez!
	Well, I only speak Portuguese!
Waiter:	**Mas é a melhor língua do mundo . . .**
	mah-eez eh ah mel-yoh ling-gwah doo moon-doh . . .
	But it's the best language in the world . . .
Maria Lucia:	**É. Eu adoro falar português.**
	eh. eh-ooh ah-doh-roo fah-lah poh-too-gez.
	It is. I love speaking Portuguese.

• •

CULTURAL WISDOM

Does it seem unusual that **alguém** (ah-ooh-*gang*) (*someone*) would say she loves speaking her **língua nativa** (*ling*-gwah nah-*chee*-vah) (*native language*)? It's like saying that you love to speak English (if English is your native language). Well, for Brazilians, it's different. When famous Brazilians are interviewed and asked what they miss most about Brazil when they're **fora do país** (*foh*-rah doo pah-*eez*) (*out of the country*), they often say they miss **falar em português** (fah-*lah* ang poh-too-*gez*) (*speaking in Portuguese*). And the truth is, I miss speaking Portuguese, too, now that I'm not living in Brazil anymore!

WORDS TO KNOW

quantas	kwahn-tuz	which
É claro!	eh klah-roh!	Of course!
mais difícil	mah-eez jee-fee-see-ooh	harder
para mim	pah-rah ming	for me
Bom, . . .	boh-oong, . . .	Well, . . .
só	soh	only
mas	mah-eez	but
melhor	mel-yoh	better
mundo	moon-doh	world
eu adoro	eh-ooh ah-doh-roo	I love

Saying Goodbye

Saying goodbye to a Brazilian is easy! Well, the expression is **fácil** (*fah*-see-ooh) (*easy*), at least. When you've made **um bom amigo** (oong *boh*-oong ah-*mee*-goo) (*a good friend*) and you realize you won't see them for a while, it's **difícil** (jee-*fee*-see-ooh) (*difficult*) to say goodbye in any language.

The quick way to say goodbye is simply **Tchau!** (chow!) (*Ciao!*)

Todo mundo (*toh*-doo *moon*-doh) (*everyone*, Literally: *all world*) in Brazil — from the guy selling **abacaxi** (ah-bah-kah-*shee*) (*pineapple*) on the street to the **dono** (*doh*-noo) (*owner*) of the restaurant where you're eating — uses **Tchau** in almost all situations. It's not like in English, where *Ciao!* can sound a little snobby.

It's also very common to say **Até** (ah-*teh*) (*until*) plus another word referring to when you think you'll see the person **de novo** (jee *noh*-voh) (*again*). (I cover the Portuguese words for date and time references in Chapter 4.) But if you want to just **memorizar** (meh-moh-ree-*zah*) (*memorize*) one of the following phrases, pick **Até logo.** It never fails.

» **Até logo.** (ah-teh *loh*-goo.) (*See you later.*)

» **Até mais.** (ah-teh *mah*-eez.) (*See you;* Literally, *Until more*)

» **Até amanhã.** (ah-*teh* ah-mahn-*yah*.) (*See you tomorrow.*)

» **Até a semana que vem.** (ah-*teh* ah seh-*mah*-nah kee *vang*.) (*See you next week.*)

SOUND NATIVE

A gente se vê (ah *zhang*–chee see *veh*) (*See you around*) is a common way of saying *bye* in a casual situation.

FUN & GAMES

Time for a crossword puzzle. It's a short one! This one will be easy — instead of clues, you get the English translations of Portuguese words that fit into the puzzle.

Across

1. Mr.

5. Tall (masculine version of this adjective)

Down

2. Verb *to be* (temporary)

3. Hi

4. Verb *to talk*

6. Name

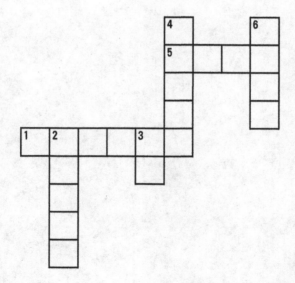

Turn to Appendix C for the answers.

numbers

» **Asking for and giving the time**

» **Expressing days of the week and calendar dates**

» **Stating size and weight using the metric system**

Chapter **4**

Getting Your Numbers, Times, and Measurements Straight

Knowing **números** (**noo**-meh-rohs) (*numbers*) in Portuguese is an easy way to make headway in learning the language. Numbers are everywhere — on price tags, clocks, weather reports, and financial news in the **jornal** (zhoh-nah-ooh) (*newspaper*). In this chapter, I tell you how to talk about numbers in Portuguese and also how to say the **dias da semana** (*jee*-us dah seh-*mahn*-ah) (*days of the week*), which, in Portuguese, involves numbers!

CULTURAL WISDOM

That's right; Brazilians refer to Monday, Tuesday, Wednesday, and so forth as "Second," "Third," "Fourth," and so on. The exceptions are **sábado** (*sah*-bah-doh) (*Saturday*) and **domingo** (doh-*ming*-goh) (*Sunday*), which have their own names.

Counting to 100 and Beyond

Good news! Numerals are the same in Portuguese as in English, so inside a Brazilian store, you can understand the price of something — even if you don't remember a single word of Portuguese. This may sound obvious, but a little familiarity when you're trying to maneuver in a new environment can provide some reassurance and maybe even the courage to initiate a little chat with the store clerk.

If you need to actually talk about a price tag, knowing how to say numbers as they're expressed in Portuguese helps. Prices are in **reáis** (hay–*ahys*), by the way — that's the name for Brazilian currency. (See Chapter 14 for details on Brazilian money. Chapters 7 and 8 cover buying food and going shopping.)

Whether you're telling the time, asking about street numbers, or talking about prices, you need to know how to say numbers. Here is how to say *one* through *ten*:

>> **um** (oong) (*one*)

>> **dois** (*doh*-eez) (*two*)

>> **três** (trehz) (*three*)

>> **quatro** (*kwah*-troo) (*four*)

>> **cinco** (*sing*-koo) (*five*)

>> **seis** (*say*-eez) (*six*)

>> **sete** (*seh*-chee) (*seven*)

>> **oito** (*oh*-ee-toh) (*eight*)

>> **nove** (*noh*-vee) (*nine*)

>> **dez** (dez) (*ten*)

Now check out the Portuguese words for 11 to 19:

>> **onze** (*ohn*-zee) (*11*)

>> **doze** (*doh*-zee) (*12*)

>> **treze** (*treh*-zee) (*13*)

>> **quatorze** (kah-*toh*-zee) (*14*)

>> **quinze** (*keen*-zee) (*15*)

>> **dezesseis** (dez-ee-*say*-eez) (*16*)

>> **dezessete** (dez-ee-*seh*-chee) (*17*)

>> **dezoito** (dez-*oh*-ee-toh) (*18*)

>> **dezenove** (dez-ee-*noh*-vee) (*19*)

And these are the numbers 20 to 100, counting by tens:

>> **vinte** (*ving*-chee) (*20*)

>> **trinta** (*treen*-tah) (*30*)

>> **quarenta** (kwah-*ren*-tah) (*40*)

>> **cinquenta** (sing-*kwen*-tah) (*50*)

>> **sessenta** (seh-*sen*-tah) (*60*)

>> **setenta** (seh-*ten*-tah) (*70*)

>> **oitenta** (oh-ee-*ten*-tah) (*80*)

>> **noventa** (noh-*ven*-tah) (*90*)

>> **cem** (sang) (*100*)

To say a double-digit number that doesn't end in zero, you just put the word **e** (ee) (*and*) in between your tens and ones digits. If you want to say *34*, for example, say **trinta e quatro** (*treen*-tah ee *kwah*-troh) (Literally: *30 and 4*).

To say *101–199*, use **cento e** (*sen*-too ee) (one hundred and) plus the rest of the number: **Cento e trinta e quatro** (*sen*-too ee *treen*-tah ee *kwah*-troh) is *134*, and **cento e oitenta e sete** (*sen*-too ee oh-ee-*ten*-tah ee *seh*-chee) is *187*.

For *201–999*, replace the **cento** with the following hundreds terms:

>> **duzentos** (doo-*zen*-tooz) (*200*)

>> **trezentos** (treh-*zen*-tooz) (*300*)

>> **quatrocentos** (kwah-troo-*sen*-tooz) (*400*)

>> **quinhentos** (keen-*yen*-tooz) (*500*)

>> **seiscentos** (say-*sen*-tooz) (*600*)

>> **setecentos** (seh-chee-*sen*-tooz) (*700*)

>> **oitocentos** (oh-ee-too-*sen*-tooz) (*800*)

>> **novecentos** (*noh*-vee-*sen*-tooz) (*900*)

One *thousand* is **mil** (*mee*-ooh), and *one million* is **um milhão** (oong meel-*yah*-ooh). For numbers in those ranges, just add an e and then the rest of the number, continuing on with the hundreds number and then the tens and the ones.

To say any number from *two million* to *one billion*, use **milhões** (meel-*yoh*-eez) (*millions*) instead of **milhão**.

Here are examples of a few numbers in the hundreds, thousands, and millions:

>> **quinhentos sessenta e quatro** (keen-*yen*-tohs seh-*sen*-tah ee *kwah*-troh) (564)

>> **seis mil duzentos e oito** (*say*-eez *mee*-ooh doo-*zen*-tooz ee *oh*-ee-toh) (6,208)

>> **dos milhões novecentos e dez** (*doh*-eez meel-*yoh*-eez noh-vee-*sen*-tohs ee *dehz*) (2,900,010)

Aside from enabling your retail therapy, knowing the Portuguese words for numbers is helpful when you need to express a certain year. If the year is in the 1900s, Brazilians say **mil novecentos e . . .** (*mee*-ooh noh-vee *sen*-tohz ee . . .) (*one thousand, nine hundred and . . .*). If the year falls in the current **século** (seh-koo-loh) (*century*), say **dois mil e . . .** (*doh*-eez *mee*-ooh ee . . .) (*two-thousand and . . .*).

If someone asks you when you were born, you can construct your answer similar to these possible answers:

>> **mil novecentos e cinquenta e dois** (*mee*-ooh noh-vee-*sen*-tohz ee sing-*kwehn*-tah ee *doh*-eez) (*1952*)

>> **mil novecentos e oitenta e três** (*mee*-ooh noh-vee-*sen*-tohz ee oh-ee-*tehn*-tah ee *trehz*) (*1983*)

>> **mil novecentos e setenta e quatro** (*mee*-ooh noh-vee-*sen*-tohz ee seh-*ten*-tah ee *kwah*-troh) (*1974*)

>> **dois mil e um** (*doh*-eez *mee*-ooh ee *oong*) (*2001*)

>> **dois mil e seis** (*doh*-eez *mee*-ooh ee *say*-eez) (*2006*)

You can shorten a year in the 1900's like we do in English by saying, for example, *I was born in '86* instead of saying *1986*: **Eu nasci em oitenta e seis** (*eh*-ooh nah-*see* ang oy-ee-*ten*-tah ee *say*-ees) (I was born in '86).

Ordering Sequences: First, Second, Third . . .

Ordinal numbers — first, second, third, and so on — apply to a wide range of conversations. A common one involves giving or getting directions. Someone may tell you to take the **primeira** (pree-*may*-rah) (*first*) left and then the **terceira** (teh-*say*-rah) (*third*) right. Or, you may need to know which floor to take an elevator to. Someone may say to take the elevator to the **sétimo** (seh-*chee*-moh) (*seventh*) floor.

Knowing how to express ordinal numbers also comes in handy when talking about the number of times you've done something. Maybe, for example, you want to tell someone it's your **segunda vez** (seh-*goon*-dah vehz) (*second time*) visiting Brazil.

Here's a helpful list for those types of situations:

» **primeiro** (pree-*may*-roh) (*first*)

» **segundo** (seh-*goon*-doh) (*second*)

» **terceiro** (teh-*say*-roh) (*third*)

» **quarto** (*kwah*-toh) (*fourth*)

» **quinto** (*keen*-toh) (*fifth*)

» **sexto** (*ses*-toh) (*sixth*)

» **sétimo** (seh-chee-moh) (*seventh*)

» **oitavo** (oh-ee-*tah*-voh) (*eighth*)

» **nono** (*noh*-noh) (*ninth*)

Try to remember to change the ending to **-a** instead of **-o** if the word that follows is feminine. (Flip back to Chapter 2 to review how feminine/masculine words work in Portuguese).

Here are some example sentences:

Pega a primeira à direita. (*peh*-gah ah pree-*may*-rah *ah* jee-*ray*-tah.) (*Take the first right.*)

Moro no quarto andar. (*moh*-roo noh *kwah*-toh ahn-*dah*.) (*I live on the fourth floor.*)

É a segunda porta. (*eh* ah seh-*goon*-dah *poh*-tah.) (*It's the second door.*)

Ele é o segundo filho da minha irmã. (eh-lee *eh* ooh seh-*goon*-doh *feel*-yoh dah *meen*-yah eeh-*mah*.) (*He's the second son of my sister.*)

CULTURAL WISDOM

In any building in Brazil, the **primeiro andar** (pree-*may*-roh ahn-*dah*) (*first floor*) is what Americans call the *second floor*. That's because Brazilians have a special term for the first floor: **o térreo** (ooh *teh*-hee-ooh) (*ground floor*). The *basement*, where parking garages are often located, is called the **subsolo** (soo-bee-*soh*-loo) (*underground*).

Telling Time

When you make social plans, the most important thing to ask may be **quando** (*kwahn*-doh) (*when*) an event will take place. This section tells you how to say what day and time you want to meet.

Saying the time of **dia** (*jee*-ah) (*day*) is easy in Portuguese. With a little practice, you can have it memorized in no time. To find out the time, say, **Que horas são?** (kee oh-rahz *sah*-ooh?) (*What time is it?*). To tell someone else what time it is, just say **São** (*sah*-ooz) (*It's*) plus the number of hours plus **e** (ee) (*and*) followed by the number of minutes. Here's an example:

> **São cinco e quinze.** (*sah*-ooh *sing*-koh ee *keen*-zee.) (*It's 5:15.*)

Just like in English, Brazilians say **horas** (*o'clock*) for each full hour of the day. In the preceding example, you wouldn't say **São cinco e quinze horas** because it's a "between time." You would, however, say **São cinco horas** (*sah*-ooh *sing*-koh *oh*-rahz) if it were 5 o'clock on the dot.

To specify *a.m.* or *p.m.*, add **da manhã** (dah mahn-*yah*) (*a.m.*; Literally: *in the morning*), **da tarde** (dah *tah*-jee) (*in the afternoon*), or **da noite** (dah noh-ee-chee) (*after about 7 p.m. — when it gets dark*; Literally: *in the night*). There's no exact translation for *a.m.* or *p.m.* — **da tarde** and **da noite** both denote *p.m.*

CULTURAL WISDOM

Brazilians often use military time, especially in formal situations, such as when checking transportation schedules. Is your **ônibus** (oh-*nee*-boos) (bus) leaving **às seis horas** (ahz *say*-eez *oh*-rahz) (at 6 a.m.) or **às 18 horas** (ahz dez-*oy*-ee-toh *oh*-rahz) (at 6 p.m.; Literally – at 18 hours)?

TIP

If it's half past the hour, say **e meia** (ee *may*-ah) (*and a half*).

Here are some time-telling examples:

> **São duas horas.** (*sah*-ooh *doo*-ahz *oh*-rahz.) (*It's two o'clock.*)
>
> **São duas e meia.** (*sah*-ooh *doo*-ahz ee *may*-ah.) (*It's 2:30.*)

São quinze para as três. (*sah*-ooh *keen*-zee pah-rah ahz *trehz*.) (*It's 15 to 3:00 [it's 2:45].*)

São onze e quinze da noite. (*sah*-ooh *ohn*-zee ee *keen*-zee *dah* noh-ee-chee.) (*It's 11:15 p.m.*)

São oito e dez da manhã. (*sah*-ooh *oh*-ee-toh ee *dez dah* mahn-*yah*.) (*It's 8:10 a.m.*)

In English, people sometimes give the time as *quarter after* or *five till* a certain hour. Brazilians sometimes use similar phrases and constructions. For times 15 minutes after the hour, you have the option of saying **e quinze** (ee *keen*-zee) (*and 15*) or **e um quarto** (ee oong *kwah*-too) (*and a quarter*) when you refer to the minutes. For times ending in 45, you can say either **quinze para a/as** (*keen*-zee *pah*-rah ah/ahz) (*15 to*) before you give the hour or **e quarenta e cinco** (ee kwah-ren-tah ee *sing*-koh) (*and 45*) after you give the hour.

Midnight is **meia-noite** (*may*-ah *noh*-ee-chee), and *noon* is **meio-dia** (*may*-oh *jee*-ah) (Literally: *midday*). In these cases — and when you say *It's one o'clock* — use **É** instead of **São,** because the number one and the words *midnight* and *noon* are singular:

É meia-noite. (eh *may*-ah *noh*-ee-chee.) (*It's midnight.*)

É meio-dia. (eh *may*-oh *jee*-ah.) (*It's noon.*)

É uma. (eh *ooh*-mah.) (*It's one.*)

É uma e vinte. (eh *ooh*-mah ee *veen*-chee.) (*It's 1:20.*)

Here are some other words and phrases that indicate time:

» **hoje à noite** (*oh*-zhee ah *noh*-ee-chee) (*tonight*)

» **noite** (*noh*-ee-chee) (*night*)

» **manhã** (mahn-*yah*) (*morning*)

» **cedo** (*seh*-doo) (*early*)

» **tarde** (*tah*-jee) (*late* and/or *afternoon,* for example, **da tarde**)

If you're meeting up with someone, you may want to ask **a que horas** (ah kee *oh*-rahz) (*at what time*) you'll be meeting. If you're responding to the question, leave out the **são** and just give the time: **Às nove e meia** (ahz *noh*-vee ee *may*-ah) (*at 9:30*), for example.

So, to review, when you're talking about what time it is, **São** means *It is . . .* and **Às** means *At. . . .*

Talking about Days of the Week

CULTURAL WISDOM

Dias da semana (*jee*-ahz dah seh-*mah*-nah) (*days of the week*) in Portuguese reflect Brazil's Catholic heritage. The explanation goes that a sixth-century bishop in Portugal wanted to break with a pagan tradition at the time in which Monday through Friday in many Latin languages were named after pagan Gods. Spanish, for example, still uses pagan terms for some of their days of the week today — **martes** in Spanish means *Tuesday*, and that word comes from the *God of Mars*, for example.

In Portugal way back when, the country's system was changed to reflect the week of Easter.

Domingo (doh-*ming*-goh) (*Sunday*) derives from *day of the lord*. **Sábado** (*sah*-bah-doh) (*Saturday*) comes from the Hebrew word for their most religious day of the week, *Shabbat* in Hebrew.

Monday through Friday in Portuguese are referred to as the *second, third, fourth, fifth, and sixth vacation days*, because during Easter week, most people historically in Portugal don't have to go to work. **Feira** (*fay*-rah) means *holiday*. **Domingo** counts as the first day of the week, so *Monday* is referred to in Portuguese as **segunda-feira** (seh-*goon*-dah *fay*-rah) (Literally: *second holiday*).

Here are the Portuguese terms for days of the week:

>> **segunda-feira** (seh-*goon*-dah-*fay*-rah) (*Monday*)

>> **terça-feira** (*teh*-sah-*fay*-rah) (*Tuesday*)

>> **quarta-feira** (*kwah*-tah-*fay*-rah) (*Wednesday*)

>> **quinta-feira** (*keen*-tah-*fay*-rah) (*Thursday*)

>> **sexta-feira** (*seh*-stah-*fay*-rah) (*Friday*)

>> **sábado** (*sah*-bah-doh) (*Saturday*)

>> **domingo** (doh-*ming*-goo) (*Sunday*)

SOUND NATIVE

Brazilians also sometimes refer to weekdays by their name without the word **feira**. People often just say **segunda** or **quarta** or **sexta** — instead of **segunda-feira**, **quarta-feira**, and **sexta-feira** to mean *Monday*, *Wednesday*, and *Friday*.

To say *on* a certain day of the week, such as *on Sunday*, say **no** (noh) or **na** (nah) before the day of the week — **no** if the day is a masculine word (if it ends in **-o**), **na** if it's feminine (if it ends in **-a**):

- » **no domingo** (noh doh-*ming*-goh) (*on Sunday*)

- » **na segunda** (nah seh-*goon*-dah) (*on Monday*)

- » **na terça** (nah *teh*-sah) (*on Tuesday*)

- » **na quarta** (nah *kwah*-tah) (*on Wednesday*)

- » **na quinta** (nah *keen*-tah) (*on Thursday*)

- » **na sexta** (nah *seh*-stah) (*on Friday*)

- » **no sábado** (noh *sah*-bah-doh) (*on Saturday*)

Here are some example sentences:

Tem um show na quarta. (tang oong *shoh* nah *kwah*-tah.) (*There's a show on Wednesday.*)

Na segunda, eu preciso trabalhar. (nah seh-*goon*-dah, eh-ooh preh-*see*-zoo trah-bal-*yah*.) (*On Monday, I need to work.*)

Vamos sair na sexta? (vah-mooz sah-*eeh* nah *seh*-stah?) (*Should we go out on Friday?*)

The following words and phrases are expressions of time that go beyond the days of the week when you're looking at a **calendário** (kah-len-*dah*-ree-ooh) (*calendar*):

- » **hoje** (*oh*-zhee) (*today*)

- » **amanhã** (ah-mahn-*yah*) (*tomorrow*)

- » **na semana que vem** (nah seh-*mah*-nah kee *vang*) (*next week*)

- » **no fim de semana** (noh *fing* jee seh-*mah*-nah) (*on the weekend*)

- » **no mês que vem** (noh *mez* kee *vang*) (*next month*)

SOUND NATIVE

Brazilians love to use the verb **combinar** (kohm-bee-*nah*), which means *to plan to get together*. It looks like it would mean *to combine*, but in reality, the word means *to arrange* or *to organize*. Here are a couple examples:

Vamos combinar para sair em breve. (*vah*-mohz kohm-bee-*nah* pah-rah sah-*eeh* ang *breh*-vee.) (*Let's plan to get together to go out soon.*)

Já combinou com ela? (*zhah* kohm-bee-*noh* koh-oong *eh*-lah?) (*Did you already make plans with her?*)

Combinado! (kohm-bee-*nah*-doo!) is a common expression that people use after deciding on a time and place to meet. It means *Agreed!*

Talkin' the Talk

AUDIO ONLINE

Valéria (vah-*leh*-ree-ah) really loves attending art events. She asks her hotel concierge what sorts of events are happening in town that she might like.

Concierge:	**Tem um espetáculo de dança moderna na semana que vem.**
	tang oong eh-speh-*tah*-koo-loh jee *dahn*-sah moh-*deh*-nah nah seh-*mah*-nah kee *vang*.
	There's a modern dance show next week.
Valéria:	**Ah é? Vale a pena ir?**
	ah *eh*? vah-*lee* ah *peh*-nah *ee*?
	Really? Is it worth going to?
Concierge:	**Sim, é uma companhia muito boa.**
	sing, *eh* ooh-mah kohm-pahn-*yee*-ah moh-*ee*-toh *boh*-ah.
	Yes, it's a very good company.
Valéria:	**Que dia, e a que horas?**
	kee *jee*-ah, ee ah kee *oh*-rahz?
	What day, and what time?
Concierge:	**Na sexta, às oito da noite.**
	nah *seh*-stah, ahz *oh*-ee-toh dah *noh*-ee-chee.
	On Friday, at 8:00 at night.
Valéria:	**Quando acaba?**
	kwahn-doh ah-*kah*-bah?
	When does it end?
Concierge:	**Às dez horas, mais ou menos.**
	ahz dehz *oh*-rahz, *mah*-eez ooh *meh*-noos.
	At around 10:00.

Valéria:	**Tá. Posso comprar o ingresso antes do show?**
	tah. poh-soo kohm-prah ooh eeng-greh-soo ahn-cheez doo shoh?
	Okay. Can I buy a ticket before the show?
Concierge:	**Pode. Mas tenta chegar meia-hora antes.**
	poh-jee. mah-eez ten-tah sheh-gah may-ah-oh-rah ahn-cheez.
	You can. But try to get there half an hour beforehand.

WORDS TO KNOW

dança moderna	dahn-sah moh-deh-nah	modern dance
companhia	kohm-pahn-yee-ah	company
Que dia?	kee jee-ah?	What day?
Quando acaba?	kwahn-doh ah-kah-bah?	When does it end?
mais ou menos	mah-eez ooh meh-noos	around (Literally: more or less)
Tá.	tah.	Okay.
Posso. . .?	poh-soo. . .?	Can I. . .?
um ingresso	oong eeng-greh-soo	a ticket
antes	ahn-cheez	before
show	shoh	show

Specifying Times and Dates

Você está planejando uma viagem? (voh–*seh* eh–*stah* plah-neh-*zhahn*-doh ooh-mah vee–*ah*-zhang?) (*Are you planning a trip?*) You may want to decide on which day of the month and at what time of day you'll be doing things. Do you want to depart on April 10th at 7 a.m.? Or on August 2nd at 3:30 p.m.? (Flip to Chapter 13 to find out how to say the Portuguese words for months of the year.)

To say *on a certain day*, use **no dia** (noo *jee*-ah) plus the day of the month, then **de** (jee) and the month (noo *jee*-ah . . . jee . . .) to say *on such-and-such day of such-and-such month*. For example, **no dia quinze de setembro** (noo *jee*-ah *keen*-zee jee seh-*tem*-broh) is *on September 15*.

Practice these phrases that include dates and times:

» **no dia três de outubro, às oito e vinte e cinco da manhã** (noo *jee*-ah *trehz* jee oh-*too*-broh, ahz *oh*-ee-toh ee *veen*-chee ee *sing*-koh dah mahn-*yah*) (*on October 3, at 8:25 a.m.*)

» **no dia vinte e dois de agosto, às vinte horas** (noo *jee*-ah *veen*-chee ee *doh*-eez jee ah-*goh*-stoh, ahz *veen*-chee *oh*-rahz) (*on August 22, at 8:00 p.m.* — here expressed in military time; Literally: *20 hours*)

» **no dia dezessete de dezembro, às vinte e uma horas e cinquenta minutos** (noo *jee*-ah dehz-ee-*seh*-chee jee deh-*zem*-broh, ahz *veen*-chee ee *ooh*-mah *oh*-rahz ee sing-*kwen*-tah mee-*noo*-tohz) (*on December 17, at 9:50 p.m.* — here expressed in military time; Literally, *21 hours and 50 minutes*)

» **no dia quatorze de maio, às dez e quinze da manhã** (noo *jee*-ah kah-*toh*-zee jee *my*-oh, ahz *dez* ee *keen*-zee dah mahn-*yah*) (*on May 14, at 10:15 a.m.*)

Brazilian Portuguese follows the European way of writing **datas** (*dah*-tuz) (*dates*): day, month, year. In the United States, most people write 5-23-76 to mean May 23, 1976. In Portuguese, the same date is written this way: 23.5.76. And yes, Brazilians use periods for dates more often than hyphens or slashes. Knowing this system of writing dates comes in handy if you're in Brazil and need to fill out a form.

Getting Familiar with the Metric System

Measuring things such as volume and weight is a necessity in any language. If you happen to be an American, you'll find that the way Brazilians measure stuff is different: They use the metric system, like most other countries in the world.

When you're at the market, fruits and vegetables are weighed in **quilos** (*kee*-lohs) (*kilos*, short for *kilograms*). Distances between towns are measured in **quilômetros** (kee-*loh*-meh-trohs) (*kilometers*). And instead of referring to inches and feet, Brazilians talk about a person's **altura** (ah-ooh-*too*-rah) (*height*) and **peso** (*peh*-zoh) (*weight*) in terms of **metros** (*meh*-trohs) (*meters*) and **quilos.**

Here are some common expressions that relate to these terms:

Quanto você pesa? (*kwahn*-toh voh-*seh peh*-zah?) (*How much do you weigh?*)

A quantos quilômetros está? (ah *kwan*-tohs kee-*loh*-meh-trohs eh-*stah?*) (*How many kilometers away is it?*)

Eu meço 1,70 metros. (eh-ooh *meh*-soo *um* pohn-toh *seh*-chee *meh*-tros.) (*I'm one point seven meters [about 5 feet and 6 inches].*)

Check out Table 4-1 for metric measurements and equivalents of the British Imperial system (used by Americans).

TABLE 4-1   **Conversion of Measurements: Metric to Imperial**

Measurement	Term	Pronunciation	Translation	Imperial Equivalent
distance	**quilômetro**	kee-*loh*-meh-troh	*kilometer*	0.62 miles
length	**centímetro**	sen-*chee*-meh-troh	*centimeter*	0.4 inches
length	**metro**	*meh*-troh	*meter*	3.28 feet
volume	**litro**	*lee*-troh	*liter*	1.06 quarts
weight/mass	**quilo**	*kee*-loh	*kilogram*	2.2 pounds
temperature	**centígrados**	sen-*chee*-grah-dohz	*degrees Celsius*	Celsius temperature × ⅑₅ + 32

Talkin' the Talk

AUDIO ONLINE

Jorginho (zhoh-*zhing*-yoh) (*"little George"*) and **Luciano** (loo-see-*ah*-noh) are at an outdoor market looking for some **limões** (lee-*moy*-eez) (*limes*) to buy to make some **caipirinhas** (kah-ee-pee-*ring*-yuz), Brazil's national cocktail, made with cachaça liquor, sugar, and lime.

Jorginho: **Quantos quilos de limão você acha que precisamos?**

            kwan-tohs *kee*-lohs jee lee-*mah*-ooh voh-seh *ah*-shah kee preh-see-*zah*-mooz?

            How many kilos of lime do you think we need?

Luciano: **Uns seis ou sete?**

oonz *say*-ees ooh *seh*-chee?

About six or seven?

Jorginho: **Temos vinte convidados, né?**

teh-mooz *veen*-chee kohn-vee-*dah*-dooz, *neh?*

We have 20 guests, right?

Luciano: **Sim.**

sing.

Yes.

Jorginho: **Eu acho que precisamos muito mais do que isso.**

eh-ooh *ah*-shoo kee preh-see-*zah*-mooz moh-*ee*-toh *mah*-eez doh kee *ee*-soh.

I think we need a lot more than that.

Luciano: **Então compramos quinze?**

en-*tah*-ooh kohm-*prah*-mooz *keen*-zee?

So let's buy 15?

- -

WORDS TO KNOW

quantos	kwan-tohs	how many
acha que	ah-shah kee	do you think that
precisamos	preh-see-zah-mooz	we need
uns	oonz	about (+ number)
temos	teh-mooz	we have
convidados	kohn-vee-dah-dooz	guests
né?	neh?	right?
Eu acho	eh-ooh ah-shoo	I think
muito mais	moh-ee-toh mah-eez	much more
isso	ee-soh	that

FUN & GAMES

Paula is a banker. On a typical day, she gets up at 6 a.m., and she heads to work at 7:15 a.m. She has lunch at 1 p.m. She leaves work at different times each day but always eats dinner at 8:30 p.m. Match each clock with the appropriate time:

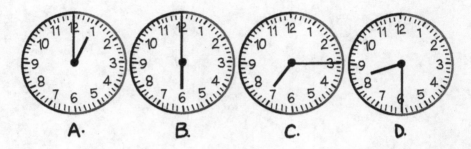

A.   B.   C.   D.

Illustration by Elizabeth Kurtzman

1 Às seis da manhã

2 Às sete e quinze da manhã

3 À uma da tarde

4 Às oito e trinta da noite

Check out the answers in Appendix C.

IN THIS CHAPTER

» **Naming the rooms and items in the home**

» **Chatting about sleeping and waking up**

» **Discussing breakfast, lunch, and dinner**

» **Talking about cleaning house**

» **Having a phone conversation**

Chapter **5**

Speaking Portuguese at Home

G et comfy, because you're about to discover all the homey words in Portuguese. Knowing how to say the parts of a **casa** (*kah*-zah) (*house*) or **apartamento** (ah-*pah*-tah-*men*-toh) (*apartment*) is the bread and butter of a new language; these are the words of everyday life.

In Brazil, like most other countries, **moradores urbanos** (moh-rah-*doh*-reez oohr-*bah*-nooz) (*city dwellers*) tend to live in apartments and people in **áreas rurais** (*ah*-ree-ahs roo-*rah*-eez) (*rural areas*) usually live in houses.

Although Brazil's **classe média** (*klah*-see meh-jah) (*middle-class*) is getting larger thanks to a growing economy, there are still a lot of **ricos** (koohs) (*rich people*) and **pobres** (oohz poh-breez) (*poor people*) in Brazil.

CULTURAL WISDOM

Os muito (oohz moh-*ee*-toh) (*the very*) **ricos** often live in gated mansions, whereas **os pobres** live clustered together in shantytowns on steep hillsides that used to be called **favelas** (fah-*veh*-lahs). **Favelas** were named after the *favela tree*, a hardscrabble plant known for withstanding drought. The idea is that the people living in **favelas** were similar to these resilient trees; they can survive in a harsh environment. Now these neighborhoods are referred to as **comunidades** (koh-moon-ee-*dah*-jees) (*shantytowns*).

Seeing What Makes Up a Home

Most Brazilian homes are like any others in the world. They're situated in a **bairro** (*bah-ee-hoo*) (*neighborhood*), and they have a front **porta** (*poh-*tah) (*door*); a place to **cozinhar** (koh-zeen-*yah*) (*cook*), **comer** (koh-*meh*) (*eat*), and **dormir** (dohr-*mee*) (*sleep*); and a **banheiro** (bahn-*yay*-roh) (*bathroom*).

The **sala de estar** (*sah*-lah jee eh-*stah*) (*living room*) is where Brazilians have their **televisão** (teh-leh-vee-*zah*-ooh) (*television*), which they use to catch the latest episode of their favorite **novela** (noh-*veh*-lah) (*soap opera*).

Take a look at Table 5-1 for a tour of the basic words used to describe different parts of a Brazilian home and the items in it.

TABLE 5-1

Living-Space Words

Term	Pronunciation	Translation
casa	*kah*-zah	*house*
apartamento	ah-*pah*-tah-*men*-toh	*apartment*
porta	*poh*-tah	*door*
janela	zhah-*neh*-lah	*window*
luz	looz	*light*
quarto	*kwah*-toh	*room* or *bedroom*
cama	*kah*-mah	*bed*
armário	ahr-*mah*-ree-ooh	*closet*
cômoda	*koh*-moh-dah	*dresser*
travesseiro	trah-veh-*say*-roh	*pillow*
lençóis	len-*soh*-eez	*sheets*
sala de estar	*sah*-lah jee eh-*stah*	*living room*
sofá	soh-*fah*	*sofa*
televisão	teh-leh-vee-*zah*-ooh	*television*
escrivaninha	es-kree-vah-*nee*-ah	*desk*
sala de jantar	*sah*-lah jee zhahn-*tah*	*dining room*
mesa	*meh*-zah	*table*

Term	Pronunciation	Translation
cadeira	kah-*day*-rah	*chair*
cozinha	koh-*zeen*-yah	*kitchen*
geladeira	zheh-lah-*day*-rah	*refrigerator*
fogão	foh-*gah*-ooh	*stove*
banheiro	bahn-*yay*-roh	*bathroom*
pia	*pee*-ah	*sink*
vaso	*vah*-soh	*toilet*
banheira	bahn-*yay*-rah	*bathtub*
varanda	vah-*rahn*-dah	*balcony*
pátio	*pah*-chee-ooh	*patio*
lavadora/secadora	lah-vah-*doh*-rah/seh-kah-*doh*-rah	*washer/dryer*
jardim	zhah-*jing*	*garden*
piscina	pee-*see*-nah	*pool*
garagem	gah-*rah*-zhang	*garage*

CULTURAL WISDOM

Here are some particular aspects of a Brazilian home:

>> All apartments have an **área de serviço** (*ah*-ree-ah jee seh-*vee*-soo) (Literally: *service area*), a nice area with a tiled floor, either **dentro** (*den*-troh) (*inside*) or **fora** (*for*-ah) outside the home on a balcony where you can put a washer/dryer, or hang wet clothes to dry, if you do not own a dryer (as is true for some Brazilians who live in the warmer regions).

>> In general, Brazilian stoves are gas-powered. Locals call a propane tank vendor to refill gas whenever it's needed. The more modern buildings have central gas. Electric cooktops are becoming more and more common these days, especially as part of mini-kitchens installed on balconies, which families use to cook special meals when entertaining.

>> Tap water is okay for cooking and cleaning, but many Brazilians do not drink it. Some people keep 5-gallon plastic jugs of filtered drinking water in their apartments; these jugs sit on top of a plastic base with a spigot. Locals call a company to come refill the water tank every week or so. In other homes, there's a wall-mounted filter connected to the tap.

Living in the Big City

São Paulo, Brazil's largest city, is home to more than 21 million **habitantes** (ah-bee-*tahn*-chees) (*residents*) and has many high-rise residential **prédios** (preh-joos) (*buildings*) with many **andares** (ahn-*dah*-reez) (*floors*). From the air, the sheer number of tall buildings is staggering — far more than you see by plane if you look down upon New York City or London, for example. The city also includes **bairros** (*bah*-ee-hoos) (*neighborhoods*) characterized by small apartment buildings that have two or three **andares**. Single-family **casas** (*kah*-zahs) (*homes*) exist as well, and on the outskirts, millions live in poverty in the shacks that make up the **comunidades** (koh-moon-ee-*dah*-jees) (*shantytowns*). But perhaps for most **paulistanos** (pah-ooh-lee-*stahn*-oos) (*people who live in São Paulo*), an **apartamento** (ah-*pah*-tah-*men*-too) (*apartment*) is what they call home.

Here are some basic words you can use to talk about living in an **apartamento**:

> » **térreo** (*teh*-hee-ooh) (*ground floor*)

> » **salão** (sah-*lah*-ooh) (*lobby*)

> » **caixa de correio** (*kah*-eeh-shah jee koh-*hay*-ooh) (*mailbox*)

> » **elevador** (eh-leh-vah-*dohr*) (*elevator*)

> » **escadas** (es-*kah*-dahs) (*stairs*)

> » **andar** (ahn-*dahr*) (*floor*, as in floors of a building)

THE LARGEST RESIDENTIAL BUILDING IN LATIN AMERICA

In São Paulo's city **centro** (*sen*-troo) (*center*), a massive, wavy building with 23 floors called **o Copan** (ooh koo-*pah*) (The Copan) has its own zip code. With about 5,000 residents, **o Copan** qualifies as the largest residential building in Latin America. O Copan was built in the 1950s by a famous architect, Oscar Niemeyer, as a social experiment, drawing both low- and high-income earners with its apartments of different sizes. I lived there for about **um ano** (*oong ahn*-yoh) (*a year*). It has many **lojas** (*loh*-zhahs) (*shops*) on the ground floor, and fantastic **vistas** (*vees*-tahs) (*views*) from the **terraço** (teh-*hah*-soh) (*rooftop area*). My **vizinhos** (vee-*zeen*-yoos) (*neighbors*) included people from all walks of life, such as filmmakers, **advogados** (ahj-voo-gah-dooz) (*lawyers*) and caregivers for the elderly. Apartment **tamanhos** (tah-*mahn*-yoos) (*sizes*) range from 300 **pés quadrados** (*pez* kwah-*drah*-dooz) (*square feet*) to 4,500 **pés quadrados**.

» **subir** (soo-*beeh*) (*to go up*)

» **descer** (deh-*seh*) (*to go down*)

» **barulho** (bah-*rool*-yoh) (*noise*)

» **bater na porta** (bah-*teh* nah *poh*-tah) (*knock on the door*)

If you're looking to **alugar** (ah-loo-*gah*) (*rent*) an **apartamento**, you may find these words helpful:

» **proprietário** (proh-pree-eh-*tah*-ree-ooh) (*landlord*)

» **inquilino/a** (een-kee-*lee*-noo) (*tenant*)

» **companheiro/a de quarto** (kohm-pahn-*yay*-roh/rah jee *kwah*-too) (*roommate*)

» **eletricidade** (eh-leh-*tree*-see-*dah*-jee) (*electricity*)

» **aquecimento** (ah-*keh*-see-*men*-toh) (*heat*)

» **ar condicionado** (*ahr* kohn-*dee*-see-ooh-*nah*-doo) (*air conditioning*)

» **renovado** (heh-noh-*vah*-doo) (*renovated*)

» **aluguel mensal** (ah-loo-*gehl* men-*sah*-ooh) (*monthly rent*)

» **depósito** (deh-*poh*-zee-toh) (*deposit*)

» **referências pessoais** (heh-feh-*ren*-see-ahs peh-soh-*ah*-eez) (*personal references*)

» **chave** (*shah*-vee) (*key*)

» **trancado** (trahn-*kah*-doo) (*locked*)

» **detector de fumaça** (deh-tek-*tohr* jee foo-*mah*-sah) (*smoke detector*)

» **alarme de incêndio** (ah-*lahr*-mee jee een-*sen*-dee-ooh) (*fire alarm*)

» **lavanderia** (lah-*vahn*-dah-*ree*-ah) (*laundry*)

» **garagem** (gah-*rah*-zhang) (*garage with assigned parking spots*)

If you visit a place and like it, you can tell the person showing you the place, **Eu gosto!** (*eh*-ooh *goh*-stoo) (*I like it!*). **Gostaria de firmar um contrato** (goh-stah-*ree*-ah jee feer-*mah oong* kohn-*trah*-too) (*I'd like to sign a contract*). If you don't like it, you can say, **Não estou interesado/a** (*nah*-ooh es-*toh* een-*teh*-reh-*sah*-doo/dah – use **interesado** if you're male and **interesada** if you're female) (*I'm not interested*). After you've moved into a new place, be sure to tell your **convidados** (kohn-vee-*dah*-dooz) (*guests*), **Bem-vindo a minha casa!** (bang *veen*-doo ah *ming*-ya *kah*-zah) (*Welcome to my house!*)

Getting Some Sleep

If you want to **dormir bem** (dohr-*mee bang*) (*sleep well*) when visiting Brazil, you should probably ask the **hotel** (oh-*tay*-ooh) (*hotel*) or **pousada** (poh-*zah*-dah) (*guesthouse*) receptionist whether to expect **barulho** (bah-*rool*-yoh) (*noise*).

TIP

Brazilians seem to have a high tolerance for **barulho.** So, another question to ask may be whether the place is close to any **bares** (*bah*-reez) (*bars*) or **música ao vivo** (*moo*-zeeh-kah ah-ooh *vee*-voh) (*live music*), especially if you'll be there **no fim de semana** (noh *fing* jee seh-*mah*-nah) (*on the weekend*).

Hopefully, conjugating **dormir** will be a good luck charm for your sound sleep in any **quarto** (*kwah*-toh) (*bedroom/room*).

Conjugation	Pronunciation
eu durmo	*eh*-ooh *duhr*-moh
você dorme	voh-*seh dohr*-mee
ele/ela dorme	*eh*-lee/*eh*-lah *dohr*-mee
nós dormimos	*nohz* dohr-*mee*-mooz
eles/elas dormem	*eh*-leez/*eh*-lahz *dohr*-mang
vocês dormem	voh-*sehz dohr*-mang

These phrases use the present tense of **dormir** as well as the infinitive (unconjugated) form of the verb:

Eu preciso dormir oito horas. (*eh*-ooh preh-*see*-zoo dohr-*mee* oh-ee-toh *oh*-rahz.) (*I need to sleep eight hours.*)

Os gatos dormem no meu quarto. (ooz *gah*-tohz *dohr*-mang noh *meh*-ooh *kwah*-toh.) (*The cats sleep in my room.*)

Adoro dormir em redes. (ah-*doh*-roo dohr-*mee* ang *heh*-jees.) (*I love to sleep in hammocks.*)

Você dorme muito ou pouco? (voh-*seh dohr*-mee moh-*ee*-toh ooh *poh*-koo?) (*Do you generally sleep a lot or a little?*)

Vou dormir. Boa noite. (*voh* dohr-*mee*. *boh*-ah *noh*-ee-chee.) (*I'm going to bed. Good night.*)

A useful sleep-related phrase is **estar com sono** (eh-*stah* kohng *soh*-noo) (*to be sleepy*):

> **Está com sono?** (eh-*stah* kohng *soh*-noo?) (*Are you sleepy?*)
>
> **Estou com sono.** (eh-*stoh* kohng *soh*-noo.) (*I'm sleepy.*)

SOUND NATIVE

Hopefully, you'll never have **pesadelos** (*peh*-zah-*deh*-looz) (*nightmares*) — only **sonhos doces** (*sohn*-yooz *doh*-seez) (*sweet dreams*)! May you **dormir com os anjinhos** (dohr-*mee* kohng ooz ahn-*zheen*-yohs) (*sleep with angels*) tonight; that's a very Brazilian expression.

Waking Up

Acorda! (ah-*kohr*-dah!) (*Wake up!*) is what a Brazilian may say if you haven't set your **despertador** (deh-*speh*-tah-doh) (*alarm clock*) properly. In **hotéis e pousadas** (oh-*tay*-eez ee poh-zah-dahz) (*hotels and guesthouses*), you can always request a wake-up call. Say **Poderia me acordar a/às . . .** (poh-deh-*ree*-ah mee ah-koh-*dah* ah/ahz . . .) (*Could you wake me up at . . .*) plus a time. (For time-related words and expressions, see Chapter 4.)

Here's how to conjugate **acordar**.

Conjugation	Pronunciation
eu acordo	*eh*-ooh ah-*kohr*-doo
você acorda	voh-*seh* ah-*kohr*-dah
ele/ela acorda	*eh*-lee/*eh*-lah ah-*kohr*-dah
nós acordamos	*nohz* ah-kohr-*dah*-mooz
eles/elas acordam	*eh*-leez/*eh*-lahz ah-*kohr*-dah-ooh
vocês acordam	voh-*sehz* ah-*kohr*-dah-ooh

Try using **acordar**:

> **Eu acordo cedo.** (*eh*-ooh ah-*kohr*-doo *seh*-doh.) (*I wake up early.*)
>
> **Ela acorda tarde.** (*eh*-lah ah-*kohr*-dah *tah*-jee.) (*She wakes up late.*)
>
> **Poderia me acordar às oito horas?** (poh-deh-*ree*-ah mee ah-kohr-*dah* ahz *oh*-ee-toh *oh*-rahz? (*Could you wake me up at 8 o'clock?*)

Chatting about Food

The word **cozinha** (koh-*zeen*-yah) (*kitchen*) comes from the verb **cozinhar** (koh-zeen-*yah*), which means *to cook*.

The food you'll find in a Brazilian **cozinha** varies from region to region and family to family. Generally speaking, because **arroz** (ah-*hohz*) (*rice*), **feijão** (fay-*zhow*) (*beans*), and **carne** (*kah*-nee) (*meat*) are staples of the national cuisine, these are the most common dishes in any Brazilian household. Many families also make easy weeknight meals such as **massa** (*mah*-sah) (*pasta*) and **salada** (sah-*lah*-dah) (*salad*), just like in many other countries in Latin America as well as North America and Europe.

CULTURAL WISDOM

For special occasions, such as a birthday, Brazilians love to host a **churrasco** (shoo-*hahs*-koh) (*Brazilian-style barbeque*) on their back outdoor **pátio** (pah-chee-ooh) (*patio*). They grill all kinds of **carne** and offer a variety of **acompanhamentos** (ah-kohm-pahn-yah-*men*-toos) (*side dishes*).

Here are some questions you might want to ask a Brazilian friend about cooking:

O quê gosta de cozinhar? (ooh *kee gohs*-tah jee koh-zeen-*yah?*) (*What do you like to cook?*) **Salada?** (sah-*lah*-dah?) (*Salad?*) **Carne?** (*kah*-nee?) (*Meat?*) **Peixe?** (*pay*-shee?) (*Fish?*) **Sobremesa?** (soh-bree-*meh*-zah?) (*Dessert?*)

Você cozinha bem? (voh-*seh* koh-zeen-yah bang?) (*Do you cook well?*)

Here's how to conjugate **cozinhar** (koh-zeen-*yah*) (*to cook*).

Conjugation	Pronunciation
eu cozinho	*eh*-ooh koh-*zeen*-yoo
você cozinha	voh-*seh* koh-*zeen*-yah
ele/ela cozinha	*eh*-lee/*eh*-lah koh-*zeen*-yah
nós cozinhamos	*nohz* koh-zeen-*yah*-mooz
eles/elas cozinham	*eh*-leez/*eh*-lahz koh-*zeen*-yah-ooh
vocês cozinham	voh-*sehz* koh-*zeen*-yah-ooh

TIP

When visiting a Brazilian home for food and drinks, you may eventually need a restroom. You can just say **O banheiro?** (ooh bahn-*yay*-roh?) (*The bathroom?*). Or, to speak in a complete sentence, you can ask, **Por favor, onde fica o banheiro?** (poh fah-*voh*, ohn-jee *fee*-kah ooh bahn-*yay*-roh?) (*Where is the bathroom, please?*) To be extra polite, substitute **toalete** (toe-ah-*leh*-chee) (*toilet*) for **banheiro**.

If you prefer going to **restaurantes** (heh-stah-ooh-*rahn*-cheez) (*restaurantes*), flip to Chapter 7 to check out some classic dishes to order at a Brazilian restaurant and find out how to order a meal. To find out what Brazilians eat at various times of day as well as how to talk about your meals in Portuguese, keep on reading!

Getting breakfast

First things first: The Portuguese phrase for **o café da manhã** (ooh kah-*feh* dah mahn-*yah*) (*breakfast*) literally means — you guessed it — *morning coffee*.

Eating **o café da manhã** is what you do after you've woken up, before heading out the door. At least that's the way Brazilians usually have their breakfast. They tend to take life slower than urban Americans, who often rush out the door and grab a bagel or muffin on their way to work.

Brazilians tend to sit down in their **sala de jantar** (*sah*-lah jee zhahn-*tah*) (*dining room*) in the morning to have **café** (kah-*feh*) (*Brazilian-style espresso coffee*). In fact, **café** is such a basic part of the Brazilian breakfast that **café da manhã** is often shortened to just **café**.

A typical Brazilian café at home is substantial and may include **frutas tropicais** (*froo*-tahs troh-pee-*kah*-eez) (*tropical fruits*), **cereal matinal** (seh-ree-*ah*-ooh mah-chee-*nah*-ooh) (*cereal*) with **leite** (*lay*-chee) (*milk*), and **iogurte** (yoh-*goor*-chee) (*yogurt*).

CULTURAL
WISDOM

The one main difference compared to what you're used to may be the appearance of **frios** (*free*-ohs) (*cold cuts*), which are eaten with **um pãozinho** (oong pah-ooh-zeen-yoo) (*a roll*) and **queijo** (*kay*-zhoh) (*cheese*). You may also see a toasted **sanduíche** (sahn-*dwee*-shee) (*sandwich*) using the same ingredients except with regular sandwich **pão** (*pah*-ooh) (*bread*) instead of a **pãozinho**. To talk about eating **café da manhã**, use the verb **tomar** (toh-*mah*) (*to take*):

Eu estou tomando café. (*eh*-ooh es-*toh* toh-*mahn*-doh kah-*feh*.) (*I'm having breakfast.*)

Eles estão tomando café na cozinha. (*eh*-leez es-*tah*-ooh toh-*mahn*-doh kah-*feh* nah koh-zeen-yah.) (*They're having breakfast in the kitchen.*)

Here are some typical breakfast items for Brazilians:

» **leite** (*lay*-chee) (*milk*)

» **café** (kah-*feh*) (*coffee*)

» **chá** (shah) (*tea*)

>> **suco de laranja** (*soo*-koh jee lah-*rahn*-zhah) (*orange juice*)

(See Chapter 7 for other types of fruits often juiced in Brazil.)

>> **cereal** (seh-ree-*ah*-ooh) (*cereal*)

>> **pão torrado** (*pah*-ooh toh-*hah*-doo) (*toast;* Literally: *toasted bread*)

>> **geléia** (zheh-*lay*-ah) (*jam*)

>> **manteiga** (mahn-*tay*-gah) (*butter*)

>> **frutas** (*froo*-tahs) (*fruit*)

>> **iogurte** (yo-*goor*-chee) (*yogurt*)

>> **ovos** (*oh*-vooz) (*eggs*)

>> **presunto** (preh-*zoon*-toh) (*ham*)

>> **queijo** (*kay*-zhoh) (*cheese*)

You may want to add some **açúcar** (ah-*soo*-kah) (*sugar*) or **leite** (*lay*-chee) (*milk*) to your **café** or **chá**. Or, if you're watching your waistline, you may want to try a popular Brazilian diet sweetener: **adoçante** (ah-doh-*sahn*-chee) (*sweetener*). This potent liquid sweetener comes in a little plastic squeeze bottle. One or two tiny drops is often plenty. It comes in many different **marcas** (*mah*-kahz) (brands).

Discussing lunch

For many Brazilians, **o almoço** (ooh ah-ooh-*moh*-soo) (*lunch*) is the biggest and most important **refeição** (heh-fay-*sah*-ooh) (*meal*) of the day.

Lunch made **em casa** (*ang kah*-zah) (*at home*) typically consists of **carne, arroz, feijão, salada,** and **suco** (*soo*-koh) (*fruit juice*) or **água** (*ah*-gwah) (*water*).

Brazilian children typically eat these same basic foods for lunch. On weekdays, most kids eat lunch at home — kids go home from school to eat lunch. But their mom may pack them a bag with **lanches** (*lahn*-sheez) (*snacks*) such as **bolachas** (boh-*lah*-shahs) (*crackers*), **suco, frutas** and **sanduíches**, to eat during **recreio** (heh-*kray*-oh) (recess). Parents who care a lot about **saúde** (sah-*ooh*-jee) (*health*) may also add cut-up **vegetais** (veh-zheh-*tah*-eez) (*vegetables*) such as **cenoura** (seh-*noh*-rah) (*carrots*), **pepino** (peh-*pee*-noh) (*cucumber*), or **pimentão verde** (pee-men-*tah*-ooh *veh*-jee) (*green bell pepper*).

CULTURAL
WISDOM

When Brazilian adults aren't having a home-cooked meal, they often have their **almoço** at a delicious, healthy, and inexpensive **restaurante a quilo** (hes-tah-ooh-*rahn*-chee ah *kee*-loh) (*a pay-by-weight buffet*). (Flip to Chapter 7 to read more about what food is served at these buffets.)

Whether at home or at a restaurant close to work, Brazilians take their time eating, usually more than **meia hora** (*may*-ah *oh*-rah) (*half an hour*). There's a theory in Brazil about American workers, who often eat lunch at their desks: If you see a group of Americans having lunch for more than half an hour together, it's a work lunch. Brazilians savor their time with friends and enjoy their mealtimes.

Cooking up dinner

CULTURAL
WISDOM

Different from **o almoço**, **o jantar** (ooh zhahn-*tah*) (*dinner*) is often eaten **em casa**. In general, Brazilians eat later than most Americans; dinnertime falls around 8 or 9 p.m.

Food prep for this last meal of the day usually begins with people peeking inside their **geladeira** (zheh-lah-*day*-rah) (*refrigerator*) to see what ingredients they have to work with. If a maid doesn't cook the family meals, dinner prep often starts with **água**, **sal** (*sah*-ooh) (*salt*), **cebola** (seh-*boh*-lah) (*onion*), and **alho** (ahl-yoh) (*garlic*).

Brazilian **jantar** is typically a lighter meal than **almoço**. **Salada**, **sopa** (*soh*-pah) (*soup*), and **massas** (*mah*-sahs) (*pasta*) are popular options, as is heating up leftovers from **almoço**.

Stepping into a kitchen in most parts of Brazil, you may smell the scent of **sopa** made with some common Brazilian ingredients: **chouriço** (choh-*ree*-sooh) (*spicy Portuguese sausage*), **couve** (*koo*-vay) (*kale or collard greens*), **batatas** (bah-*tah*-tahs) (*potatoes*), and **coentro** (koh-*en*-troh) (*cilantro*).

Regionally, dinner dishes vary widely. In the northeast of the country, for example, where **peixe** (*pay*-shee) (*fish*) is very popular, you're sure to find a woman any night of the week cooking up a **moqueca** (moh-*keh*-kah) (*seafood stew*) that includes **azeite de dendê** (ah-*zay*-chee jee den-*deh*) (*palm oil; a very strong taste that isn't for those with a weak stomach*), **tomate** (toh-*mah*-chee) (*tomato*), **cebola**, and slow-cooked **peixe**.

In São Paulo, you'd surely smell the flavors of Japanese, Korean, and Italian cuisine in many home kitchens, reflecting the sizeable immigrant groups that have settled there.

CULTURAL
WISDOM

All over Brazil, you'd hear the sound of the latest Brazilian **novela** (noh-*veh*-lah) (*soap opera*) on the television at dinnertime! The Brazilian **novela** industry is huge and produces very high-quality shows that are exported all over the world.

Here are some other dishes common to most parts of Brazil when it comes to **jantar** staples:

>> **carne grelhada** (*kah*-nee grel-*yah*-dah) (*grilled meat*)

>> **macarrão ao molho de tomate** (mah-kah-*hah*-ooh ah-ooh *mol*-yoh jee toh-*mah*-chee) (*spaghetti with tomato sauce*)

>> **arroz e feijão** (ah-*hohz* ee fay-*zhow*) (*rice and beans*)

>> **puré de batata** (puh-*ray* jee bah-*tah*-tah) (*mashed potatoes*)

Use these words to express basic cooking techniques:

>> **assar** (ah-*sah*) (*to bake*)

>> **cortar** (kohr-*tah*) (*to cut*)

>> **ferver** (fehr-*ver*) (*to boil*)

>> **fritar** (free-*tahr*) (*to fry*)

>> **picar** (pee-*kah*) (*to dice*)

Here's how to talk about standard **utensílios de cozinha** (ooh-ten-*see*-lee-ooz jee koh-*zeen*-yah) (*kitchen utensils*):

>> **faca** (*fah*-kah) (*knife*)

>> **forno** (*fohr*-noh) (*oven*)

>> **frigideira** (free-zhee-*day*-rah) (*frying pan*)

>> **medidor** (meh-jee-*doh*) (*measuring cup*)

>> **microondas** (mee-*krohn*-dahs) (*microwave*)

>> **panela** (pah-*neh*-lah) (*pot*)

>> **ralador** (hah-lah-*doh*) (*grater*)

>> **tábua de cortar** (*tah*-boo-ah jee kohr-*tah*) (*cutting board*)

>> **tesoura** (teh-*zoh*-rahs) (*scissors*)

Before you take a seat at the **mesa** (*meh*-zah) (*table*), here are the Portuguese words for place-setting items in case you need to ask for any of them:

>> **garfo** (*gah*-foh) (*fork*)

>> **faca** (*fah*-kah) (*knife*)

>> **colher** (kool-*yeh*) (*spoon*)

>> **prato** (*prah*-toh) (*plate*)

> » **prato fundo** (*prah*-toh *foon*-doh) (*bowl*)

> » **copo** (*koh*-poo) (*cup/glass*)

> » **taça de vinho** (*tah*-sah jee *veen*-yoh) (*glass of wine*)

> » **guardanapo** (gwah-dah-*nah*-poh) (*napkin*)

Cleaning House

In most middle- and upper-class households in Brazil, people pay a **diarista** (jee-ah-*rees*-tah) (*cleaning woman*) to **limpar** (leem-*pah*) (*clean*) the house once a week. Some tools that a **diarista** uses are an **aspirador de pó** (ah-spee-rah-*doh* jee poh) (*vacuum cleaner*), **esponja** (es-*pohn*-zhah) (*sponge*), **pano** (*pah*-noh) (*rag*), **esfregão** (es-freh-*gah*-ooh) (*mop*), and **balde** (*bah*-ooh-jee) (*bucket*).

The **diarista** typically **limpa** these parts of a home or apartment:

> » **janelas** (zhah-*neh*-lahs) (*windows*)

> » **espelhos** (eh-*spel*-yohs) (*mirrors*)

> » **portas** (*poh*-tahs) (*doors*)

> » **lixeiras** (lee-*shay*-rahs) (*garbage cans*)

> » **azulejos** (ah-zoo-*lay*-zhohs) (*tiles in a tiled floor or wall*)

> » **paredes** (pah-*reh*-jeez) (*walls*)

> » **geladeira** (zheh-lah-*day*-rah) (*refrigerator*)

A **diarista** also tends to **lavar louças** (lah-*vah* loh-sahs) (*wash the dishes*); **fazer a cama** (fah-*zeh* ah *kah*-mah) (*make the bed*); and scrub the **banheira** (bahn-*yeh*-rah) (*bathtub*), **pia** (*pee*-ah) (*sink*), and **vaso** (*vah*-soh) (*toilet*) in the **banheiro** (bahn-*yay*-roh) (*bathroom*).

She may also **passar roupa** (pah-*sah hoh*-pah) (*iron clothing*), **lavar roupas** (lah-*vah hoh*-pahs) (*wash clothes*), and **cozinhar** (koh-zeen-*yah*) (*cook*), but typically only if the client pays a bit extra for these **serviços** (seh-*vee*-soos) (*services*).

CULTURAL WISDOM

For people in the middle class and up, Brazilian apartments have a **máquina de lavar** (*mah*-kee-nah jee lah-*vah*) (*washing machine*) for clothing but not for dishes. There's always a big sink in the service area where clothes can be washed by hand.

Going for a Walk Around the Neighborhood

One of the most **agradável** (ah-grah-*dah*-vah-ooh) (*pleasurable*; Literally: *agreeable*) things to do in a new place is to go for a **passeio** (pah-*say*-oh) (*stroll*) in the **bairro** (*bah*-ee-hoo) (*neighborhood*) **a pé** (ah peh) (*by foot*). While enjoying your **passeio**, you'll see street **placas** (*plah*-kahs) (*signs*) with names that include words like **Rua** (*hoo*-ah) (*Street*) and **Avenida** (ah-veh-*nee*-dah) (*Avenue*). You can **atravesser** (ah-trah-veh-*seh*) (*cross*) the **rua** when you see **uma faixa de pedestre** (*ooh*-mah *fah*-ee-shah jee peh-*des*-tree) (*a crosswalk*), and if **a luz** (ah loos) (*the light*) is **verde** (*vehr*-jee) (*green*), not **vermelha** (vehr-*mel*-yah) (*red*).

To learn more about getting around towns and cities in Brazil, check out Chapter 15's section, "Navigating Cityscapes." You may notice lovely **árvores** (ah-*vohr*-eez) (*trees*) or **pássaros** (*pah*-sah-roos) (*birds*). You may see people walking their **cachorro** (kah-*shoh*-hoo) (*dog*). How's the **clima** (*klee*-mah) (*weather*)? You may be out when there's **sol** (*soh*-ooh) (*sun*) and **nuvens** (*noo*-vangz) (*clouds*), or there may be **chuva** (*shoo*-vah) (*rain*). How is the **vento** (*ven*-toh) (*wind*)? Is there a nice **brisa** (*bree*-zah) (*breeze*)? If you're at the beach, you may be walking on **areia** (ah-*ray*-ah) (*sand*). You may be walking **devagar** (deh-vah-*gah*) (*slowly*) or **rápido** (*ha*-pee-doh) (*fast*). Hopefully, you're wearing **zapatos confortáveis** (sah-*pah*-toos kohn-fohr-*tah*-vay-eez) (*comfortable shoes*).

Are you in a **bairro residencial** (*bah*-ee-hoo heh-zee-den-see-*ah*-ooh) (*residential neighborhood*) or in an **área comercial** (*ah*-ray-ah koh-mehr-see-*ah*-ooh) (*commercial area*)? It's always fun to glimpse through the **vitrines** (vee-*tree*-nees) (*windows*) of **lojas** (*loh*-zhahs) (*stores*) in a new place.

Here are some **perguntas** (pehr-*goon*-tahs) (*questions*) you can ask locals before your **passeio**:

> **É seguro caminhar por este bairro?** (eh seh-*goo*-roh kah-ming-*yah* pohr es-chee *bah*-ee-hoo) (*Is it safe to walk around this neighborhood?*)

> **Qual direção recomenda para um passeio?** (*kwah*-oo dee-rek-*sah*-ooh heh-koh-men-dah pah-rah oong pah-*say*-oh) (*Which direction do you recommend to take a walk?*)

A fun place to walk around is the famous **Ipanema** (ee-pah-*neh*-mah) neighborhood of Rio. It's on the beach, dotted with places to buy fresh **sucos** (*soo*-kohs) (*juices*) and **vitaminas** (vee-tah-*meen*-uz) (*milkshakes*) made from tropical **frutas** (*froo*-tahs) (*fruits*) you may have never heard of, and places to buy **Havaianas** (ah-vah-ee-*ah*-nahs) (a famous Brazilian flip-flop brand). On the **praia** (*prah*-ee-ah) (beach) there, you can see the famous **Morro Dois Irmãos** (*moh*-hoo *doh*-eez eeh-*mah*-ooz) (Literally: *Two Brothers Mountain*). While walking around Rio's **Ipanema** and **Copacabana** (coh-pah-kah-*bah*-nah) neighborhoods, you may catch a glimpse of the famous **Cristo Redentor** (*kree*-stoh heh-den-*tohr*) (*Christ the Redeemer*) **estatua** (es-*tah*-too-ah) (*statue*) and the **Pão de Açúcar** (*pah*-ooh jee ah-*soo*-kah) (famous distinctive Sugarloaf Mountain). These two fun neighborhoods are located right next to each other and are easy to **caminhar** (*walk*) around and not too large to **explorar** (ek-sploh-*rahr*) (*explore*).

GIRL FROM IPANEMA (1962)

Let's dive into the lyrics of the most famous song internationally that Brazil has produced. It describes a true story. The songwriters Antônio Carlos Jobim and Vinícius de Moraes used to sit in a **café** (kah-*feh*) (*cafe*) and admire a young woman who would pass by. The real woman, **Heloísa Eneida de Menezes Paes Pinto** (eh-loh-*ee*-zah eh-*nay*-ee-dah jee men-*eh*-zees *pah*-ees peen-toh) (born in 1945), is **famosa** (fah-*moh*-zah) (*famous*) in Brazil. She even carried an Olympic torch for Brazil during the 2016 Olympic Games, which were held in Rio. The song's style is **bossa nova** (*boh*-sah *noh*-vah) and **jazz** (pronounced the same as in English). Go ahead, play the song! Enjoy!

Portuguese	English
Olha, que coisa mais linda, (*ohl*-yah kee *koh*-ee-zah my-eez *leen*-dah)	*Look, such a sight, so beautiful,*
Mais cheia de graça, (my-eez *shay*-yah jee *grah*-sah)	*So filled with grace,*
É ela, menina, que vem e que passa, (eh *eh*-lah, meh-*nee*-nah, kee *vang* ee kee *pah*-sah)	*It's her, this girl who comes and who passes,*
Num doce balanço, a caminho do mar. (noong *doh*-see bah-*lahn*-soo, ah kah-*ming*-yoh doo *mahr*)	*With a sweet swing, on her way to the sea.*
Moça do corpo dourado, (*moh*-sah doo *koh*-poo doh-*rah*-doo)	*Girl with a body of gold*
Do sol de Ipanema, (doo *sohl* jee ee-pah-*neh*-mah)	*From the sun of Ipanema,*
O seu balançado (ooh seh-oo bah-lahn-*sah*-doo)	*Her swing*
É mais que um poema (eh *my*-eez kee oong poh-*eh*-mah)	*Is more than a poem,*

(continued)

(continued)

Portuguese	English
É a coisa mais linda (eh ah *koy*-zah my-eez *leen*-dah)	*Is a sight more beautiful*
Que eu já vi passar (kee eh-oo *jah* vee pah-*sah*)	*Than I have ever seen pass by.*
Ah, por que estou tão sozinho? (*ah*, poh kay eh-*stoh* tah-ooh soh-*zeen*-yoo)	*Ah, why am I so alone?*
Ah, por que tudo é tão triste? (*ah*, poh kay *too*-doo eh tah-oo *trees*-chee)	*Why is there so much sadness?*
Ah, a beleza que existe (*ah*, ah beh-*leh*-zah kee eeg-*zees*-chee)	*This beauty that exists,*
A beleza que não é só minha, (ah beh-*leh*-zah kee nah-ooh eh soh *ming*-ya)	*This beauty that is not only mine,*
Que também passa sozinha. (*kee* tahm-bang *pah*-sah soh-*zeen*-ya)	*That also passes by alone.*
Ah, se ela soubesse (*ah*, see *eh*-lah soo-*beh*-see)	*Ah, if she but knew,*
Que quando ela passa, (kee *kwan*-doh eh-la *pah*-sah)	*That when she passes by,*
O mundo sorrindo (ooh *moon*-doh soh-*heen*-doo)	*The world smiles,*
Se enche de graça (seh *ang*-shee jee *grah*-sah)	*Is filled with grace,*
E fica mais lindo (ee *fee*-kah my-eez *leen*-doh)	*And becomes more beautiful,*
Por causa do amor. (poh *cow*-zah doo ah-*mohr*)	*Because of love.*

Making a Phone Call

Whether you're lounging on your **sofá** (soh–*fah*) (*couch*) at home, or on a busy **rua** (*hoo*–ah) (*street*) trying to make a business **chamada** (shah-*mah*-dah) (*call*), **falar no celular** (fah-*lah* noo sel-ooh-*lah*) (*talking on a cellphone*) in a different language can be intimidating. But **você está com sorte!** (voh-*seh* eh-*stah* kohng soh-chee!) (*you're in luck!*) You've picked a great learners' language; I'll tell you why I think so.

First, most Brazilians tend to talk **devagar** (deh-vah-*gah*) (*slowly*), or at least at a reasonable pace, and clearly enunciate their syllables. Most locals slow their speech automatically when talking with someone who's not fluent in Portuguese. But best of all, Brazilians typically *love* foreigners and are **contentes** (kohn-*ten*-cheez) (*happy*) to talk to you.

So go native: Relax. **Fique tranquilo** (*fee*-kee trahn-*kwee*-loh) (*Don't worry*). Here's what you say to answer the phone:

>> **Alô?** (ah-*loh?*) (*Hello?*)

>> **Sim?** (sing?) (*Yes?*) (formal)

>> **Pois não?** (*poh*-eez *nah*-ooh) (How can I help you?) (formal)

>> **Oi.** (*oy*-ee.) (*Hi.*) (very informal)

Before you hang up the phone, use these words to say goodbye:

>> **Tchau.** (chow.) (*Bye*; Literally: *Ciao,* like in Italian)

>> **Até logo.** (ah-*teh* loh-goo.) (*Bye*; Literally: *Until soon.*)

>> **Até mais.** (ah-*teh mah*-eez.) (*Bye*; Literally: *Until more.*)

>> **Até amanhã.** (ah-*teh* ah-mahn-*yah*.) (*Talk to/See you tomorrow*; Literally: *Until tomorrow.*)

CULTURAL WISDOM

Brazilians are very social people, so talking on the phone comes naturally to them. The **telefone** (teh-leh-*foh*-nee) (*telephone*) itself even holds an important place in Brazilian history. The very first samba tune ever recorded was titled **"Pelo Telefone"** (*peh*-loo teh-leh-*foh*-nee) (*"On the Phone"*) (Rio, 1917).

This section gives you the basics of navigating Brazil's telephone system and following Brazilian phone etiquette.

CALLING INSIDE OR OUTSIDE BRAZIL

In Brazil, most phone numbers have either seven or eight digits and a two-digit prefix for the **cidade** (see-*dah*-jee) (city) or a **código de área** (*koh*-jee-goo jee *ah*-ree-ah) (*regional code*), which often has a zero in front. The phone number of a famous hotel in Rio called Copacabana Palace, for example, looks like this: (021) 2548-7070. The **código internacional** (*koh*-jee-goh een-teh-nah-see-oh-*nah*-ooh) (*international calling code*) for Brazil is 55, so the phone number for Copacabana Palace is (55-21) 2548-7070 when the caller is located outside Brazil.

Not only are Brazilians intensely social but they're also very **carinhosos** (kah-reen-*yoh*-zooz) (*affectionate*). When a **chamada** (shah-*mah*-dah) (*phone call*) ends between two female friends, a male and a female friend, or two family members, Brazilians often say **Um beijo** (oong *bay*-zhoh) (*A kiss*), or, if the call is between two men, **Um abraço** (oong ah-*brah*-soo) (*A hug*).

Try out these useful phrases when talking about using the phone in Portuguese:

» **atender o telefone** (ah-ten-*deh* ooh teh-leh-*foh*-nee) (*to answer the phone*)

» **deixar um recado** (day-*shah* oong heh-*kah*-doh) (*to leave a voice-mail message*)

» **está correto** (ehs-*tah* koh-*heh*-toh) (*it's correct*)

» **está errado** (ehs-*tah* eh-*hah*-doh) (*it's wrong*)

» **dar um telefonema** (*dah oong* teh-leh-foh-*neh*-mah) (*to make a phone call*) (**telefonema** is a rare example of a noun that ends in **–a**, yet is masculine! Hence, even though it might look strange, **um telefonema** is correct, not **uma telefonema.**)

» **ligar para alguém** (lee-*gah* pah-rah ah-ooh-*gang*) (*to call someone*)

» **número do telefone** (*noo*-meh-roh doo teh-leh-*foh*-nee) (*phone number*)

» **uma cabine telefônica** (ooh-mah kah-*bee*-neh teh-leh-*foh*-nee-kah) (*public phone booth*), also known as **orelhão** (or-el-*yah*-ooh) (*phone booth;* Literally: *big ear* because of the way the booths are shaped). Like elsewhere in the world, public phones are gradually becoming museum pieces, because most everyone has a cellphone.

Talkin' the Talk

Patricia (pah-*tree*-see-ah) is calling a hotel near Ipanema beach in Rio. She wants to meet up with her friend **Roberta** (hoh-*beh*-tah).

Operator: **Bom dia. Hotel do Sol Ipanema.**

boh-oong *jee*-ah. oh-*teh*-ooh doo *soh*-ooh eeh-pah-*neh*-mah.

Good morning. Sun Hotel, Ipanema.

Patricia:	**Bom dia. Poderia falar com a Roberta Fernandes, quarto número sete oito três, por gentileza?**
	boh-oong *jee*-ah. poh-deh-*ree*-ah fah-*lah* koh-oong ah hoh-*beh*-tah feh-*nahn*-jeez, *kwah*-toh *noo*-meh-roh seh-chee *oh*-ee-toh *trehz*, poh zhehn-chee-*leh*-zah?
	Good morning. Could you connect me with Roberta Fernandes, room number 783, please?
Operator:	**Quem está falando?**
	kang *es-tah* fah-*lahn*-doh?
	Who's this calling?
Patricia:	**É Patricia Assunção.**
	eh pah-*tree*-see-ah ah-soong-*sah*-ooh.
	This is Patricia Assunção.
Operator:	**Só um momento, por favor.**
	soh oong moh-*men*-toh, poh fah-*voh*.
	Just a moment, please.

• •

WORDS TO KNOW

Poderia falar com. . .?	poh-deh-<u>ree</u>-ah <u>fah</u>-<u>lah</u> koh-oong. . .?	Could you connect me with. . .?
por gentileza	poh zhehn-chee-<u>leh</u>-zah	please (formal)
por favor	poh fah-<u>voh</u>	please (informal)
Quem está falando?	kang es-<u>tah</u> fah-<u>lahn</u>-doh?	Who's this calling?
É . . .	eh . . .	It's . . . (name)
Só um momento.	soh oong moh-<u>men</u>-toh.	Just a moment.

Connecting with the calling verb: Ligar

In this section, you get to know the verb **ligar** (lee-*gah*) (*to call*). It's a great **-ar** verb you can use to practice verb conjugation because **-ar** verbs are a piece of cake. (See Chapter 2 for more on verb conjugation).

Ligar is almost always packaged with **para** — as in **ligar para** (lee-*gah* pah-rah) (*to call*) someone or someplace. To use this expression, use **ligar para** plus the name of the person or place.

First, here are the conjugations of **ligar**.

Conjugation	Pronunciation
eu ligo	eh-ooh *lee*-goh
você liga	voh-*seh lee*-gah
ele/ela liga	*eh*-lee/*eh*-lah *lee*-gah
nós ligamos	*nohz* lee-*gah*-mohz
eles/elas ligam	*eh*-leez/*eh*-lahz *lee*-gah-ooh
vocês ligam	voh-*sehz lee*-gah-ooh

Practice these example sentences that use **ligar**:

Ligo para os Estados Unidos todos os dias. (*lee*-goh pah-rah ooz eh-*stah*-dooz ooh-*nee*-dohz *toh*-dooz ooz *jee*-ahz.) (*I call the U.S. every day.*)

Ela liga para o namorado dela cinco vezes por dia. (*eh*-lah *lee*-gah pah-rah ooh nah-moh-*rah*-doh *deh*-lah *seen*-koh *veh*-zeez poh *jee*-ah.) (*She calls her boyfriend five times a day.*)

Você liga para a sua mãe muito? (voh-*seh lee*-gah *pah*-rah ah *soo*-ah *mah*-ee moh-*ee*-toh?) (*Do you call your mom often?*)

SOUND NATIVE

The expression **ligar para** has a colloquial meaning, *to pay attention to* someone or something. For example, **Eu não ligo para o futebol** (eh-ooh *nah*-ooh *lee*-goh pah-rah ooh foo-chee-*bah*-ooh) translates to *I don't care about soccer.*

The verb **ligar** also means *to plug in* something: **Liga o computador, por favor.** (*lee*-gah ooh kohm-*poo*-tah-*doh*, po hah-*voh.*) (*Plug in the computer, please.*) Similarly, **desligar** means *to unplug* or *to turn off* something: **Desliga a tevê!** (des-*lee*-gah ah teh-*veh!*) (*Turn off the TV!*)

SOUND NATIVE

Se liga (see *lee*-gah) is another popular slang expression that uses the verb **ligar.** It means *Get with it* or *Wake up to the facts.* Someone obsessed with celebrity gossip may say, "You don't know about that [insert name of new hot nightclub]?" **Se liga!** The expression literally means *Plug yourself in.*

Dealing with verbal mush

The first phone **conversa** (kohn-*veh*-sah) (*conversation*) in any new language is tough. You can't see the person's face or body language as they're talking. You feel **nervoso** (neh-*voh*-zoo) (*nervous*) that you're taking up their valuable time. The connection may be bad. Their **palavras** (pah-*lahv*-rahz) (*words*) come out sounding like mush.

The Brazilian **sotaque** (soh-*tah*-kee) (*accent*) sounds particularly unfamiliar in the beginning. Though natives tend to speak slowly, the abundance of nasal vowels throws off even people with a good knowledge of Portuguese words and grammar. All the talking through the **nariz** (nah-*reez*) (*nose*) sometimes causes people to mistake Brazilian Portuguese for **russo** (*hoo*-soh) (*Russian*) or **francês** (frahn-*say*-ees) (*French*)!

On top of all the different vowels, you also experience the difficulty encountered by people listening to any new language: Where do the words **começam** (koh-*meh*-sah-ooh) (*begin*) and **acabam** (ah-*kah*-bah-ooh) (*end*)? At first, words sound like they're all strung together, with no breaks. And on the phone, distinguishing words is especially tough.

TIP

Be easy on yourself for the first few days you're in Brazil (if you're one of the lucky ones with plans to visit) or when you first begin to communicate in Portuguese with a Brazilian. Watch Brazilian **televisão** (teh-leh-vee-*zah*-ooh) (*TV*) while you're getting ready to go out, and pay attention to people speaking around you. Soak up the sounds of the language. Pay attention to body language, which often provides useful clues about the content of what a person's saying.

Slowly, you can begin to recognize repeated **sons** (soh-oongz) (*sounds*) and repeated words. With a little effort on the listening end, you may be surprised by how many words you recognize with ease after just **uma semana** (*ooh*-mah seh-mah-nah) (*one week*). Then talking on the phone won't be so hard.

TIP

Se você não entende (see voh-*seh* nah-ooh en-*ten*-jee) (*if you don't understand*) what the person on the other end of the line is saying, try asking whether they speak English. Say **Fala inglês?** (*fah*-lah eeng-*glehz?*) (*Do you speak English?*)

I remember hearing the word **teatro** (chee-*ah*-troh) (*theater*) for the first time. I had seen the word written on paper **muitas vezes** (moo-*ee*-tahz *veh*-zeez) (*many times*), and it seemed like one of the easier words to **aprender** (ah-pren-*deh*) (*learn*) — it's not so different from the English word. Yet my friend repeated the word probably four times, and I still didn't get it! She then translated to English, and I felt a little **envergonhada** (en-veh-gohn-*yah*-dah) (*embarrassed*). But it was worth it; I was able to recognize the word the very next time I heard it.

Talkin' the Talk

Flavia (*flah*-vee-ah) tries to call her co-worker **Carlos** (*kah*-looz) about a work project. The phone line is bad, and the conversation turns to mush.

Flavia:	**Olá, Carlos, por favor?**
	oh-lah, *kah*-looz, poh fah-*voh*.
	Hello, Carlos, please.
Voice on other side:	**Krnha estrn galades.** (Unintelligible.)
Flavia:	**Poderia falar um pouco mais devagar, por favor?**
	poh-deh-*ree*-ah fah-*lah* oong *poh*-koh *mah*-eez deh-vah-*gah*, poh fah-*voh*?
	Can you speak a little slower, please?
Voice on other side:	**Sod snod manjekof.** (Unintelligible.)
Flavia:	**Não estou te escutando. Está ruim a linha.**
	nah-ooh es-*toh* chee es-koo-*tahn*-doh. es-*tah* hoo-*ing* ah *leen*-yah.
	I can't hear you. The connection is bad.
Voice on other side:	**No momento, não se encontra.**
	noh moh-*men*-toh, *nah*-ooh see en-*kohn*-trah.
	He's not here right now.

Flavia: **Ligo mais tarde, obrigada.**

lee-goh mah-eez *tah*-jee, oh-bree-*gah*-dah.

I'll call later, thanks.

WORDS TO KNOW

não se encontra	<u>nah</u>-ooh see en-<u>kohn</u>-trah	he/she isn't here (formal)
não está	<u>nah</u>-ooh eh-<u>stah</u>	he/she isn't here (informal)
a linha	ah <u>leen</u>-yah	the phone line
devagar	deh-vah-<u>gah</u>	slowly
mais tarde	<u>mah</u>-eez <u>tah</u>-jee	later
no momento	noh moh-<u>men</u>-toh	right now (formal)

SOUND
NATIVE

If you want to say *right now* and you're not talking on the phone, you can say **agora mesmo** (ah-*goh*-rah *mez*-moh) (*right now*). **No momento** is frequently used on the phone with strangers because it sounds more formal.

Being a Gracious Guest

Brazilians are social, generous people, so you may find yourself at one of their homes — whether you're in Brazil or London, Miami, or Mexico City — to attend a **festa** (*fes*-tah) (*party*) or **jantar** (zhahn-*tah*) (*dinner*). Brazilians love to **convidar** (kohn-vee-*dah*) (*invite*) guests to their living spaces!

When you enter the home of a Brazilian, they're likely to say this very common phrase of hospitality: **Fique à vontade** (*fee*-kee ah vohn-*tah*-jee) (*Make yourself comfortable*). To which you can say, **Muito obrigado/a** (moh-*ee*-toh oh-bree-*gah*-doo/dah – use **obrigado** if you're male and **obrigada** if you're female) (*Thank you very much*).

Then you may want to add one of the following phrases:

>> **Que casa linda!** (kee *kah*-zah *leen*-dah!) (*What a beautiful home!*)

>> **Adoro a sua casa!** (ah-*doh*-roo ah *soo*-ah *kah*-zah!) (*I love your home!*)

>> **Você é muito gentil.** (voh-*seh* eh moh-*ee*-toh zhang-*chee*-ooh.) (*You are very kind.*)

FUN & GAMES

Name the rooms of the house that are illustrated in the following drawing.

Illustration by Elizabeth Kurtzman

A. _____

B. _____

C. _____

D. _____

E. _____

Find the answers in Appendix C.

2

Brazilian Portuguese in Action

IN THIS PART . . .

Keep the conversation going.

Visit restaurants and farmer's markets.

Make purchases.

Go out on the town.

Keep in touch with the help of technology.

Talk about work.

Enjoy the natural world.

Chapter **6**

Getting to Know You: Small Talk

When you're learning a language, talking to people — even about the most basic things — can be a little stressful. But if you think about it, the first few minutes of talking to anybody new usually involves the same old questions. This chapter covers the questions that Brazilian Portuguese speakers are most likely to ask you as well as how to answer and what questions you'll probably want to ask them!

Where Are You From?

The first question you're likely to be asked in Brazil is **De onde você é?** (jee *ohng-jee voh-seh eh?*) (*Where are you from?*). Brazilians are very proud that people from all over the **mundo** (*moon-*doh) (*world*) come to visit their country. They're always curious to imagine how **longe** (*lohn-*zhee) (*far*) you came. They may also ask **De que país você é?** (jee kee pah-*eez* voh-seh *eh?*) (*Which country are you from?*).

Here's how you can answer:

Eu sou inglês. (*eh*-ooh *soh* eeng-*glehz*.) (*I'm English.*)

Eu sou da Inglaterra. (*eh*-ooh *soh* dah *eeng*-glah-*teh*-hah.) (*I'm from England.*)

Here are Portuguese words for some countries and nationalities that you may find useful:

» **alemão/alemã** (ah-leh-*mah*-ooh/ah-leh-*mah*) (*German;* male/female)

» **Alemanha** (ah-leh-*mahn*-yah) (*Germany*)

» **americano/americana** (ah-meh-ree-*kahn*-oh/ah-meh-ree-*kahn*-ah) (*American;* male/female)

» **Estados Unidos** (ehs-*tah*-dooz ooh-*nee*-dooz) (*United States*)

» **australiano/australiana** (ah-oo-strah-lee-*ah*-noh/ah-oo-strah-lee-*ah*-nah) (*Australian;* male/female)

» **Austrália** (ah-oo-*strah*-lee-ah) (*Australia*)

» **canadense** (kah-nah-*den*-see) (*Canadian;* male or female)

» **Canadá** (kah-nah-*dah*) (*Canada*)

» **chinês/chinesa** (shee-*nez*/shee-*neh*-zah) (*Chinese;* male/female)

» **China** (*shee*-nah) (*China*)

» **francês/francesa** (frahn-*sehz*/frahn-*seh*-zah) (*French;* male/female)

» **França** (*frahn*-sah) (*France*)

» **inglês/inglesa** (eeng-*glehz*/eeng-*gleh*-zah) (*English;* male/female)

» **Inglaterra** (eeng-glah-*teh*-hah) (*England*)

» **japonês/japonesa** (zhah-poh-*nehs*/zhah-poh-*nehz*-ah) (*Japanese;* male/female)

» **Japão** (zhah-*pah*-ooh) (*Japan*)

CULTURAL WISDOM

Don't be surprised if a Brazilian from a touristy place like Rio responds **Eu sabia** (*eh*-ooh sah-*bee*-ah) (*I knew it*) when you say which country you're from. With so many tourists around, Brazilians get plenty of practice at pinpointing nationalities.

Did you notice that in Portuguese, the first letter of nationalities isn't capitalized? In English, people write *American* with a capital A. In Portuguese, it's **americano.** Oh, and while I'm talking about Americans, be aware that a few Brazilians get offended by the term **americano.** They say, "We're Americans too!" These folks prefer the term **norte-americano** (*noh*-chee ah-meh-ree-*kah*-noh) to describe someone from the United States. If you're Canadian though, stick with **canadense**, because Brazilians use **norte-americano** to refer to people from the United States.

Brazilians often tell you where they're from by using the nickname for people from their city or state. Here are the most common ones:

- **bahiano/a** (bah-ee-*ah*-noh/bah-ee-*ah*-nah) (someone from Bahia state)

- **carioca** (kah-ree-*oh*-kah) (someone from the city of Rio; male or female)

- **gaúcho/a** (gah-*ooh*-shoh/gah-*ooh*-shah) (someone from Rio Grande do Sul state)

- **mineiro/a** (mee-*nay*-roh/mee-*nay*-rah) (someone from Minas Gerais state)

- **paulista** (pow-*lee*-stah) (someone from São Paulo state; male or female)

- **paulistano/a** (pow-lee-*stahn*-oh/pow-lee-*stahn*-ah) (someone from the city of São Paulo)

After telling you where they're from, Brazilians often try to tell you that their part of Brazil is the best. Their food and beaches are the best. And of course, the people are the coolest where they're from.

The truth is, Brazilians are **legais** (lay-*gah*-eez) (*cool:* use **legal** — lay-*gah*-ooh — when the cool person/thing is singular and **legais** when you're talking about more than one person/thing) and **simpáticos** (seem-*pah*-chee-koos) (*nice*) in all parts of the country. But **mineiros** are famously the nicest. They have a reputation among Brazilians as being particularly nice. The common phrase is **Mineiros, gente boa** (mee-*nay*-rohz, *zhang*-chee *boh*-ah) (*people from Minas Gerais state are really nice, cool people;* Literally: *Mineiros, good people*).

Talkin' the Talk

AUDIO ONLINE

Juliana (zhoo-lee-*ah*-nah) is a waitress at a **churrascaria** (shoo-*hahs*-kah-*ree*-ah) (*Brazilian barbeque restaurant*) in Rio Grande do Sul state, where **churrasco** (shoo-*hah*-skoh) (*all-you-can-eat grilled cuts of meat, fish, chicken, and an extensive side-dish buffet*) originates. Samir, from Ohio, just sat down.

Juliana: **Tudo bem? De onde você é?**

           too-doh *bang?* jee *ohn*-jee voh-*seh* eh?

           How are you? Where are you from?

Samir:	**Sou americano.**
	soh ah-meh-ree-*kahn*-oh.
	I'm American.
Juliana:	**De que lugar?**
	jee kee loo-*gah?*
	From whereabouts?
Samir:	**De Ohio. E você, é daqui?**
	jee oh-*hah*-ee-oh. ee voh-*seh*, *eh* dah-*kee?*
	From Ohio. And you, are you from here?
Juliana:	**Sim, sou gaúcha. De onde vem?**
	sing, *soh* gah-*ooh*-shah. jee *ohn*-jee *vang?*
	Yes, I'm Gaucha (from Rio Grande do Sul state). Where are you coming from?
Samir:	**Do Rio. Vou passar uma semana aqui no Rio Grande do Sul.**
	doo *hee*-ooh. voh pah-*sah* ooh-mah seh-*mah*-nah ah-*kee* noh hee-ooh *grahn*-jee doo *soo.*
	From Rio. I'm going to stay here in Rio Grande do Sul for a week.
Juliana:	**Ótimo. Está gostando do Brasil?**
	ah-chee-moh. eh-*stah* goh-*stahn*-doh dooh brah-*zee*-ooh?
	Great. Are you liking Brazil?
Samir:	**Claro! Estou adorando esse país.**
	klah-roh! es-*toh* ah-doh-*rahn*-doh eh-see pah-*eez*.
	Of course! I'm loving this country.

● ●

WORDS TO KNOW		
De que lugar?	jee <u>kee</u> loo-gah?	From whereabouts? Literally, "From which place?"
De onde vem?	jee <u>ohn</u>-jee <u>vang</u>?	Which part of Brazil have you just been to?
Está gostando do Brasil?	eh-<u>stah</u> gohs-<u>tahn</u>-doh dooh brah-<u>zee</u>-ooh?	Are you liking Brazil?
Estou adorando esse país.	ehs-<u>toh</u> ah-doh-<u>rahn</u>-doh eh-see pah-<u>eez</u>.	I'm loving this country.

Figuring Out Family Connections

Brazilian families are very tight-knit; they tend to live in the same cities as their **pais** (*pah-eez*) (*parents*) and **irmãos** (*ee-mah-ooz*) (*siblings/brothers and sisters*) and see each other at least once a week.

CULTURAL WISDOM

Brazilians like to ask new friends how many siblings they have and where their **mãe** (*mah-ee*) (*mom*) and **pai** (*pah-ee*) (*dad*) live, right off the bat. This practice is different from some countries, where asking about **familiares** (*fah-mee-lee-ah-reez*) (*family members*) can seem too intimate — or even too boring — for the first few minutes of a conversation.

Take a look at Table 6-1 for some words to express family **relações** (*heh-lah-soh-eez*) (*relationships*).

TIP

In Brazil, street kids often call any adult **tia** (*chee*-ah) (*aunt*) or **tio** (*chee*-ooh) (*uncle*), especially when they're asking for money or help. If you find yourself in this situation, it's okay to give the child a small amount of money. Otherwise, just say, **Agora não** (ah-*goh*-rah *nah*-ooh) (*I can't*). If you do want to give a little money to a child, make sure you take the money out before they see where you keep it. Don't give anyone a chance to grab your wallet on the street.

TABLE 6-1 ## Relatives

Portuguese Word	Pronunciation	English Word
irmão	ee-*mah*-ooh	*brother*
irmã	ee-*mah*	*sister*
primo	*pree*-moh	*male cousin*
prima	*pree*-mah	*female cousin*
primos	*pree*-mooz	*cousins*
avô	ah-*voh*	*grandfather*
avó	ah-*vah*	*grandmother*
avós	ah-*vohz*	*grandparents*
filho	*feel*-yoo	*son*
filha	*feel*-yah	*daughter*
filhos	*feel*-yooz	*children*
marido	mah-*ree*-doh	*husband*
mulher/esposa	mool-*yeh*/es-*poh*-zah	*wife*
neto	*neh*-toh	*grandson*
neta	*neh*-tah	*granddaughter*

Using Possessives: "My . . ."

In Portuguese, it's easy to identify whether the sister you're talking about is **a sua irmã** (*ah soo*-ah ee-*mah*) (*your sister*), **a irmã do seu amigo** (ah ee-*mah* doo *seh*-ooh ah-*mee*-goo) (*your friend's sister*), or **a irmã dela** (ah ee-*mah deh*-lah) (*her sister*).

The **exemplos** (eh-*zem*-plooz) (*examples*) in Table 6-2 use family relationships to **mostrar** (moh-*strah*) (*show*) how to say *my, your, his, her,* and *their* in Portuguese. But these **palavras** (pah-*lahv*-rahz) (*words*) come up in tons of situations that have nothing to do with family, **é claro** (eh *klah*-roh) (*of course*).

Possessives come up in conversation all the time. You may want to use such phrases as **a minha ideia** (ah *ming*-yah ee-*day*-ah) (*my idea*), **os meus amigos** (ooz *meh*-ooz ah-*mee*-gooz) (*my friends*), **a sua profissão** (ah *soo*-ah proh-fee-*sah*-ooh) (*your profession*), **o apartamento dela** (ooh ah-*pah*-tah-*men*-toh *deh*-lah) (*her apartment*), or **os preços da loja** (ooz *preh*-sooz dah *loh*-zhah) (*the store's prices*).

To express *my* plus the *type of relative*, say the phrases in Table 6-2.

TABLE 6-2   **Phrases That Mean "My"**

Phrase	Pronunciation	Type of Relative	Example
a minha	ah *ming*-ya	one female	a minha irmã (*my sister*)
o meu	ooh *meh*-oo	one male	o meu irmão (*my brother*)
as minhas	ahz *ming*-yahs	multiple females	as minhas irmãs (*my sisters*)
os meus	oohz *meh*-ooz	multiple males or males and females	os meus irmãos (*my brothers*)

To express *your* plus the *type of relative* use the phrases in Table 6-3.

TABLE 6-3   **Phrases That Mean "Your"**

Phrase	Pronunciation	Type of Relative	Example
a sua	ah *soo*-ah	one female	a sua irmã (*your sister*)
o seu	ooh *seh*-oo	one male	o seu irmão (*your brother*)
as suas	ahz *soo*-ahz	multiple females	as suas irmãs (*your sisters*)
os seus	oohz *seh*-ooz	multiple males	os seus irmãos (*your brothers*)

To express *our*, say the phrases in Table 6-4.

TABLE 6-4   **Phrases That Mean "Our"**

Phrase	Pronunciation	Type of Relative	Example
a nossa	ah *noh*-sah	one female	a nossa irmã (*our sister*)
o nosso	ooh *noh*-soo	one male	o nosso irmão (*our brother*)
as nossas	ahz *noh*-sahz	multiple females	as nossas irmãs (*our sisters*)
os nossos	oohz *noh*-sooz	multiple males	os nossos irmãos (*our brothers*)

To express *his*, *her*, or *their* instead of *my*, *your*, or *our*, use the phrases in Table 6-5. In these cases, Brazilians reverse the order of *who* has *what*. Instead of mentioning the owner first and then what's theirs, as in *my notebook* and *our house*, the owned thing is mentioned before the owner in Portuguese.

TABLE 6-5 Phrases that Mean "'s," "Her," "His," and "Their"

Phrase	Pronunciation	Translation	Example
de (name)	jee	(name)'s (Literally: of [name])	**irmã de José** (José's sister; Literally: sister of José)
dela	deh-lah	her (Literally: of her)	**irmã dela** (her sister; Literally: sister of her)
dele	deh-lee	his (Literally: of him)	**irmã dele** (his sister; Literally: sister of him)
deles	deh-leez	their (Literally: of them)	**irmã deles** (their sister; Literally: sister of them)

For example, with **os nossos irmãos** (oohz noh-sooz ee-mah-ooz), the literal translation is our brothers. Our comes first, then brothers — just like in English. But if you want to talk about Tatiana's brother, the correct translation is **o irmão da Tatiana** (oo ee-mah-ooh dah tah-chee-ah-nah) (the brother of Tatiana). Say first what the owner owns, and then name the owner. Another example of this format is **as casas deles** (ahz kah-zahz deh-leez) (their houses).

Sometimes, the owner isn't a person but rather a thing or even a place: **os resultados financeiros da empresa** (ooz heh-zool-tah-dooz fee-nahn-say-rooz dah em-preh-zah) (the company's financial results) or **as praias do Rio** (ahz prah-ee-ahz doo hee-ooh) (Rio's beaches).

In English, you can technically say the beaches of Rio as well as Rio's beaches; but in Portuguese, you can only say the beaches of Rio. But if you make a mistake in the word order, a Brazilian will still most likely understand you, so don't sweat it.

The word **de** (of) in Portuguese often gets attached to the next word in what people call a contraction. In the case of his and hers, Brazilians say **dela** instead of **de ela**, **dele** instead of **de ele**, and so on. It's sort of fun to pronounce! Try it.

To express It's mine, say **É meu/minha** (eh meh-ooh/meen-yah) while pointing to the item. To say It's yours, use **É seu/sua** (eh seh-ooh/soo-ah). It's ours is **É nosso/nossa** (eh noh-soo/sah). Use the masculine form (**meu/seu/nosso**) if the thing you're talking about is masculine (nouns that generally end in –o) and use the feminine form (**minha/sua/nossa**) if you're referring to a feminine "thing" (words ending generally in –a).

In a general context — not only when you're talking about relatives — if you want to specify what exactly is whose, change the **meu, seu,** or **nosso** to match the item: Is it masculine or feminine? Singular or plural? Check out Table 6-6 for possibilities of combinations for talking about my things, your things, and our things.

TABLE 6-6   **Possessive Words — My, Your, and Our**

Meaning	Singular Masculine Object	Singular Feminine Object	Plural Masculine Object	Plural Feminine Object
my	**o meu** (*ooh meh*-ooh)	**a minha** (*ah ming*-yah)	**os meus** (*ooz meh*-ooz)	**as minhas** (*ahz ming*-yahz)
your	**o seu** (*ooh seh*-ooh)	**a sua** (*ah soo*-ah)	**os seus** (*ooz seh*-ooz)	**as suas** (*ahz soo*-ahz)
our	**o nosso** (*ooh noh*-soo)	**a nossa** (*ah noh*-sah)	**os nossos** (*ooz noh*-sooz)	**as nossas** (*ahz noh*-sahz)

Here are some general example phrases to reinforce how to use possessives in Portuguese. Notice again how the noun — the thing you're talking about — goes after *my*, *our*, and *your* but before *his*, *hers*, or *theirs*:

» **o cabelo dela** (ooh kah-*beh*-loo *deh*-lah) (*her hair*)

» **os carros deles** (ooz kah-hohz *deh*-leez) (*their cars*)

» **o livro dele** (ooh *leev*-roh *deh*-lee) (*his book*)

» **o meu telefone** (ooh *may*-ooh teh-leh-*foh*-nee) (*my phone*)

» **a minha casa** (ah *ming*-yah *kah*-zah) (*my house*)

» **os nossos planos** (ooz *noh*-sooz *plah*-nooz) (*our plans*)

» **o seu relógio** (ooh seh-ooh heh-*loh*-zhee-ooh) (*your watch*)

Knowing Who, What, and Where

If you're visiting Brazil, you may want to ask locals about the best events and beaches around. You'll want to know things like **onde** (*ohn*-jee) (*where*), **quando** (*kwahn*-doh) (*when*), and **quanto** (*kwahn*-toh) (*how much*).

Here are some other basic words to help you get information:

» **como?** (*koh*-moo?) (*how?*)

» **o que?** (ooh *kee?*) (*what?*)

» **por quê?** (poo-*keh?*) (*why?*)

» **qual?** (*kwah*-ooh?) (*which?*)

» **quem?** (kang?) (*who?*)

The following examples demonstrate how to use these words:

O que é isso? (ooh *kee* eh *ee*-soh?) (*What is this?*)

Onde fica a praia? (*ohn*-jee *fee*-kah ah *prah*-ee-ah?) (*Where is the beach?*)

Quando é o show? (*kwahn*-doh *eh* ooh show?) (*When is the concert?*)

Quem é ele? (kang eh *eh*-lee?) (*Who is he?*)

Por que é assim? (poh *keh* eh ah-*sing*?) (*Why is it like that?*)

Como é ela? (*koh*-moo eh eh-lah?) (*What is she like?*)

Quanto é? (*kwahn*-toh *eh*?) (*How much does it cost?*)

Qual carro é o seu? (*kwah*-ooh *kah*-hoh *eh* ooh *seh*-ooh?) (*Which car is yours?*)

TIP

If you want to ask someone what something means, say **O que quer dizer. . .?** (ooh *keh* keh jee-*zeh*. . .?). It literally means *What does . . . mean to say?*

For example, imagine that you're at one of Brazil's millions of drink stands on the street and you see the word **vitamina**. It looks like the word *vitamin* in English, but surely they're not selling vitamins? So you ask **O que quer dizer vitamina?**

Vitamina (vee-tah-*mee*-nah), by the way, means *smoothie*. **Vitaminas** come in more than 20 flavors in Brazil! You'll be glad to know what the word means, because your favorite flavor is just waiting for you to discover it. Find out more about Brazilian drinks in Chapter 7.

Talking in the Past Tense

Not everything happens in the **aqui** (ah-*kee*) (*here*) and **agora** (ah-*goh*-rah) (*now*). Sometimes you want to say that you've *already called* the hotel or to ask your friend whether your mom *called you yesterday*. This is stuff that happened in the **passado** (pah-*sah*-doh) (*past*), so you need to change the verb conjugation.

For **-ar** verbs, just take off the **-ar** and add the endings shown in the following table to make the verb past tense.

Subject Pronoun	Past Tense Verb Ending
eu	-ei
você	-ou
ele/ela	-ou

Subject Pronoun	Past Tense Verb Ending
nós	-amos (same as in present tense)
eles/elas	-aram
vocês	-aram

Specifically, here are the conjugations for the past tense of **ligar** (*to call someone*).

Conjugation	Pronunciation
eu liguei	eh-ooh *lee*-gay
você ligou	voh-*seh* lee-*goh*
ele/ela ligou	*eh*-lee/*eh*-lah lee-*goh*
nós ligamos	*nohz* lee-*gah*-mohz
eles/elas ligaram	*eh*-leez/*eh*-lahz lee-*gah*-rah-ooh
vocês ligaram	voh-*sehz* lee-*gah*-rah-ooh

REMEMBER

Don't worry that the **eu** (*I*) form uses the stem **ligu–** even though the others use the simple **lig–** stem. It just means that the verb **ligar** is *irregular* for the **eu** form. But spoken out loud, you can't hear the **u**. So don't sweat it.

Check out some examples of **ligar** in the past tense:

Ligaram para você ontem. (lee-*gah*-rah-ooh pah-rah voh-*seh ohn*-tang.) (*They called you yesterday.*)

Já liguei para ele. (zhah lee-*gay* pah-rah *eh*-lee.) (*I already called him.*)

Você não me ligou. (voh-*seh nah*-ooh mee lee-*goh*.) (*You didn't call me.*)

Now take a peek at some other common **-ar** verbs and examples of their usage in the past tense:

» **deixar** (day-*shah*) (*to leave*)

Deixou recado? (day-*shoh* heh-*kah*-doh?) (*Did you leave a message?*)

» **encontrar** (ehn-kohn-*trah*) (*to find/to meet*)

Finalmente encontrei a rua certa. (fee-nah-ooh-*men*-chee en-kohn-*tray* ah *hoo*-ah *seh*-tah.) (*I finally found the right street.*)

» **escutar** (eh-skoo-*tah*) (*to listen*)

Ela escutou um som estranho. (eh-lah eh-skoo-*toh* oong *soh*-oong eh-*strahn*-yoh.) (*She heard a strange sound.*)

» **falar** (fah-*lah*) (*to talk/to tell*)

Ele me falou que hoje vai ter festa. (*eh*-lee mee fah-*loh* kee *oh*-zhee vah-ee teh *feh*-stah.) (*He told me that there's a party today.*)

» **fechar** (feh-*shah*) (*to close*)

Fecharam a porta. (feh-*shah*-rah-oong ah *poh*-tah.) (*They closed the door.*)

Browse Table 6-7 for some common time references that signal the past tense and come in handy with everyday conversations.

TABLE 6-7

Past Tense Time References

Term	Pronunciation	Meaning
ontem	*ohn*-tang	*yesterday*
na semana passada	nah seh-*mah*-nah pah-*sah*-dah	*last week*
hoje de manhã	*oh*-zhee jee mahn-*yah*	*this morning*
ontem à noite	*ohn*-tang ah *noh*-ee-chee	*last night*
faz alguns dias	*fah*-eez ah-ooh-*goonz* jee-ahz	*a few days ago*
faz vinte minutos	*fah*-eez *veen*-chee mee-*noo*-tohz	*20 minutes ago*
faz muito tempo	*fah*-eez moh-*ee*-toh *tem*-poh	*a long time ago*
no ano passado	noh *ah*-noh pah-*sah*-doh	*last year*

An important irregular verb in the past tense is **ir** (ee) (*to go*). This verb comes in handy when you're talking about where you've been and what you've done.

Here are the conjugations for the past tense of **ir**.

Conjugation	Pronunciation
eu fui	*eh*-ooh *fwee*
você foi	voh-*seh foh*-ee
ele/ela foi	*eh*-lee/*eh*-lah *foh*-ee

Conjugation	Pronunciation
nós fomos	*nohz foh*-mooz
eles/elas foram	*eh*-leez/*eh*-lahz *foh*-rah-ooh
vocês foram	voh-*sehz foh*-rah-ooh

Here are some phrases that include **ir** in the past tense:

Eu fui para o Brasil em abril. (*eh*-ooh *fwee* pah-rah ooh brah-*zee*-ooh ang ah-*bree*-ooh.) (*I went to Brazil in April.*)

Nós fomos para a praia no domingo. (nohz *foh*-mooz pah-rah ah *prah*-ee-ah noh doh-*ming*-goh.) (*We went to the beach on Sunday.*)

Para onde ela foi? (pah-rah *ohn*-jee eh-lah *foh*-ee?) (*Where did she go?*)

Eles foram jantar num restaurante. (eh-leez *foh*-rah-ooh zhahn-*tah* noong heh-stah-ooh-*rahn*-chee.) (*They went to have dinner at a restaurant.*)

Talkin' the Talk

Eliana (eh-lee-*ah*-nah) and **Leila** (*lay*-lah) are office co-workers. **Leila** just got back from a vacation in **Bahia** (bah-*ee*-ah) state. Notice the past-tense uses of the verbs **gostar** (goh-*stah*) (*to like*) and **ir** (ee) (*to go*).

Eliana:	**Gostou da Bahia?**
	goh-*stoh* dah bah-*ee*-ah?
	Did you like Bahia?
Leila:	**Sim, gostei muito.**
	sing, goh-*stay* moh-*ee*-too.
	Yeah, I liked it a lot.
Eliana:	**Aonde você foi?**
	ah-*ohn*-jee *voh*-seh *foh*-ee?
	Where did you go?

CHAPTER 6 Getting to Know You: Small Talk **115**

Leila:	**Nós fomos para Itacaré.**	
	nohz *foh*-mooz pah-rah ee-tah-kah-*reh*.	
	We went to Itacaré.	
Eliana:	**Eu nunca fui para a Bahia.**	
	eh-ooh *noon*-kah *fwee pah*-rah ah bah-*ee*-ah.	
	I've never been to Bahia (state).	
Leila:	**Nunca foi? Vale a pena.**	
	noon-kah *foh*-ee? *vah*-lee ah *peh*-nah.	
	You've never been? It's worth it.	
Eliana:	**No ano passado fui para os Lençóis Maran-henses. Que delícia!**	
	noo *ah*-noh pah-*sah*-doo *fwee pah*-rah oohz len-*soy*-eez mah-rah-oong-*yang*-seez. kee deh-*lee*-see-ah!	
	Last year I went to Lençóis Maranhenses (a sand dune area with pools of water, in Maranhão state). What a treat!	

● ●

WORDS TO KNOW

Gostou. . .?	goh-<u>stoh</u>. . .?	Did you like. . .?
gostei	goh-<u>stay</u>	I liked
aonde	ah-<u>ohn</u>-jee	to where
além de	ah-<u>lang</u> jee	in addition to/besides
nunca	<u>noon</u>-kah	never
Vale a pena.	<u>vah</u>-lee ah <u>peh</u>-nah.	It's well worth it.
Que delícia!	<u>kee</u> deh-<u>lee</u>-see-ah!	What a treat!

Pulling It Together with Connector Words

As with any language, little connector words, grammatically known as conjunctions and prepositions, pull together main words to make a sentence sound right. You may recognize some of the words in Table 6-8 because some appear many times in this book. These connector words are small but very important.

TABLE 6-8 ## Connector Words (Conjunctions and Prepositions)

Term	Pronunciation	Meaning
e	ee	*and*
além de	ah-*lang* jee	*in addition to*
mas	*mah*-eez	*but*
para	*pah*-rah	*to/in order to*
se	see	*if*
mesmo se	*mez*-moh see	*even if*
embora	em-*boh*-rah	*although*
que	kee	*that*
só que	soh *kee*	*except that*
desde	*dez*-jee	*since*
porque	poh-*keh*	*because*
até	ah-*teh*	*until*
com	koh-oong	*with*
por	poh	*through/by*
de	jee	*of*
sobre	*soh*-bree	*about/on top of*

Here are a few phrases that use connectors:

>> **café com leite** (kah-*feh* koh-oong *lay*-chee) (*coffee with milk*)

>> **desde a primeira vez que eu te vi** (*dez*-jee ah pree-*may*-rah *vehz* kee *eh*-ooh chee *vee*) (*ever since I first saw you*)

» **é para você** (eh *pah*-rah voh-*seh*) (*it's for you*)

» **Romeu e Julieta** (*hoh*-mee-ooh ee zhoo-lee-*eh*-tah) (*Romeo and Juliet*)

Three "Save Me!" Phrases

A few days after arriving in Brazil, I was sent as a reporter to cover a business conference. I had some familiarity with Portuguese because I was already a fluent Spanish speaker, but I still didn't understand much of the language and I felt helpless. **De repente** (deh heh-*pen*-chee) (*Suddenly*), a speaker got up to the podium, and I could **compreender** (kohm-pree-en-*deh*) (*understand*) a lot more Portuguese than normal. I wondered whether **talvez** (*tah*-ooh *vehz*) (*maybe*) the guy was from some region of Brazil that's easier to understand.

It turned out that the guy was American! He spoke Portuguese very well but had an American **sotaque** (soh-*tah*-kee) (*accent*), which made it easier for me to understand his Portuguese. The Brazilian accent is hard to understand at first, and sometimes you'll want to ask the person you're speaking with to **falar mais devagar, por favor** (fah-*lah mah*-eez deh-vah-*gah*, poh fah-*voh*) (*speak more slowly, please*).

When you're feeling frustrated, pull these phrases out of your pocket:

Desculpe, não entendi. (jees-*kool*-pee, *nah*-ooh en-ten-*jee*.) (*I didn't understand.*)

Como? (*koh*-moh?) (*What did you say?* [informal])

Poderia repetir, por favor? (poh-deh-*ree*-ah heh-peh-*chee*, poh fah-*voh*?) (*Could you repeat that, please?*)

Sharing Your Contact Information

After your first conversation with some people who speak Portuguese, you may decide you'd like to keep in touch with them. Or they may ask for your contact info first. If you hear, **Qual o seu número?** (*kwah*-oo ooh seh-oo *noo*-meh-roh?) (*What's your number?*), you can respond **O meu número é . . .** (ooh *meh*-oo *noo*-meh-roh *eh . . .*) (*My number is . . .*). (Flip to Chapter 4 to find out how to say numbers in Portuguese.) Or, they may say, **Você tem Instagram/WhatsApp/Facebook?**

(voh-*seh tang een*-stah-grahm/wat-*sahp*/fay-see-*boo*-kee). You can respond, **O meu** + [app] you want them to contact you on + **é. . .** (ooh *meh*-ooh + [app] + *eh*. . .) + your username/handle. To learn more social media vocab and know-how, flip to Chapter 10.

Here are some other follow-up questions you can ask new friends. Notice the use of **seu** (*your*) in the questions and **meu** (*my*) in the responses, which I cover earlier in this chapter:

> **Qual é o seu sobrenome?** (*kwah*-ooh *eh* ooh *seh*-oo soh-bree-*noh*-mee?) (*What's your last name?*)
>
> **Onde mora?** (ohn-jee *moh*-rah?) (*Where do you live?*)
>
> **Qual é o seu email?** (*kwah*-ooh *eh* ooh *seh*-oo ee-*may*-oh?) (*What's your email?*)

And here's how you can respond if you're asked these questions:

> **O meu sobrenome é . . .** (ooh *meh*-oo soh-bree-*noh*-mee *eh* . . .) (*My last name is . . .*)
>
> **Eu moro . . .** (eh-ooh *moh*-roo . . .) (*I live . . .*)
>
> **O meu email é . . .** (ooh *meh*-oo ee-*may*-oh *eh* . . .) (*My email is . . .*)

You may need to spell out your name for your new Brazilian friends. Or you may need to **pedir** (peh-*jee*) (*ask*) someone to spell their name for you. Luckily, spelling in Brazilian Portuguese is pretty **fácil** (*fah*-see-ooh) (*easy*) because things are spelled the way they sound (unlike in English where two words can sound the same but have different spellings and meanings), and the vast majority of Brazilians have common Portuguese **nomes** (*noh*-meez) (*first names*).

CULTURAL WISDOM

Be prepared to raise an eyebrow: Some of the names you hear in Brazil may surprise you. There are **bastantes** (bah-*stahn*-cheez) (*quite a few*) Brazilian men with interesting names like **Givanildo** or **Washington,** alongside the more classic Portuguese names like **João** or **Roberto.**

Brazil is also home to many foreign immigrants, including the large Japanese population in São Paulo, who have non-Portuguese names. Don't let **a pronúncia** (ah proh-*noon*-see-ah) (*the pronunciation*) throw you off. Ask someone to spell out their name if you're unsure about what to call them.

FUN & GAMES

Use the illustration as a guide to practice using your possessives — *my, your, his/her, their,* and *our.* Translate the English phrases into Portuguese. (Hint: You're allowed to look back in the chapter for help!)

Illustration by Elizabeth Kurtzman

A. my dad _____

B. your mom _____

C. his brother _____

D. their sister _____

E. our grandma _____

Turn to Appendix C for the answers.

Chapter **7**

Dining Out and Going to the Market

Está com fome? (eh-*stah* koh-*oong foh*-mee?) (*Are you hungry?*) **Quer comer?** (*keh* koh-*meh*?) (*Do you want to eat?*) Well, **se fala** (see *fah*-lah) (*they say*) that you can't really get to know a **cultura estrangeira** (kool-*too*-rah ehs-trahn-*zhey*-rah) (*foreign culture*) until you've eaten its **comida** (koh-*mee*-dah) (*food*). This chapter is all about helping you become acquainted with Brazilian cuisine. Find out how to order it, talk about it, shop for it, and enjoy it.

Trying Brazilian Foods

The classic Brazilian **comida** (koh-*mee*-dah) (*meal/food*) is **simples** (seem-pleez) (*basic*): a piece of **carne** (*kah*-nee) (*beef*) served with **feijão** (fay-zhow) (*beans*), **arroz** (ah-*hohz*) (*rice*), and **salada** (sah-*lah*-dah) (*salad*). Brazilian cuisine gets its inspiration mainly from Portuguese, African, and indigenous culinary traditions. It's generally not **apimentada** (ah-*pee*-men-*tah*-dah) (*spicy*) and varies a bit by region.

In this section, I describe Brazilian staples as well as the different types of Brazilian eateries and the food you can find there.

Sampling the classics

CULTURAL WISDOM

No dish is more typical of Brazil than **feijoada**, (fay-zhow-*ah*-dah), a black bean stew that uses various parts of a pig. **Feijoada** was first whipped up in **cozinhas** (koh-*zeen*-yahz) (*kitchens*) by **escravos** (ehs-*krah*-vohz) (*slaves*) brought from Africa starting in the 16th century. The **escravos** were **pobres** (poh-breez) (*poor*), and they made sure they ate almost all parts of every animal. **Feijoada** is traditionally served in restaurants on **quarta-feira** (kwah-tah *fay*-rah) (*Wednesday*) and **sábado** (*sah*-bah-doh) (*Saturday*).

Churrasco (choo-*hah*-skoo) (*Brazilian barbecue*) is also popular throughout the country. And you cannot leave Brazil without trying **mandioca frita** (mahn-jee-oh-kah *free*-tah), or *fried manioc root. Manioc* is a slightly sweet root vegetable indigenous to Brazil. Move over French fries, **mandioca frita** are way better!

A popular Brazilian lunch includes a **sanduíche na chapa** (sahn-*dwee*-shee nah *shah*-pah) (*pressed hot sandwich*) that combines meat, cheese, and other ingredients in a **pão francês** (*pah*-ooh frahn-*say*-eez) (*small baguette*), pressed on a hot grill.

Here are some other classic Brazilian foods:

» **açaí na tigela com granola** (ah-sah-*ee* nah tee-*zheh*-lah *koh*-oong grah-*noh*-lah): Amazonian fruit sorbet in a large bowl, topped with granola and sometimes honey, this dish is a favored beach food of Brazilian surfers. **Açaí** is a small, eggplant-colored berry that's now available in the United States, too.

» **acarajé** (ah-*kah*-rah-*zheh*): This popular treat from Bahia state is sold on beaches and on the street and looks like a falafel sandwich. It consists of deep-fried black-eyed-pea cakes filled with a savory paste made from nuts called **vatapá** (vah-tah-*pah*), tiny dried shrimp, and diced tomatoes. They usually offer **pimenta** (pee-*men*-tah) (*hot sauce*), which you can add or not. The cakes are fried in **azeite de dendê** (ah-*zay*-chee jee den-*day*) (*palm oil*).

WARNING

Beware the **azeite de dendê**. It's very strong and can cause stomachaches for those who've never tried it before.

» **coco** (*koh*-koh): Brazilians love *coconut*. They drink coconut water out of a whole green coconut, through a straw. Vendors chop off a top slice of the coconut with a machete and then sell it for very cheap on the beach and on the street. **Coco** is also used in lots of main dishes from Bahia state and the rest of the Northeast.

» **coxinha** (koh-*sheen*-yah): **Coxinhas** are made by mixing flour, butter and seasonings, then shaping the mixture into a teardrop, stuffed with shredded chicken, then fried. You can find this dish at most corner **botecos** (boo-*teh*-kooz) (*cheap restaurants*) (see the section "Bom apetite! Ordering and enjoying your meal" later in this chapter) or bakeries in Brazil.

» **farofa** (fah-*roh*-fah): This is toasted manioc flour sautéed in butter. Sometimes people add bits of fried bacon, onion, or even scrambled eggs. **Farofa** is served with **feijoada** or on the side with steak. Mmmm, a not-to-miss item!

» **moqueca** (moh-*keh*-kah): This thick seafood or fish stew from the coast of Bahia state is made with **azeite de dendê** (ah-*zay*-chee jee den-*deh*) (*red palm oil*) — which can be hard on a stomach that's unfamiliar with it — and **leite de coco** (*lay*-chee jee *koh*-koo) (*coconut milk*).

» **pão de queijo** (*pah*-ooh jee *kay*-zhoh): Pão de queijo is *cheese bread* that's sold either as little balls or in pieces the size of a biscuit. This treat is unbelievably delicious and addictive. The warm, chewy bread originates in the state of Minas Gerais but has become popular all over Brazil.

Finding a place to eat

If you want to make plans to grab a bite to eat with your Brazilian friends, you may need to know how to talk about the basic meals:

» **café da manhã** (kah-*feh* dah mahn-*yah*) (*breakfast;* Literally: *morning's coffee*)

» **almoço** (*ah*-ooh-*moh*-soo) (*lunch*)

» **jantar** (zhahn-*tah*) (*dinner*)

» **lanche** (*lahn*-shee) (*snack*)

Then it's time to decide what kind of eatery you want to go to. You can get a **refeição** (heh–fay–*sah*–ooh) (*meal*) at five basic types of eateries in Brazil:

» **boteco** (boo-*teh*-koo): A cheap restaurant serving simple meals where people also go to drink beer or take shots of liquor.

» **padaria** (pah-dah-*ree*-ah) (*bakery*): At some Brazilian **padarias,** you can sit down for a meal.

» **lanchonete** (lahn-shoh-*neh*-chee) (*casual restaurant, Brazilian-style diner*): An informal restaurant — Brazil's answer to fast food — that tends to be busiest during the lunch hour.

ASKING ABOUT RESTAURANT VIRUS PRECAUTIONS

Before sitting down at a **restaurante** (heh-stah-ooh-*rahn*-chee) (*restaurant*), you may want to ask staff about their **protocolo sanitário** (proh-toh-*koh*-loo sah-nee-*tah*-ree-ooh) (sanitary protocol) surrounding **COVID-19** (same spelling as in English) (*koh*-vee-jee dez-ee-*noh*-vee). You can ask, **Preciso mascara?** (preh-*see*-zoo mahs-kah-rah) (*Do I need a mask?*) or **Preciso documento de vacinação?** (preh-*see*-zoo doh-koo-*men*-toh jee vah-see-nah-*sah*-ooh) (*Do I need proof of vaccination?*) You might also want to ask for a **mesa** (*meh*-zah) (*table*) that is **fora** (*foh*-rah) (*outside*) or **dentro** (*den*-troh) (*inside*). You can also specify that you want to **comer aqui** (koh-*meh* ah-*kee*) (*eat here*) or ask for **comida** (koh-*mee*-dah) (*food*) that is **para viagem** (*pah*-rah vee-*ah*-zhang) (*to go*). Some restaurants may require that you **medir temperatura** (meh-*jee* tem-peh-rah-*too*-rah) (*take your temperature*) before you **entrar** (en-*trah*) (*enter*) to keep the **vírus** (*veeh*-roos) (*virus*) at bay. I am hoping that if you pick up this book a year or more after it's published (that would be 2023 or later, since this book was published in 2022), our global **pandemia** (pahn-deh-*mee*-ah) (*pandemic*) will have cooled off, and you (fingers crossed) might not need COVID vocab (that's a tongue-twister; try saying "COVID vocab" quickly a few times!).

>> **restaurante à quilo** (heh-stah-ooh-*rahn*-chee ah *kee*-loh) (*pay-by-weight restaurant*): A self-serve buffet where the price of your food is based on its weight in kilos; a delicious, healthy, fast, and cheap option in Brazil.

>> **restaurante** (heh-stah-ooh-*rahn*-chee) (*restaurant*): A traditional dining option, where you gather with friends and family for a sit-down meal that's served to you by a **garçon** (gah-*sohng*) (*waiter*) or **garçonete** (gah-soh-*neh*-chee) (*waitress*).

Perusing the menu

As in other places in the world, food on the **cardápio** (kah-*dah*-pee-oh) (*menu*) in a Brazilian eatery is likely grouped into the following familiar sections:

>> **bebidas** (beh-*bee*-dahz) (*drinks*)

>> **entradas** (en-*trah*-dahz) (*appetizers*)

>> **pratos principais** (*prah*-tohz preen-see-*pah*-eez) (*main dishes*)

>> **sobremesas** (soh-bree-*meh*-zahz) (*desserts*)

You may also see the term **especialidades da casa** (eh-speh-see-ah-lee-*dah*-jeez dah *kah*-zah) (*house specialties*).

If you visit a Brazilian **lanchonete**, expect the **cardápio** to offer **hamburgers** (ahm-booh-gehrz) (*hamburgers*), **sanduíches** (sahn-*dwee*-sheez) (*sandwiches*), **salgados** (sah-ooh-*gah*-dohz) (*savory pastries*), **pratos feitos** (prah-tohz *fay*-tohz) (*combo plates*, usually consisting of rice, beans, meat, and salad), and **sucos** (soo-kohz) (*fruit juices*).

Don't be surprised to see **pizza** or **sushi** — both spelled and pronounced the same in Portuguese as in English — in Brazilian restaurants, especially in São Paulo, where lots of Italian and Japanese immigrants (and descendants of immigrants) live. The robust presence of these populations also means that you can find excellent **italiano** (ee-tah-lee-*ah*-noh) (*Italian*) and **japonês** (zhah-poh-*nehz*) (*Japanese*) **restaurantes** in São Paulo.

TIP

If you want to ask for something specific, say **Tem. . .?** (tang. . .?) (*Do you have. . .?*) You can fill in the blank with one of the following words or phrases:

>> **algo para crianças** (*ah*-ooh-goh *pah*-rah kree-*ahn*-sahz) (*something for kids*)

>> **frango** (*frahn*-goh) (*chicken*)

>> **legumes refogados** (lay-*goo*-meez ray-foh-*gah*-doos) (*sautéed vegetables*)

>> **massas** (*mah*-sahz) (*pasta*)

>> **peixe** (*pay*-shee) (*fish*)

>> **pratos vegetarianos** (*prah*-tohz veh-zheh-teh-ree-*ah*-nohz) (*vegetarian dishes*)

>> **salada** (sah-*lah*-dah) (*salad*)

>> **sopa** (*soh*-pah) (*soup*)

You can also use **Tem**, from the verb **ter** (teh) (*to have*), to ask whether a **prato** (prah-toh) (*dish*) contains a specific **ingrediente** (eeng-greh-jee-*en*-chee) (*ingredient*) that you may or may not want.

Here's how to conjugate **ter**.

Conjugation	Pronunciation
eu tenho	*eh*-ooh *tang*-yoh
você tem	voh-*seh tang*
ele/ela tem	*eh*-lee/*eh*-lah *tang*
nós temos	*nohz teh*-mohz
eles/elas têm	*eh*-leez/*eh*-lahz *tang*
vocês têm	voh-*sehz tang*

Here are some practice questions for finding out more about a dish:

Tem carne? (tang *kah*-nee?) (*Does it have meat in it?*)

Tem frutos do mar? (tang *froo*-tohz doo *mah*?) (*Does it have any seafood in it?*)

Tem azeite de dendê? (tang ah-*zay*-chee jee den-*deh*?) (*Does it have palm oil?*)

Tem coentro? (tang koh-*en*-troh?) (*Does it have cilantro?*)

Bom apetite! Ordering and enjoying your meal

When you're **pronto** (*prohn*-toh) (*ready*) to **pedir** (peh-*jeeh*) (*order*; Literally: *to ask for*), you can just say, **Quero . . . por favor** (*keh*-roo . . . poh-fah-*voh*) (*I want . . . please*).

REMEMBER

Quero comes from the verb **querer** (keh-*reh*) (*to want*), which comes in handy in lots of **situações** (see-too-ah-*soh*-eez) (*situations*), not just when **tem fome** (tang *foh*-mee) (*you're hungry*).

You can use **querer** at a store to tell the clerk what you want, to tell an **amigo** (ah-*mee*-goh) (*male friend*) what kind of **bebida** (beh-*bee*-dah) (*drink*) you'd like when you're visiting his **casa** (*kah*-zah) (*house*), or to tell someone about your **trabalho** (trah-*bahl*-yoh) (*job*) or **metas para a vida** (*meh*-tahs *pah*-rah ah *vee*-dah) (*life aspirations*).

Here's how to conjugate **querer**.

Conjugation	Pronunciation
eu quero	*eh*-ooh *keh*-roo
você quer	voh-*seh keh*
ele/ela quer	*eh*-lee/*eh*-lah *keh*
nós queremos	*nohz* keh-*reh*-mohz
eles/elas querem	*eh*-leez/*eh*-lahz *keh*-rang
vocês querem	voh-*sehz keh*-rang

SOUND NATIVE

Brazilians often just say **Quer?** (keh?) (*Do you want?*) to ask whether you want something. So you can offer your Brazilian colleague a slice of cake by pointing to it and saying **Quer?** Similarly, Brazilians generally say **Vou querer** (voh keh-*reh*) (*I will have*; Literally: *I will want*) instead of **Quero**. But **Quero** is easier to memorize, and it's a useful word for many other situations.

You can practice **querer** with these questions and phrases:

Quer um Guaraná? (*keh* oong *gwah*-rah-*nah?*) (*Do you want a Guaraná?*) (a popular Brazilian soda made from the seeds of the **guaraná** plant, which is local to the Amazon region and contains caffeine)

Sim, quero. (*sing, keh*-roo.) (*Yes, please.* Literally: *Yes, I want.*)

Não, não quero, obrigada. (*nah*-ooh, nah-ooh *keh*-roo, oh-bree-*gah*-dah.) (*No thanks.*)

TIP

If the **cardápio** is too confusing, you may just want a recommendation. Say **O que você recomenda?** (ooh *kee* voh-*seh* heh-koh-*men*-dah?) (*What do you recommend?*). If you want to go with what the person recommends, say **OK, tá bom** (oh-kay tah *boh*-oong) (*Okay, I'll go with that;* Literally: *That's good*).

Here are some things you may want to **pedir** (peh-*jee*) (*ask for*) at a **restaurante** (heh-stah-ooh-*rahn*-chee) (*restaurant*) or someone's **casa** (kah-zah) (*house*):

>> **sal** (*sah*-ooh) (*salt*)

>> **pimenta do reino** (pee-*men*-tah doo *hay*-noo) (*black pepper*)

>> **pimenta** (pee-*men*-tah) (*Brazilian hot sauce* — hot red peppers soaking in oil; Literally: *pepper*)

>> **limão** (lee-*mah*-ooh) (*lime*)

>> **pão** (*pah*-ooh) (*bread*)

>> **gelo** (*zheh*-loh) (*ice*)

>> **azeite de oliva** (ah-*zay*-chee jee oh-*lee*-vah) (*olive oil*)

>> **vinagre** (vee-*nah*-gree) (*red or white wine vinegar*)

>> **vinagrete** (vee-nah-*greh*-chee) (*vinaigrette;* made of chopped tomato, onion, and green bell pepper with vinegar — Brazilians put **vinagrete** on barbecued meat)

If you know a **prato** has a specific **ingrediente** that you want **retirado** (heh-chee-*rah*-doh) (*taken out*), say **sem** (sang) (*without*) followed by the name of the ingredient, which may be one of the following words:

>> **açúcar** (ah-*soo*-kah) (*sugar*)

>> **alho** (*ahl*-yoh) (*garlic*)

>> **cebola** (seh-*boh*-lah) (*onion*)

>> **leite** (*lay*-chee) (*milk*)

>> **maionese** (mah-ee-oh-*neh*-zee) (*mayonnaise*)

>> **manteiga** (mahn-*tay*-gah) (*butter*)

>> **molho** (*mohl*-yoh) (*sauce*)

>> **óleo** (*oh*-lee-oh) (*vegetable oil*)

>> **queijo** (*kay*-zhoh) (*cheese*)

When enjoying a meal with your Brazilian friends, you may want to use these phrases at the **mesa** (*meh*-zah) (*table*):

Que gostoso! (kee gohs-*toh*-zoo!) (*How delicious!*)

É delicioso. (eh deh-lee-see-*oh*-zoo.) (*It's delicious.*)

Eu adoro chocolate (or any food you love)! (*eh*-ooh ah-*doh*-roo shoh-koh-*lah*-chee!) (*I love chocolate!* Literally: *I adore chocolate!*)

Eu detesto ovos. (*eh*-ooh deh-*teh*-stoh *oh*-vooz.) (*I hate eggs.* Literally: *I detest eggs.*)

Qual a sua comida favorita? (*kwah*-ooh ah *soo*-ah koh-*mee*-dah fah-voh-*ree*-tah?) (*What's your favorite food?*)

Está quente. (es-*tah kang*-chee.) (*It's hot.*)

Está frio. (eh-*stah free*-oh.) (*It's cold.*)

Bom apetite! (boh-oong ah-peh-*tee*-chee!) (*Bon appetite!*)

Saúde! (sah-*oo*-jee!) (*Cheers!* Literally: *Health!*)

Satisfying your sweet tooth

When you've finished your meal and want a bit more time to enjoy the company of your friends or family that gathered with you for your Brazilian meal, be sure to enjoy **sobremesa** (soh-bree-*meh*-zah) (*dessert*). Here are some of my favorite Brazilian desserts:

>> **bolo de laranja** (boh-loo jee lah-*rahn*-zhah) (*orange-flavored pound cake*)

>> **bolo de limão** (boh-loo jee lee-*mah*-ooh) (*lime-flavored pound cake*)

>> **musse de chocolate** (mooz jee sho-koh-*lah*-chee) (*chocolate mousse*)

>> **musse de maracujá** (mooz jee mah-rah-koo-*jah*) (*passion-fruit mousse*)

» **pizza doce** (*peet*-zah *doh*-see) (*pizza with sweet toppings*)

In Brazil, pizza joints usually offer several dessert pizzas. **Chocolate e morango** (sho-koh-*lah*-chee ee moh-*rahn*-goh) (*chocolate and strawberry*) is an experience not to be missed.

» **pudim de leite** (poo-*jing* jee *lay*-chee) (*flan custard*)

» **Romeo e Julieta** (*hoh*-mee-oh ee zhoo-lee-*eh*-tah) (*guava paste with a piece of hard white cheese; Literally: Romeo and Juliet*)

» **sorvete** (soh-*veh*-chee) (*ice cream*)

You may even want a **cafezinho** (kah-feh-*zeen*-yoh), a shot of Brazilian coffee served in a tiny cup or glass to go with your **sobremesa**. In good restaurants, you can ask for your coffee to be **sem açúcar** (sang ah-*soo*-kah) (*unsweetened*). And if you're in a really decadent mood, you can ask for **chantily** (shan-chee-*lee*) (*whipped cream*) with your coffee.

CULTURAL WISDOM

Brazilians usually leave a 10 percent **gorjeta** (goh-*zheh*-tah) (*tip*) at a restaurant, even the simpler ones. Most restaurants include the tip in the **conta** (kohn-tah) (*bill*), which says **serviço incluído** (seh-*vee*-soh een-kloo-*ee*-doh) (*tip included*). If service is terrible, though, you can refuse to pay the extra charge. *Sales tax* on a **conta** shows up as **I.V.A.** (*ee*-vah).

Talkin' the Talk

AUDIO ONLINE

Paying the bill isn't the most fun part of eating out, but it's a necessity nevertheless. **Alberto** (ah-ooh-*beh*-too) and **Marina** (mah-*ree*-nah) are surprised when their tasty seafood meal ends in an expensive bill.

Alberto:	**A conta, por favor.**
	ah *kohn*-tah, poh fah-*voh*.
	The check, please.
Waiter:	**Um momento, por favor.**
	oong moh-*men*-toh, poh fah-*voh*.
	Just a moment, please.
Alberto:	**Aceita cartão?**
	ah-*say*-tah kah-*tah*-ooh?
	Do you accept credit cards?

Waiter:	**Aceitamos.**
	ah-say-*tah*-mohz.
	Yes, we do (Literally: we accept).
Alberto:	**Que caro! Noventa e sete reais?**
	kee *kah*-roh! noh-*ven*-tah ee *seh*-chee hay-*ahys*?
	How expensive! Ninety-seven reals (about US$50)?
Marina:	**O serviço está incluído?**
	ooh seh-*vee*-soh eh-*stah* eeng-kloo-*ee*-doo?
	Is the tip included?
Alberto:	**Ah, foi por isto. É de dez por cento.**
	Ah, *foh*-ee poh *ees*-toh. eh jee *dehz* poh *sen*-toh.
	Ah, that's why. It's 10 percent.
Marina:	**Tem caneta?**
	tang kah-*neh*-tah?
	Do you have a pen?
Waiter:	**Aqui está.**
	ah-*kee* eh-*stah*.
	Here you go.

• •

WORDS TO KNOW

a conta	ah <u>kohn</u>-tah	the bill
vou	voh	I will
trazê-la	trah-<u>zeh</u>-lah	bring it
aceita	ah-<u>say</u>-tah	do you accept/he or she accepts
cartão	kah-<u>tah</u>-ooh	credit card (Literally: card)
aceitamos	ah-say-<u>tah</u>-mohz	we accept
uma porção	<u>ooh</u>-mah poh-<u>sah</u>-ooh	an order (one portion of food)
cada	<u>kah</u>-dah	each

caro	<u>kah</u>-roh	expensive
o serviço	ooh seh-<u>vee</u>-soh	obligatory tip (Literally: service)
incluído	eeng kloo-<u>ee</u>-doo	included
foi por isto	<u>foh</u>-ee poh <u>ee</u>-stoh	that's why
caneta	kah-<u>neh</u>-tah	pen

Buying Drinks

The incredible **variedade** (vah-ree-eh-*dah*-jee) (*variety*) of **sucos** (*fruit juices*) that Brazilian eateries offer is my favorite aspect of eating and drinking in Brazil. The average **restaurante** has between 10 and 20 types of **sucos** to choose from, and the selection varies depending on the region. Brazilians love their **sucos** and **vitaminas** (vee-tah-*mee*-nahz) (*fruity milkshakes/smoothies*). Juice bars are everywhere. Rio seems to have one on every block.

Here are the most common **frutas** (*froo*-tahz) (*fruits*) in Brazil. If you want to ask for the fruit in **suco** form, say **suco de . . .** (*soo*-koh jee . . .) (*juice of . . .*). Just plug one of these fruits into the blank:

>> **abacaxi** (ah-bah-kah-*shee*) (*pineapple*)

>> **goiaba** (goy-*ah*-bah) (*guava*)

>> **laranja** (lah-*rahn*-zhah) (*orange*)

>> **mamão** (mah-*mah*-ooh) (*papaya*)

>> **manga** (*mahn*-gah) (*mango*)

>> **maracujá** (mah-rah-koo-*zhah*) (*passion fruit*)

>> **melancia** (meh-lahn-*see*-ah) (*watermelon*)

TIP

Don't leave Brazil without trying my favorite **suco**: **cupuaçu** (koo-poo-ah-*soo*), a milky white Amazonian fruit with a tangy taste.

Aside from **suco**, to help you wash down all the wonderful Brazilian food, you may want one of the following **bebidas** (beh-*bee*-dahz) (*drinks*):

>> **água sem gás** (*ah*-gwah *sang* gahz) (*still mineral water*)

>> **água com gás** (*ah*-gwah *kohng* gahz) (*sparkling mineral water*)

- **Guaraná Antártica** (gwah-rah-*nah* ahn-*tah*-chee-kah), (Brazil's most popular brand-name soda, made from the Amazonian berry **guaraná**; **Antártica** is the brand name)

- **Guaraná diet** (gwah-rah-*nah dah*-ee-chee) (*diet Guaraná*)

- **Coca-Cola** (koh-kah *koh*-lah) (*Coke*)

- **Coca light** (koh-kah *lah*-ee-chee) (*Diet Coke*)

- **cerveja** (seh-*veh*-zhah) (*beer*)

- **chope** (*shoh*-pee) (*light draft beer*)

- **vinho branco/tinto** (*veen*-yoh *brahn*-koh/*cheen*-toh) (*white/red wine*)

- **café** (kah-*feh*) (*coffee*)

- **chá** (shah) (*tea*)

- **leite** (*lay*-chee) (*milk*)

SOUND NATIVE

If you go to a bar in Brazil, you may notice people saying **Mais um** (*mah*-eez *oong*) or **Mais uma** (*mah*-eez *ooh*-mah) a lot. The phrases mean *I'll have another* (Literally: *More one*).

A note about Brazilian **cerveja**: Brazilians often joke that beer has to be **estupidamente gelada** (eh-*stoo*-pee-dah-*men*-chee zheh-*lah*-dah) (*stupidly cold*). A Brazilian sends back a beer that's not ice cold. And the only time you can possibly get good **cerveja escura** (seh-*veh*-zhah es-*koo*-rah) (*dark beer*) in Brazil is during the German beer festival Oktoberfest, held each year in **Blumenau** (*bloo*-meh-*now*), which is in Santa Catarina state (southern Brazil, where many descendants of German immigrants live).

REMEMBER

Then, of course, there's the national drink of Brazil, the **caipirinha** (kah-ee-pee-*ring*-yah). It's made with **cachaça** (kah-*shah*-sah) (*sugar cane liquor*), **gelo** (*zheh*-loh) (*ice*), **limão** (lee-*mah*-ooh) (*lime*), and **açúcar** (ah-*soo*-kah) (*sugar*). You can also order a **caipifruta** (kah-ee-pee-*froo*-tah), which is a **caipirinha** made with a fruit of your choice instead of lime. Or, as is the preference of many Brazilians, you can specify that you'd like a **caipiroska** (kah-ee-pee-*roh*-ska) (**caipirinha** made from vodka instead of **cachaça**).

Basking in Brazilian Barbeque

You can't talk about Brazilian food without mentioning the beloved **churrascaria** (choo-*hah*-skeh-*ree*-ah), a Brazilian-style barbeque restaurant that is usually rather fancy. It's a **comer à vontade** (koh-*meh* ah vohn-*tah*-jee) (*all-you-can-eat*) affair, and **churrascarias** are popping up in cities all over the world.

Waiters come by your **mesa** (*meh*-zah) (*table*) with a trolley holding about ten different **cortes** (*koh*-cheez) (*cuts*) of meat or even a whole **salmão** (sah-ooh-*mah*-ooh) (*salmon*) every five minutes or so.

Sometimes you're given a round card that's **verde** (*veh*-jee) (*green*) on one side and **vermelho** (veh-*mel*-yoh) (*red*) on the other. When you want to **comer mais** (koh-*meh mah*-eez) (*eat more*), place the card with the **verde** side up. When you're **satisfeito** (sah-tees-*fay*-toh) (*full*), be sure to have the **vermelho** side showing. Otherwise, it'll be hard to fend off the **garçon** (gah-*sohng*) (*waiter*)!

Here are the typical **cortes** the **garçon** may bring by your **mesa:**

>> **picanha** (pee-*kahn*-yah) (*rump steak*)

>> **alcatra** (ow-*kah*-trah) (*top sirloin*)

>> **fraldinha** (frah-ooh-*jeen*-yah) (*flank steak*)

>> **linguiça** (ling-*gwee*-sah) (*Brazilian chorizo-style sausage*)

>> **lombo** (*lohm*-boh) (*pork loin*)

>> **coxa de frango** (*koh*-shah jee *frahn*-goh) (*chicken thighs*)

>> **peito de frango** (*pay*-toh jee *frahn*-goh) (*chicken breast*)

>> **coração de frango** (koh-rah-*sah*-ooh jee *frahn*-goh) (*chicken hearts*)

>> **cordeiro** (koh-*day*-roh) (*lamb*)

Carne is most often served **grelhada** (greh-ooh-*yah*-dah) (*grilled*).

CULTURAL WISDOM

You may wonder what you're supposed to do with the bowl of yellow powdery stuff that looks like corn meal on your **mesa**. It's **farinha** (fah-*reen*-yah) (*manioc flour*). Dip your meat into coarse flour? I personally didn't like **farinha** for about a year. But now when I eat a steak without it, I miss this accompaniment. It's definitely an acquired taste, but once acquired, you'll find it impossible to **viver sem** (vee-*veh sang*) (*live without*). It gives nice texture to steak.

Vegetarianos (veh-zheh-teh-ree-*ah*-nohz) (*vegetarians*), never fear: **Churrascarias** always have a wonderful salad buffet for you to enjoy.

Mastering Eating and Drinking Verbs

I've included the word **comida** (koh-*mee*-dah) (*food*) in this chapter already. It comes from the verb **comer** (koh-*meh*) (*to eat/to have a meal*). Here's how to conjugate **comer**.

Conjugation	Pronunciation
eu como	*eh*-ooh *koh*-moo
você come	voh-*seh koh*-mee
ele/ela come	*eh*-lee/*eh*-lah *koh*-mee
nós comemos	*nohz* koh-*meh*-mohz
eles/elas comem	*eh*-leez/*eh*-lahz *koh*–mang
vocês comem	voh-*sehz koh*-mang

Try out these sentences to use **comer:**

Vamos comer. (*vah*-mohz koh-*meh*.) (*Let's eat.*)

O meu cachorro come cenoura. (ooh *meh*-ooh kah-*shoh*-hoo *koh*-mee seh-*noh*-rah.) (*My dog eats carrots.*)

Como muito. (*koh*-moo moh-*ee*-toh.) (*I eat a lot.*)

Ela come pouco. (*eh*-lah *koh*-mee *poh*-koh.) (*She doesn't eat much;* Literally: *She eats little.*)

Next, glance at the verb **beber** (beh–*beh*) (*to drink*). Depending on the context, **beber** can also specifically mean *to drink alcohol*, much like when people in the United States say "He drinks a lot" to mean *He drinks a lot of alcohol.* The Portuguese equivalent is **Ele bebe muito** (*eh*-lee *beh*–bee moh-*ee*-toh). Here's how to conjugate **beber.**

Conjugation	Pronunciation
eu bebo	*eh*-ooh *beh*-boh
você bebe	voh-*seh beh*-bee
ele/ela bebe	*eh*-lee/*eh*-lah *beh*-bee
nós bebemos	*nohz* beh-*beh*-mohz
eles/elas bebem	*eh*-leez/*eh*-lahz *beh*-bang
vocês bebem	voh-*sehz beh*-bang

Here are some basic phrases that use **beber:**

> **O que você quer para beber?** (ooh kee voh-*seh keh* pah-rah beh-*beh?*) (*What do you want to drink?*)

> **É preciso beber muita água todos os dias.** (eh preh-*see*-zoh beh-*beh* moh-*ee*-tah *ah*-gwah toh-dooz ooz *jee*-ahz.) (*It's necessary to drink a lot of water every day.*)

SOUND NATIVE

Brazilians often also use the verb **tomar** (toh–*mah*) to mean *to drink*. It's okay to use **tomar** when you'd say *to have a drink*, as in these examples:

> **Gostaria de tomar uma Coca-Cola?** (gohs-tah-*ree*-ah jee toh-*mah* ooh-mah koh-kah *koh*-lah?) (*Would you like to have a Coke?*)

> **Vamos tomar um drinque.** (*vah*-mohz toh-*mah* oong *dring*-kee.) (*Let's have a drink/ cocktail.*)

Tomar also means *to take*. Brazilians and North Americans use some of the same expressions that use *take:*

>> **tomar a iniciativa** (toh-*mah* ah ee-*nee*-see-ah-*chee*-vah) (*to take the initiative*)

>> **tomar conta de** (toh-*mah kohn*-tah jee) (*to take care of*)

>> **tomar remédios** (toh-*mah* heh-*meh*-jee-ooz) (*to take medicine*)

Shopping at the Market

Brazilians shop at **supermercados** (*soo*-peh-meh-*kah*-dooz) (*supermarkets*), but they also love to buy **frutas** (*froo*-tahz) (*fruits*) and **legumes e verduras** (leh-*goo*-meez ee veh-*doo*-rahz) (*vegetables*) at **feiras** (*fay*-rahz) (*outdoor markets*), where the food is usually **mais barata** (mah-eez bah-*rah*-tah) (*cheaper*) and **mais fresca** (mah-eez *fres*-kah) (*fresher*). (Flip to Chapter 14 to find out about Brazilian money.)

CULTURAL WISDOM

The biggest supermarket chain in Brazil is called **Pão de Açúcar** (*pah*-ooh jee ah-*soo*-kah) (*The Sugarloaf*), named after the famous rock that distinguishes Rio's skyline.

Picking up practical items

Here are some items you can buy at a **supermercado** besides **produtos frescos** (proh–*doo*–toos *fres*–kohs) (*fresh food items*):

>> **adoçante** (ah-doh-*sahn*-chee) (*popular sugar substitute*)

>> **aparelho de barbear** (ah-pah-*rel*-yoh jee bah-bee-*ah*) (*shaving razor*)

>> **coisas congeladas** (*koy*-zahz kohn-zheh-*lah*-dahz) (*frozen things*)

>> **escova de dente** (eh-*skoh*-vah jee *den*-chee) (*toothbrush*)

>> **fralda** (*frah*-ooh-dah) (*diapers*)

>> **legumes enlatados** (leh-*goo*-meez en-lah-*tah*-doos) (*cans of vegetables*)

>> **massas** (*mah*-sahz) (*pasta*)

>> **papel higiênico** (pah-*peh*-ooh ee-*zheh*-nee-koh) (*toilet paper*)

>> **pasta de dente** (*pah*-stah jee *den*-chee) (*toothpaste*)

>> **produtos de limpeza** (proh-*doo*-tohz jee leem-*peh*-zah) (*cleaning products*)

>> **revistas** (heh-*vee*-stahz) (*magazines*)

>> **sabonete** (sah-boh-*neh*-chee) (*soap*)

>> **temperos** (tem-*peh*-rooz) (*herbs and spices*)

>> **xampu** (shahm-*poo*) (*shampoo*)

Visit www.paodeacucar.com/ to discover the names of more supermarket items in Portuguese.

Buying produce at an outdoor market

Now check out the **feira**. Here are some typical **verduras** (veh–*dooh*–rahz) (*leafy veggies*) and **legumes** (leh–*goo*–meez) (*veggies that grow underground*) you can often find at this type of market:

>> **abóbora** (ah-*boh*-boh-rah) (*pumpkin*)

>> **batata** (bah-*tah*-tah) (*potato*)

>> **berinjela** (beh-ren-*zheh*-lah) (*eggplant*)

>> **brócolis** (*broh*-koh-leez) (*broccoli*)

- **coentro** (koh-*en*-troh) (*cilantro*)
- **couve** (*koh*-ooh-vee) (*collard greens or kale*)
- **espinafre** (es-pee-*nah*-free) (*spinach*)
- **feijão** (fay-*zhow*) (*beans*)
- **pepino** (peh-*pee*-noh) (*cucumber*)
- **repolho** (heh-*pol*-yoh) (*cabbage*)
- **salsinha** (sah-ooh-*seen*-yah) (*parsley*)

TIP

Fry shredded **couve** with garlic and eat it with **feijoada**, a black bean stew that's a staple of Brazilian cuisine.

A **feira** also usually sells some types of fish and meat:

- **peixe** (*pay*-shee) (*fish*)
- **frutos do mar** (*froo*-tohz doo *mah*) (*seafood*; Literally: *fruits of the sea*)
- **marisco** (mah-*rees*-koh) (*shellfish*)
- **atum** (ah-*toong*) (*tuna*)
- **salmão** (sah-ooh-*mah*-ooh) (*salmon*)
- **camarão** (kah-mah-*rah*-ooh) (*shrimp*)
- **caranguejo** (kah-rahn-*gay*-zhoh) (*crab*)
- **lula** (*loo*-lah) (*squid*)
- **polvo** (*pohl*-voh) (*octopus*)
- **cortes de carne** (*koh*-cheez jee *kah*-nee) (*cuts of meat*)
- **carne moída** (*kah*-nee moh-*ee*-dah) (*ground beef*)
- **aves** (*ah*-veez) (*poultry*)
- **frango sem osso** (*frahn*-goh sang *oh*-soo) (*boneless chicken*)
- **frango com osso** (*frahn*-goh koh-oong *oh*-soo) (*boned chicken*)

Sometimes a butcher asks whether you want your meat **de primeira ou de segunda** (jee pree–*may*–rah ooh jee seh–*goon*–dah) (*highest quality or regular quality*). You can answer, **de primeira, por favor**, or **de segunda, por favor**.

Talkin' the Talk

AUDIO ONLINE

Luiza (loo-*ee*-zah) and **Susana** (soo-*zah*-nah) are friends. They decide to visit the local outdoor **feira** (*fay*-rah) (*market*) together. All around them, vendors are shouting out what they're selling.

Luiza: **O que você precisa?**

ooh *kee* voh-*seh* preh-*see*-zah?

What do you need?

Susana: **Preciso de tomates e muita fruta.**

preh-*see*-zoo jee toh-*mah*-cheez ee moh-*ee*-tah *froo*-tah.

I need some tomatoes and a lot of fruit.

Luiza: **Vamos lá.**

vah-mooz *lah*.

Let's get to it.

Susana: (To the vendor) **Os tomates, quanto custam?**

oohz toh-*mah*-cheez, *kwahn*-toh *koos*-tah-oong?

How much for the tomatoes?

Vendor: **Dois e cinquenta o quilo.**

doh-eez ee sing-*kwen*-tah ooh *kee*-loo.

Two-fifty a kilo.

Susana: **Dois quilos, por favor.**

doh-eez *kee*-looz, poh fah-*voh*.

Two kilos, please.

Vendor: **Quer eles numa sacola ou duas?**

keh *eh*-leez noo-mah sah-*koh*-lah ooh *doo*-ahz?

Do you want them in one or two bags?

Susana: **Duas, por favor. Senão vai ser pesado demais.**

doo-ahz, poh fah-*voh*. see-*now* vah-ee *seh* peh-*zah*-doh jee-*mah*-eez.

Two, please. It'll be too heavy otherwise.

Luiza:	**Agora as frutas . . .**
	ah-*goh*-rah ahz *froo*-tahz . . .
	Now the fruit . . .
Another seller:	**Pêssego docinho, dois por um real! Pêssego bem docinho!**
	peh-seh-goh doh-*seen*-yoh, *doh*-eez poh oong hay-*ow*! peh-seh-goh bang doh-*seen*-yoh!
	Sweet peaches, two for one real! Really sweet peaches!

WORDS TO KNOW

precisa	preh-<u>see</u>-zah	you need
preciso	preh-<u>see</u>-zoo	I need
Vamos lá.	vah-mooz <u>lah</u>.	Let's get to it.
Quanto custam?	<u>kwahn</u>-toh <u>koos</u>-tah-oong?	How much do they cost?
quilo	<u>kee</u>-loh	kilogram
sacola	sah-<u>koh</u>-lah	bag
pesado	peh-<u>zah</u>-doh	heavy
demais	jee-<u>mah</u>-eez	too much
senão	see-<u>now</u>	otherwise
pêssego	<u>peh</u>-seh-goh	peach
docinho	doh-<u>seen</u>-yoh	sweet
bem	bang	very (Literally: well)

FUN & GAMES

You're at a business meeting at a hotel in Florianópolis, Brazil. Your clients have provided lunch for you. Identify each type of food in Portuguese.

A.

B.

C.

D.

E.

Illustrations by Elizabeth Kurtzman

A. _____

B. _____

C. _____

D. _____

E. _____

Flip to Appendix C for the answers.

Chapter **8**

Shopping

I n Brazil, you can shop for **prazer** (prah-*zeh*) (*pleasure*) or out of **necessidade** (neh-seh-see-*dah*-jee) (*necessity*). In this chapter, you get an overview of your shopping options and discover the vocabulary you need to shop with style. I also introduce some of Brazil's most popular souvenirs that you may want to check out and give you tips on when bargaining is appropriate and how to negotiate successfully.

Scoping Out the Shopping Scene

As in most countries, in Brazil you can **fazer compras** (fah-*zeh* kohm-prahz) (*shop*) in four main settings:

» **uma feira** (*ooh*-mah *fay*-rah) (*an outdoor market*)

» **uma loja na rua** (*ooh*-mah *loh*-zhah nah hoo-ah) (*a store on the street*)

» **um shopping** (*oong shoh*-ping) (*a shopping mall*)

» **online** (ohn-*lah*-ee-nee) (*online*)

CULTURAL
WISDOM

Brazil's **shoppings** are very similar to malls in the United States and other Western countries. They have **lojas de roupas** (loh-zhahz jee *hoh*-pahz) (*clothing stores*), **livrarias** (lee-vrah-*ree*-ahz) (*bookstores*), **farmácias** (fah-*mah*-see-ahz) (*drugstores*), **salas de cinema** (sah-lahz jee see-*neh*-mah) (*movie theaters*), and a **praça** de alimentação (*prah*-sah jee ah-lee-mehn-tah-*sah*-ooh) (*food court*). One thing's a little different though: In Brazil, **shoppings** are more associated with the middle and upper classes. Most Brazilians prefer **lojas na rua** or **feiras,** where **coisas** (*koy*-zahz) (*things*) are **mais baratas** (*mah*-eez bah-*rah*-tahz) (*cheaper*).

At Brazil's **feiras,** in addition to finding **comida** (koh-*mee*-dah) (*food*), you can **comprar** (kohm-*prah*) (*buy*) locally made **artesanato** (ah-teh-zah-*nah*-toh) (*handicrafts*), which vary according to region. You can find **bonecos feitos à mão** (boo-*neh*-kooz *fay*-tohz ah *mah*-ooh) (*handmade dolls*) in Pernambuco state, lots of items made from **pedra** (*peh*-drah) (*stone*) in Minas Gerais state, and excellent **redes** (*heh*-jeez) (*hammocks*) in practically any Brazilian **povoado** (poh-voh-*ah*-doh) (*small town*).

Saying What You're Looking For

In this section, I start with shopping for **roupas** (*hoh*-pahz) (*clothes*). When you enter a **loja** (*loh*-zhah) (*store*), expect to hear **Posso ajudar?** (*poh*-soo ah-zhoo-*dah?*) (*Can I help you?*). The **atendente** (ah-ten-*den*-chee) (*salesperson*) may then say one of the following phrases:

> **Está procurando algo em específico?** (eh-*stah* proh-koo-*rahn*-doh ah-ooh-goh ang eh-speh-*see*-fee-koh?) (*Are you looking for something in particular?*)

> **Já conhece a nossa loja?** (zhah kohn-*yeh*-see ah *noh*-sah *loh*-zhah?) (*Are you already familiar with our store?*)

> **Temos uma promoção.** (*teh*-mohz *ooh*-mah proh-moh-*sah*-ooh.) (*We're having a sale.*)

And here are some things you can say to the **atendente:**

> **Estou só olhando.** (eh-*stoh* soh ohl-*yahn*-doh.) (*I'm just looking.*)

> **Estou procurando. . . .** (eh-*stoh* proh-koo-*rahn*-doh. . . .) (*I'm looking for. . . .*)

> **Tem. . . ?** (tang. . . ?) (*Do you have. . . ?*)

Talking about what you want to buy

Now for the goods. **O que precisa?** (ooh *keh* preh-*see*-zah?) (*What do you need?*). Say you need **roupas** (*hoh*-pahz) (*clothing*). You can tell the salesperson, **Estou procurando** (eh-*stoh* proh-koo-*dahn*-doh) (*I'm looking for*) one of the following items:

- **biquini** (bee-*kee*-nee) (*bikini*)
- **blusa** (*bloo*-zah) (*woman's shirt*)
- **calça jeans** (*cow*-sah *jeenz*) (*jeans*)
- **calças** (*kah*-ooh-sahz) (*pants*)
- **camisa** (kah-*mee*-zah) (*man's shirt*)
- **camiseta** (kah-mee-*zeh*-tah) (*T-shirt*)
- **chapéu** (shah-*peh*-ooh) (*hat*)
- **cinto** (*seen*-too) (*belt*)
- **meias** (*may*-ahz) (*socks*)
- **relógio** (heh-*law*-zhee-oh) (*watch*)
- **saia** (*sah*-ee-ah) (*skirt*)
- **sapatos** (sah-*pah*-tohz) (*shoes*)
- **sunga** (*soong*-gah) (*men's swim briefs*)
- **vestido** (ves-*chee*-doo) (*dress*)

You may want to specify a **tamanho** (tah-*mahn*-yoh) (*size*). **Os tamanhos** can be either European (numbers, which are used for both clothing and shoes; see Chapter 4 for the rundown on Brazilian words for numbers) or generic (small to extra large). Here's how to express generic sizes:

- **pequeno (P)** (peh-*keh*-noh) (*small*)
- **médio (M)** (*meh*-jee-oh) (*medium*)
- **grande (G)** (*grahn*-jee) (*large*)
- **extra grande (GG)** (*ehz*-trah *grahn*-jee) (*extra large*)
- **tamanho único** (tah-*mahn*-yoh *oo*-nee-koh) (*one size fits all*)

CULTURAL WISDOM

Brazilian sizes run smaller than those in North America and some European countries. A size medium shirt in the United States is the equivalent of a large in Brazil. Don't feel like you need to go on a **regime** (heh-*zhee*-mee) (*diet*) after you hit a Brazilian clothing store!

Naming colors in Portuguese

When shopping, you may want to talk about a certain **cor** (koh) (*color*). Here are some words you can use to request **cores** (koh-reez) (*colors*) or describe an item:

>> **amarelo/a** (ah-mah-*reh*-loo/lah) (*yellow*)

>> **azul** (ah-*zoo*) (*blue*)

>> **branco/a** (*brahn*-koh/kah) (*white*)

>> **laranja** (lah-*rahn*-zhah) (*orange*)

>> **lilás** (lee-*lahz*) (*purple*)

>> **marrom** (mah-*hoh*-oong) (*brown*)

>> **preto/a** (*preh*-toh/tah) (*black*)

>> **rosa** (*hoh*-zah) (*pink*)

>> **verde** (*veh*-jee) (*green*)

>> **vermelho/a** (veh-*mel*-yoo/yah) (*red*)

If you want a different shade, just add **claro** (*klah*-roh) (*light*) or **escuro** (eh-*skoo*-roh) (*dark*) after the name of the **cor**:

>> **azul claro** (ah-*zoo klah*-roh) (*light blue*)

>> **vermelho escuro** (veh-*mel*-yoo eh-*skoo*-roh) (*dark red*)

CULTURAL WISDOM

Brazilian **atendentes** can actually be a bit annoying on your first encounter. They never seem to leave you alone. Just keep in mind that they're being friendly and trying to be helpful.

What happens if your **cinto** or **camiseta** is too small or too big? You can use the following phrases to tell the **atendente**:

É pequeno demais. (eh peh-*keh*-noh jee-*my*-eez.) (*It's too small.*)

É grande demais. (eh *grahn*-jee jee-*my*-eez.) (*It's too big.*)

Putting the word **demais** after a word is like adding the word *too* or *really* in front of an adjective in English. Check it out:

É caro demais. (eh *kah*-roh jee-*my*-eez.) (*It's too expensive.*)

É bonito demais. (*eh* boo-*nee*-too jee-*my*-eez.) (*It's really beautiful.*)

SOUND NATIVE

É bom demais! (eh *boh-oong* jee-*my*-eez!) (*It's fantastic!*) is a common phrase that literally means *It's too good!*

Trying and Trying On: The Verb Experimentar

The verb for trying on clothes is **experimentar** (eh-*speh*-ree-men-*tah*). It's easy to remember; what does the word look like? **Tá certo** (tah *seh*-toh) (*That's right*) — *experiment*. In Portuguese, you experiment with new **cores** (*koh*-reez) (*colors*) and new looks by **experimentando** (eh-speh-ree-men-*tahn*-doh) (*trying on*) **peças de roupa** (*peh*-sus jee *hoh*-pah) (*articles of clothing*).

Experimentar has a second meaning that's useful to know as well: *to try*, as in to try **uma comida nova** (*ooh*-mah koh-*mee*-dah *noh*-vah) (*a new food*). Here are some common phrases using **experimentar**:

» **Quer experimentar. . .?** (*keh* eh-*speh*-ree-men-*tah*. . .?) (*Would you like to try/try on. . .?*)

» **Posso experimentar. . .?** (*poh*-soo eh-*speh*-ree-men-*tah*. . .?) (*Can I try/try on. . .?*)

» **Tem que experimentar. . . .** (*tang* kee eh-*speh*-ree-men-*tah*. . . .) (*You've got to try/try on. . . .*)

» **Experimenta!** (eh-*speh*-ree-*men*-tah!) (*Try it!*)

The following table shows you how to conjugate **experimentar**.

Conjugation	Pronunciation
eu experimento	*eh*-ooh eh-*speh*-ree-*men*-too
você experimenta	voh-*seh* eh-*speh*-ree-*men*-tah
ele/ela experimenta	*eh*-lee/*eh*-lah eh-*speh*-ree-*men*-tah
nós experimentamos	*nohz* eh-*speh*-ree-men-*tah*-mohz
eles/elas experimentam	*eh*-leez/*eh*-lahz eh-*speh*-ree-men-*tah*-ooh
vocês experimentam	voh-*sehz* eh-speh-ree-*men*-tah-ooh

Practice these phrases that use **experimentar:**

Posso experimentar essa blusa? (*poh*-soo eh-*speh*-ree-men-*tah* eh-sah *bloo*-zah?) (*Can I try on this [women's] shirt?*)

Gostaria de experimentá-lo? (goh-stah-*ree*-ah jee eh-*speh*-ree-men-*tah*-loh?) (*Would you like to try it on?*)

É só experimentar. (eh *soh* eh-*speh*-ree-men-*tah*.) (*It won't hurt just to try it/try it on.* Literally: *It's just trying.*)

After you leave the **provador** (proh-vah-*doh*) (*dressing room*), you need to decide whether you want to **comprar ou não** (kohm-*prah* ooh *nah*-ooh) (*buy or not*).

Taking It: The Verb Levar

After you've tried on an item, the salesperson may use the verb **levar** (leh-*vah*) (*to get/to take,* as in to buy something) to ask whether you want to buy it. She may ask, **Quer levar?** (keh leh-*vah*?) (*Would you like to take it?*). Respond using **levar:**

Vou levar. (voh leh-*vah*.) (*I'll take it.*)

Não, não vou levar, mas obrigado/a. (*nah*-ooh, *nah*-ooh voh leh-*vah,* mah-eez oh-bree-*gah*-doh/dah – use **obrigado** if you're male and **obrigada** if you're female) (*No, I'm not going to get it, but thanks.*)

Levar is an **-ar** verb (the easiest kind of verb to conjugate — see Chapter 2). Here's what **levar** looks like conjugated.

Conjugation	Pronunciation
eu levo	*eh*-ooh *leh*-voh
você leva	voh-*seh leh*-vah
ele/ela leva	*eh*-lee/*eh*-lah *leh*-vah
nós levamos	*nohz* leh-*vah*-mohz
eles/elas levam	*eh*-leez/*eh*-lahz leh-*vah*-ooh
vocês levam	voh-*sehz leh*-vah-ooh

Levar also means *to take* in the general sense, and it's used in Portuguese the same way *to take* is in English. Here are some examples of how to use **levar** to mean either *to buy* or *to take:*

Vai levar tudo ou só as calças? (*vah*-ee leh-*vah too*-doh ooh *soh* ahz *kah*-ooh-sahz?) (*Are you going to get everything or just the pants?*)

Levou aqueles sapatos? (leh-*voh* ah-*keh*-leez sah-*pah*-dohz?) (*Did you get those shoes?*)

Leva uma toalha. (*leh*-vah *ooh*-mah toh-*ahl*-yah.) (*Take a towel.*)

Leva ela para a escola, por favor. (*leh*-vah *eh*-lah *pah*-rah ah eh-*skoh*-lah, poh fah-*voh*.) (*Take her to school, please.*)

Talkin' the Talk

Dudu (doo-*doo*) (the nickname for Eduardo — like saying Ed for Edward) is looking for a new pair of sunglasses. He stops at a stall on the street near a beach and is approached by a **vendedora** (ven-deh-*doh*-rah) (*salesperson*).

Dudu:	**Gosto muito desse.**
	goh-stoo moh-*ee*-too *deh*-see.
	I really like this one.
Vendedora:	**É bonito. Quer experimentar?**
	eh boo-*nee*-too. keh eh-*speh*-ree-men-*tah*?
	It's nice. Do you want to try them on?
Dudu:	**Posso?**
	poh-soo?
	Can I?
Vendedora:	**Claro.**
	klah-roo.
	Of course.
Dudu:	**Obrigado. É muito legal.**
	oh-bree-*gah*-doh. eh moh-*ee*-toh lay-*gow*.
	Thanks. It's really cool.
Vendedora:	**Estou vendendo muito desse modelo.**
	eh-*stoh* ven-*den*-doh moh-*ee*-too *deh*-see moh-*deh*-loo.
	I'm selling a lot of that brand.

Dudu:	**Quanto custa?**
	kwahn-toh koo-stah?
	How much does it cost?
Vendedora:	**Custa oito reais. Quer levar?**
	koos-tah oh-ee-toh hay-ahys. keh leh-vah?
	It costs eight reals. You wanna take it?
Dudu:	**Vou sim. Tem troco para cinquenta reais?**
	voh sing. tang troh-koo pah-rah sing-kwen-tah hay-ah-eez?
	Yeah. Do you have change for fifty reais?

WORDS TO KNOW

gosto	goh-stoo	I like
desses	deh-seez	of these
estou	eh-stoh	I am
vendendo	ven-den-doh	selling
troco	troh-koo	change (for money)

TIP

The verb **gostar** (goh–*stah*) (*to like*) is always followed by **de** (*jee*), which means *of*. But in English, saying something like "I like of these" sounds odd, so when you translate **Gostar desses** (*I like these*) to English, just leave out the *of*.

Making Comparisons and Expressing Opinions

If you're shopping with an **amigo** (ah–*mee*–goh) (*friend*), you may want to share your **opinião** (oh–pee–nee–*ah*–ooh) (*opinion*) about things in the **loja** (*loh*–zhah) (*shop*).

If you think something is just so-so, you can use one of these phrases:

Gosto. (*gohs*-doo.) (*I like it [fine].*)

Está bem. (eh-*stah bang.*) (*It's okay.*)

Não está mau. (*nah*-ooh eh-*stah mah*-ooh.) (*It's not bad.*)

If you see something that you like even more, you can express your opinion by saying:

Esse é melhor. (*es*-ee *eh* meh-ooh-*yoh*.) (*This one's better.*)

Esse eu gosto mais. (*eh*-see ee-ooh *goh*-stoo *mah*-eez.) (*I like this one more.*)

É bem bonito esse. (eh *bang* boo-*nee*-too *eh*-see.) (*This one's really nice.*)

When you see the best one, let your **amigo** know by using one of these phrases:

Esse é o melhor. (*eh*-see *eh* ooh meh-ooh-*yoh*.) (*This one's the best.*)

É perfeito esse. (eh peh-*fay*-toh *eh*-see.) (*This one's perfect.*)

REMEMBER

Better is **melhor** (meh-ooh-*yoh*), and *the best* is **o melhor** (ooh meh-ooh-*yoh*).

Now comes the fun part. In Portuguese, adding the ending **-íssimo/a** or **-érrimo/a** to the end of some adjectives exaggerates whatever's being said.

Brazilians love to **exagerar** (eh-zah-zheh-*rah*) (*exaggerate*). Something that's nice but not really **caro** (*kah*-roh) (*expensive*) is suddenly **chiquérrimo** (shee-*keh*-hee-moh) (*really glamorous*). This exaggeration is all about Brazilians' great quality of making the most of **a vida** (ah *vee*-dah) (*life*). Whatever's in front of them is **o melhor**.

SOUND NATIVE

Here are some common expressions you can use while shopping:

» **Caríssimo!** (kah-*ree*-see-moh!) (*So expensive!* — from the word **caro**)

» **Chiquérrimo!** (shee-*keh*-hee-moh!) (*Really glamorous/expensive-looking!* — from the word **chique**)

You can use the following exaggerating expressions in many kinds of situations:

» **Divertidíssimo!** (jee-*veh*-chee-*jee*-see-moh!) (*Incredibly fun!* — from **divertido**)

» **Gostosérrimo!** (goh-stoh-*zeh*-hee-moh!) (*Really delicious!* — from **gostoso**)

Talkin' the Talk

AUDIO ONLINE

Luis (loo-*eez*) and **Fabiano** (fah-bee-*ah*-noh) are checking out a used CD store.

Luis: **Legal. Eles têm muitos do Caetano.**

lay-*gow*. eh-leez *tang* moh-*ee*-tooz doo kah-eh-*tah*-noh.

Cool. They have a lot of Caetano (Caetano Veloso, one of Brazil's most famous singers).

Fabiano: **Tem** *Outras Palavras***?**

tang *oh*-trahz pah-*lahv*-rahz?

Do they have (the album) Other Words?

Luis: **Tem. Mas acho melhor os CDs mais recentes dele.**

tang. mah-eez *ah*-shoo mel-*yoh* oohz say-*dayz* mah-eez heh-*sen*-cheez *deh*-lee.

They have it. But I think his more recent albums are better.

Fabiano: **Bom, o melhor de todos é** *Fina Estampa***.**

boh-oong, ooh mel-*yoh* jee *too*-dooz eh *fee*-nah eh-*stahm*-pah.

Well, the best of all is Elegant Look.

Luis: **Cada qual tem a sua opinião.**

kah-dah *kwah*-ooh tang ah *soo*-ah oh-pee-nee-*ah*-ooh.

Each to his own opinion.

Fabiano: **Nossa, esse da Metállica é baratíssimo! Dois reais!**

noh-sah, *eh*-see dah meh-*tah*-lee-kah eh bah-rah-*chee*-see-moh! *doh*-eez hay-*ahys*!

Wow, this Metallica one is so cheap! Two reais!

Luis: **Que bom.**

kee *boh*-oong.

Great.

Fabiano: **Esqueça o Caetano!**

eh-*skeh*-sah ooh kah-ee-*tah*-noh!

Forget Caetano!

WORDS TO KNOW

legal	lay-<u>gow</u>	cool
Caetano Veloso	kah-eh-<u>tah</u>-noh veh-<u>loh</u>-zoo	Caetano Veloso
acho melhor	<u>ah</u>-shoo mel-<u>yoh</u>	I prefer
recentes	heh-<u>sehn</u>-cheez	recent
melhor de todos	meh-ooh-<u>yoh</u> jee <u>too</u>-dooz	the best of all
baratíssimo	bah-rah-<u>chee</u>-see-moh	really cheap
esqueça	eh-<u>skeh</u>-sah	(you) forget

Exploring Brazilian Treasures

Brazilian **mercados** (meh-*kah*-dooz) (*markets*) have plenty of **artesanato** (ah-teh-zah-*nah*-toh) (*handicrafts*) that you may want to **levar** (leh-*vah*) (*take*) with you. The type of **objetos** (ohb-*zheh*-tohz) (*objects*) you'll find depends on the **região** (hey-zhee-*ow*) (*region*) of Brazil in which you're shopping.

REMEMBER

The two most popular **lembranças** (lem-*brahn*-sahz) (*souvenirs*) from Brazil are probably **redes** (*heh*-jeez) (*hammocks*) and **berimbaus** (beh-reem-bah-ooz) (*musical instruments from the state of Bahia*).

A **berimbau** looks like the bow from a bow and arrow with a semi-open wooden gourd at the bottom. To play it, you pluck the bowstring with a metal coin and a thin wooden stick. The sound has an unusual twang, and the instrument is only capable of veering a note or two up or down. The **berimbau** is a beautiful instrument, with striped colors on the gourd and on the bow. And beginners, delight! It's impossible to make a bad sound on the instrument.

Also in Bahia are the famous, colorful **fitas do Bonfim** (*fee*-tahz doo *boh*-oong-*feeng*) (*ribbons of Bonfim*), which come from a church called Bonfim in the city of Salvador. When you buy a **fita**, the seller ties it around your wrist and tells you to make three wishes. The vendor then warns you **nunca** (*noon*-kah) (*never*) to take it off; otherwise, the wishes won't come true. On the upside, if you let it disintegrate naturally, they say the wishes you made will become reality!

Havaianas (ah-vah-ee-*ah*-nahz) (*Hawaiians*), a brand of beach flip-flops, are also a popular Brazilian item.

Many people enjoy the inexpensive **bijouteria** (bee–*zhoo*-teh-*ree*-ah) (*jewelry*) sold in outdoor markets. You can find handmade **anéis** (ah-*nay*-eez) (*rings*), **brincos** (*breeng*-kohz) (*earrings*), and **colares** (koh-*lah*-reez) (*necklaces*).

Check out some of these other classic Brazilian souvenirs:

>> **um biquini** (oohng bee-*kee*-nee) (*a bikini*)

>> **uma camiseta de um time de futebol** (*ooh*-mah kah-mee-*zeh*-tah jee oong *chee*-mee jee foo-chee-*bah*-ooh) (Literally: *a T-shirt of a soccer team*)

TIP

Soccer T-shirts with the team's name are sold all over Brazil. The shirts sold on the street are probably knockoffs. The official team shirts are very expensive. Check out Chapter 16 for more on talking about sports in Portuguese.

>> **uma canga com a bandeira brasileira** (*ooh*-mah *kahn*-gah *koh*-oong ah bahn-*day*-rah brah-zee-*lay*-rah) (*a beach sarong* used as a towel or skirt, printed *with the Brazilian flag*)

>> **música brasileira** (*moo*-zee-kah brah-zee-*lay*-rah) (*Brazilian music*)

>> **uma pintura** (*ooh*-mah peen-*too*-rah) (*a painting*)

>> **pó de guaraná** (*poh* jee gwah-rah-*nah*) (*guarana berry powder,* used to make a traditional natural energy drink)

>> **produtos dos índios** (proh-*doo*-tohz dooz een-jee-ohz) (*products made by native Brazilian tribes;* Literally: *products of Indians*)

In Brazil, you can find tons of knickknacks made from a wide variety of materials, including the following:

>> **barro** (*bah*-hoh) (*clay*)

>> **cerâmica** (seh-*rah*-mee-kah) (*ceramics*)

>> **madeira** (mah-*day*-rah) (*wood*)

>> **palha** (pahl-*yah*) (*straw*)

>> **pedra** (*peh*-drah) (*stone*)

>> **renda** (*hen*-dah) (*lace*)

>> **sementes** (seh-*men*-cheez) (*seeds*)

>> **vidro** (*vee*-droh) (*glass*)

TIP

If you want to know whether an item is *handmade*, ask whether it's **feito à mão** (*fay*-toh ah *mah*-ooh). For food, the term for *homemade* is **caseiro** (kah-*zay*-roh), which comes from the word **casa** (*kah*-zah) (*house*).

Negotiating Price in Outdoor Markets

CULTURAL WISDOM

As a rule of thumb, you can bargain in Brazil in **feiras** (*fay*-rahs) (*outdoor markets*) but not inside **lojas** (*loh*-zhahz) (*stores*). At **feiras**, most locals don't try to negotiate prices, but you can always try; it isn't considered offensive. (To find out how to say numbers in Portuguese, flip to Chapter 4.)

Start out by asking how much something costs and then offer a lower price (see Chapter 4 for Portuguese terms for numbers and Chapter 14 to find out about money). Or you can tell a vendor that you have only a certain amount of money. The following phrases are helpful for bargaining.

> **Quanto custa?** (*kwahn*-toh *koo*-stah?) (*How much does it cost?*)
>
> **Quanto que é?** (*kwahn*-toh kee *eh?*) (*How much is it?*)
>
> **Posso pagar [number] reais?** (*poh*-sooh pah-*gah* [number] hay-*ahys?*) (*Can I pay [number] reais?*)
>
> **Só tenho vinte reais.** (*soh tang*-yoh *veen*-chee hay-*ahys.*) (*I have only 20 reais.*)

You can then accept the price the vendor gives you or make a final offer.

TIP

Of course, if you tell a vendor that you only have 15 reais, you don't want to pay with a 20-real bill. Separate the bills you want to use to buy an item before approaching the stall.

When bargaining, keep your cool. If you make the first move, your first offer should be about half of what you're prepared to pay; you can then accept the vendor's counteroffer or state your final price. Be firm but polite. Few vendors will give you their best price if they feel you're disrespecting them.

FUN & GAMES

The following words in Portuguese have been scrambled. Unscramble them!
They are all color words:

Colors:

1. EDVER

2. RCNBAO

3. HMLEVREO

4. ZALU

5. SRAO

6. MMRROA

Try to identify all the items of clothing in the following illustration:

Illustration by Elizabeth Kurtzman

A. _____

B. _____

C. _____

D. _____

E. _____

F. _____

G. _____

See Appendix C for the answers.

See Appendix T for the answers.

» Checking out the music scene

» Enjoying museums, galleries, and movies

» Falling in love

Chapter **9**

Going Out on the Town

When you think of Brazil, you probably think first of its **praias** (*prah-ee-ahz*) (*beaches*) (check out Chapter 12) and then **Carnaval** (kah-nah-*vah*-ooh) (see Chapter 17). But there's so much more to Brazilian culture! For starters, the country has fabulous **museus** (moo-*zay*-ooz) (*museums*) and a vibrant arts scene as well as lots of domestic **filmes** (*fee*-ooh-meez) (*movies*).

Brazilians also have an uncanny knack for enjoying themselves. Listening to **música ao vivo** (*moo*-zee-kah ah-ooh *vee*-voo) (*live music*) and taking in the atmosphere at a bar or enjoying tunes by local DJs at a **boate** (boh-*ah*-chee) (*nightclub*) are great cultural experiences, too. This chapter tells you what you need to know to explore and appreciate the art and culture of Brazil and to enjoy yourself as much as any Brazilian.

Talking about Going Out

Está a fim de sair? (es-*tah* ah *fing* jee sah-*eeh?*) (*Are you in the mood to go out?*)

Whether you're itching for **música ao vivo** (*moo*-zee-kah ah-ooh *vee*-voo) (*live music*) or something else, you can use the following phrase to ask locals what there is to do around town:

> **O que você recomenda para fazer hoje à noite?** (ooh *kee* voh-*seh* heh-koh-*men*-dah pah-rah fah-*zeh* oh-zhee ah *noh*-ee-chee?) (*What do you recommend to do tonight?*)

The locals may ask, **O que você gosta?** (ooh *kee* voh–*seh* goh–stah?) (*What do you like?*). You can respond **Gosto de . . .** (*goh*–stoh *jee . . .*) (*I like . . .*) followed by one of the following:

>> **bares** (*bah*-reez) (*bars*)

>> **boates** (boh-*ah*-cheez) (*nightclubs*)

>> **cinema** (see-*neh*-mah) (*cinema*)

>> **espectáculos** (eh-spek-*tah*-koo-lohz) (*shows*)

>> **eventos culturais** (eh-*ven*-tohz kool-too-*rah*-eez) (*cultural events*)

>> **festas** (*fes*-tahz) (*parties*)

>> **teatro** (chee-*ah*-troh) (*theater*)

If you're new in town and just want to ask how to get to the **centro** (*sen*–troh) (*downtown*), say **Onde fica o centro?** (*ohn*–jee *fee*-kah ooh *sen*–troh?) (*Where's the downtown area?*).

Inviting someone out and being invited

Of course, the best scenario happens not when you have to ask a local about things around town but when a local **te convida** (chee kohn-*vee*-dah) (*invites you*) to some event. They may say:

Estou te convidando! (eh-*stoh* chee kohn-vee-*dahn*-doh!) (*I'm inviting you!*)

Vem com a gente! (*vang koh*-oong ah *zhang*-shee!) (*Come with us!*)

Vem comigo! (*vang* koh-*mee*-goo!) (*Come with me!*)

If you're the one who's doing the inviting, you can use one of the preceding expressions or any of the following:

Quer ir comigo? (*keh ee* koh-*mee*-goo?) (*Do you want to go with me?*)

Quer vir conosco? (*keh vee* koh-*noh*-skoh?) (*Do you want to come with us?*)

Quero te convidar. (*keh*-roo chee kohn-vee-*dah*.) (*I want to invite you* — though this phrase doesn't mean the person inviting will pick up the tab)

Here are more specific examples of common expressions using **convidar** (kohn-vee-*dah*) (*to invite*):

Quero convidar a todos para a minha casa. (*keh*-roo kohn-vee-*dah* ah *toh*-dooz *pah*-rah ah *meen*-yah *kah*-zah.) (*I want to invite everyone to my house.*)

Estão convidando a gente para a praia. (eh-*stah*-ooh kohn-vee-*dahn*-doh ah *zhang*-chee pah-rah ah *prah*-ee-ah.) (*They're inviting us to go to the beach.*)

SOUND
NATIVE

Brazilians often say **a gente** (ah *zhang*-chee) rather than **nós** (nohz) to mean *we* or *us*. **A gente** literally means *the people*. It's as if you're talking about another group of people to talk about yourself and a friend, then you conjugate it as if it's one person. Here's an example: A woman tells her husband that she and a friend are going to the beach: **A gente vai a para praia** (ah *zhang*-chee *vah*-ee pah-rah *prah*-ee-ah) (*We are going to the beach*). The textbook way of saying the same thing (which Brazilians use as well) is **Nós vamos para a praia** (nohz *vah*-mooz pah-rah *prah*-ee-ah) (*We are going to the beach*).

Asking what a place or event is like

After you have an idea about the **evento** (eh-*ven*-toh) (*event*) or **lugar** (loo-*gah*) (*place*) that a person from the area is recommending, you may want to ask for **mais detalhes** (*mah*-eez deh-*tahl*-yeez) (*more details*).

Here are a few questions that can help you gather details:

Como é o lugar? (koh-moo *eh* ooh loo-*gah*?) (*What's the place like?*)

Quando começa? (*kwahn*-doh koh-*meh*-sah?) (*When does it start?*)

Onde fica? (*ohn*-jee *fee*-kah?) (*Where is it?*)

Tem algum motivo? (*tang* ah-ooh-goong moh-*chee*-voh?) (*Why is it being put on?*)

O que é, exatamente? (ooh *kee eh*, eh-zah-tah-*men*-chee?) (*What is it, exactly?*)

Try these additional phrases to get even more clues:

Custa caro? (*koo*-stah *kah*-roh?) (*Is it expensive?*)

Vai ter muitas pessoas? (*vah*-ee *teh* moh-*ee*-tahz peh-*soh*-ahz?) (*Will there be a lot of people?*)

Que tipo de música vai ter? (kee *chee*-poh jee moo-zee-kah vah-ee *teh*?) (*What type of music will there be?*)

Que tipo de gente? (kee *chee*-poh jee *zhang*-chee?) (*What type of people?*)

É informal ou formal? (eh een-foh-*mah*-ooh ooh foh-*mah*-ooh?) (*Is it informal or formal?*)

Vale a pena ir? (*vah*-lee ah *peh*-nah ee?) (*Is it worth going to?*)

You're likely to hear these answers to your questions about an event:

Não custa caro. (*nah*-ooh *koo*-stah *kah*-roh.) (*It's not expensive.*)

Vai ser muito bom. (*vah*-ee *seh* moh-*ee*-toh *boh*-oong.) (*It's going to be really good.*)

Vale a pena. (*vah*-lee ah *peh*-nah.) (*It's worth going.*)

Deve ter bastante gente. (deh-vee *teh* bah-*stahn*-chee *zhang*-chee.) (*There should be a lot of people.*)

O lugar é pequeno. (ooh loo-*gah* eh peh-*keh*-noh.) (*The place is small.*)

É muito jovem. (*eh* moh-*ee*-toh *zhoh*-vang.) (*It's a young crowd* — typically meaning people in their 20s.)

É para todas as idades. (*eh pah*-rah *toh*-dahz ahz ee-*dah*-jeez) (*It's for all ages.*)

É um bar gay. (*eh* oong *bah gay*.) (*It's a gay bar.*)

Other important questions to ask about bars or events are whether there's an **entrada** (en-*trah*-dah) (*cover charge*) and whether the place has a **consumação mínima** (kohn-soo-mah-*sah*-ooh *mee*-nee-mah) (*minimum charge*; Literally: *minimum consumption*), meaning you must spend a certain amount of money on drinks or food while you're there. Ask **Paga para entrar?** (*pah*-gah pah-rah en-*trah*?) (*Does it have a cover charge?*) or **Tem consumação mínima?** (*tang* kohn-soo-mah-*sah*-ooh *mee*-nee-mah?) (*Is there a minimum charge?*). If the bar or restaurant features **música ao vivo** (*moo*-zee-kah ah-ooh *vee*-voh) (*live music*), ask if there is a **couvert artístico** (koh-ooh-*vert* ahr-*chees*-chee-koh) (*live music surcharge*) as well.

CULTURAL WISDOM

At many bars in Brazil, you receive a paper card called a **comanda** (koh-*mahn*-dah) when you walk in. Instead of paying for food and drinks when you order them, the bartender or waiter marks your orders on the card. Each person gets a card; they aren't for groups. When you're ready to leave, you wait in line by the cashier and pay for everything at once.

Taking in Brazil's Musical Culture

The one thing you shouldn't miss doing in Brazil **de noite** (*jee* noh-ee-chee) (*at night*) is listening to **música ao vivo** (*moo*-zee-kah ah-ooh *vee*-voh) (*live music*). Normally this involves going to a restaurant or bar where there's a **cantor** (kahn-toh) (*singer*). Most often, the **cantor** plays the **violão** (vee-oh-*lah*-ooh) (*acoustic guitar*) while singing. Sometimes there's a **baterista** (bah-teh-*rees*-tah) (*drummer*) and someone playing the **baixo** (*bah*-ee-shoh) (*bass guitar*) to accompany the **cantor.**

CULTURAL WISDOM

Live singers in Brazil repeat ad infinitum about 40 Brazilian top hits that span the past several decades. The **plateia** (plah-*tay*-ah) (*crowd*) always loves these songs and often sings along. For a long time after I moved to Brazil, I recognized only a few **canções** (kahn-*soh*-eez) (*songs*). But before I left, after three years of living in Brazil, I realized in a bar one night that I knew all the songs! It's true that the top hits are drummed into your brain over the years (you even hear them in the super-markets), but learning them was still a small victory for me.

Using the musical verb: Tocar

Você toca algum instrumento? (voh-*seh* toh-kah ah-ooh-*goong een*-stroo-*men*-toh?) (*Do you play an instrument?*) In Brazil, the **violão** is by far the most common instrument played. But Brazilians appreciate all kinds of music, and anything having to do with music is a great conversation starter.

Here's how you conjugate **tocar** (toh-*kah*) (*to play [an instrument]*).

Conjugation	Pronunciation
eu toco	*eh*-ooh *toh*-koo
você toca	voh-*seh toh*-kah
ele/ela toca	*eh*-lee/*eh*-lah *toh*-kah
nós tocamos	nohz toh-*kah*-mohz
eles/elas tocam	*eh*-leez/*eh*-lahz *toh*-kah-ooh
vocês tocam	voh-*sehz toh*-kah-ooh

This is how you say the names of popular instruments in Portuguese:

>> **o violão** (ooh vee-ooh-*lah*-ooh) (*acoustic guitar*)

>> **o baixo** (ooh *bah*-ee-shoh) (*bass guitar*)

>> **a guitarra** (ah gee-*tah*-hah) (*electric guitar*)

>> **a bateria** (ah *bah*-teh-*ree*-ah) (*drums*)

>> **a flauta** (ah *flah*-ooh-tah) (*flute*)

>> **o piano** (ooh pee-*ah*-noh) (*piano*)

>> **o violino** (ooh vee-ooh-*lee*-noh) (*violin*)

Here are some phrases you can use to talk about playing instruments:

Eu toco piano. (*eh*-ooh *toh*-koo pee-*ah*-noh.) (*I play the piano.*)

Ela toca bateria. (*eh*-lah *toh*-kah bah-teh-*ree*-ah.) (*She plays the drums.*)

Eles tocam violão. (*eh*-leez *toh*-kah-ooh vee-oh-*lah*-ooh.) (*They play the guitar.*)

CULTURAL WISDOM

Brazilians talk about the shape of the guitar as similar to a woman's body. English-speakers say *hourglass figure*; Brazilians say **corpo de violão** (*koh*-poo jee vee-ooh-*lah*-ooh) (*guitar-shaped body*).

Now for Brazilian instruments, here are some of the most famous music-makers:

>> **o berimbau** (ooh *beh*-reem-*bah*-ooh): A large bow that's played with a wooden stick. It's used to accompany the Brazilian martial arts form **capoeira** (kay-poh-*ay*-rah).

>> **o cavaquinho** (ooh kah-vah-*keen*-yoh): An instrument similar to a ukulele. It's used in bands that play **samba** (*sahm*-bah), Brazil's national rhythm, a three-step beat that can either be moderate tempo or fast, and **chorinho** (shoh-*heen*-yoh), an older form of samba popular in the 19th century until the 1920s in Brazil.

>> **a cuíca** (ah *kwee*-kah): A stick that's rubbed through what looks like a small drum. It makes a donkey hee-haw or whine, depending on how it's moved.

>> **o pandeiro** (ooh pahn-*day*-roh): A tambourine.

>> **o paxixi** (ooh pah-shee-*shee*): A woven rattle.

>> **a sanfona** (ah sahn-*foh*-nah): An accordion used for **forró** music.

SOUND NATIVE

If you want to talk about children (or adults!) *playing*, avoid the verb **tocar**, which is only for playing instruments. Instead, use the verb **brincar** (bring-*kah*), as in the following example:

As crianças gostam de brincar. (ahz kree-*ahn*-sahz *goh*-stah-ooh jee bring-*kah*.) (*Children like to play.*)

Brincar also means *to kid around.* **Está brincando?** (eh-*stah* bring-*kahn*-doh?) is a popular phrase that means *Are you kidding?*

And if you want to talk about *playing sports*, use the verb **jogar** (zhoh-*gah*). Flip to Chapter 16 to learn all about **jogar**.

Using the dancing verb: Dançar

Especially if you're **solteiro/a** (sohl-*tay*-roh/rah) (*a single person*), you'll probably want to know how to ask someone to **dançar** (dahn-*sah*) (*dance*). You also need to know how you'll be asked to **dançar**.

REMEMBER

Couple-dancing is common in Brazil. The most popular form is probably **forró** (foh-*hoh*), a fast-paced, country-sounding music and accompanying dance form that originates in the northeast. **Samba** (*sahm*-bah), the best-known music and dance from Brazil, is for **casais** (kah-*zah*-eez) (*couples*) and to dance **sozinho** (soh-*zeen*-yoh) (*alone*).

Take a peek at the conjugations for **dançar**.

Conjugation	Pronunciation
eu danço	*eh*-ooh *dahn*-soh
você dança	voh-*seh dahn*-sah
ele/ela dança	*eh*-lee/*eh*-lah *dahn*-sah
nós dançamos	*nohz* dahn-*sah*-mohz
eles/elas dançam	*eh*-leez/*eh*-lahz *dahn*-sah-ooh
vocês dançam	voh-*sehz dahn*-sah-ooh

Practice these common expressions that include **dançar**:

Vamos dançar? (*vah*-mohz dahn-*sah?*) (*Shall we dance?*)

Quer dançar comigo? (keh dahn-*sah* koh-*mee*-goo?) (*Do you want to dance with me?*)

Não sei dançar. (*nah*-ooh *say* dahn-*sah*.) (*I don't know how to dance.*)

Using the singing verb: Cantar

Você gosta de cantar? (voh-*seh goh*-stah jee kahn-*tah?*) (*Do you like to sing?*) The verb **cantar** (kahn-*tah*) (*to sing*) is a great, basic verb to practice. Its ending is **-ar**, so the conjugations are a piece of cake (find information on conjugating verbs in Chapter 2).

Conjugation	Pronunciation
eu canto	*eh*-ooh *kahn*-toh
você canta	voh-*seh kahn*-tah
ele/ela canta	*eh*-lee/*eh*-lah *kahn*-tah
nós cantamos	nohz kahn-*tah*-mohz
eles/elas cantam	*eh*-leez/*eh*-lahz *kahn*-tah-ooh
vocês cantam	voh-*sehz kahn*-tah-ooh

Here are some ways you can use **cantar:**

Ela canta super bem. (eh-lah *kahn*-tah *soo*-peh *bang*.) (*She sings really well.*)

Eu não canto muito bem. (*eh*-ooh *nah*-ooh *kahn*-toh moh-*ee*-toh *bang*.) (*I don't sing very well.*)

Você canta? Não sabia. (voh-*seh kahn*-tah? *nah*-ooh sah-*bee*-ah.) (*You sing? I didn't know.*)

Nós cantamos no chuveiro. (nohz kahn-*tah*-mohz noh shoo-*vay*-roh.) (*We sing in the shower.*)

Exploring Art

Brazil has plenty of **galerias de arte** (gah-leh-*ree*-ahz jee *ah*-chee) (*art galleries*) and **museus** (moo-*zeh*-oohz) (*museums*). The biggest and most famous ones are in some of the country's largest cities, São Paulo and Rio, and its capital, Brasilia; but intriguing smaller museums are in all sorts of nooks and crannies of the country. Brazil also has great **centros culturais** (*sen*-trohz kool-too-*rah*-eez) (*cultural centers*), which host their own **exposições de arte** (es-poh-zee-*soh*-eez jee *ah*-chee) (*art exhibitions*).

Inside Brazil's **galerias de arte, museus,** and **centros culturais,** you can find **quadros** (*kwah*-drohz) (*paintings*), **esculturas** (eh-skool-*too*-rahz) (*sculptures*), **fotografias** (foh-toh-grah-*fee*-ahz) (*photographs*), and **objetos históricos** (ohb-*zheh*-tohz ee-*stoh*-ree-kohz) (*historic objects*) — just like in any major art institution in the world.

Check out some phrases that deal with **arte** (*ah*–chee) (*art*):

Você gosta de arte? (voh-*seh* goh-stah jee *ah*-chee?) (*Do you like art?*)

Tem uma exposição muito boa no Itaú Cultural. (*tang* ooh-mah es-poh-zee-*sah*-ooh moh-*ee*-toh *boh*-ah noh ee-tah-*ooh* kool-too-*rah*-ooh.) (*There's a really good exhibition at Itaú Cultural Center.*)

Tem uns quadros famosos do Picasso naquele museu. (*tang* oonz *kwah*-drohz fah-*moh*-zooz doo pee-*kah*-soh nah-*keh*-lee moo-*zeh*-ooh.) (*There are some famous Picasso paintings in that museum.*)

Eu adoro as vernissages. (*ee*-ooh ah-*doh*-roo ahz veh-nee-*sah*-zhez.) (*I love art exhibition opening nights.*)

Going to the Movies

What type of **filmes** (*fee*-ooh-meez) (*movies*) do you like? Have you ever seen **um filme brasileiro** (oong *fee*-ooh-mee brah-zee-*lay*-roh) (*a Brazilian movie*)? You may be surprised to find out that the Brazilian **indústria de filmes** (een-*doo*-stree-ah jee *fee*-ooh-meez) (*movie industry*) is very large and produces many high-quality movies every year. (Check out Chapter 19 for a list of some classic Brazilian movies you can download/stream.)

CULTURAL WISDOM

At most **salas de cinema** (*sah*-lahz jee see-*neh*-mah) (*movie theaters*) in Brazil, about half of the **filmes** playing are Brazilian. Several **filmes novos** (*fee*-ooh-meez *noh*-vooz) (*new films*) come out every month. In addition to domestic films, you can also see **filmes americanos** (*fee*-ooh-meez ah-meh-ree-*kah*-nohz) (*American movies*) and **filmes europeus** (*fee*-ooh-meez eh-ooh-roh-*peh*-ooz) (*European movies*).

You may want to ask whether a movie is **legendado** (leh-zhang-*dah*-doo) (*subtitled*) or **dublado** (doo-*blah*-doo) (*dubbed over*). Subtitled films are also sometimes referred to as **versão original** (veh-*sah*-ooh oh-*ree*-zhee-*nah*-ooh) (*original version*).

Here are some handy phrases you can use to talk about **filmes**:

Vamos ao cinema? (*vah*-mohz ah-ooh see-*neh*-mah?) (*Do you want to go to the movies?*)

Quer assistir um filme? (*keh* ah-sees-*chee* oong *fee*-ooh-mee?) (*Do you want to see a movie?*)

Que tipo de filmes você gosta? (kee *chee*-poh jee *fee*-ooh-meez voh-seh *goh*-stah?) (*What type of movies do you like?*)

Qual filme você gostaria de ver? (*kwah*-ooh *fee*-ooh-mee voh-*seh* gohs-tah-*ree*-ah jee *veh?*) (*Which movie do you want to see?*)

Talkin' the Talk

AUDIO ONLINE

Diogo (jee-*oh*-goh) and **Catarina** (kah-tah-*ree*-nah) talk about going to the movies together.

Diogo:	**Vamos ao cinema?**
	vah-mohz ah-ooh see-*neh*-mah?
	Should we go to the movies?
Catarina:	**Vamos. Qual filme gostaria de assistir?**
	vah-mohz. *kwah*-ooh *fee*-ooh-mee gohs-tah-*ree*-ah jee ah-sees-*chee?*
	Let's go. What movie do you want to see?
Diogo:	**Estou com vontade de assistir uma comédia.**
	eh-*stoh koh*-oong vohn-*tah*-jee jee ah-sees-*chee* ooh-mah koh-*meh*-jah.
	I feel like seeing a comedy.
Catarina:	**Para mim, qualquer filme fila tá bom.**
	pah-rah *mee*, *kwah*-keh *fee*-ooh-mee *fee*-lah tah *boh*-oong.
	For me, any movie line is good.
Diogo:	**É verdade. Hoje é sábado.**
	eh veh-*dah*-jee. *oh*-zhee eh *sah*-bah-doh.
	That's right. Today is Saturday.
Catarina:	**Bom, vamos para a Sala UOL?**
	boh-oong, *vah*-mohz pah-rah ah *sah*-lah ooh-*oh*-ooh?
	Well, should we go to the UOL (name of a movie theater)?

Diogo:	**Tá bom. Você espera na fila, e eu compro a pipoca.**
	tah *boh*-oong. voh-*seh* eh-*speh*-rah nah *fee*-lah, ee *eh*-ooh *kohm*-proh ah pee-*poh*-kah.
	Okay. You wait in the line, and I'll buy the popcorn.
Catarina:	**Acha justo isso?**
	ah-shah *zhoo*-stoh *ee*-soh?
	Do you think that's fair?
Diogo:	(With a laugh) **Acho.**
	ah-shoo.
	Yes, I do (Literally: *I think*).

●●

WORDS TO KNOW

Estou com vontade . . .	eh-<u>stoh</u> koh-oong vohn-<u>tah</u>-jee . . .	I feel like . . . (what you feel like doing)
assistir	ah-sees-<u>chee</u>	to watch (a movie, a show, TV)
uma comédia	<u>ooh</u>-mah koh-<u>meh</u>-jah	a comedy
para mim	<u>pah</u>-rah <u>mee</u>	for me
qualquer	<u>kwah</u>-keh	any/whichever
fila	<u>fee</u>-lah	line (of people)
verdade	veh-<u>dah</u>-jee	true/truth
bom	<u>boh</u>-oong	so/well
vamos	<u>vah</u>-mohz	let's go/should we go?
ver	veh	to see
espera	eh-<u>speh</u>-rah	wait
pipoca	pee-<u>poh</u>-kah	popcorn
Acha. . .?	<u>ah</u>-shah. . .?	Do you think. . .?
justo	<u>zhoo</u>-stoh	fair
isso	<u>ee</u>-soh	this/that

Names of non-Brazilian **filmes,** such as American and European ones, are often translated into Portuguese with a funny result. My favorite is the movie *O Brother, Where Art Thou?* (2000), which was translated as **E Aí, Irmão, Cadê Você?** (ee ah-*ee* eeh-*mah*-ooh, kah-*deh* voh-*she?*) (*Hey Dude, Where Are You?*). Of course, Brazilians probably laugh at how we translate their movie titles, too!

Falling in Love — in Portuguese

Speaking of going out at night, this section touches on dating. They say **o amor** (ooh ah-*moh*) (*love*) is the international **língua** (ling-gwah) (*language*). And I believe that's true, but why would anyone want to love **sem falar** (*seen* fah-*lah*) (*without talking*), when saying **palavras carinhosas** (pah-*lahv*-rahs kah-reen-yoh-zahs) (*lovey-dovey words*) in Portuguese is so much fun?

Brazilian Portuguese is an extremely romantic **língua.** Not only are the sounds beautiful and melodic, but Brazilians themselves are very **românticos** (hoh-mahn-chee-kooz) (*romantic*). And you can't separate the **língua** from its **cultura** (kool-*too*-rah) (*culture*). The language **é cheia de poesia** (eh *shay*-ah jee poh-eh-zee-ah) (*is full of poetry*).

CULTURAL WISDOM

In Brazil, most people are up-to-date on the television **novelas** (noh-*veh*-lahz) (*soap operas*). And with the vast majority of Brazilian **novelas** dealing with **a paixão** (ah pah-ee-*shah*-ooh) (*passion*), most Brazilians think about romance a lot. The stories are **alegres** (ah-*leh*-greez) (*happy*) and **tristes** (*trees*-cheez) (*sad*), of course, with a touch of **tragédia** (trah-*zheh*-jee-ah) (*tragedy*).

SOUND NATIVE

Brazilians even have a specific verb to describe the act of walking around town in a love-lock with your honey: **namorar** (*nah*-moh-*rah*). That could mean either smooching in public or just walking hand in hand, gazing into each other's eyes. The root of the verb is **amor.** What did **Jaqueline** (zhah-keh-*lee*-nee) do Saturday? **Ela foi namorar** (*eh*-lah *foh*-ee nah-moh-*rah*).

Girlfriend, by the way, is **namorada** (nah-moh-*rah*-dah), and *boyfriend* is **namorado** (nah-moh-*rah*-doo). After things move along, the happy couple may decide to have a **casamento** (kah-zah-*men*-toh) (*wedding*). At that point, they become **noivo** (*noy*-ee-voh) (*fiancé*) and **noiva** (*noh*-ee-vah) (*fiancée*), or two of each sex. Husband is **marido** (mah-*ree*-doo) and wife is **mulher/esposa** (mool-*yeh*/es-*poh*-zah). To discover how to respectfully talk about a non-binary person, see Chapter 2.

Check out some classic romantic phrases in Portuguese:

> **Eu te amo.** (*eh*-ooh chee *ah*-moo.) (*I love you.*)

> **Você quer casar comigo?** (voh-*seh* see *keh* kah-*zah* koh-*mee*-goo?) (*Will you marry me?*)

Eu estou apaixonado/a. (*eh*-ooh eh-*stoh* ah-pah-ee-shee-ooh-*nah*-doo/dah.) (*I'm in love.*)

Estou com muita saudade de você. (*eh*-stoh koh-oong moh-*ee*-tah sah-ooh-*dah*-jee jee voh-*seh*.) (*I miss you very much.*)

Me dá um beijo. (mee *dah* oong *bay*-zhoh.) (*Give me a kiss.*)

Eu vou te amar por toda a minha vida. (*eh*-ooh *voh* chee ah-*mah* poh *toh*-dah ah ming-yah *vee*-dah.) (*I'm going to love you for the rest of my life.*)

And here's how Brazilians say sweet nothings:

» **meu amor** (*meh*-ooh ah-*moh*) (*my love*)

» **meu querido/ minha querida** (*meh*-ooh keh-*ree*-doo/ *ming*-yah keh-*ree*-dah) (*my honey;* Literally: *my loved one*)

» **meu fofinho/ minha fofinha** (*meh*-ooh foh-*fing*-yoh/ *ming*-yah foh-*fing*-yah) (*my sweetie;* Literally: *my soft, fluffy one*)

SOUND
NATIVE

Try out these classic romantic phrases that Brazilians use to **paquerar** (pah–keh–*rah*) (*flirt*):

Você é muito lindo/a. (voh-*seh* eh moh-*ee*-toh *leen*-doh/dah.) (*You're really handsome/beautiful.*)

Você tem olhos muito bonitos. (voh-*seh* tang *ohl*-yooz moh-*ee*-toh boo-*nee*-tooz.) (*You have very pretty eyes.*)

Gostei muito de você. (goh-*stay* moh-*ee*-toh jee voh-*seh*.) (*I really like you.*)

Here are some practical phrases, too, for when you meet someone you're interested in:

Me dá o seu número de celular? (mee *dah* ooh *seh*-ooh *noo*-meh-roh jee sel-ooh-*lah*?) (*Will you give me your cell number?*)

O que vai fazer amanhã? (ooh *kee vah*-ee fah-*zeh* ah-mahn-*yah*?) (*What are you doing tomorrow?*)

Quer ir ao cinema comigo? (*keh* ee ah-ooh see-*neh*-mah koh-*mee*-goo?) (*Do you want to go to the movies with me?*)

Of course, these are all things you say after the very first question: **Qual é seu nome?** (*kwah*–ooh *eh* seh-ooh *noh*-mee?) (*What's your name?*) or **Quer dançar?** (*keh* dahn–*sah*?) (*Do you want to dance?*)

Talkin' the Talk

AUDIO ONLINE

Pay attention as **Jorge** (*zhoh*-zhee) and **Glória** (*gloh*-ree-ah) flirt with each other.

Jorge:	**Olá, quer dançar?**
	oh-*lah*, *keh* dahn-*sah*?
	Hi, do you want to dance?
Glória:	**Tá bom.**
	tah *boh*-oong.
	Okay.
Jorge:	**Você é muito linda. Qual é seu nome?**
	voh-*seh* eh moh-*ee*-toh *leen*-dah. *kwah*-ooh *eh seh*-ooh *noh*-mee?
	You're very pretty. What's your name?
Glória:	**Obrigada. Sou a Glória. E você?**
	oh-bree-*gah*-dah. *soh* ah *gloh*-ree-ah. ee voh-*seh*?
	Thanks. I'm Gloria. And you?
Jorge:	**Jorge. Você vem muito aqui? Nunca te vi aqui.**
	zhoh-zhee. voh-*seh vang* moh-*ee*-toh ah-*kee*? *noong*-kah chee *vee* ah-*kee*.
	Jorge. Do you come here often? I've never seen you here.
Glória:	**Só vim uma vez antes.**
	soh *ving ooh*-mah vehz *ahn*-cheez.
	I only came once before.

Jorge: **Espero te ver mais por aqui.**

eh-*speh*-roo chee *veh mah*-eez poh ah-*kee*.

I hope to see you here more.

Glória: **Eu também.**

eh-ooh tahm-*bang*.

Me, too.

WORDS TO KNOW		
Você vem muito aqui?	voh-<u>seh</u> <u>vang</u> moh-<u>ee</u>-toh ah-<u>kee</u>?	Do you come here often?
vim	ving	I came
uma vez	<u>ooh</u>-mah <u>vehz</u>	one time
Espero te ver mais.	eh-<u>speh</u>-roo chee <u>veh</u> <u>mah</u>-eez.	I hope to see you more.

FUN & GAMES

Match the following fun activities with their English translation. **Relaxe** (heh-*lah*-shee) (*relax*); you probably know more answers than you realize!

1. **exposição de arte**
2. **cinema**
3. **boate**
4. **bar**
5. **festa**

a. *bar*
b. *nightclub*
c. *party*
d. *art exhibition*
e. *movies*

Turn to Appendix C for the answers.

IN THIS CHAPTER

» **Connecting with a new friend**

» **Arranging to see someone again**

» **Calling someone to leave a message**

» **Figuring out tech preferences for a call**

» **Using common texting abbreviations**

Chapter **10**

Using Technology To Keep In Touch

Many people in Brazil, and around the world, don't have a fixed telephone line anymore. Everyone seems to use a **celular** (sel-ooh-*lahr*) (*cellphone*) these days. For those in the privileged classes, it's an **iPhone** (*ah*-ee-fohn). Others may communicate using their **relógio smartwatch** (heh-*loh*-zhee-ooh smaht-*wah*-chee) (*smartwatch*; Literally: *watch smartwatch*), **iPad** (ee-*pah*-jee) or **computador** (kohm-poo-tah-*dohr*) (*computer*).

There are so many options these days to stay connected. Say you want to **falar** (fah-*lahr*) (*talk*) with someone on your **celular**. Do you want the **chamada** (shah-*mah*-dah) (*call*) to be **voz** (vohz) (*voice*) only? Or will it be a **chamada de vídeo** (shah-*mah*-dah jee *vee*-joh) (*video call*)? Are you going to call them using a regular **número de telefone** (*noo*-meh-roh jee teh-leh-*foh*-nee) (*telephone number*), or would it be easier to find their profile on a calling app such as **Whatsapp** (wut-*sapp*-ee)?

The medium may change, but the **palavras** (pah-*lahv*-rus) (*words*) you need to communicate will remain the same.

Talking and Texting with a Digital Device

Calling someone in a different language can be intimidating, but **você está com sorte!** (voh-*seh* eh-*stah* kohng *soh*-chee!) (*you're in luck!*) You've picked a great learners' language; I'll tell you why I think so.

Brazilians are used to talking with **estrangeiros** (ehs-trahn-*zhay*-rohz) (*foreigners*). Most locals slow their speech automatically when talking with someone who's not fluent in Portuguese. But best of all, Brazilians typically *love* foreigners and are **contentes** (kohn-*ten*-cheez) (*happy*) to talk to you. You can always ask the person you're talking to to speak **devagar** (deh-vah-*gah*) (*slowly*), if they just aren't slowing down for you. **Pode falar devagar, por favor?** (poh-jee fah-*lah* deh-vah-*gah*, poh fah-*voh*) (*Can you speak slowly, please?*)

So go native: Relax. **Fique tranquilo** (*fee*-kee trahn-*kwee*-loh) (*Don't worry*). Here's what you say to answer the phone:

>> **Alô?** (ah-*loh?*) (*Hello?*) (formal)

>> **Sim?** (sing?) (*Yes?*)

>> **Oi.** (*oy*-ee.) (*Hi.*) (informal)

Before you hang up, use these words to say goodbye:

>> **Tchau.** (chow.) (*Bye; Literally: Ciao*, like in Italian)

>> **Até logo.** (ah-*teh* loh-goo.) (*Bye; Literally: Until soon.*)

>> **Até mais.** (ah-*teh* mah-eez.) (*Bye; Literally: Until more.*)

>> **Até amanhã.** (ah-*teh* ah-mahn-*yah*.) (*Talk to/See you tomorrow; Literally: Until tomorrow.*)

CULTURAL WISDOM

Brazilians are very social people, so talking on the phone comes naturally to them. The **telefone** (teh-leh-*foh*-nee) (*telephone*) itself even holds an important place in Brazilian history. The very first samba tune ever recorded was titled **"Pelo Telefone"** (*peh*-loo teh-leh-*foh*-nee) (*"On the Phone"*) (Rio, 1917).

This section gives you the basics to navigate Brazil's area code system and to follow Brazilian phone etiquette.

SOUND NATIVE

Not only are Brazilians intensely social but they're also very **carinhosos** (kah-reen-*yoh*-zooz) (*affectionate*). When a **chamada** (shah-*mah*-dah) (*phone call*) ends between two female friends, a male and a female friend, or two family members, Brazilians often say **Um beijo** (oong *bay*-zhoh) (*A kiss*), or, if the call is between two men, **Um abraço** (oong ah-*brah*-soo) (*A hug*).

CALLING INSIDE OR OUTSIDE BRAZIL

In Brazil, most phone numbers have either seven or eight digits and a two-digit prefix for the **cidade** (see-*dah*-jee) (*city*) or a **código regional** (koh-jee-goo heh-jee-oh-*nah*-ooh) (*regional code*), which often has a zero in front. The phone number of a famous hotel in Rio called Copacabana Palace, for example, looks like this: (021) 2548-7070. The **código internacional** (koh-jee-goh een-teh-nah-see-oh-*nah*-ooh) (*international calling code*) for Brazil is 55, so the phone number for Copacabana Palace is (55-21) 2548-7070 when the caller is located outside Brazil.

Try out these useful phrases when talking about calling in Portuguese:

» **atender o telefone** (ah-ten-*deh* ooh teh-leh-*foh*-nee) (*to answer the phone*)

» **deixar um recado** (day-*shah* oong heh-*kah*-doh) (*to leave a voice-mail message*)

» **está correto** (ehs-*tah* koh-*heh*-toh) (*it's correct*)

» **está errado** (ehs-*tah* eh-*hah*-doh) (*it's wrong*)

» **dar um telefonema** (*dah* oong teh-leh-foh-*neh*-mah) (*to make a phone call*)

» **ligar para alguém** (lee-*gah* pah-rah ah-ooh-*gang*) (*to call someone*)

» **número do telefone** (*noo*-meh-roh doo teh-leh-*foh*-nee) (*phone number*)

» **uma cabine telefônica** (ooh-mah kah-*bee*-neh teh-leh-*foh*-nee-kah) (*public phone booth*), also known as **orelhão** (or-el-*yah*-ooh) (*phone booth; Literally: big ear* because of the way the booths are shaped).

Talkin' the Talk

**AUDIO
ONLINE**

Patricia (pah-tree-see-ah) is calling a hotel near Ipanema beach in Rio. She wants to meet up with her friend Roberta (hoh-beh-tah).

Operator:

Bom dia. Hotel do Sol Ipanema.

boh-oong jee-ah. oh-teh-ooh doo soh-ooh eeh-pah-neh-mah.

Good morning. Sun Hotel, Ipanema.

Patricia:	Bom dia. Poderia falar com a Roberta Fernandes, quarto número sete oito três, por gentileza?
	boh-oong jee-ah. poh-deh-ree-ah fah-lah koh-oong ah hoh-beh-tah feh-nahn-jeez, kwah-toh noo-meh-roh seh-chee oh-ee-toh trehz, poh zhehn-chee-leh-zah?
	Good morning. Could you connect me with Roberta Fernandes, room number 783, please?
Operator:	Quem está falando?
	kang es-tah fah-lahn-doh?
	Who's this calling?
Patricia:	**É Patricia Assunção.**
	eh pah-tree-see-ah ah-soong-sah-ooh.
	This is Patricia Assunção.
Operator:	Só um momento, por favor.
	soh oong moh-men-toh, poh-fah-voh.
	Just a moment, please.

WORDS TO KNOW

Poderia falar com . . .	poh-deh-ree-ah fah-lah koh-oong . . .	Could you connect me with . . .
por gentileza	poh zhehn-chee-leh-zah	please (formal)
por favor	poh fah-voh	please (informal)
Quem está falando?	kang es-tah fah-lahn-doh?	Who's this calling?
É . . .	eh . . .	It's . . . (name)
Só um momento.	soh oong moh-men-toh.	Just a moment.

Dealing with verbal mush

The first voice call **conversa** (kohn-*veh*-sah) (*conversation*) in any new language is tough. You can't see the person's face or body language as they're talking. You feel **nervoso** (neh-*voh*-zoo) (*nervous*) that you're taking up their valuable time. The connection may be bad. Their **palavras** (pah-*lahv*-rahz) (*words*) come out sounding like mush.

The Brazilian **sotaque** (soh-*tah*-kee) (*accent*) is particularly unfamiliar-sounding in the beginning. Though natives tend to speak slowly, the abundance of nasal vowels throws off even people with a good knowledge of Portuguese words and grammar. All the talking through the **nariz** (nah-*reez*) (*nose*) sometimes causes people to mistake Brazilian Portuguese for **russo** (ooh *hoo*-soh) (*Russian*) or **francês** (frahn-*say*-ees) (*French*)!

On top of all the different vowels, you also experience the difficulty encountered by people listening to any new language: Where do the words **começam** (koh-*meh*-sah-ooh) (*begin*) and **acabam** (ah-*kah*-bah-ooh) (*end*)? At first, words sound like they're all strung together, with no breaks. And on the phone, distinguishing words is especially tough.

Be easy on yourself for the first few days you're in Brazil (if you're one of the lucky ones with plans to visit) or when you first begin to communicate in Portuguese with a Brazilian. Watch Brazilian **televisão** (teh-leh-vee-*zah*-ooh) (*TV*) stations while you're getting ready to go out, and pay attention to people speaking around you. Soak up the sounds of the language. Pay attention to body language, which often provides useful clues about the content of what a person's saying.

Slowly, you can begin to recognize repeated **sons** (soh-oongz) (*sounds*) and repeated words. With a little effort on the listening end, you may be surprised by how many words you recognize with ease after just **uma semana** (*ooh*-mah seh-mah-nah) (*one week*). Then making a voice call won't be so hard.

TIP

Se você não entende (see voh-*seh* nah-ooh en-*ten*-jee) (*if you don't understand*) what the person on the other end of the line is saying, try asking whether they speak English. Say **Fala inglês?** (*fah*-lah eeng-*glehz?*) (*Do you speak English?*)

I remember hearing the word **teatro** (chee-*ah*-troh) (*theater*) for the first time. I had seen the word written on paper **muitas vezes** (moo-*ee*-tahz *veh*-zeez) (*many times*), and it seemed like one of the easier words to **aprender** (ah-pren-*deh*) (*learn*) — it's not so different from the English word. Yet my friend repeated the word probably four times, and I still didn't get it! She then translated to English, and I felt a little **envergonhada** (en-veh-gohn-*yah*-dah) (*embarrassed*). But it was worth it; I was able to recognize the word the very next time I heard it.

Talkin' the Talk

AUDIO ONLINE

Flavia (flah-vee-ah) tries to call her co-worker Carlos (kah-looz) about a work project. The phone line is bad, and the conversation turns to mush.

Flavia:	Olá, Carlos, por favor?
	oh-lah, kah-looz, poh fah-voh.
	Hello, Carlos, please.
Voice on other side:	Krnha estrn galades. (Unintelligible.)
Flavia:	Poderia falar um pouco mais devagar, por favor?
	poh-deh-ree-ah fah-lah oong poh-koh mah-eez deh-vah-gah, poh fah-voh?
	Can you speak a little slower, please?
Voice on other side:	Sod snod manjekof. (Unintelligible.)
Flavia:	Não estou te escutando. Está ruim a linha.
	nah-ooh es-toh chee es-koo-tahn-doh. es-tah hoo-ing ah leen-yah.
	I can't hear you. The connection is bad.
Voice on other side:	No momento, não se encontra.
	noh moh-men-toh, nah-ooh see en-kohn-trah.
	He's not here right now.
Flavia:	Ligo mais tarde, obrigada.
	lee-goh mah-eez tah-jee, oh-bree-gah-dah.
	I'll call later, thanks.

WORDS TO KNOW

não se encontra	nah-ooh see en-kohn-trah	he/she isn't here (formal)
não está	nah-ooh eh-stah	he/she isn't here (informal)
a linha	ah leen-yah	the phone line
devagar	deh-vah-gah	slowly
mais tarde	mah-eez tah-jee	later
no momento	noh moh-men-toh	right now (formal)

SOUND NATIVE

If you want to say *right now* and you're not talking on the phone, you can say **agora mesmo** (ah-*goh*-rah *mez*-moh) (*right now*). **No momento** is frequently used on the phone with strangers because it sounds more formal.

Connecting with the calling verb: Ligar

In this section, you get to know the verb **ligar** (lee-*gah*) (*to call*). It's a great **-ar** verb you can use to practice verb conjugation because **-ar** verbs are a piece of cake. (See Chapter 2.)

Ligar is almost always packaged with **para** — as in **ligar para** (lee-*gah* pah-rah) (*to call*) someone or someplace. To use this expression, use **ligar para** plus the name of the person or place.

First, here are the conjugations of **ligar**.

Conjugation	Pronunciation
eu ligo	eh-ooh *lee*-goh
você liga	voh-*seh lee*-gah
ele/ela liga	*eh*-lee/*eh*-lah *lee*-gah
nós ligamos	*nohz* lee-*gah*-mohz
eles/elas ligam	*eh*-leez/*eh*-lahz *lee*-gah-ooh
vocês ligam	voh-*sehz lee*-gah-ooh

Practice these example sentences that use **ligar**:

Ligo para os Estados Unidos todos os dias. (*lee*-goh pah-rah ooz eh-*stah*-dooz ooh-*nee*-dohz *toh*-dooz ooz *jee*-ahz.) (*I call the U.S. every day.*)

Ela liga para o namorado dela cinco vezes por dia. (*eh*-lah *lee*-gah pah-rah ooh nah-moh-*rah*-doh *deh*-lah *seen*-koh *veh*-zeez poh *jee*-ah.) (*She calls her boyfriend five times a day.*)

Você liga para a sua mãe muito? (voh-*seh lee*-gah *pah*-rah ah *soo*-ah *mah*-ee moh-*ee*-toh?) (*Do you call your mom often?*)

SOUND NATIVE

The expression **ligar para** has a colloquial meaning, *to pay attention to* someone or something. For example, **Eu não ligo para o futebol** (*eh*-ooh *nah*-ooh *lee*-goh pah-rah ooh foo-chee-*bah*-ooh) translates to *I don't care about soccer.*

The verb **ligar** also means *to plug in* something: **Liga o computador, por favor.** (*lee*-gah ooh kohm-*poo*-tah-*doh*, poh-fah-*voh*.) (*Plug in the computer, please.*) Similarly, **desligar** means *to unplug* or *to turn off* something: **Desliga a tevê!** (des-*lee*-gah ah teh-*veh!*) (*Turn off the TV!*)

SOUND NATIVE

Se liga (see *lee*-gah) is another popular slang expression that uses the verb **ligar**. It means *Get with it* or *Wake up to the facts.* Someone obsessed with celebrity gossip may say, "You don't know about that [insert name of new hot nightclub]?" **Se liga!** The expression literally means *Plug yourself in.*

Telling Someone to Call You

You can also use the calling verb **ligar** to make plans. Use the formula **Pode me ligar?** (*poh*-jee mee lee-*gahr*) (*Can you call me?*) to ask someone to call you. Or, if you want to let a person know that you plan to call, you can use the formula **Eu te ligo** (*eh*-ooh chee *lee*-goo) (*I'll call you*) if the person is a friend, or **Eu vou ligar** (*eh*-ooh voh lee-*gahr*) (*I'll call*) in a more formal situation, such as in business dealings.

Let's check out some specific phrases you might hear, or want to use, which use **ligar**:

Pode me ligar quando a mesa estiver pronto, por favor? (*poh*-jee mee lee-*gahr* *kwahn*-doh ah *meh*-zah es-chee-vehr *prohn*-toh, poh fah-*vohr*) (*Can you call me when the table is ready, please?*)

Pode me ligar quando tiver mais informações? (*poh*-jee mee lee-*gahr* kwahn-doh tee-*vehr mah*-eez een-for-mah-see-*oh*-neez) (*Can you call me when you have more information?*)

Pode me ligar mais tarde, por favor? Estou ocupado/a. (*poh*-jee mee lee-*gahr mah*-eez tah-jee, poh fah-*vohr*. eh-*stoh* oh-koo-*pah*-doo/dah.) (*Can you call me later, please? I'm busy.*) (See Chapter 2 to learn about how to choose the o/a ending. **Hint:** If you're male, use the **–o** ending for adjectives that describe yourself, and if you're female, use the **–a** ending).

Pode me ligar amanhã? (*poh*-jee mee lee-*gahr* ah-mahn-*yah*) (*Can you call me later?*)

Eu te ligo amanhã. (*eh*-ooh chee *lee*-goo ah-mahn-*yah*.) (*I'll call tomorrow.* [informal])

Eu te ligo mais tarde. (*eh*-ooh chee *lee*-goo *mah*-eez tah-jee.) (*I'll call later.* [informal])

Eu vou ligar amanhã. (*eh*-ooh voh lee-*gahr* ah-mahn-*yah*.) (*I'll call tomorrow.*)

Posso ligar amanhã? (*poh*-soo lee-*gahr* ah-mahn-*yah*?) (*Can I call tomorrow?*)

Leaving a Message

It almost seems like a thing of the past these days to **deixar um recado** (day-*shah* oong heh–*kah*–doh) (*leave a message*) on someone's **caixa de mensagem** (*kah*–ee-shah jee men–*sah*–zhang) (*voice mail*).

Here's how to do it: First, say hi: **Olá** (oh–*lah*) (*Hi;* formal) or **Oi** (oh–ee) (*Hi;* informal). Then, identify yourself: **Sou + your name** (*soh*–ooh + your name) (*It's + your name*). Literally, you're saying, "I'm + your name," which seems odd, but that's the beauty of learning other languages — you find that regular old ideas can be expressed in totally different ways.

Then get to why you're calling . . .

Eu estou ligando porque . . . (eh-ooh es-*toh* lee-*gahn*-doh pohr-*keh* . . .) (*I'm calling because . . .*)

Eu estou ligando para perguntar . . . (eh-ooh es-*toh* lee-*gahn*-doh pah-rah pehr-goon-*tahr* . . .) (*I'm calling to ask . . .*)

Eu queria dizer . . . (eh-ooh keh-*ree*-ah jee-*zehr* . . .) (*I wanted to say . . .*)

Then you can close your **recado** by asking the person to call you back (refer to the preceding section, "Telling someone to call you"). It may be a simple, **Me ligue,**

por favor (mee *lee*-gee, poh fah-*voh*) (*Please call me*). Finally, say **obrigado/a** (oh-bree-*gah*-doo/dah) (*thank you*) and **Até logo** (ah-*tay loh*-goo) or **Tchau** (chow) (*Ciao*).

Of course, you may be leaving a voice message with a live person, such as a receptionist at a company, or a relative or roommate of an **amigo** (ah-*mee*-goo) (*friend*). In that case, first, you can ask if the person you're looking for is available: **O/A [+ name of person you're looking for] está?** (ooh/ah + name + eh-*stah*) (*Is + name of person . . . available?*) Use **o** if the person is male and use **a** if the person you're looking for is female. For example, if someone were calling me, and my husband answered, they could ask, **Está Karen?** (*Is Karen there?*)

If the person isn't there, you're likely to hear, **Não, não está. Quer deixar um recado?** (*nah*-ooh, *nah*-ooh es-*tah*. keh day-*shah* oong heh-*kah*-doo?) (*No, they're not here. Do you want to leave a message?*) If they don't ask if you want to leave a message, you can say, **Posso deixar um recado?** (*poh*-soo day-*shah* oong heh-*kah*-doo?) (*Can I leave a message?*)

If they say, **Sim, quem gostaria?** (*sing, kay*-eeng goh-stah-*ree*-uh?), that means *Yes, who's speaking?* Then, bingo! You don't have to leave a message. You get to speak to the person you're looking for.

In other cases, you may need to ask a **recepcionista** (hay-sep-see-ooh-*nees*-tah) (*receptionist*) for a **ramal** (hah-*mah*-ooh) (*extension*) first.

The live person may respond:

> **Só um minutinho** (*soh* oong mee-noo-*cheen*-yoo) (*Just a minute;* Literally: *Just a little minute*)

> **Aguarde um momento.** (ah-*gwah*-jee oong moh-*men*-toh.) (*Wait a moment.*)

> **Deixa-eu checar se ele/ela está.** (*day*-shah eh-ooh sheh-*kah* see eh-lee/eh-lah es-*tah*.) (*Let me check if he/she is here.*)

> **Vou passar a ligação para o/a [+ name of person you're looking for]** (voh pah-*sah* ah lee-gah-*sah*-ooh *pah*-rah ooh/ah + who you're looking for.) (*I'm going to pass you to + name of person;* the speaker will use **o** if it's a male and **a** if it's a female.)

If the person isn't there, you may want to say:

> **Pode dizer para ele/ela que . . .** (poh-jee jee-*zeh* pah-rah *eh*-lee/*eh*-lah kee . . .) (*Can you tell him/her that . . .*)

> **Pode falar para ele/ela para me ligar?** (poh-jee fah-*lah* pah-rah *eh*-lee/*eh*-lah pah-rah mee lee-*gah*?) (*Can you tell him/her to call me?*)

Making Arrangements over the Phone

Lucky you — you made a Brazilian friend and want to **combinar** (kohm-bee-*nah*) (*schedule a get together/meet up*).

Here are some phrases to use over the phone to figure out **detalhes** (deh-*tahl-yees*) (*details*) of the next hang-out:

> **Eu te queria convidar a . . .** (eh-ooh chee keh-*ree*-ah kohn-vee-*dah* ah . . .) (*I want to invite you to . . .*)

> **O que está fazendo amanhã?** (ooh *kee* es-*tah* fah-*zen*-doh ah-mahn-*yah?*) (*What are you doing tomorrow?*)

> **Você quer que a gente se veja de novo?** (voh-*seh keh* kee ah *zhayn*-shee see *veh*-zhah jee *noh*-voo?) (*Do you want to meet up again?*)

> **A que horas você quer combinar?** (ah kee *hoh*-rahs voh-seh *keh* kohm-bee-*nah?*) (*What time do you want to meet up?*)

> **Que dia é bom para você?** (kee *jee*-ah eh *boh*-oong pah-rah voh-*seh?*) (*Which day is good for you?*)

> **Onde combinamos?** (*ohn*-jee kohm-bee-*nah*-moos?) (*Where should we meet?*)

> **O que vamos fazer?** (ooh *keh vah*-moos fah-*zeh?*) (*What should we do?*)

To discuss **que dia** (kee *jee*-ah) (*which day*) and **hora** (*hoh*-rah) (*time*) you want to meet up, check out Chapter 4. Chapter 4 also goes over essential words such as **hoje** (*oh*-zhee) (*today*) and **amanhã** (ah-mahn-*yah*) (*tomorrow*).

As for what you may want to do together, here are some common **atividades** (ah-tee-vee-*dah*-jees) (*activities*):

> **ir jantar** (*eeh* zhan-*tah*) (*to go out to dinner*)

> **ir almoçar** (*eeh* ahl-moh-*sah*) (*to go to lunch*)

> **ir tomar café** (*eeh* toh-*mah* kah-*feh*) (*to go have coffee*)

> **ir passear** (*eeh* pah-see-*ah*) (*to go for a stroll*)

> **ir à praia** (eeh ah *prah*-ee-ah) (*to go to the beach*)

> **ir ao cinema** (*eeh* ah-ooh see-*neh*-mah) (*to go to the movies*)

For more ideas of stuff to do, check out Chapter 9.

Texting to Check In

You can use the same phrases in the preceding section if you want to text someone, instead of call, whether that's on your smartphone, iPad, smartwatch, or on any instant messaging service.

Look at the bright side: When you **digitar** (dee-zhee-*tahr*) (*type*) in Portuguese, you don't have to worry about pronunciation!

Here are some additional phrases that may come in handy once you're ready to text (and of course, you can use these phrases when you speak, too!):

> **Prazer em conhecê-lo/la!** (prah-*zeh* ang kohn-yeh-*seh*-loo/lah!) (*It was great to meet you!*)
>
> **Obrigado/a por . . .** (oh-bree-*gah*-doo/dah pohr . . .) (*Thank you for . . .*)
>
> **Eu me divertei muito!** (eh-ooh mee jee-veh-*tay* moo-ee-toh!) (*I had so much fun!*)
>
> **Como vai?** (koh-moo *vah*-ee?) (*How are you?*)
>
> **O que está fazendo hoje?** (ooh *kee* es-*tah* fah-*zen*-doh *oh*-zhee?) (*What are you up to today?*)

Digital Talk Know-How

FaceTime, Skype, WhatsApp: So many **opções** (op-*soh*-eez) (*options*), so little **tempo** (*tem*-poh) (*time*)! Before the real meat of a conversation, you'll want to get contact info for the other person, decide which tech platform to meet on, and whether you want to chat with **somente de voz** (soh-*men*-shee *jee* vohz) (*audio/voice only*), or go bold and make it a **chamada de vídeo** (shah-*mah*-dah jee *vee*-joh) (*video call*).

Check out the following handy phrases:

> **Qual o seu número de telefone?** (*kwah*-ooh ooh seh-ooh *noo*-meh-roh jee teh-leh-*foh*-nee?) (*What's your phone number?*) (See Chapter 4 to find out how to express numbers in Portuguese.)
>
> **Vou te adicionar aos meus contatos.** (*voh* chee ah-jee-shee-ooh-*nahr* ah-ooz meh-ooz kohn-*tahk*-toos.) (*I'll add you to my contacts.*)
>
> **Vou te enviar uma mensagem de texto.** (*voh* chee en-vee-*ah* ooh-mah men-*sah*-zhang jee *tek*-stoh.) (*I'm going to send you a text message.*)

Vou compartilhar o link. (*voh* kohm-pahr-cheel-*yahr* ooh *leen*-kee.) (*I'll share the link.*)

Qual é o seu Zap? (*kwah*-ooh *eh* ooh seh-ooh *sah*-pee?) (*What's your WhatsApp info?* Literally: *What's your Zap?*)

Posso te enviar uma mensagem de texto no Zap? (*poh*-soo chee en-vee-*ah* ooh-mah men-*sah*-zhang jee *tex*-toh noo *sah*-pee?) (*Can I text you on WhatsApp?*)

Falamos pelo vídeo chat? (fah-*lah*-mooz peh-loo vee-joh *shah*-chee?) (*Let's talk by video chat?*)

Você tem FaceTime? (voh-seh *tang* fay-see-*tah*-ee-mee?) (*Do you have FaceTime?*)

Here are some more basic tech communication words and phrases:

>> **cellular** (sel-ooh-*lah*) (*cellphone*)

>> **mensagem** (men-*sah*-zhang) (*message*)

>> **voz** (vohz) (*voice*)

>> **video** (*vee*-joh) (*video*)

>> **tirar uma foto** (chee-*rahr* ooh-mah *foh*-toh) (*to take a photo*)

>> **compartilhar** (kohm-*pahr*-cheel-*yahr*) (*to share*)

>> **vídeo chat** (*vee*-joh *shah*-chee (*video chat*)

>> **transmissão ao vivo** (trahnz-mee-*sah*-ooh ah-ooh *vee*-voh) (*livestream*)

>> **webcam** (*veh*-bee *kah*-mee) (*webcam*)

>> **camera** (*kah*-meh-rah) (*camera*)

>> **chamada de voz** (shah-*mah*-dah jee *vohz*) (*voice call*)

>> **chamada de video** (shah-*mah*-dah jee *vee*-joh) (*video call*)

CULTURAL WISDOM: WHAT'S UP WITH WhatsApp?

In Brazil, as in many countries around the world, many people use the free app WhatsApp. In Brazil, the app is known by its nickname, **Zap** (*sah*-pee). If you want to keep in contact with people you meet while you're visiting the country as well as after you come home, WhatsApp makes it easy (I'm not paid to say this, promise!). As of press time (2022), WhatsApp had 2 billion **usuários** (oo-zoo-*ah*-ree-oos) (*users*) worldwide.

>> **mensagem de áudio** (men-*sah*-zhang jee *ah*-ooh-*joh*) (*audio message*)

>> **enviado** (en-vee-*ah*-doo) (*delivered; as in a text message*)

SOUND NATIVE

Sound like a native: Just for fun, check out some abbreviations you can use while texting. No pronunciation guide necessary!

>> **hj: hoje** (*today*)

>> **bjs: beijos** (*kisses*)

>> **abs: abraços** (*hugs*)

>> **blz: Beleza** (*sounds good*)

>> **vcs: vocês** (*you guys*)

>> **vc: você** (*you;* informal)

>> **brinks: brincadeira** (*joke; as in Just kidding*)

>> **tranks: tranquilo** (*calm; as in, It's all good*)

>> **kkkkkk: ka ka ka** (*hahaha*)

>> **pq?: Por quê** (*why?*)

Staying Informed through the Internet

Just like the average English speaker, Brazilians like to find out what's going on in the **mundo** (*moon*-doh) (*world*) by clicking around on the **Internet** (een-teh-*neh*-chee) (*Internet*). They may want to find out which **ofertas** (oh-*fehr*-tuz) (*sales*) are going on, discover **escándalos políticos** (es-*kahn*-dah-looz poh-*lee*-chee-kooz) (*political scandals*), or check in on how their personal financial **investimentos** (een-ves-tee-*men*-toos) (*investments*) are doing.

Here are some basic words you can use to describe what you do **online** (ohn-*lah*-ee-nee) (*online*):

>> **pesquisar** (pes-kee-*zah*) (*to research*)

>> **procurar** (proh-koo-*rah*) (*to search*)

>> **notícias** (noh-*chee*-see-uz) (*news*)

>> **esportes** (es-*poh*-cheez) (*sports*)

>> **jornal** (joh-*nah*-ooh) (*newspaper*)

- **banco** (*bahn*-koh) (*bank*)

- **YouTube** (yoo-*too*-bee) (*YouTube*)

- **quadro de bate-papo** (*kwah*-droo jee bah-chee-*pah*-poh) (*chat/discussion board*)

- **entretenimento** (en-treh-ten-ee-*men*-toh) (*entertainment*)

- **o clima** (ooh *klee*-mah) (*the weather*)

- **comprar** (kohm-*prah*) (*to buy*)

And, maybe just like you, most Brazilians use **Google** (pronounced the same, how about that?) to find information they are looking for.

Emailing

Mandar um email (mahn–*dah* oong ee-*may*-oh) (*sending an email*) is a great way to practice Brazilian Portuguese. You can use an online dictionary to help you discover translations, and you won't feel the pressure you might in a spoken, face-to-face conversation.

CULTURAL WISDOM

Something that may seem different to you is how affectionate Brazilians sound when they're emailing. Don't be afraid of using kisses and hugs to **fechar** (feh-*shah*) (*end*) your email!

Here are some common emailing terms and abbreviations:

- **Olá** (oh-*lah*) (*Hello*)

- **Oi!** (*oh*-ee!) (*Hi!*)

- **Prezado/a** . . . (preh-*zah*-doo/dah) (*Dear . . .*; Use **Prezado** if you're writing a man, and **Prezada** if you're emailing a woman)

- **Um abraço** (*oong* ah-*brah*-soo) (*a hug*; this ending is appropriate for an informal closing to a business or personal email.)

- **Abs,** an abbreviation for **abraços,** (ah-*brah*-soos) (*hugs*; sending multiple hugs is also appropriate for an informal closing to a business or personal email.)

- **Um beijo** (oong *bay*-zhoh) (*a kiss*; this ending should be used only with a close friend.)

- **Bjs,** an abbreviation for **beijos** (*bay*-zhos) (*kisses*; sending multiple kisses is appropriate only for messages to a close friend.)

>> **Atensiosamente** (ah-*ten*-zee-oh-zah-*men*-chee) (*Sincerely*)

>> **Encaminho em anexo** (en-kah-*ming*-yoh oong ah-*nex*-oh) (*I'm sending an attachment*)

The symbol @ in Portuguese is called the **arroba** (ah-*hoh*-bah). If you have a *period* in your email, you may want to remember that's called a **ponto** (*pohn*-toh). *Underscore* is **sublinha** (soo-bee-*leen*-yah), and hyphen is **hífen** (*ee*-fen). Check out Chapter 1 to review how to say letters of the alphabet in Portuguese, so that you can easily spell out your email to a Brazilian.

TIP

Talkin' the Talk

**AUDIO
ONLINE**

Diogo (jee-*oh*-goo) and **Zeca** (*zeh*-kah) are samba music fanatics. They like an old type of samba called **chorinho** (shoh-*reen*-yoh). They just met each other in the audience of a **chorinho** show. **Zeca** is telling **Diogo** about a **chorinho** concert next week. Notice that even Brazilians themselves have trouble understanding each other. (It's a loud concert.)

Zeca:	**Tem um concerto de chorinho na semana que vem, sabia?**
	tang oong kohn-*seh*-toh jee shoh-*reen*-yoh nah
	seh-*mah*-nah kee *vang*, sah-*bee*-ah?
	There's a chorinho concert next week, did you know?
Diogo:	**Ah é? Quando e onde?**
	ah *eh*? *kwahn*-doh ee *ohn*-jee?
	Really? When and where?
Zeca:	**Na noite da quarta-feira, no bairro das Laranjeiras.**
	nah *noh*-ee-chee dah *kwah*-tah *fay*-rah, noh *bah*-ee-hoo dahz lahr-ang-*zhay*-rahz.
	On Wednesday night, in the neighborhood of Laranjeiras.
Diogo:	**Poderia me mandar um email com os dados?**
	poh-deh-*ree*-ah mee mahn-*dah* oong ee-*may*-oh koh-oong ooz *dah*-dooz?
	Could you send me an email with the details?

Zeca:	**Claro. Qual é o seu email?**
	klah-roh. *kwah*-ooh *eh* ooh *seh*-ooh ee-*may*-oh?
	Sure. What's your email?
Diogo:	**É diogo.conrado@uol.com.br**
	eh jee-*oh*-goh *pohn*-toh kohng-*hah*-doh ah-*hoh*-bah *ooh*-oh-*eh*-lee *pohn*-toh *koh*-oong *pohn*-toh beh *eh*-hee.
	It's diogo.conrado@uol.com.br.
Zeca:	**Não entendi.**
	nah-ooh en-ten-*jee*.
	I didn't understand.
Diogo:	**É diogo.conrado@uol.com.br.**
	eh jee-*oh*-goh *pohn*-toh kohng-*hah*-doh ah-*hoh*-bah *ooh*-oh-*eh*-lee *pohn*-toh kohng *pohn*-toh beh *eh*-hee.
	It's diogo.conrado@uol.com.br.

· ·

WORDS TO KNOW

na semana que vem	nah seh-mah-nah kee vang	next week
sabia?	sah-bee-ah?	Did you know?
Ah é?	ah eh?	Really?
noite	noh-ee-chee	night
bairro	bah-ee-hoo	neighborhood
mandar	mahn-dah	to send
claro	klah-roh	of course
Não entendi.	nah-ooh en-ten-jee.	I don't understand.

Socializing on Social Media

Logging onto **Facebook** (*fay*-ee-see *boo*-kee), **Instagram** (Brazilians refer to it as **Insta** (*een*-stah) or **Twitter** (twee-tehr) **em** português (ang poh-too-*gehz*) (*in Portuguese*) can be a great way to practice Portuguese. Of course, the thumbs-up and heart buttons on Facebook need no translation. And what's hashtag in Portuguese?: #. Easy. To say it, Brazilians even use the English word **hashtag** (*ash*-ee-*tah*-gee).

A fun way to learn some basic Brazilian social media words is to change your language setting to **português** (poh-too-*gehz*) (*Portuguese*) on your favorite social media app.

Here are some common social media terms:

>> **um post** (oong *pohs*-chee) (*a post*)

>> **online** (on-*lah*-ee-nee) (*online*)

>> **foto** (*foh*-too) (*photo*)

>> **vídeo** (vee-joh) (*video*)

>> **página** (*pah*-zhee-nah) (*page*)

>> **amigos** (ah-*mee*-gooz) (*friends*)

>> **cadastre-se** (kah-*dah*-strah-see) (*register*)

>> **uma conta** (*ooh*-mah *kohn*-tah) (*an account*)

>> **notícias** (noh-*chee*-see-uz) (*news*)

>> **colocar tag** (koh-loh-*kah* tag) (*to put a tag*)

>> **grupos** (*groo*-pooz) (*groups*)

>> **adicionar** (ah-*jee*-see-oh-*nah*) (*to add*)

>> **remover** (heh-moh-*veh*) (*to remove*)

>> **editar** (eh-jee-*tah*) (*to edit*)

>> **site de relacionamento** (*sah*-ee-chee jee heh-lah-see-ooh-nah-*men*-toh) (*social networking site*)

>> **procurar** (proh-koo-*rahr*) (*to search*)

>> solicitações **de amizade** (soh-lee-see-tah-*soh*-eez jee ah-mee-*zah*-jee) (*friend requests*)

>> **status** (*stah*-tooz) (*status* – yes, they just use the English word)

» **comentar** (koh-men-*tah*) (*comment*)

» **compartilhar** (kohm-pah-cheel-*yah*) (*share*)

» **curtir** (koo-*chee*) (*to like*)

» **ao vivo** (ah-ooh *vee*-voh) (*live – as in live video*)

And here are some social media terms that may come in handy:

» **Me add no Face?** (mee *ah*-jee noh *fay*-ee-see) (*Will you add me on Facebook?*)

» **Você está nas redes sociais?** (voh-*seh* es-*tah* nahz *heh*-jees soh-see-*ah*-ees) (*Are you on social media?*)

» **Qual o seu nome de usuário?** (*kwah*-ooh ooh seh-ooh *noh*-mee jee oo-zoo-*ah*-ree-ooh) (*What's your username?*)

» **Vou te escrever em messenger** (voh-ooh chee es-kreh-*veh* ang *mes*-en-zheh) (*I'll write you over messenger*)

» **Posso colocar tag em você no meu post?** (poh-soo koh-loh-kah *tag* ang voh-*seh* noo meh-ooh *pos*-chee) (*Can I tag you in my post?*)

» **Você se importa se eu postar esta foto?** (voh-*seh* see eem-pohr-*tah* see eh-ooh poh-*stah* es-tah *foh*-too) (*Do you mind if I post this photo?*)

If you visit Brazil, hopefully you'll make a Brazilian **amigo** (ah-*mee*-goo) (*male friend*) or **amiga** (ah-*mee*-gah) (*female friend*) and keep in touch over **mídia social** (*mee*-jah soh-see-*ah*-ooh) (*social media*) after you leave.

Keeping Your Tablet at Your Fingertips

As you might imagine, the word **iPad** is spelled exactly the same in Brazilian Portuguese, except that when you hear a native pronounce it, you're more likely to think they're saying the name of an exotic bird: ee-*pah*-jee. Totally different **pronúncia** (proh-*noon*-see-ah) (*pronunciation*). But, **é claro** (eh *klah*-roo) (*of course*), Brazilians use **tablets** (*tah*-bleh-cheez) (yes, again, they use the English word, and the pronunciation is almost unrecognizable) for the same reasons as you.

Here are some terms that Brazilians use to talk about tablets:

» **conectar a WiFi** (koh-nek-*tah* ah *wee*-fee) (*connect to Wi-Fi*)

» **alta velocidade** (*ah*-ooh-tah veh-loh-see-*dah*-jee) (*high-speed*)

- >> **Internet** (een-teh-*neh*-chee) (*Internet*)

- >> **rede** (*heh*-jee) (*network*)

- >> **senha** (*sen*-yah) (*password*)

- >> **tomada** (toh-*mah*-dah) (*outlet* – as in, where you plug in the tablet)

- >> **apps** (ahps) (*apps*)

- >> **podcast** (pod-*kas*-chee) (*podcast*)

- >> **tela** (*teh*-lah) (*screen*)

- >> **câmera** (*kah*-meh-rah) (camera)

- >> **baterias** (bah-teh-*ree*-us) (*batteries*)

- >> **desconectado** (des-kohn-ek-*tah*-doo) (*offline*)

- >> **digitar** (dee-zhee-*tah*) (*to type*)

- >> **loja da Apple** (*loh*-zhah dah *ah*-poh-ooh) (*Apple store*)

- >> **email** (ee-*may*-oh) (*email*)

- >> **configurações** (kohn-fee-goo-rah-*soh*-eez) (*settings*)

- >> **navegador** (nah-veh-gah-*dor*) (*browser*)

- >> **baixar** (bah-ee-*shah*) (*download*)

- >> **estojo** (es-*toh*-zhoh) (*carrying case*)

Talking about Feelings Using Words and Emoji

Social media definitely brings out our emoções (eh-moh-*soh*-eez) (*emotions*). Whether you're watching a video of **cachorros ou gatos fofinhos** (kah-*shoh*-hoos ooh *gah*-tooz foh-*fing*-yooz) (*cute dogs or cats*) or watching footage of **guerra** (*geh*-hah) (*war*), we may experience intense feelings. We may want to tell people about our feelings by reacting to a video or online **conteúdo** (kohn-tay-*ooh*-doh) (*content*) in a post.

Here's are a sampling of feelings words you may want to use when you're online (or offline). You can write or say, **Eu estou** (*eh*-ooh es-*toh*) (*I am*) + [feelings word]:

>> **feliz** (feh-*lees*) (*happy*)

>> **triste** (*trees*-chee) (*sad*)

>> **envergonhado**/a (en-veh-gohn-*yah*-doo/dah) (*embarrassed*)

>> **irritado**/a (ee-hee-*tah*-doo/dah) (*irritated*)

>> **com raiva** (koh-oong *hah*-ee-vah) (*angry*)

>> **decepcionado**/a (deh-sep-see-ooh-*nah*-doo/dah) (*disappointed*)

>> **assustado**/a (ah-soos-*tah*-doo/dah) (*scared*)

>> **calmo**/a (*kah*-ooh-moh/mah) (*calm*)

>> **apaixionado**/a (ah-pah-ee-see-ooh-*nah*-doo/dah) (*in love – as in romantic love*)

>> **surpreso**/a (soor-*preh*-zoo/zah) (*surprised*)

>> **tímido**/a (*chee*-mee-doh/dah) (*shy*)

>> **orgulhoso**/a (or-gool-*yoh*-zoo/zah) (*proud*)

>> **entusiasmado**/a (en-*too*-zee-ahz-*mah*-doo/dah) (*excited*)

>> **confuso**/a (kohn-*foo*-zoh/zah) (*confused*)

>> **preocupado**/a (preh-oh-koo-*pah*-doo/dah) (*worried*)

If you're male, use the –o ending of the feeling word, and if you're female, use the –a ending. For expressing yourself as a *não-binário* (*nah*-ooh bee-*nah*-ree-ooh) (*non-binary*) person, see Chapter 2.

Psiu. . . (that's how you write *Psst*. . .in Portuguese): Flip ahead to the Fun & Games section on the next page to try to match emojis with their "feeling word" names in Portuguese.

You may want to react to a social media post (or offline situation) with a feelings expression such as one of those below:

>> **Adorável!** (ah-doh-*rah*-veh-ooh) (*Adorable!*)

>> **Eu adoro + what you love** (*eh*-ooh ah-*doh*-rooh) (*I love . . .*)

>> **Eu detesto + what you hate** (*eh*-ooh deh-*tes*-too) (*I hate . . .*)

>> **Legal!** (lay-*gow*) (*Cool!*)

>> **Que lindo!** (kee *leen*-doh) (*How beautiful!*)

>> **Engracado!** (een-grah-*sah*-doo) (*Funny!*)

>> **Que chato!** (kee *shah*-toh) (How annoying!)

FUN & GAMES

Match the emoticon to the Portuguese word to describe the emoji.

1. **triste**   **a.**

2. **com raiva**   **b.**

3. **confuso/a**   **c.**

4. **preocupado/a** **d.**

5. **surpreso/a**   **e.**

6. **apaixonado/a** **f.**

7. **entusiasmado/a** **g.**

8. **feliz**   **h.**

Flip to Appendix C for the answers.

Chapter **11**

Chatting About Business

I f you bought this book because you're going to Brazil on a **viagem de negócios** (vee-*ah*-zhang *jee* neh-*goh*-see-ooz) (*business trip*), then you must already know that the **economia** (eh-koh-no-*mee*-ah) (*economy*) there is one of the world's largest. São Paulo is the best known among Brazil's business-oriented cities — no doubt because it's the country's headquarters for **bancos** (bahn-koos) (*banks*) and other **indústrias** (een-*doo*-stree-ahs) (*industries*). Yet other parts of Brazil are vital to the country's economy, too. Brazil's **recursos naturais** (heh-koo-sohs nah-too-*rah*-ees) (*natural resources*), for instance, are concentrated in the Amazon region, whereas the nation's rapidly growing **setor de petróleo e gás** (seh-*toh* jee peh-*troh*-lee-ooh e *gah*-eez) (*oil and gas sector*) is located in Rio.

Brazil boasts the highest gross domestic product (GDP) in Latin America, and a big part of this economy is the nation's considerable financial services sector. The country's main **bolsa de valores** (bohl-sah jee vah-*loh*-reez) (*stock market*), the **Bolsa de Valores de São Paulo** (BM&FBovespa), is located in São Paulo, which is the trading center for stock in the country's banks as well as its oil and gas sector. The **Índice Bovespa** (*een*-jee-see boh-*veh*-spah) is Brazil's equivalent to Standard & Poor's 500 stock index of major companies.

Qual a sua profissão? What Do You Do?

Whether you're going to Brazil for **negócios** (neh-*goh*-see-ooz) (*business*) or **prazer** (prah-*zeh*) (*pleasure*), you may want to explain to someone what type of **trabalho** (trah-*bahl*-yoo) (*work*) you do.

Here's a list of some common **profissões** (proh-fee-*soh*-eez) (*professions*). Remember to change the last **-o** to an **-a** if you're a female:

>> **advogado/a** (ahj-voh-*gah*-doo/dah) (*lawyer*)

>> **arquiteto/a** (ah-kee-*teh*-too/tah) (*architect*)

>> **artista** (ah-*chees*-tah) (*artist*)

>> **designer de interiores** (dee-*zah*-een-eh jee een-teh-ree-*oh*-reez) (*interior designer*)

>> **estudante** (es-too-*dahn*-chee) (*student*)

>> **especialista em TI** (es-peh-see-ah-ooh-*lee*-stah ang tay ee) (*IT specialist*)

>> **engenheiro/a** (en-zhen-*yeh*-roo/rah) (*engineer*)

>> **jornalista** (zho-nah-*lees*-tah) (*journalist*)

>> **médico/a** (*meh*-jee-koo/kah) (*doctor*)

>> **professor/a** (proh-feh-*soh*/soh-rah) (*teacher*)

>> **psicólogo/a** (psee-*koh*-loh-goo/gah) (*psychologist*)

>> **voluntário/a** (voh-loon-*tah*-ree-oh/ah) (*volunteer*)

If you work for a not-for-profit, you can say Eu **trabalho para uma organização sem fins lucrativos** (eh-oo trah-*bahl*-yoo pah-rah ooh-mah oh-gah-nee-zah-*sah*-ooh *sang feengs* loo-krah-*chee*-vohz) (*I work for a not-for-profit*). Brazilians also refer to non-profits as **ONGs** (*ong*-geez, short for **organização não governamental** or *non-governmental organization — what we call NGOs*).

Businesspeople can start off by saying Eu **sou da área de negógios** (eh-oo soh dah ah-ree-ah jee neh-*goh*-see-ooz) (*I work in business*). Then they may add their **posição** (poh-zee-*sah*-oo) (*position*) within the **empresa** (em-*preh*-zah) (*company*):

>> **analista** (ah-nah-*lee*-stah) (*analyst*)

>> **assistente** (ah-sees-*tang*-chee) (*assistant*)

>> **chefe** (*sheh*-fee) (*head*)

» **consultor/a** (kohn-sool-*toh*/*toh*-rah) (*consultant*)

» **contador** (kohn-tah-*doh*) (*accountant*)

» **diretor/a** (jee-rek-*toh*/jee-rek-*toh*-rah) (*director*)

» **dono/a** (*doh*-noo/*doh*-nah) (*owner*)

» **gerente** (zheh-*ren*-chee) (*manager*)

» **gerente de contas** (zheh-*ren*-chee jee *kohn*-tahs) (*account manager*)

» **porta-voz** (poh-tah *vohz*) (*spokesperson*)

» **presidente** (preh-zee-*dang*-chee) (*president*)

» **sócio/a** (*soh*-see-oh/ah) (*partner*)

» **sócio/a fundador/a** (*soh*-see-oh/ah foon-dah-*doh*/*doh*-rah) (*founding partner*)

» **vendedor/a** (ven-deh-*doh*/*doh*-rah) (*salesperson*)

Applying the doing verb: Fazer

After you disclose what your basic **trabalho** is, you may want to explain a little more about what your company **faz** (fahz) (*makes/does*). The verb **fazer** (fah–*zeh*) (*to do/make*) is one that Brazilians use often to talk about work and many other things, too.

Conjugation	Pronunciation
eu faço	*eh*-ooh *fah*-soo
você faz	voh-*seh fahz*
ele/ela faz	*eh*-lee/*eh*-lah *fahz*
nós fazemos	*nos* fah-*zeh*-moos
eles/elas fazem	*eh*-leez/*eh*-lahs *fah*-zang
vocês fazem	voh-*sehz fah*-zang

Here's how to use the past tense of **fazer**. (See Chapter 6 for more on using the past tense.)

Conjugation	Pronunciation
eu fiz	*eh*-ooh *fis*
você fez	voh-*seh fehz*

Conjugation	Pronunciation
ele/ela fez	*eh*-lee/*eh*-lah *fehz*
nós fizemos	*nos* fih-*zeh*-moos
eles/elas fizeram	*eh*-leez/*eh*-lahs fee–*zeh*–rahm
vocês fizeram	voh-*sehz* fee-*zeh*-rah-rahm

Check out some example sentences that use both the present and past tenses of **fazer:**

O que você faz? (ooh *kee* voh-*seh fahz?*) (*What do you do?*)

A minha empresa faz relatórios para a indústria de telecomunicações. (ah *meen*-yah em-*preh*-zah *fahz* heh-lah-*toh*-ree-ooz pah-rah ah een-*doos*-tree-ah jee teh-leh-koh-moo-nee-kah-*soy*-eez.) (*My company does reports for the telecommunications industry.*)

Nós fizemos um anúncio para a Coca-Cola aqui no Brasil. (nos fih-*zeh*-moos oong ah-*noon*-see-oh pah-rah ah koh-kah *koh*-lah ah-kee noo brah-*zee*-ooh.) (*We did an ad for Coca-Cola here in Brazil.*)

Vou fazer uma apresentação amanhã; estou nervosa! (voh fah-*zeh* ooh-mah ah-preh-zen-tah-*sah*-ooh ah-mahn-*yah*; eh-stow neh-*voh*-zah!) (*I'm doing a presentation tomorrow; I'm nervous!*)

Eu faço esculturas feitas de metal. (eh-ooh *fah*-soo eh-skool-*too*-rahs *fay*-tahs jee meh-*tah*-ooh.) (*I make sculptures made of metal.*)

And now, some non–work–related ways you can use **fazer:**

Vou fazer uma salada. (voh fah-*zeh* ooh-mah sah-*lah*-dah.) (*I'm going to make a salad.*)

Como as ostras fazem pérolas? (*koh*-moo ahz *ohs*-trahs *fah*-zang *peh*-roh-lahs?) (*How do oysters make pearls?*)

O quê vocês fizeram ontem no Rio? (ooh *kee* voh-*sehz* fee-*zeh*-rahm *ohn*-tang noo *hee*-ooh?) (*What did you guys do yesterday in Rio?*)

O que posso fazer? (ooh *kee poh*-soo fah-*zeh?*) (*What can I do?*)

SOUND NATIVE

Sometimes, **fazer** is used to mean something besides *to make/do*. **Fazer uma festa** (fah–*zeh* ooh–mah *fes*–tah), for example, means *to throw a party.*Using the working verb: Trabalhar

Similar to the word **trabalho**, the verb **trabalhar** (trah–bahl–*yah*) (*to work*) can help you explain your responsibilities.

Conjugation	Pronunciation
eu trabalho	*eh*-ooh trah-*bahl*-yoo
você trabalha	voh-*seh* trah-*bahl*-yah
ele/ela trabalha	*eh*-lee/*eh*-lah trah-*bahl*-yah
nós trabalhamos	*nos* trah-bahl-*yah*-moos
eles/elas trabalham	*eh*-leez/*eh*-lahs trah-*bahl*-yah-ooh
vocês trabalham	voh-*sehz* trah-*bahl*-yah-ooh

Here's how to use the past tense of **trabalhar**. (See Chapter 6 for more on using the past tense.)

Conjugation	Pronunciation
eu trabalhei	*eh*-ooh trah-bahl-*yay*
você trabalhou	voh-*seh* trah-bahl-*yoh*
ele/ela trabalhou	*eh*-lee/*eh*-lah trah-bahl-*yoh*
nós trabalhamos	*nos* trah-bahl-*yah*-moos
eles/elas trabalharam	*eh*-leez/*eh*-lahs trah-bahl-*yah*–rah-oong
vocês trabalham	voh-*sehz* trah-*bahl*-yah-ooh

Here are some example sentences:

Em que você trabalha? (ang *kee* voh-*seh* trah-*bahl*-yah?) (*What kind of work do you do?*)

Eu trabalho na área de marketing. (eh-ooh trah-*bahl*-yoo nah *ah*-ree-ah jee *mah*-keh-ching.) (*I work in marketing. Literally: I work in the area of marketing.*)

Você trabalha muito! (voh-*seh* trah-*bahl*-yah moo-*ee*-too!) (*You work a lot!*)

Eu preciso trabalhar este fim de semana; que saco! (eh-ooh preh-*see*-zoo trah-bahl-*yah* es-chee *fing* jee seh-*mah*-nah; kee *sah*-koo!) (*I have to work this weekend; what a drag!*)

Talkin' the Talk

AUDIO
ONLINE

Bruno (*broo*-noh) and **Carolina** (*kah-roh*-lee-nah) are on a first date. They ask each other questions about what kind of work they do.

Bruno: **E . . . você trabalha na área de comunicação para uma empresa de internet que vende sapatos, é isso?**

ee . . . voh-*seh* trah-*bahl*-yah nah *ah*-ree-ah jee koh-moo-nee-kah-*sah*-ooh pah-rah ooh-mah em-*preh*-zah jee een-teh-*netch*-ee kee *ven*-jee sah-*pah*-tohs, eh *ee*-soh?

So . . . you work in communications for an internet company that sells shoes, right?

Carolina: **Isso. Eu sou assessora de imprensa.**

ee-soh. *eh*-ooh *soh* ah-seh-*soh*-rah jee eem-*pren*-sah.

That's right. I'm a press liaison.

Bruno: **Gosta do trabalho?**

goh-stah doo trah-*bahl*-yoo?

Do you like your job?

Carolina: **Normal, eu gosto do meu chefe, então não está mal.**

noh-*mah*-ooh, eh-ooh *gost*-oo doo meh-ooh *sheh*-fee, en-*tah*-ooh *nah*-ooh eh-*stah mah*-ooh.

So-so, I like my boss, so it's not bad.

Bruno: **Bom, eu sou engenheiro civil. Adoro o que faço. Além disso, me dão sete semanas de férias ao ano.**

boh-oong, eh-ooh *soh* en-zhen-*yeh*-roo see-*vee*-ooh. Ah-*doh*-roo ooh *kee fah*-soo. ah-*lang jee*-soh, mee *dah*-ooh *seh*-chee seh-*mahn*-ahs jee *feh*-ree-uz ah-ooh *ah*-noh.

Well, I'm a civil engineer. I love what I do. Besides, they give me seven weeks of vacation each year.

Carolina: **Nossa, que legal!**

noh-sah, kee lay-*gow*!

Wow, how cool!

Bruno: **Só que eu trabalho todos os sábados. . . .**

soh kee eh-ooh trah-*bahl*-yoo *toh*-doos ooz *sah*-bah-dohs. . . .

Except that I work every Saturday. . . .

• •

WORDS TO KNOW		
comunicação	koh-<u>moo</u>-nee-kah-<u>sah</u>-ooh	communications
vende	<u>ven</u>-jee	sells
assessora de imprensa	ah-seh-<u>soh</u>-rah jee eem-<u>pren</u>-sah	press liaison
normal	noh-<u>mah</u>-ooh	so-so
engenheiro civil	en-zhen-<u>yeh</u>-roo see-<u>vee</u>-ooh	civil engineer
Adoro	ah-<u>doh</u>-roo	I love
além disso	ah-<u>lang</u> <u>jee</u>-soh	besides
férias	<u>feh</u>-ree-uz	vacation
Que legal!	kee lay-<u>gah</u>-ooh!	How cool!
só que	<u>soh</u> kee	except that

Mailing Things the Old-Fashioned Way

Even though **email** (ee-*may*-oh) (*email*) is how people most often communicate these days, occasionally, when it comes to business and other practical matters, **enviar uma carta** (en-vee-*ah* ooh-mah *kah*-tah) (*sending/to send a letter*) is the most **profissional** (proh-*fee*-see-ooh-*nah*-ooh) (*professional*) or **oficial** (oh-*fee*-see-*ah*-ooh) (*official*) way to send a **resposta** (hes-*pohs*-tah) (*response*), **mensagem** (men-*sah*-zhang) (*message*), or **pergunta** (peh-*goon*-tah) (*inquiry; Literally: question*).

Here are some useful terms when it comes to sending a formal letter:

» **Atenciosamente** (ah-*ten*-see-*ooh*-zah-*men*-chee) (*Sincerely*)

» **CEP** (*seh*-pee) (*zip code*) (CEP is an acronym for **Código de Endereçamento Postal** or *Postal Address Code*.)

>> **correio** (koh-*hay*-ooh) (*post office*)

>> **data** (*dah*-tah) (*date*)

>> **endereço** (en-deh-*res*-ooh) (*address*)

>> **Prezado/a senhor/senhora** (preh-*zah*-doo/dah sen-*yoh*/sen-*yoh*-rah) (*Dear Sir/Madame*)

>> **Querido/a** + friend's name (keh-*ree*-doo/dah) (*Dear + friend's name*; informal)

>> **selo do correio** (*seh*-loo doo koh-*hay*-ooh) (*postal stamp*)

When you start a formal letter, you may want to address a specific person. In that case, you can use abbreviations for **Senhor** and **Senhora: Prezado Sr.** (fill in the name) if the addressee is a man or **Prezada Sra.** (fill in the name) if you're writing to a woman.

Check out some polite terms you may consider using to begin your letter:

>> **Eu estou escrevendo esta carta porque** . . . (*eh*-ooh es-*toh* es-kreh-*ven*-doh eh-stah *kah*-tah poh-*keh* . . .) (*I'm writing this letter because . . .*)

>> **Eu gostaria de solicitar** . . . (*eh*-ooh goh-sta-*ree*-ah jee soh-lee-see-*tah* . . .) (*I'd like to ask for . . .*)

>> **Eu gostaria de saber** . . . (*eh*-ooh goh-sta-*ree*-ah jee sah-*beh* . . .) (*I'd like to know . . .*)

>> **Muito obrigado/a por** . . . (moh-*ee*-too oh-bree-*gah*-doo/dah poh . . .) (*Thank you very much for . . .*)

TIP

Try to use the term **por gentileza** (*poh* zhen-chee-*lay*-zah) (*would you be so kind as to*) at some point to express your gratitude. It's just an extra-polite way of saying *please.* You can also use **por gentileza** over the phone or in a retail store when you want to say *please* and sound extra **cortês** (kor-*tes*) (*polite*).

Placing a Business Call

When you're making a business call, be sure to use **senhor/senhora** (seen-*yoh*/seen-*yoh*-rah) (*Mr./Mrs.*) followed by the person's name when you're asking to speak to someone you don't know well or at all.

Here are some common phrases you may want to know during a business phone call:

>> **Olá, meu nome é (insert your name).** (oh-*lah*, meh-ooh *noh*-mee *eh* [insert your name].) (*Hello, this is [insert your name].*)

>> **O Senhor/Senhora (fill in name) está?** (ooh *sen*-yoh/sen-*yoh*-rah [fill in name] eh-*stah*?) (*Is Mr./Mrs. [fill in name] there?*)

>> **Estou procurando alguém da área de. . . .** (eh-*stoh* proh-koo-*rahn*-doh ah-ooh-*gang* dah ah-ree-ah *jee*. . . .) (*I'm looking for someone in the [fill in the blank] department.*)

>> **Eu gostaria de deixar um recado para ele/ela.** (eh-ooh gohs-tah-*ree*-ah *jee* day-*shah* oong hay-*kah*-doo *pah*-rah eh-lee/eh-lah.) (*I'd like to leave him/her a message.*)

>> **Eu agradeço** (eh-ooh ah-grah-*deh*-soo) (*I thank you very much;* extra polite)

You can end the phone conversation with a polite **Até logo** (ah–*teh* loh–goo) (*Goodbye; Literally: Until later*).

Making Appointments and Conducting Meetings

When it comes time for a face–to–face business **reunião** (hay–oo-–nee–*ah*–ooh) (*meeting*), you need to schedule an **hora** (oh–rah) (*time*), a **lugar** (loo–*gah*) (*place*), and the estimated **duração** (doo–rah–*sah*–ooh) (*length/duration*).

Here are some questions and statements you can use to set up the meeting:

>> **Podemos marcar uma reunião?** (poh-*deh*-mooz mah-*kah* ooh-mah hay-oon-ee-*ah*-ooh?) (*Shall we schedule a meeting?*)

>> **Onde?** (ohn-jee?) (*Where?*)

>> **A que horas?** (ah kee *oh*-rahs?) (*What time?*)

>> **Por quanto tempo?** (poh *kwahn*-toh *tem*-poh?) (*For how long?*)

SOUND NATIVE

You can end the conversation with an enthusiastic **Até lá!** (ah–*tay lah!*) (*See you; Literally: Until then!*)

Hopefully, you and your meeting partner will be **pontuais** (pohn-too-*ah*-eez) (*on time/punctual*) and not **adiantado** (ah-jee-ahn-*tah*-doo) (*early*) or **atrasado** (ah-trah–*zah*-doo) (*late*)!

Expressing profit, loss, revenue, and expenses

At your business meeting, you may need to talk about the nitty-gritty details of finance. Here are some basic business terms to know:

>> **balanço** (bah-*lahn*-soo) (*expense report*)

>> **custos** (*koos*-tohs) (*costs*)

>> **gastos** (*gas*-tohs) (*expenses*)

>> **impostos** (eem-*pohs*-tooz) (*taxes*)

>> **lucro** (*loo*-kroh) (*profit*)

>> **perdas** (*peh*-dahs) (*losses*)

>> **receita** (heh-*say*-tah) (*revenue*)

>> **relatório anual** (heh-lah-*toh*-ree-ooh ahn-ooh-*ah*-ooh) (*annual report*)

>> **resultados financeiros** (heh-zool-*tah*-dooz fee-nahn-*say*-rohs) (*financial results*)

Here are some questions and a statement you may want to use when asking about the **desempenho** (des-em-*pen*-yoh) (*performance*) of a company:

Quando sai o relatório anual? (kwahn-doh *sah*-ee ooh heh-lah-*toh*-ree-ooh ahn-oo-*ah*-ooh?) (*When does the annual report come out?*)

É possível aumentar as receitas? (*eh* poh-*see*-veh-ooh ah-ooh-men-*tah* ahz heh-*say*-tahs?) (*Is it possible to increase revenue?*)

Os gastos da empresa são muito altos? (ooz *gahs*-toos dah em-*preh*-zah *sah*-ooh moh-*ee*-toh *ah*-ooh-tohs?) (*Are the company's costs really high?*)

Os impostos municipais são bastante baixos. (oohz eem-*pohs*-tooz moon-ee-see-*pah*-eez *sah*-ooh bah-*stahn*-chee *bah*-ee-shos.) (*The city taxes are pretty low.*)

Luckily, in Brazil, lots of people in the business sector speak English very well. Because Portuguese isn't as commonly known around the world as, say, English, Spanish, or French, many Brazilians learn English at an early age.

In fact, when I first moved to Brazil as a business journalist, I did all my **entrevistas** (en-treh-*vees*-tahs) (*interviews*) in English for the first several months, before I started to get the hang of Portuguese. But don't let that discourage you from learning this beautiful language. It's always more fun and respectful to speak the native language when traveling for business or leisure.

Asking about business goals

When talking shop in Brazil, you may want to ask someone about the future of a company, or what the **objetivos** (ohb-zheh-*chee*-voos) (*goals*) of the company are. You may already know whether the company is **grande** (*grahn*-jee) (*big*) or **pequena** (peh-*keh*-nah) (*small*), how many **empregados** (em-preh-*gah*-doos) (*employees*) it has, and where its **sede** (*seh*-jee) (*headquarters*) is located.

Try using these questions to ask about a company's upcoming **planos** (*plah*-noos) (*plans*) and **expectativas em geral** (es-pek-tah-*chee*-vahs ang zheh-*rah*-ooh) (*outlook in general*):

> **Qual é a previsão de lucro da empresa para este ano?** (*kwah*-ooh *eh* a preh-vee-*zah*-ooh jee *loo*-kroh dah em-preh-zah pah-rah *es*-chee *ah*-noo?) (*What is the company's estimated profit for this year?*)

> **Quando esperam atingir fluxo de caixa positivo?** (*kwahn*-doh es-*peh*-rah-oong ah-teen-*zheeh floo*-shoh jee *kah*-eeh-shah poh-zee-*chee*-voh?) (*When do you expect to reach positive cash flow?*)

> **Vocês têm planos para comprar outra empresa?** (voh-*say*-eez tang *plah*-nooz pah-rah kom-*prah oh*-trah em-*preh*-zah?) (*Do you guys have plans to buy another company?*)

> **Quais são as maiores dificultades da empresa hoje e no futuro?** (*kwah*-eez *sah*-ooh ahz my-*oh*-reez jee-fee-kool-*dah*-jeez dah em-*preh*-zah *oh*-zhee ee no foo-*too*-roo?) (*What are the biggest challenges for the company today and in the future?*)

Working from Home

Here's an easy one: In Brazil, they call a home office . . . **home office** (*hoh*-mee *oh*-fee-see)! The pronunciation is different, but they just lift our phrase from English, which makes things easier! Office is technically **escritório** (es-kree-*toh*-ree-ooh). *Work from home* is **trabalhar de casa** (trah-bahl-*yah* jee *kah*-zah). For more vocabulary about features of a home, see Chapter 5.

If you **trabalhar de casa**, what are some of the **vantagens** (ven-*tah*-zhangz) (*advantages*), **na sua opinião** (nah *soo*-ah oh-pee-nee-*ah*-ooh) (*in your opinion*)? Many people say their **qualidade de vida** (kah-lee-*dah*-jee jee *vee*-dah) (*quality of life*) is better. It may be easier to **fazer exercício** (fah-*zeh* eh-zeh-*see*-see-ooh) (*do exercise*) or to eat an **alimentação saudável** (ah-lee-men-tah-*sah*-ooh sah-ooh-*dah*-veh-ooh) (*healthy diet*).

Here are some handy phrases you can use to talk about where you work:

>> **Eu trabalho em casa.** (*eh*-ooh trah-*bahl*-yoh ang *kah*-zah.) (*I work from home.*)

>> **Eu trabalho num escritório.** (*eh*-ooh trah-*bahl*-yoh noong es-kree-*toh*-ree-ooh.) (*I work at an office.*)

>> **Posso trabalhar em casa?** (*poh*-soo trah-bahl-*yah* ang *kah*-zah?) (*Can I work from home?*)

>> **Você trabalha em casa, ou num escritório?** (voh-*seh* trah-*bahl*-yah ang *kah*-zah oh noong es-kree-*toh*-ree-ooh?) (*Do you work from home, or in an office?*)

>> **Eu tenho um home office.** (eh-ooh *tang*-yoh oong *oh*-mee *oh*-fee-see.) (*I have an office in my house.*)

>> **A minha empresa tem escritório.** (ah *ming*-yah em-*preh*-zah tang es-kree-*toh*-ree-ooh.) (*My company has an office.*)

>> **Nos fazemos reuniões no escritório.** (nohz fah-*zeh*-mooz hay-ooh-nee-*oh*-eez noo es-kree-*toh*-ree-ooh.) (*We do meetings at the office.*)

>> **Eu trabalho em casa a maioria dos dias.** (*eh*-ooh trah-*bahl*-yoh ang *kah*-zah ah my-oh-*ree*-ah dohz *jee*-ahz.) (*I work at home most days.*)

Here are some words you may need to use when talking about your home office:

>> **caneta** (kah-*neh*-tah) (*pen*)

>> **computador** (kohm-poo-tah-*doh*) (*computer*)

>> **laptop** (lah-pee-*toh*-pee) (*laptop*)

>> **tela** (*teh*-lah) (*screen*)

>> **impressora** (eem-preh-*soh*-rah) (*printer*)

>> **copiadora** (koh-pee-ah-*doh*-rah) (*copier*)

>> **escrivaninha** (es-*kree*-vah-*neen*-yah) (*desk*)

>> **cadeira ergonômica** (kah-*day*-rah ehr-goh-*noh*-mee-kah) (*ergonomic chair*)

And finally, here's what to say during a virtual **reunião** (hay–ooh–nee–*ah*–ooh) (*meeting*) over a video conferencing platform, potential bloopers included:

>> **Eu volto já.** (eh-ooh *voh*-ooh-toh *zhah*.) (*I'll be right back.*)

>> **Estou desligando a webcam para almoçar.** (es-*toh* des-lee-*gahn*-doh ah veh-bee-*kah*-mee pah-rah ah-ooh-moh-*sah*.) (*I'm turning off the camera to eat lunch.*)

» **Desculpe, eu estava em mute.** (jees-*kool*-pee, eh-ooh es-*tah*-vah ang mee-*oot* (*Sorry, I was on mute.*)

» **Todo mundo, vamos silenciar, por favor.** (toh-doo *moon*-doh, *vah*-mohz see-len-see-*ahr*, poh fah-*voh*.) (*Everyone, let's go on mute.*)

» **Pode ativar o som?** (*poh*-jee ah-chee-*vah* ooh *soh*-oong?) (*Can you unmute yourself? Literally, Can you activate the sound?*)

» **Você está silenciado.** (voh-*seh* es-*tah* see-len-see-*ah*-doo.) (*You're on mute.*)

» **Fica/Fique à vontade para fazer perguntas no chat.** (*fee*-kah/*fee*-kee ah vohn-*tah*-jee pah-rah fah-*zeh* pehr-*goon*-tuz noo *shah*-chee.) (*Feel free to ask questions in the chat.*) (**Fica** is informal; **Fique** is formal)

» **Não posso te ouvir.** (nah-ooh *poh*-soo chee ooh-*vee*.) (*I can't hear you.*)

» **Ligue seu vídeo.** (*lee*-gee seh-ooh *vee*-joh.) (*Turn on your video.*)

» **Está travando.** (es-*tah* trah-*vahn*-doh.) (*It's glitchy.*)

» **Vou aumentar o meu volume.** (*voh* ah-ooh-men-*tah* ooh meh-ooh voh-*loo*-mee.) (*I will turn up my volume.*)

» **Você congelou.** (voh-*seh* kohn-zheh-*loh*) (*You're frozen.*)

» **Desculpe, os meus meninos estão fazendo barulho.** (jees-*kool*-pee, ooz meh-ooz men-*nee*-nooz es-*tah*-ooh fah-*zen*-doh bah-*rool*-yoh.) (*Sorry, my kids are making noise.*)

» **Você pode ouvir o meu cachorro latindo?** (voh-*seh* *poh*-jee ooh-*veeh* ooh meh-ooh kah-*shoh*-hoh lah-*cheen*-doh?) (*Can you hear my dog barking?*)

To discover what you can do when you have **férias** (*feh*–ree–uz) (*vacation*), see Chapter 13. Or, if a regular weekend is coming up, Chapter 9 can help you talk about deciding what to do.

FUN & GAMES

Imagine that you're planning a business meeting. You need to pick a date as well as discussion items to put on the agenda. Match these Portuguese words you might use in your note with their English translation.

1. **reunião**   a. *performance*

2. **fazer**   b. *profit*

3. **trabalho**   c. *job*

4. **data**   d. *company*

5. **empresa**   e. *taxes*

6. **lucro**   f. *date (as in calendar date)*

7. **planos**   g. *meeting*

8. **impostos**   h. *plans*

9. **desempenho**   i. *to do/make*

10. **receita**   j. *revenue*

Flip to Appendix C for answers.

Chapter **12**

Recreation and the Outdoors

Most of Brazil's population is concentrated near its **litoral** (lee-toh-*rah*-oo) (*coastline*), making **praias** (*prah*-ee-ahz) (*beaches*) a focus of daily life for many Brazilians. That's why a Brazilian beach is an ideal place to practice your Portuguese. Tons of people are there who, because they're probably enjoying themselves, are generally **de bom humor** (jee *boh*-oong ooh-*moh*) (*in a good mood;* Literally: *of good humor*).

When talking with a Brazilian — whether you're sipping **água de coco** (*ah*-gwah jee *koh*-koh) (*coconut water*) through a straw out of a green coconut in **Rio** (*hee*-ooh) or enjoying a **cerveja** (seh-*veh*-zhah) (*beer*) in Hawaii — watch your companion's eyes light up at the mention of a beach.

But don't make the mistake of thinking that Brazilians are limited to the beach for outdoor fun. Other interesting places in Brazil for outdoor recreation include the **Amazônia** (ah-mah-*zoh*-nee-ah) (*Amazon rainforest*) and the **Pantanal** (pahn-tah-*nah*-ooh), a safari-like wetlands landscape with rare animal species in Brazil's central-west region.

In this chapter, I point out how you can talk about beaches, plants, and animals as well as a bit about soccer and other sports in Portuguese. And, yes, you also find out how to ask people what they like to do.

Finding Out What's Really on a Brazilian Beach

Beaches in Brazil are packed with people enjoying the company of old friends and making new acquaintances. At urban beaches, you're likely to see **surfistas** (soo-*fee*-stahs) (*surfers*) and people **correndo** (koh-*hen*-doh) (*jogging*) on the beach-front avenue.

In this section I teach you the names of things you may see on a Brazilian beach, as well as stuff people do on them.

Rio (*hee*-ooh) is home to Brazil's most famous beaches. Yet almost all of Brazil's beaches are lovely.

TIP

To get away from the tourists and **ladrões** (lah-*droh*-eez) (*pickpockets*) in Rio, locals and tuned-in visitors head to **Barra da Tijuca** (*bah*-hah *dah* tee-*zhoo*-kah), which is several beaches over from **Ipanema** (ee-pah-*neh*-mah). Barra da Tijuca is known for having the cleanest water. This beach is located in front of one of the newest high-rise developments in Rio's **Zona Sul** (*soh*-nah *soo*) (*South Zone*), Rio's fanciest area, with nice apartment buildings and hotels.

Getting outfitted for a day at the beach

It's a myth that all Brazilian **mulheres** (moo-*yeh*-reez) (*women*) wear itsy-bitsy, teeny-weeny, thong bikini bottoms. You may see this type of bathing suit on many **Rio de Janeiro** (*hee*-ooh jee zhah-*nay*-roo) state beaches but only in isolated cases on other Brazilian beaches. That said, it's true that the average top and bottom pieces of a Brazilian **biquini** (bee-*kee*-nee) (*bikini*) are **menor** (meh-*noh*) (*smaller*) than the average American or European bikini.

HOT SPOTS ON POPULAR BRAZILIAN BEACHES

In Rio, the two main beaches are named **Copacabana** (koh-pah-kah-*bah*-nah) and **Ipanema** (ee-pah-*neh*-mah). Copacabana draws many types of people, whereas Ipanema is favored by the **jovens** (*joh*-vangs) (*young*) and **gente legal** (zhang-chee lay-*gah*-ooh) (*hip people*). Post markers are located on Ipanema beach, each with a different number, to help situate people. **Posto 9** (*poh*-stoh *noh*-vee) (*post number 9*) is considered the trendiest. But whatever part of Ipanema beach you're on, be sure to see the unforgettable **pôr do sol** (*poh* doo *soh*-oo) (*sunset*).

In Portuguese, thong bikini bottoms are called **fio dental** (*fee*-oh dang-*tah*-ooh) (*dental floss*) — Brazilians always have a sense of humor!

Most Brazilian men wear **sungas** (*soong*-gahz) (*small, tight-fitting swim briefs, like Speedos*), and young male surfers tend to wear **bermudas** (beh-*moo*-dahz) (*Bermuda shorts*) — longer, American-style swimming shorts.

Though Brazilians are known for being **vaidosos** (*vah*-ee-*doh*-zooz) (*vain*) and are famous for wearing skimpy bathing suits (both men and women), they're incredibly **de mente aberta** (jee *men*-chee ah-*beh*-tah) (*open-minded*). People of all shapes and sizes can feel **confortável** (kong-foh-*tah*-veh-ooh) (*comfortable*) and enjoy themselves on a Brazilian beach.

So don't feel pressured to buy a Brazilian bathing suit if it's not your thing. Brazilians are plenty used to **turistas** (too-*rees*-tahz) (*tourists*) expressing a different **estilo** (ehs-*chee*-loh) (*style*) and cultural background. In fact, most Brazilians are **curiosos** (koo-ree-*oh*-zooz) (*curious*) about differences in style and may be eager to discuss them with you.

Here are some words you can use to talk with people about beach attire and accessories:

>> **canga** (*kang*-gah) (*sarong*)

>> **chinelos** (shee-*neh*-looz) (*flip-flops*)

>> **óculos de sol** (oh-koo-lohz jee *soh*-oo) (*sunglasses*)

>> **prancha de surf** (*prahn*-shah jee *sooh*-fee) (*surfboard*)

>> **protetor solar** (proh-teh-*toh* soh-*lah*) (*sunblock*)

>> **toalha** (toh-*ahl*-yah) (*towel*)

Brazilians tend to sit on **cangas** (*kang*-gahz) (*sarongs*) more often than actual **toalhas** (toh-*ahl*-yahz) (*towels*) at the beach. **Camelôs** (kahm-eh-*lohs*) (*street vendors*) often sell **cangas** on the beach. Or you can find one at a nearby **loja** (*loh*-zhah) (*store*).

Brazil's most popular flip-flop brand, **Havaianas** (ah-vah-ee-*ah*-nahz), has become hugely successful worldwide. You can see thousands of people wearing the famous brand on Brazilian beaches as well as on the streets of New York and Paris. The name **Havaianas** means *Hawaiians*, oddly enough. That's because Hawaii is the most exotic beach location Brazilians can think of. Never mind that to non-Brazilians, Brazil is a super exotic locale.

Checking out other beach attractions

Of course, bikinis aren't the only attraction on a Brazilian beach. You may be pretty excited to find and rent a **cadeira de praia** (kah-*deh*-rah jee *prah*-ee-ah) (*beach chair*) and **sombrinha** (sohm-*breen*-yah) (*beach umbrella; Literally: little shade*) from a vendor on the beach.

REMEMBER

You can also buy beach snacks, which are cheap. You may hear someone walking by, shouting **Cinco reais! Cinco reais!** (*sing*-koh hay-*ah*-eez! *sing*-koh hay-*ah*-eez!) (*five reais! five reais!*) along with the name of the food they're selling. Typical beach snack foods include **queijo coalho** (*kay*-zhoh koh-*ahl*-yoh) (*grilled cheese cubes*), **espetinhos de carne** (eh-speh-*cheen*-yohs jee kah-nee) (*beef shish kabobs*), **amendoim** (ah-*mang*-doh-*eeng*) (*peanuts*), and **picolé** (pee-koh-*leh*) (*fruity popsicles*). See Chapters 5 and 7 for more about Portuguese words for different kinds of food.

Here are a few other terms you may want to use when talking with a Brazilian about the beach:

>> **areia** (ah-*ray*-ah) (*sand*)

>> **barraca** (bah-*hah*-kah) (*beach shack [that serves food/drinks]*)

>> **castelo de areia** (kah-*steh*-loo jee ah-*ray*-ah) (*sand castle*)

>> **crianças** (kree-*ahn*-sahz) (*kids*)

>> **frescobol** (*freh*-skoo-*bah*-ooh) (*beach paddle ball*)

>> **futebol** (foo-chee-*bah*-ooh) (*soccer*)

>> **golfinhos** (goh-ooh-*feen*-yohs) (*dolphins*)

>> **livros** (*leev*-rohz) (*books*)

>> **peixes** (*pay*-ee-shees) (*fish*)

>> **pescadores** (pehs-kah-*doh*-reez) (*fishermen*)

>> **pôr do sol** (poh doo soh-ooh) (*sunset*)

>> **revista** (heh-*vee*-stah) (*magazine*)

>> **tubarão** (too-bah-*rah*-ooh) (*shark*)

>> **vôlei de praia** (*voh*-lay jee *prah*-ee-ah) (*beach volleyball*)

WHAT'S FRESCOBOL?

Imagine playing ping-pong without the net, on the beach. That's basically **frescobol**, a **Carioca** (kah-ree-*oh*-kah) (person from Rio) favorite. Two people (of any age) try to volley a small, hard ball (heavier than a ping-pong ball) using wooden paddles. **Fresco** (*fres*-koh) means *fresh* and refers to the fresh air and wind you feel as you play. If you change the **-o** to an **-a**, you have the American soda *Fresca*. Guess why the soda makers named it that way? The bubbles and citric flavors are like a hit of "fresh" air. Good thing Fresca isn't salty, though. Learning Portuguese can help you better understand the roots of English!

Talkin' the Talk

AUDIO ONLINE

Paula (*pah*-ooh-lah) and **Rogério** (hoh-*zheh*-ree-ooh) are heading to Post 9 on Ipanema beach, in Rio. They discuss whether they remembered to bring everything they'll need from home for a day at the beach.

Paula: **Temos protetor solar?**

teh-mohz proh-teh-*toh* soh-*lah*?

Do we have sunblock?

Rogério: **Sim, mas só fator oito. Tá bom para você?**

sing, *maz soh* fah-*toh* oh-ee-toh. tah *boh-oong* pah-rah voh-*seh*?

Yeah, but it's just SPF 8. Is that okay for you?

Paula: **Sim, tá bom. Eu estou com uma canga, mas acho suficiente para nós dois.**

sing, tah *boh-oong*. eh-ooh es-*toh* kohng ooh-mah *kahng*-gah, maz ah-shoo soo-fee-see-*en*-chee pah-rah *nooz doh*-eez.

Yeah, that's fine. I have one sarong (to lay on), but I think it's enough for the two of us.

Rogério: **Ótimo. Agora só quero uma cerveja.**

oh-chee-moh. ah-*goh*-rah soh keh-roo ooh-mah seh-*veh*-zhah.

Great. Now I just want a beer.

Paula: **Eu estou de regime. Vou tomar uma água de coco.**

eh-ooh es-*toh* jee heh-*zhee*-mee. voh toh-*mah* oo-mah
ah-gwah jee *koh*-koo.

I'm on a diet. I'm going to have coconut water.

WORDS TO KNOW		
temos	<u>teh</u>-mohz	do we have
fator	fah-<u>toh</u>	SPF
para ti	pah-rah <u>chee</u>	for you
tá bom	tah <u>boh-oong</u>	that's fine
acho	<u>ah</u>-soo	I think
ótimo	<u>oh</u>-chee-moh	great
agora	ah-<u>goh</u>-rah	now
regime	heh-<u>zhee</u>-mee	diet

Describing beautiful beaches

Determining which regions of Brazil have the best beaches is a matter of opinion.
If you like lush green mountain landscapes and **turquesa** (too-*keh*-zah) (*turquoise*) water, head for southeast Brazil (Rio or **São Paulo** (sah-ooh *pah*-oo-loh)
states). If you prefer **água quente** (ah-gwah *kang*-chee) (*warm water*) and lots of
coqueiros (koh-*kay*-rohz) (*coconut trees*), head for the northeast — north of (and
including) **Bahia** (bah-*ee*-ah) state or west of (and including) **Rio Grande do Norte**
(hee-ooh *grahn*-jee doo *noh*-chee) state.

REMEMBER

Brazilians themselves tend to glorify beaches in the northeast, where the ocean is
often a bright blue-green color and **palmeiras** (pah-ooh-*may*-rahs) (*palm trees*)
dot white sandy beaches and the local culture is particularly **relaxado** (heh-lah-
shah-doo) (*relaxed*). Bahia state would probably win the prize as the favorite beach
férias (*feh*-ree-ahz) (*vacation*) destination of Brazilians themselves because of the
state's reputation for throwing a good **festa** (*feh*-stah) (*party*).

Other destinations in Brazil that are known for their beaches include **Florianópolis** (floh-ree-ah-*noh*-poh-lees), an island off the coast of **Santa Catarina** (*sahn*-
tah kah-tah-*ree*-nah) state in the south, **Ceará** (say-ah-*rah*) state in the north,

and **Fernando de Noronha** (feh-*nahn*-doh jee noh-*rohn*-yah), a northeastern island that's about an hour away by **avião** (ah-vee-*ah*-oo) (*plane*) from the Brazilian mainland, near **Rio Grande do Norte** (hee-oh *grahn*-jee doo *noh*-chee) state. Only a certain number of tourists are allowed to visit **Fernando de Noronha** each day, so make plans well in advance.

All beaches have a unique beauty, of course. Here are some phrases you can use to talk about how pretty a beach is:

> **Que bonita!** (kee boh-*nee*-tah!) (*How pretty!*)
>
> **É maravilhosa!** (eh mah-rah-vee-lee-*oh*-zah!) (*It's amazing!*)
>
> **Incrível!** (eeng-*kree*-veh-ooh!) (*Unbelievable!*)
>
> **Nossa senhora!** (noh-sah seen-*yoh*-rah!) (*Wow!*)
>
> **Que legal!** (kee leh-*gah*-ooh!) (*How cool!*)
>
> **Meu Deus!** (meh-oo *deh*-ooz!) (*Oh my God!*)
>
> **Não acredito!** (*nah*-ooh ah-kreh-*jee*-toh!) (*I can't believe it!*)

SOUND NATIVE

Nossa senhora! literally means *Our lady!* and would be the English equivalent of saying *Holy Mary, mother of God!* It's very common in Brazil, and people often just say **Nossa!**

...........Talkin' the Talk...........

AUDIO ONLINE

Marta (*mah*-tah) and **Fabiana** (fah-bee-*ah*-nah) have just reached **Ilha Grande** (*eel*-yah *grahn*-jee), a beautiful island off the coast of Rio de Janeiro state.

Marta: **Nossa, que bonita!**

noh-sah, kee boo-*nee*-tah!

Wow, how pretty!

Fabiana: **Incrível!**

eeng-kree-*veh*-ooh!

Unbelievable!

Marta:	**É a praia mais bonita que eu já vi.**
	eh ah *pray*-ee-ah mah-eez boo-*nee*-tah kee eh-ooh zhah *vee*.
	It's the prettiest beach I've ever seen.
Fabiana:	**Isso eu não sei, mas acho super legal.**
	ee-soh eh-ooh nah-ooh *say*-ee, *mah*-eez ah-shoh soo-peh lay-*gow*.
	I don't know about that, but I think it's really cool.
Marta:	**A água é azul turquesa mesmo.**
	ah *ah*-gwah eh ah-*zoo* too-*keh*-zah *mez*-moh.
	The water is really turquoise.

WORDS TO KNOW

mais bonita	mah-eez boo-nee-tah	prettiest
Isso	ee-soh	this/that
eu não sei	eh-ooh nah-ooh say-ee	I don't know
super legal	soo-peh lay-gow	really cool
água	ah-gwah	water
azul turqueza	ah-zoo too-keh-zah	turquoise

Exploring the Amazon Rainforest

The world's largest rainforest, **a Amazônia** (ah ah–mah–*soh*–nee–ah) (*the Amazon rainforest*), provides the planet with a rich supply of oxygen and is one of the most biodiverse spots in the **mundo** (*moon*–doh) (*world*). Lucky Brazil is the owner of the majority of this magnificent natural resource.

CULTURAL WISDOM

As famous as **a Amazônia** is, very few Brazilians have ever visited it! This is in part because getting there is expensive, and it's very far from where most Brazilians live, which is near the **litoral** (lee-toh-*rah*-ooh) (*coast*).

When traveling to a **Amazônia**, most people fly into **Manaus** (mah-*nah*-oohs), the largest city in the Amazon with about two million residents. If you actually make it to this **lugar remoto** (loo-*gah* heh-*moh*-too) (*remote location*), you'll have a lot to tell Brazilians about their own country.

When you're ready to explore the rainforest, check out these cool things to do:

>> **assistir shows de dança indígena** (ah-sees-*chee* shows jee *dahn*-sah een-*dee*-zhee-nah) (*watch shows of indigenous dancers*)

>> **observar macacos nas árvores** (ohb-seh-*vah* mah-*kah*-kooz nooz *ah*-voh-reez) (*observe monkeys in the trees*)

>> **pescar piranhas** (pes-*kah* pee-*rahn*-yahs) (*go pirana fishing*)

>> **relaxar em cruzeiros pelos rios Amazonas e Negro** (heh-lah-*shah* ang kroo-*zay*-rohs peh-lohs *hee*-ooz ah-mah-*soh*-nahs ee *neh*-groo) (*relax on river cruises on the Amazon River and the Rio Negro*)

>> **ver golfinhos rosas** (veh gohl-*feen*-yohs *hoh*-zahs) (*see pink dolphins*)

Another big tourist draw is seeing the point of first contact between the **Rio Solimões** (*hee*-ooh soh-lee-*moh*-eez) and the **Rio Negro** (*hee*-ooh neg-roh) (known as Rio Negro in English, too; Literally: *black river*). The former is brown and the latter is black, and for a while, the two rivers flow side by side in their respective colors.

One thing that really amazed me when I was in the Amazon was the fact that I didn't get bitten by **mosquitos** (mohs-*kee*-tohs) (*mosquitoes*). Turns out, the Rio Negro's pH and acidity levels aren't great for mosquito egg-laying. I got bitten by more mosquitos in São Paulo than in the Amazon!

Talking about Biodiversity

The Brazilian government estimates that the country is home to at least 43,000 types of animal species alone and a few million different types of insects! In this section I can't go through the whole list, obviously, but I can give you the Portuguese names of some typical **plantas** (*plahn*-tahs) (plants) and **animais** (ah-nee-*mah*-eez) (*animals*) that live in Brazil and make up one of the most biodiverse regions of the planet.

Considering plant life

Visiting the Amazon is a terrific way to see Brazil's abundance of wild flora and fauna because this rainforest is home to many rare species of plant and animal life. Another option is to visit the **Pantanal** (pahn-tah-*nah*-ooh) (*the Pantanal*), a vast **pântano** (*pahn*-tah-noh) (*wetland*) area in the central-west part of the country, near Bolivia, that's also rich with biodiversity.

Plant life is so much a part of the **Pantanal** that the name of the Brazilian state in which it's located has a word related to *mata* (*mah*-tah) (*forest*) in it: **Mato Grosso do Sul** (*mah*-toh *groh*-soo doo *soo*), which translates to *Thick Southern Forest*.

Here are some words to help you speak about the most basic types of plant life in Portuguese:

>> **árvore** (*ah*-voh-ree) (*tree*)

>> **coqueiro** (koh-*kay*-roh) (*coconut tree*)

>> **flor** (floh) (*flower*)

>> **mangues** (*mang*-geez) (*mangroves*)

>> **a selva** (ah *seh*-ooh-vah) (*the jungle*)

Identifying wildlife

Aside from domestic **cachorros** (kah-*shoh*-hooz) (*dogs*) and **gatos** (gah-tooz) (*cats*), many other **animais** (ah-nee-*mah*-eez) (*animals*) live in Brazil. Here are some of the classics that inhabit the **Amazônia** and the **Pantanal** as well as some wild areas in other parts of the country:

>> **arara-azul** (ah-*rah*-rah ah-*zoo*) (*Hyacinth Macaw*), the largest flying parrot in South America

>> **bicho preguiça** (bee-shoo preh-*gee*-sah) (*sloth*)

>> **capivara** (kah-pee-*vah*-rah) (*capybara*), the largest rodent in the world

>> **serpente** (seh-*pen*-chee) (*snake*)

>> **jacaré** (zhah-kah-*reh*) (*cayman*), a small alligator

>> **macaco** (mah-*kah*-koo) (*monkey*)

>> **onça-preta** (*ohn*-sah *preh*-tah) (*jaguar*)

>> **pássaro** (*pah*-sah-roh) (*bird*)

>> **rã** (*hah*) (*frog*)

>> **tamanduá bandeira** (tah-mahn-doo-*ah* bahn-*day*-rah) (*anteater*)

>> **tatu** (tah-*too*) (*armadillo*)

>> **tucano** (too-*kah*-noh) (*toucan*)

I have a soft spot in my **coração** (koh-rah-*sah*-ooh) (*heart*) for the **capivara**, because I spotted many in the **Rio Tietê** (*hee*-ooh chee-eh-*teh*) (*Tiete River*), a very polluted river that runs through **São Paulo** (sah-ooh *pah*-oo-loh). They must have amazing survival instincts to live in such an urban environment.

Asking People What They Like to Do

When you're making friends with Brazilians, you may want to figure out what you have in common. An easy thing to ask new acquaintances is what sports or forms of recreation they enjoy. After all, Brazilians like to play and enjoy other sports besides soccer.

Here are some words in Portuguese to use to talk about other **esportes** (eh-*spoh*-cheez) (*sports*) and types of recreation you can do in many different parts of the world:

>> **alpinismo** (ah-ooh-pee-*nees*-moh) (*rock climbing*)

>> **basquete** (bahs-*keh*-chee) (*basketball*)

>> **beisebol** (*bay*-eez-bah-ooh) (*baseball*)

>> **correr** (koh-*heh*) (*to jog*)

>> **futebol americano** (foo-chee-*bah*-ooh ah-meh-ree-*kah*-noh) (*American football*)

>> **esquiar** (es-kee-*ah*) (*to ski*)

>> **acampar** (ah-kahm-*pah*) (*to go camping*)

>> **golfe** (*gohl*-fee) (*golf*)

>> **ir pescar** (*eeh* pes-*kah*) (*to go fishing*)

>> **natação** (nah-tah-*sah*-ooh) (*to swim*)

>> **andar de bicicleta** (ahn-*dah* jee bee-see-*kleh*-tah) (*to go bike riding*)

>> **patinar no gelo** (pah-tee-*nah* noh *zheh*-loh) (*to ice skate*)

>> **surfe/surfar** (*soo*-fee) (*surfing*)

>> **tênis** (*teh*-neez) (*tennis*)

>> **vôlei** (*voh*-lay) (*volleyball*)

Of course, you may just want to talk about **exercício** (eh-seh-*see*-see-ooh) (*exercise*) and recreation. Perhaps you want to get to know someone better or extend an invitation to join you for some outdoor activity for the sake of **boa saúde** (*boh*-ah sah-*ooh*-jee) (*good health*) and **diversão** (jee-veh-*sah*-ooh) (*fun*). These words can come in handy:

>> **academia** (ah-kah-deh-*mee*-ah) (*gym*)

>> **fazer caminhada** (fah-*zeh* kahm-een-*yah*-dah) (*to go for a walk or a hike*)

>> **malhar** (mahl-*yah*) (*to lift weights*)

>> **passear de buggy** (pah-see-*ah* jee *boo*-gee) (*sand dune buggy*), common in northeastern Brazil

>> **jangada** (zhahng-*gah*-dah) (*tiny sailboat*), common in northeastern Brazil

>> **andar de barco** (ahn-*dah* jee *bah*-koh) (*to take a boat ride*)

>> **fazer snorkeling** (fah-*zeh* snoh-keh-leeng) (*to snorkel*)

>> **fazer mergulho** (fah-*zeh* meh-*gool*-yoh) (*to scuba dive*)

>> **escalada em rocha** (es-kah-*lah*-dah ang *hoh*-shah) (*rock climbing*)

>> **andar de bicicleta** (ahn-*dah* jee bee-see-*kleh*-tah) (*to go bicycling*)

>> **stand up paddle** (*stahn*-jee *up*-ee *pah*-dohl) (*stand-up paddleboard*)

You can also participate in **esportes radicais** (eh-*spoh*-cheez hah-jee-*kah*-eez) (*extreme sports*) in a number of places in Brazil. One of my favorites is **voar de asa delta** (voh-*ah* jee ah-zah *deh*-ooh-tah) (*to go hang gliding*) in Rio, over Ipanema Beach.

TIP

To find out what someone likes to do, just ask, **Você gosta de. . .?** (voh-seh *goh*-stah jee. . .?) (*Do you like. . .?*) and then add the activity, as in these examples:

Você gosta de surfar? (voh-seh *goh*-stah jee soo-*fah*?) (*Do you like to surf?*)

Você gosta de ir à academia? (voh-*seh goh*-stah jee *ee* ah ah-kah-deh-*mee*-ah?) (*Do you like to go to the gym?*)

Você gosta de correr? (voh-*seh goh*-stah jee koh-*heh*?) (*Do you like to go running?*)

Você gosta de jogar futebol? (voh-*seh goh*-stah jee zhoh-*gah* foo-chee-*bah*-ooh?) (*Do you like to play soccer?*)

If someone asks you one of these questions, you can answer **Sim, gosto** (*sing, goh-stoo*) (*Yeah, I like it*) or **Não, não gosto** (*nah*-ooh, *nah*-ooh *goh*-stoo) (*No, I don't like it*).

You can use the **você gosta de . . .** format for a ton of fun activities, including these:

> **Você gosta de viajar?** (voh-seh *goh*-stah jee vee-ah-*zhah?*) (*Do you like to travel?*)

> **Você gosta de ir ao cinema?** (voh-*seh goh*-stah jee *ee* ah-ooh see-*neh*-mah?) (*Do you like to go to the movies?*)

> **Você gosta de praticar o seu inglês?** (voh-*seh goh*-stah jee prah-chee-*kah* ooh seh-ooh eeng-*glehz?*) (*Do you like practicing your English?*)

> **Você gosta de cozinhar?** (voh-*seh goh*-stah jee koh-zing-*yah?*) (*Do you like to cook?*)

**SOUND
NATIVE**

It can be difficult to express your most passionate feelings in another language. But here are a few easy tricks: To say you love doing something, use **Eu adoro . . .** (eh-ooh ah-*doh*-roo . . .) (*I love . . .*). If you hate it, say **Eu detesto . . .** (eh-ooh deh-*tes*-toh . . .) (*I hate . . .*). Can you guess what the roots of these Portuguese words are? That's right — to *adore* and to *detest*.

Talkin' the Talk

**AUDIO
ONLINE**

Erika (*eh*-ree-kah) and **Daniel** (dahn-ee-*eh*-ooh) are teenagers who are just meeting at a new summer lifeguarding job. They get acquainted by asking each other questions.

Erika:	**Daniel, o quê você gosta de fazer?**
	dahn-ee-*eh*-ooh, ooh *kee* voh-seh *goh*-stah jee fah-*zeh?*
	Daniel, what do you like to do?
Daniel:	**Na realidade, eu gosto muito de esquiar.**
	nah hay-ahl-ee-*dah*-jee, eh-ooh *gohs*-too moh-*ee*-toh jee es-kee-*ah.*
	Actually, I really like to ski.
Erika:	**É sério? Que engraçado.**
	eh *seh*-ree-ooh? kee en-grah-*sah*-doo.
	Really? That's funny.

Daniel:	**Quais esportes você gosta mais?**
	kwah-eez es-*poh*-cheez voh-*seh goh*-stah *mah*-eez?
	And you, which sports do you like most?
Erika:	**Eu adoro surfar. Eu detesto esquiar.**
	eh-ooh ah-*doh*-roo soor-*fah*. eh-ooh deh-*tes*-too es-kee-*ah*.
	I love to surf. I hate skiing.
Daniel:	**Por quê?**
	poh-*keh*?
	Why?
Erika:	**É frio demais!**
	eh *free*-ooh jee-*mah*-eez!
	It's too cold!

WORDS TO KNOW

na realidade	nah hay-ahl-ee-<u>dah</u>-jee	actually
eu gosto muito	eh-ooh gohs-too moh-ee-toh	I really like
esquiar	es-kee-<u>ah</u>	to ski
É sério?	eh seh-ree-ooh?	Really?
que engraçado	kee en-grah-sah-doo	how funny
quais	<u>kwah</u>-eez	which
esportes	es-<u>poh</u>-cheez	sports
frio	<u>free</u>-oh	cold
adjective + demais	jee-mah-eez	too + adjective

FUN & GAMES

You've just arrived at the fabled island Fernando de Noronha, which lies an hour by plane from Brazil's northeast. It's known locally as **o Havaí brasileiro** (ooh ah-vah-*ee* brah-zee-*lay*-roh) (*the Brazilian Hawaii*). You head for the beach, an hour before sunset, to take a dip. On your way, you see unusual birds and trees. But on the beach, you see the same things you've already seen on other Brazilian beaches. Name the things you can see in the picture.

Illustration by Elizabeth Kurtzman

FUN & GAMES

A. _____

B. _____

C. _____

D. _____

E. _____

F. _____

G. _____

H. _____

I. _____

See Appendix C for the answers.

3
Brazilian Portuguese on the Go

Plan that trip to Brazil.

Count your *reais.*

Travel the country in style.

Enjoy a soccer game.

Celebrate Carnaval.

Deal with emergencies.

Chapter **13**

Planning a Trip

I don't know whether it's **verdade** (veh-*dah*-jee) (*true*) that the **vaso sanitário** (*vah*-soh sah-nee-*tah*-ree-ooh) (*toilet*) flushes in the opposite direction in the Southern Hemisphere. I wanted to do an experiment before taking off to live in Brazil, but I never got around to it. Maybe you can try it. . . .

What I do know firsthand, though, is how strange it feels to sweat under the hot **sol** (*soh*-ooh) (*sun*) in mid-January. That's right — wintertime in the Northern Hemisphere is summertime in Brazil, which is located in the **hemisfério sul** (eh-mees-*feh*-ree-ooh doo *soo*) (*southern hemisphere*). When you're planning a **viagem** (vee-*ah*-zhang) (*trip*) to Brazil, this seasonal switcheroo is important to consider. In this chapter I point out how to choose the best time for your Brazilian getaway and describe the characteristics of Brazil's main regions.

I also give you the lowdown on passports and visas, help you choose the right accommodations for your stay, and offer some tips on what to take with you to Brazil. Along the way, I cover how to use the pertinent verb **ir** (ee) (*to go/to be going*) and how to form possessives (*my, your, her, his, ours, theirs*).

Picking the Best Time for Your Trip

REMEMBER

Prices are double, sometimes triple, for traveling in Brazil during summer in the Southern Hemisphere — **dezembro até março** (deh-*zem*-broh ah-*teh mah*-soh) (*December to March*). But the summertime price hike is due more to the surge of Brazilian vacationers than foreign tourists. People flock to Brazil year-round, whereas most Brazilians go **de férias** (jee *feh*-ree-ahz) (*on vacation*) in the **verão** (veh-*rah*-ooh) (*summer*) only.

Here are the Portuguese words for the different **estações** (eh-stah-*soh*-eez) (*seasons*):

>> **primavera** (pree-mah-*vay*-rah) (*spring*)

>> **verão** (veh-*rah*-ooh) (*summer*)

>> **outono** (oh-*toh*-noo) (*fall/autumn*)

>> **inverno** (een-*veh*-noo) (*winter*)

TIP

If you like crowds and **festas** (*feh*-stahz) (*parties*) and want to meet lots of native Brazilians at the vacation hotspots, visit Brazil during its **verão**. If you prefer to travel on the cheap, go during the Northern Hemisphere's summer months, the Brazilian **inverno** (een-*veh*-noh) (*winter*).

In Brazil's North and Northeast, the weather is **quente** (*kang*-chee) (*hot*) year-round. In the Amazon, it usually rains at some point each day all year, so bring your **guarda-chuva** (*gwah*-dah *shoo*-vah) (*umbrella*). If you visit the Northeast from **abril até julho** (ah-*bree*-ooh ah-*teh* joo-lyoh) (*April to July*), the chance of **chuva** (*shoo*-vah) (*rain*) is very high, too. But the rain usually doesn't last all day. And waiting out a tropical storm can be kind of relaxing.

Check out the **mapa do Brasil** (*mah*-pah doh brah-*zee*-ooh) (*map of Brazil*) in Figure 13-1.

In the Southeast [where **Rio** (*hee*-ooh) and **São Paulo** (sah-ooh-*pah*-oo-loh) are located], weather patterns are a bit different; **dezembro até março** (deh-*zem*-broh ah-*teh mah*-soh) (*December to March*) is hot and humid with a high probability of rainstorms, whereas **junho até setembro** (*zhoon*-yoh ah-*teh* seh-*tem*-broh) (*June to September*) is typically **ensolarado** (en-sohl-ah-*rah*-doo) (*sunny*) and **seco** (*seh*-koh) (*dry*).

South of Rio has a real **inverno** from **abril até julho** (ah-*bree*-ooh ah-*teh* joo-lyoh) (*April to July*); temperatures get pretty **frio** (*free*-oh) (*cold*) the higher you go in altitude. It even **neva** (*neh*-vah) (*snows*) some years in **Rio Grande do Sul** (*hee*-ooh *grahn*-jee doo *soo*) state, the southernmost part of the country.

FIGURE 13-1:
This map shows the five regions of Brazil and popular destinations.

Illustration by Elizabeth Kurtzman

Here are a few more terms you can use to ask about or describe the weather while you're planning your Brazilian getaway:

>> **nublado** (nooh-*blah*-doo) (*cloudy*)

>> **o vento** (ooh ven-to) (*wind*)

>> **úmido** (*ooh*-mee-doh) (*humid*)

>> **a neve** (ah *neh*-vee) (*snow*)

>> **gelado** (zheh-*lah*-doh) (*icy*)

REMEMBER

When talking about the best time to visit Brazil, knowing how to say the months of the year in Portuguese comes in handy. Notice that, in Portuguese, the first letter of the name of each month isn't capitalized like it is in English:

>> **janeiro** (zhah-*nay*-roh) (*January*)

>> **fevereiro** (feh-veh-*ray*-roh) (*February*)

>> **março** (*mah*-soo) (*March*)

>> **abril** (ah-*bree*-ooh) (*April*)

>> **maio** (*my*-oh) (*May*)

>> **junho** (*zhoon*-yoh) (*June*)

>> **julho** (*zhool*-yoh) (*July*)

>> **agosto** (ah-*goh*-stoh) (*August*)

>> **setembro** (seh-*tem*-broh) (*September*)

>> **outubro** (oh-*too*-broh) (*October*)

>> **novembro** (noh-*vem*-broh) (*November*)

>> **dezembro** (deh-*zem*-broh) (*December*)

To say *in* a certain month, use **em** (ang) plus the name of the month. Here are a couple example sentences:

Vou para o Brasil em maio. (*voh pah*-rah ooh brah-*zee*-ooh ang *my*-oh.) (*I'm going to Brazil in May.*)

Ela retornou do Canadá em novembro. (*eh*-lah heh-toh-*noh* doo kah-nah-*dah* ang noh-*vem*-broh.) (*She returned from Canada in November.*)

Or, you may want to say, I'm going to return home **em agosto** (ang ah–*goh*–stoh) (*in August*) or ask, Does it rain a lot in the Amazon **em março** (ang *mah*–soo) (*in March*)?

Talkin' the Talk

AUDIO ONLINE

Caio (*ky*-oh) dreams about visiting the Amazon, but he only has vacation days off in June — right during the rainy season. He asks his friend **Fábio** (*fah*-bee-ooh), a biologist who has spent a lot of time in the Amazon, for advice.

Caio: **Oi Fábio, já foi para o Amazonas no inverno?**

oh-ee fah-bee-ooh, *zhah foh*-ee pah-rah ooh ah-mah-*zoh*-nahz noo een-*veh*-noh?

Hey Fabio, have you been to the Amazon in the winter?

Fábio: **Já. Por quê?**

zhah. poh *keh?*

Yeah. Why?

Caio:	**Qual mês foi?**	
	kwah-ooh mez foh-ee?	
	What month was it?	
Fábio:	**Fui em junho.**	
	fwee ang zhoon-yoh.	
	I went in June.	
Caio:	**Choveu muito?**	
	shoh-veh-ooh moh-ee-too?	
	Did it rain a lot?	
Fábio:	**Choveu muito pela manhã, mas fez sol pela tarde.**	
	shoh-veh-ooh moh-ee-too peh-lah mahn-yah, mah-eez fez soh-ooh peh-lah tah-jee.	
	It rained a lot in the morning, but it was sunny in the afternoon.	
Caio:	**Ah é? Que bom.**	
	ah eh? kee boh-oong.	
	Really? Great.	

● ●

WORDS TO KNOW

Já foi. . . ?	zhah foh-ee. . . ?	Have you been. . . ?
no inverno	noo een-veh-noh	in the winter
choveu	shoh-veh-ooh	rained
pela manhã	peh-lah mahn-yah	in the morning
fez sol	fez soh-ooh	it was sunny
pela tarde	peh-lah tah-jee	in the afternoon

Obtaining a Passport and Visa

REMEMBER

If you plan to visit Brazil, you'll need a **passaporte** (pah-sah-*poh*-chee) (*passport*). If you don't have one, be sure to get one far in advance of your trip; passports can take weeks to get finalized. If you already have a **passaporte**, check to make sure that the **data de vencimento** (*dah*-tah jee ven-see-*men*-toh) (*expiration date*) won't come before your trip starts! As of press time, Brazil requires visitors to show passports that are valid on the day of entrance to the country. (Some countries require validity that extends to 3-6 months past the return date, but this isn't the case with Brazil.)

If you're curious about how to say some of the personal identification details listed on a passport in Portuguese, take a look here:

>> **nome** (*noh*-mee) (*name*)

>> **sobrenome** (*soh*-bree-*noh*-mee) (*last name*)

>> **nacionalidade** (nah-see-oh-nah-lee-*dah*-jee) (*nationality*)

>> **endereço** (en-deh-*reh*-soh) (*address*)

>> **data de nascimento** (*dah*-tah jee nah-see-*men*-toh) (*date of birth*)

As far as getting your **visto** (*vees*-toh) (*visa*), first check on the website of the Brazilian **embaixada** (em-bah-ee-*shah*-dah) (*embassy*) in your **país** (pah-*eez*) (*country*) to find out whether you need one to enter Brazil. As of 2022, Americans visiting Brazil for tourism or business purposes didn't need a visa.

REMEMBER

If you plan to travel to any developing countries within 90 days prior to your visit to Brazil that might be host to **febre amarela** (*feh*-bree ah-mah-*reh*-lah) (*yellow fever*), you may be required to show **prova de vacinação de febre amarela** (*proh*-vah jee vah-see-nah-*sah*-ooh jee *feh*-bree ah-mah-*reh*-lah) (*proof of yellow fever vaccination*) in order to get a visa to enter Brazil.

Researching Public Health Concerns

You may want to check the U.S. Centers for Disease Control website for recommended vaccines for travelers going to Brazil. As of press time, these included:

>> **hepatite A** (eh-pah-*chee*-chee ah) (*hepatitis A*)

>> **hepatite B** (eh-pah-*chee*-chee beh) (*hepatitis B*)

» **febre tifóide** (*feh*-bree chee-*foh*-ee-jee) (*typhoid*)

» **febre amarela** (*feh*-bree ah-mah-*reh*-lah) (*yellow fever*) (recommended if you plan to visit near any rivers in Brazil)

Here are some other terms that you may want to know as you assess health **riscos** (*heez*–goos) (*risks*) when planning an upcoming trip to Brazil:

» **malária** (mah-*lah*-ree-ah) (*malaria*)

» **chicungunha** (shee-keen-*goon*-yah) (*chikungunya* — a mosquito-driven infectious disease common in tropical climates)

» **zika** (*see*-kah) (*Zika*)

» **SIDA** (*see*-dah) (*AIDS*)

» **dengue** (*dang*-gee) (*dengue*)

» **COVID-19** (*koh*-vee-jee dez-ee-*noh*-vee) (*COVID-19*)

» **taxa de transmissão** (*tah*-shah jee trahnz-mee-*sah*-ooh) (*transmission rate*)

» **quarentena** (kwah-ren-*ten*-ah) (*quarantine*)

Packing for Your Brazilian Getaway

You lucky duck, are you really planning a trip to Brazil? Starting to pack your **mala** (*mah*–lah) (*suitcase*) already? No doubt you got some new **roupas** (*hoh*–pahs) (*clothes*) for the voyage!

Here are some other things you may want to pack:

» **biquini/sunga** (bee-*kee*-nee/*soong*-gah) (*bikini/tight-fitting swim briefs for men* — if you want to look like Brazilian men on the beach!)

» **repelente** (heh-peh-*len*-chee) (*insect repellant*)

» **chapéu** (shah-*peh*-ooh) (*hat*)

» **chinelos** (shee-*neh*-looz) (*flip-flops*)

» **protetor solar** (proh-teh-*toh* soh-*lah*) (*sunblock*)

» **tênis** (*teh*-nees) (*sneakers;* Literally: *tennis shoes*)

» **óculos de sol** (*oh*-koo-lohs jee *soh*-ooh) (*sunglasses*)

» **prova de vacinação de febre amarela** (*proh*-vah jee vah-see-nah-*sah*-ooh jee *feh*-bree ah-mah-*reh*-lah) (*proof of yellow fever vaccination*)

» **câmera** (*kah*-meh-rah) (*camera*)

» **carregador de bateria** (kah-heh-gah-*doh* jee bah-teh-*ree*-ah) (*battery charger*)

» **conversor de voltagem** (kohn-veh-*soh* jee vol-*tah*-zhang) (*power converter*)

» **adaptador de tomada** (ah-*dahp*-tah-*doh* jee toh-*mah*-dah) (*plug*)

REMEMBER

Many electrical outlets in Brazil use the round-prong (not rectangular) kind of plug, so get an **adaptador** if necessary. Voltage in the electric current varies widely in Brazil; it can be anywhere from 100 to 240 volts. Check the power adaptors of your laptop before you get on the plane. You may need to buy a **conversor de voltagem.**

In general, anything related to technology is more expensive in Brazil than in the United States and in some European countries. Photography aficionados, better to bring extra **baterias** for your single-lens reflex **câmera,** for example, than deal with finding the right store and unloading more of your **carteira** (kah-*tay*-rah) (*wallet*) than you'd like to. **Protetor solar** (proh-teh-*toh* soh-*lah*) (*sunscreen*) tends to be more expensive in Brazil, too, so it may be worth bringing extra.

However, **roupas, sapatos** (sah-*pah*-tohs) (*shoes*), and most things you'd buy in a **farmácia** (fah-*mah*-see-ah) (*drugstore*) are reasonably priced in Brazil and easy to replenish if you need to.

Deciding Where to Go

Brazil has it all: beaches, hiking, natural wonders, history, great food, infectious music, urban life, and rural solitude. Each region has its strong points, so do a little research before your trip to Brazil to decide which parts of the country you should visit.

In this section, you find highlights of places to go in Brazil as well as some insight about what you can expect from the various destinations, all of which feature intriguing wonders of the natural, urban, and historical varieties. Of course, veering off the beaten path is fun, too; this overview is a good starting point for planning your Brazilian vacation.

Fortunately for people who like variety, Brazil's airlines offer daily flights to all parts of Brazil, so it's easy to visit more than one region during a single trip. The largest airlines in Brazil are **LATAM Brazil** (lah-*tahm* brah-see-ooh), **Gol** (gohl) and **Azul** (ah-*zoo*). Check out Chapter 15 for more on traveling by air.

The North

Brazil's North region is known for its vast expanses of land without a lot of human population and includes some interesting towns as well as the Amazon rainforest. The North is not a very touristy area, which may delight travelers who like to make their own tracks.

Pará (pah-*rah*) state has beautiful beaches, and the North is also where the world-famous Amazon rainforest is located. When visiting this area, most people fly into **Manaus** (mah-*nah*-ooz), the capital of **Amazonas** (ah-mah-*soh*-nahz) state and the biggest city in the Brazilian part of the Amazon.

From Manaus, you can reach several jungle lodges within a couple of hours. Most lodges are located near the **Rio Amazonas** (*hee*-ooh ah-mah-*soh*-nahz) (*Amazon River*). Here, you can see local indigenous culture as well as exciting animals, including **piranhas** (pee-*rahn*-yahz) (*piranas*), **macacos** (mah-*kah*-kooz) (*monkeys*), and **bichos-preguiça** (*bee*-shoo preh-*gee*-sahz) (*sloths*). **Parintins** (pah-reen-*cheenz*), a town a few hours from Manaus, is famous for its Carnaval in July. Flip to Chapter 17 for details on Brazil's different Carnaval celebrations.

The Northeast

If you want to see what many people consider to be Brazil's best beaches, visit the Northeast region. Tourists often make a holiday in Brazil just by connecting the dots between the following places:

>> **Bahia** (bah-*ee*-ah) is the most popular destination in the Northeast. It's the place for relaxing and listening to music; many of Brazil's most famous musicians are from Bahia. This is the place to see **capoeira** (kah-poh-*ay*-rah), a world-famous martial arts form.

Popular beachy places to go in Bahia include **Morro de São Paulo** (*moh*-hoo jee sah-ooh *pah*-ooh-loo), **Praia do Forte** (*prah*-ee-ah doo *foh*-chee), **Itacaré** (ee-tah-kah-*reh*), and **Trancoso** (trahn-*koh*-zoo), which are all rustic; **Porto Seguro** (*poh*-too seh-*goo*-roo) is urban and relatively expensive. In the interior of the state is a majestic, plateau-filled area called **Chapada Diamantina** (shah-*pah*-dah jee-ah-mahn-*chee*-nah), which hikers and those looking for solitude will appreciate.

Salvador (*sah*-ooh-vah-*doh*) is the capital of the Bahia State. Its city center, known as **Pelourinho** (peh-loh-*ring*-yoh), boasts beautiful old colonial architecture that is protected by its designation as a UNESCO world heritage site. Salvador was Brazil's very first city and served as the country's colonial capital for more than 200 years.

>> **Recife e Olinda** (heh-*see*-fee ee oh-*leen*-dah) is composed of two neighboring cities along the state of **Pernambuco** (peh-nahm-*boo*-koh) coast. Recife is very urban, while Olinda may be the most charming little town in Brazil, with its amazing views, narrow streets, colonial architecture, and emphasis on local art.

>> **Rio Grande do Norte** (hee-ooh *grahn*-jee doo *noh*-chee) boasts sand dunes and dolphins. My personal favorite beach in this state is **Pipa** (*pee*-pah). It's pure magic with dolphins, views of turquoise waters from a bluff, rainbow-colored rocks, a fun little town, and a perfect mix of locals and tourists. With just a few places to go out, you meet them all!

>> **Ceará** (see-ah-*rah*) has turquoise water and is one of the areas that makes the northeastern states famous for their beaches.

>> **Lençóis Maranhenses** (lehn-*soh*-eez mah-rahn-*yen*-seez) in **Maranhão** (mah-rahn-*yah*-ooh) boasts turquoise lagoons amid white sand dunes that are like nothing else on Earth. **Belém** (beh-*lang*), the capital of Pará state, and **São Luis** (*sah*-ooh loo-*eez*), the capital of Maranhão state, are relaxed, culturally interesting cities to check out.

The Central-West

The Central-West region is home to Brazil's capital **Brasília** (brah-*zee*-lee-ah), a city founded in 1960 that is known for its modernist architecture and is not a big tourist draw. Within the region lies the **Pantanal** (pahn-tah-*nah*-ooh), known locally as Brazil's Serengeti — its African plains, home to exotic animals that thrive in the plains and wetlands. By far, the Central-West region is the best place to see wild animals in Brazil. Spotting animals here is easier than in the Amazon simply because the Pantanal has more open space. The Pantanal is a bit of a secret and doesn't see many tourists despite its riches. It is a bit of a trek to get here, and tourist packages are more expensive here compared to the beach destinations.

Campo Grande (*kahm*-poh *grahn*-jee) and **Bonito** (boo-*nee*-too) are the two main towns in the Pantanal; both are located in **Mato Grosso do Sul** (*mah*-toh *groh*-soo doo *soo*) state. The area is huge, so visiting with a tour rather than exploring on your own by car is the way to go. Tour guides can lead you to all the magnificent flocks of rare **pássaros** (*pah*-sah-rohz) (*birds*), giant **pintados** (peen-*tah*-dooz) (*catfish*), gargantuan **tamuandás bandeiras** (tah-moo-ahn-*dahz* bahn-*day*-rahz) (*anteaters*), and fearsome **serpentes** (seh-*pen*-cheez) (*snakes*) and **jacarés** (zhah-kah-*res*) (*alligators*)!

The Southeast

REMEMBER

The Southeast region is considered the most sophisticated in Brazil; it contains the country's two richest and most famous cities: **Rio de Janeiro** (*hee*-ooh jee zhah-*nay*-roo) and **São Paulo** (sah-ooh *pah*-ooh-loo). Here you can find the best restaurants in the country as well as the cultural joys and poverty-based downers that exist in most every megalopolis in the world.

Rio (*hee*-ooh) is a gorgeous city, known for its hills, fabulous urban beaches, **o Cristo Redentor** (ooh *krees*-too heh-den-*toh*) (*Christ the Redeemer statue*, shown in Figure 13-2), **Pão de Açúcar** (*pah*-ooh jee ah-*soo*-kah) (*Sugarloaf Mountain* — with a cable car to get there), and lively locals. Popular beach areas to visit near Rio are rustic **Ilha Grande** (*eel*-yah *grahn*-jee), sophisticated **Búzios** (*boo*-zee-oohz), and historic **Paraty** (pah-rah-*chee*). Also be sure to take a quick trip to **Petrópolis** (peh-*troh*-poh-leez), established by Pedro II, the last Emperor of Brazil, as the imperial residence in 1843.

FIGURE 13-2:
The Christ the Redeemer statue is a hallmark of Rio de Janeiro.

Illustration by Elizabeth Kurtzman

SOUND NATIVE

Some visitors to Brazil are surprised to find out that many Brazilians refer to Rio by its full name, Rio de Janeiro, and not the nickname *Rio*.

NAMING RIO

Do you know what **Rio de Janeiro** (*hee*-ooh jee zhah-*nay*-roo) means? The literal translation is *River of January*. The Portuguese discovered the area on January 1, 1552, and mistook Rio's Guanabara Bay for the mouth of a river.

São Paulo is great for anthropologists. This city has huge immigrant populations from Japan, Lebanon, and Italy, among other parts of the world. It's also one of the largest cities on Earth, with more than 12 million people. Art and restaurant buffs appreciate São Paulo's nightlife and cultural institutions — the best Brazil has to offer. But the heavy traffic makes transportation difficult, and the city isn't among Brazil's prettiest. São Paulo's state beaches are at least two hours from the city, but they're gorgeous, with emerald mountains tumbling into turquoise water.

The Southeast is also home to **Minas Gerais** (*mee*-nahz zheh-*rah*-eez) (Literally: *General Mines*) state, which has no beaches, but it does have some of the tastiest food in Brazil and very friendly locals. It's full of old mines and historic towns with colonial Portuguese architecture. The most famous town is **Ouro Preto** (*oh*-ooh-roh *preh*-toh) (Literally: *Black Gold*), named after the gold mines there. There's even a town in Minas (the state's nickname) that's famous for UFO sightings; it's called **São Tomé das Letras** (*sah*-ooh toh-*meh* dahz *leh*-trahz). Some locals think there's something otherworldly about Minas state because of all the minerals in the ground there.

The South

This region of Brazil has a higher concentration of German and Polish immigrants' descendants. The sea water in the south is also a bit different from the rest of the country; it's colder.

Rio Grande do Sul (*hee*-ooh *grahn*-jee doo *soo*) state shares a border, as well as many cultural traditions, with Argentina and Uruguay. Here's where the famous Brazilian **churrascarias** (choo-hahs-kah-*ree*-ahs), Brazilian all-you-can-eat steakhouses with salad buffets, originate. The capital, **Porto Alegre** (*poh*-too ah-*leh*-gree), is a clean, safe, and pleasant city, and the people are polite but a bit more introverted compared to Brazilians in the rest of the country. Rio Grande do Sul hosts Brazil's most famous film festival in **Gramado** (grah-*mah*-doo), a town in the interior. Hikers enjoy the **Serra Gaúcha** (*seh*-hah gah-*ooh*-shah), located in the interior of the state and known for its vast plains and plateaus that resemble the American West. By the way, Rio Grande do Sul is the only Brazilian state on the Atlantic coast that's not known for its beaches!

Florianópolis (floh–ree-ah-*noh*-poh–lees) is the capital of **Santa Catarina** (*sahn*-tah kah–tah-*ree*-nah). The city is located on an island that boasts at least 32 stunning beaches — one for every day of the month! **Floripa** (floh-*ree*-pah), the local nickname for Florianópolis, is very modern; it attracts Argentine tourists in the summer.

The world–famous Iguaçu Falls are located in southern Brazil, too, on the border of **Paraná** (pah-rah-*nah*) state and Argentina. The name in Portuguese is **Foz do Iguaçu** (*fohz* doo ee-gwah-*soo*). This canyon is filled with 250 breathtaking **cataratas** (kah–tah-*rah*-tahz) (*waterfalls*), making it, in my opinion, much more impressive than Niagara Falls in the United States, which has just two waterfalls.

Talkin' the Talk

AUDIO ONLINE

Vinicius (vee-*nee*-see-ooz) is from **Florianópolis** (floh-ree-ah-*noh*-poh-lees), a city on a beautiful island in southern Brazil. It's July, and he's just arrived in **Manaus** (mah-*nah*-ooz) — the biggest city in Brazil's share of the Amazon. During breakfast, **Vinicius** chats with a hotel worker about local weather.

Vinicius:	**Que calor! Estava esperando chuva.**
	kee kah-*loh*! es-*dah*-vah es-peh-*rahn*-doh *shoo*-vah.
	It's so hot! I was expecting rain.
Worker:	**Não é só chuva aqui como todo mundo pensa.**
	nah-ooh eh soh *shoo*-vah ah-*kee* koh-moh *toh*-doo *moon*-doh *pen*-sah.
	It's not all rain here like everyone thinks.
Vinicius:	**Mas estamos em temporada de chuva, né?**
	mah-eez ehs-*tahm*-ohz ang tem-poh-*rah*-dah jee *shoo*-vah, neh?
	But we're in the rainy season, right?
Worker:	**Estamos. Na verdade, não é típico fazer sol em julho.**
	ehs-*tah*-mohz. nah veh-*dah*-jee, *nah*-ooh eh *chee*-pee-koh fah-*zeh soh*-ooh ang *zhoo*-lee-oh.
	We are. Actually, it's not normal to have sunny weather in July.

Vinicius:	**Tenho sorte, então.**
	tang-yoh *soh*-chee, en-*tah*-ooh.
	I'm lucky, then.
Worker:	**Sim, mas quem sabe — pela tarde pode precisar de um guarda-chuva.**
	sing, mah-eez kang *sah*-bee — peh-lah *tah*-jee poh-jee preh-see-*zah* jee oong goo-*ah*-dah *shoo*-vah.
	Yeah, but who knows — in the afternoon you may need an umbrella.
Vinicius:	**Obrigado pela dica. Vou levar um.**
	oh-bree-*gah*-doh peh-lah *jee*-kah. *voh* leh-*vah* oong.
	Thanks for the tip. I'll bring one along.

WORDS TO KNOW

sol	*soh*-ooh	sun
quente	*kang*-chee	hot
calor	kah-*loh*	heat
frio	*free*-ooh	cold
chuva	*shoo*-vah	rain
chover	shoh-*veh*	to rain
guarda-chuva	goo-*ah*-dah *shoo*-vah	umbrella
nuvens	*noo*-vangz	clouds
a umidade	ah ooh-mee-*dah*-jee	humidity

Talking about Going: The Verb Ir

The verb **ir** (ee) (*to go/to be going*) is so useful; I'm excited to talk about this one. Hopefully you'll feel like you're advancing your Portuguese by leaps and bounds after discovering what's in this section.

Take a look at the present tense conjugations for **ir**.

Conjugation	Pronunciation
eu vou	*eh*-ooh *voh*
você vai	voh-*seh vah*-ee
ele/ela vai	*eh*-lee/*eh*-lah *vah*-ee
nós vamos	nohz *vah*-mohz
eles/elas vão	*eh*-leez/*eh*-lahz *vah*-ooh
vocês vão	voh-*sehz vah*-ooh

Try out these sample sentences using **ir**:

> **Ela vai para a praia.** (*eh*-lah *vah*-ee *pah*-rah ah *prah*-ee-ah.) (*She's going to the beach.*)

> **Você vai para o show?** (voh-*seh vah*-ee pah-rah ooh *shoh*?) (*Are you going to the show?*)

> **Eu vou para a minha casa.** (*eh*-ooh *voh pah*-rah ah ming-yah *kah*-zah.) (*I'm going to my house.*)

> **Nós vamos ao cinema.** (nohz *vah*-mooz *ah*-ooh see-*neh*-mah.) (*We're going to the movies.*)

> **Eles vão para o show de rock.** (*eh*-leez *vah*-ooh *pah*-rah ooh show jee *hoh*-kee.) (*They're going to the rock concert.*)

REMEMBER Ir often goes with **para** (*pah*-rah). **Ir para** (*eeh pah*-rah) means *to go to.*

You can talk about the future by conjugating **ir** and adding another verb. Voilá! For example, **Nós vamos dançar** (*nohz* vah-*mohz* dahn-*sah*) means *We're going to dance.* Easy, right?

Try this formula with the verb **viajar** (vee-ah-*zhah*) (*to travel/to take a trip*), because that's what this chapter's about. In each of these phrases, someone is *going to take a trip/travel.*

Conjugation	Pronunciation
eu vou viajar	*eh*-ooh *voh* vee-ah-*zhah*
você vai viajar	voh-*seh vah*-ee vee-ah-*zhah*
ele/ela vai viajar	*eh*-lee/*eh*-lah *vah*-ee vee-ah-*zhah*
nós vamos viajar	*nohz* vah-mohz vee-ah-*zhah*
eles/elas vão viajar	*eh*-leez/*eh*-lahz *vah*-ooh vee-ah-*zhah*
vocês vão viajar	voh-*sehz vah*-ooh vee-ah-*zhah*

Here are some examples that use the future tense:

> **Eu vou viajar de trem.** (*eh*-ooh *voh* vee-ah-*zhah* jee *trang.*) (*I'm going to travel by train.*)

> **Você vai viajar de ônibus.** (voh-*seh vah*-ee vee-ah-*zhah* jee *oh*-nee-boos.) (*You're going to travel by bus.*)

> **Ela vai viajar de avião.** (*eh*-lah *vah*-ee vee-ah-*zhah* jee ah-vee-*ah*-ooh.) (*She's going to travel by plane.*)

Now you can talk about all kinds of things in the future:

> **Vamos fazer o jantar.** (*vah*-mohz fah-*zeh* ooh zhan-*tah.*) (*We're going to make dinner.*)

> **Você vai cantar para nós?** (voh-*seh vah*-ee kahn-*tah pah*-rah *nohz?*) (*You're going to sing for us?*)

> **Ele vai ligar para ela.** (*eh*-lee *vah*-ee lee-*gah pah*-rah *eh*-lah.) (*He's going to call her.*)

> **Vamos sair?** (*vah*-mohz sah-*eeh?*) (*Are we going to go out?*)

> **Vou para a Europa no mês que vem.** (*voh pah*-rah ah eh-ooh-*roh*-pah noh *mez* kee *vang.*) (*I'm going to Europe next month.*)

Talkin' the Talk

AUDIO ONLINE

Today is **Pedro's** (*ped*-roh's) first day of school. His mom is asking him what he's promised to do and not do today. Pay attention to how they use the verb **ir** to talk about the future.

Mom: **O que vai fazer hoje, meu filho?**

ooh *kee vah*-ee fah-*zeh* oh-zhee, *meh*-ooh *feel*-yoh?

What are you going to do today, my son?

Pedro: **Vou ser um bom menino.**

voh *seh* oong *boh*-oong meh-*nee*-noh.

I'm going to be a good boy.

Mom: **E o que mais?**

ee ooh *kee mah*-eez?

And what else?

Pedro: **Vou comer tudo no almoço.**

voh koh-*meh too*-doo noh ah-ooh-*moh*-soo.

I'm going to eat everything at lunch.

Mom: **Muito bem. E o que não vai fazer?**

moh-*ee*-toh *bang*. eeh ooh *kee nah*-ooh *vah*-ee fah-*zeh*?

Very good. And what are you not going to do?

Pedro: **Não vou falar em voz alta.**

nah-ooh *voh* fah-*lah* ang *vohz* ah-*ooh*-tah.

I won't talk loudly.

Mom: **E o que mais?**

ee ooh *kee mah*-eez?

And what else?

Pedro: **Vou te esperar na frente da escola no final do dia.**

voh chee eh-speh-*rah* nah *fren*-chee dah eh-*skoh*-lah noo fee-*nah*-ooh doo *jee*-ah.

I'm going to wait for you in front of the school at the end of the day.

Mom:	**Muito bom, Pedro. Eu te amo.**
	moh-*ee*-toh *boh*-oong, *ped*-roh. *eh*-ooh chee *ah*-moh.
	Very good, Pedro. I love you.
Pedro:	**Eu te amo também, mamãe.**
	eh-ooh chee *ah*-moh tahm-*bang*, *mah*-ee.
	I love you too, Mommy.

Going Through Customs

Getting through **a alfândega** (ah ah-ooh-*fahn*-deh-gah) (*customs*) at a Brazilian airport or bus station is a cinch. Authorities first review **o formulário** (ooh foh-moo-*lah*-ree-ooh) (*the form*) that you filled out on the plane. Most likely you checked the box that indicates you have **nada a declarar** (*nah*-dah ah deh-klah-rah) (*nothing to declare*), and you'll sail through.

Be careful about bringing new expensive items into Brazil — think **laptop** (*lahp-top*-ee) (*laptop computer*) or **câmera** (*kah*-meh-rah) (*camera*). By law, any person, whether Brazilian or foreigner, must pay taxes on items worth over a certain amount. Don't chance it. **Segurança** (seh-goo-*rahn*-sah) (*security*) may decide to check your **bagagem** (bah-*gah*-zhang) (*luggage*) by opening a **mala** (*mah*-lah) (*suitcase*). You could get fined an arm and a leg in **impostos** (eem-*poh*-stooz) (*taxes*).

Choosing a Place to Sleep

When you're looking for a place to hang your hat during your Brazilian vacation, it helps to know that most people choose to stay at one of these two main types of **hospedagem** (oh-speh-*dah*-zhang) (*lodging*) in Brazil:

> » **hotéis** (oh-*tay*-eez) (*hotels*) tend to be large and impersonal.
>
> » **pousadas** (poh-*zah*-dahz) (*guesthouses*) are often small and friendly.

Do I seem biased? Well, I really recommend staying at a **pousada** because the close quarters and chatty **donos** (*doh*-nooz) (*owners*) make for an excellent Portuguese classroom. The **donos** often work in the **pousada** themselves because it's their livelihood. So choosing a **pousada** can feel like staying in another family's home. They're similar to what North Americans refer to as a B&B (bed and breakfast — a small inn), except that most Brazilian **pousadas** are larger — up to 20 **quartos** (*kwah*-tooz) (*rooms*) or so.

REMEMBER

Pousadas are generally **baratas** (bah-*rah*-tahz) (*inexpensive*). A **simples** (*seem*-pleez) (*modest*) room during most of the year typically costs 150–500 reais (about $35–100) for two people **por noite** (poh noh-ee-chee) (*per night*). In popular beach spots or historic touristy towns, like **Olinda** (oh-*leen*-dah), **pousadas** can be pricier. During the high season, expect to pay about 20 percent more anywhere you go.

At large chain **hotéis**, the going rates are typically higher than at **pousadas**. Expect to pay 450 reais (about $100) and up for chain **hotéis** in major cities for most of the year; add that 20 percent or so spike if you're visiting during the high season (from the week before Christmas until after Carnaval).

Making reservations

TIP

If you plan to visit Brazil for **Réveillon** (heh-vay-*yohn*) (*New Year's Eve*) or **Carnaval** (*kah*-nah-*vah*-ooh) (*Carnival*), **faça uma reserva com antecedência** (*fah*-sah ooh-mah heh-*seh*-vah kohng ahn-teh-seh-*den*-see-ah) (*make a reservation ahead of time*)! In the case of **Carnaval**, it's best to book lodging and air travel about six months in advance. **Hotéis** and **pousadas** often offer a five-day **pacote** (pah-*koh*-chee) (*package*) that covers Saturday through Ash Wednesday. For more on **Carnaval**, see Chapter 17.

Regardless of when you're traveling, try to make a **reserva** before you **chegar** (sheh-*gah*) (*arrive*) in Brazil. That said, unless you're staying during a holiday or some special event is going on, you should be fine just showing up and scouting out the area.

You can use these questions and phrases about **hospedagem** (oh-speh-*dah*-zhang) (*accomodations*) on the phone when you're making a **reserva** or in person at the **recepção do hotel** (heh-sep-*sah*-ooh doo oh-*teh*-ooh) (*hotel reception desk*). (For more on talking on the phone in Portuguese, see Chapter 10.) The most important thing, of course, is to find out whether the place has a **vaga** (*vah*-gah) (*vacancy*):

> **Tem vaga para hoje à noite?** (tang *vah*-gah pah-rah *oh*-zhee ah *noh*-ee-chee?) (*Do you have a vacancy for tonight?*)
>
> **Tem vaga para o fim de semana?** (*tang vah*-gah pah-rah ooh *fing* jee seh-*mah*-nah?) (*Do you have a vacancy for the weekend?*)
>
> **Tem vaga para o mês que vem?** (tang *vah*-gah pah-rah ooh *mehz* kee *vang*?) (*Do you have a vacancy for next month?*)

Here are some questions that the hotel clerk may ask you:

> **Quantas pessoas?** (*kwahn*-tahz peh-*soh*-ahz?) (*How many people?*)
>
> **Por quantas noites?** (poh *kwahn*-tahz *noh*-ee-cheez?) (*For how many nights?*)
>
> **Cama de casal, ou duas camas de solteiro?** (*kah*-mah jee kah-*zah*-ooh, ooh *doo*-ahz *kah*-mahz jee soh-ooh-*tay*-roh?) (*A double bed, or two twin beds?*)

Use these phrases to respond:

> **Eu queria fazer uma reserva.** (*eh*-ooh kee-*ree*-ah fah-*zeh ooh*-mah heh-*seh*-vah.) (*I want to make a reservation.*)
>
> **É para duas pessoas.** (*eh* pah-rah *doo*-ahz peh-*soh*-ahz.) (*It's for two people.*)
>
> **Só para uma pessoa.** (*soh* pah-rah *ooh*-mah peh-*soh*-ah.) (*Just for one person.*)

Checking in and out: Registration

Checking into a **hotel** or **pousada** in Brazil follows the same process as it does in most places in the world. First, you give the desk clerk your **nome** (*noh*-mee) (*name*). If you have a **reserva**, the clerk will probably check the **detalhes** (deh-*tahl*-yeez) (*details*) on file for you and then give you the **chaves** (*shah*-veez) (*keys*) to the **quarto** (*kwah*-too) (*room*).

SOUND NATIVE

Most Brazilians refer to *the check-in process* as **o check-in** (ooh sheh-*king*). **Fazer o check-in** (fah-*zeh* ooh sheh-*king*) means *to check in*.

The hotel clerk may use these phrases:

>> **Aqui tem duas chaves.** (ah-*kee* tang *doo*-ahz *shah*-veez.) (*Here are two keys.*)

>> **Preencha essa ficha, por favor.** (*pren*-sha *eh*-sah *fee*-shah, poh fah-*voh*.) (*Fill out this form, please.*)

By federal law, each **hotel** and **pousada** must give every **hóspede** (*oh*-speh-jee) (*guest*) a **ficha** (*fee*-shah) (*form*) to fill out; you must write down basic information about yourself and list the places you've visited in Brazil and where you plan to go. This **ficha** helps **Embratur** (em-brah-*too*) (*the federal tourism board*) understand the activity of its tourists. The **ficha** uses the following terms:

>> **nome** (*noh*-mee) (*first name*)

>> **sobrenome** (*soh*-bree *noh*-mee) (*last name/surname*)

>> **país de origem** (pah-*eez* jee oh-*ree*-zhang) (*country of origin*)

>> **data** (*dah*-tah) (*date*)

>> **próximo destino** (*proh*-see-moh des-*chee*-noo) (*next destination*)

>> **número do passaporte** (*noo*-meh-roh doo pah-sah-*poh*-chee) (*passport number*)

Asking about amenities

One nice thing about Brazilian **hospedagem** is that **o café da manhã** (ooh kah-*feh* dah mahn-*yah*) (*breakfast*) almost always comes with the per-night rate. The term **café da manhã** is often shortened to just **café**, so you can ask the receptionist, **Vem incluído o café?** (*vang* een-kloo-*ee*-doh ooh kah-*feh*?) (*Is breakfast included?*). Brazilian breakfasts are ample and delicious; see Chapter 5 to find out what you can expect on the menu.

REMEMBER

What you don't generally get with a **pousada** that you do get with a **hotel** are an **academia** (ah-kah-deh-*mee*-ah) (*fitness room/gym*), a **piscina** (pee-*see*-nah) (*pool*), and a full-service **restaurante** (heh-stah-ooh-*rahn*-chee) (*restaurant*).

Before you decide where to stay, you may want to ask some **perguntas** (peh-*goon*-tahz) (*questions*) about amenities. The expression **Tem. . . ?** (tang. . . ?) (*Does it have/Do you have. . . ?*) is useful for asking about amenities. Here are some **perguntas** you can use to ask about **o quarto**:

>> **Tem banheira?** (*tang* bahn-*yay*-rah?) (*Does it have a bathtub?*)

>> **Tem ar condicionado?** (tang *ah* kohn-*dee*-see-ooh-*nah*-doo?) (*Does it have air conditioning?*)

O quarto tem ventilador? (ooh *kwah*-too *tang* ven-chee-lah-*doh?*) (*Does the room have a fan?*)

Tem cofre? (tang *koh*-free?) (*Does it have a safe deposit box?*)

Tem vista? (tang *vee*-stah?) (*Does it have a view?*)

Tem Wifi? (tang *wee*-fee?) (*Does it have WiFi?*)

O quarto tem TV à cabo? (ooh *kwah*-too *tang* teh-*veh* ah *kah*-boh?) (*Does the room have cable TV?*)

Tem Jacuzzi? (*tang* zhah-koo-zee?) (*Does it have a Jacuzzi?*)

And here are some questions you can ask about the **hotel** or **pousada** in general:

Tem piscina? (tang pee-*see*-nah?) (*Do you have a pool?*)

Tem quarto para não fumantes? (tang *kwah*-toh pah-rah *nah*-ooh foo-*mahn*-cheez?) (*Do you have non-smoking rooms?*)

Tem academia? (tang ah-kah-deh-*mee*-ah?) (*Do you have a gym?*)

To ask about transportation services, ask, **Oferecem traslado?** (oh–feh–*reh*–sah–ooh trahz–*lah*–doo?) (*Do you offer a pick–up service from the airport?*).

Getting Possessive

Now it's time to get possessive and find out how to say words like *my, yours,* and *ours.* If you're traveling with a companion, you may want to tell hotel staff what your individual requests are. For example, you may want to specify that there's a problem with **a sua cama** (ah *soo*–ah *kah*–mah) (*your bed*) or that your friend wants to put **as coisas dela** (ahz koy–zahz *deh*–lah) (*her things*) in a safe deposit box. Or maybe your towels are missing and you want to ask about **as nossas toalhas** (ahz *noh*–sahz toe–*ahl*–yahz) (*our towels*).

For all these situations, you want to use a possessive term. To express *It's mine,* say **É meu** (eh *meh*–ooh) while pointing to the item. To say *It's yours,* use **É seu** (eh *seh*–ooh). *It's ours* is **É nosso** (eh *noh*–soo).

If you want to specify what exactly is yours, change the **meu, seu,** or **nosso** to match the item; is it masculine or feminine and singular or plural? Check out Table 13-1 for possibilities of combinations for talking about *my* things, *your* things, and *our* things.

TABLE 13-1   Possessive Words — My, Your, and Our

Meaning	Singular Masculine Object	Singular Feminine Object	Plural Masculine Object	Plural Feminine Object
my	**o meu** (ooh *meh*-ooh)	**a minha** (ah *ming*-yah)	**os meus** (ooz *meh*-ooz)	**as minhas** (ahz *ming*-yahz)
your	**o seu** (ooh *seh*-ooh)	**a sua** (ah *soo*-ah)	**os seus** (ooz *seh*-ooz)	**as suas** (ahz *soo*-ahz)
our	**o nosso** (ooh *noh*-soo)	**a nossa** (ah *noh*-sah)	**os nossos** (ooz *noh*-sooz)	**as nossas** (ahz *noh*-sahz)

Here are examples of possessive terms that may come up when talking in a **hotel** or **pousada**:

>> **o meu passaporte** (ooh *meh*-ooh pah-sah-*poh*-chee) (*my passport*)

>> **as nossas bagagens** (ahz *noh*-sahz bah-*gah*-zhangz) (*our baggage*)

>> **os nossos planos** (ooz *noh*-sooz *plah*-nohz) (*our plans*)

>> **o seu cartão de crédito** (ooh *seh*-ooh kah-*tah*-ooh jee *kreh*-jee-toh) (*your credit card*)

REMEMBER

When you want to talk about *his*, *her*, or *their* things, be sure to switch the word order. Instead of putting the possessive word in front of the thing — for example, **o meu quarto** (ooh *meh*-ooh *kwah*-too) (*my room*) — name the item first and then say **de** (deh) (*of*) plus the owner. Attach the **de** to the **ele**, **ela**, or **eles/elas** (the *him*, *her*, or *them*), and drop the **e** between the words. Here are some examples:

>> **dele** (*deh*-lee) (*his*; Literally: *of him*)

>> **dela** (*deh*-lah) (*her*; Literally: *of her*)

>> **deles** (*deh*-leez) (*their*; Literally: *of them* — for all males or males and females)

>> **delas** (*deh*-lahz) (*their*; Literally: *of them* — for all females)

Technically, when you say **o quarto dele** (ooh *kwah*-toh *deh*-lee) (*his room*), you're saying *the room of him*. Name the thing first and then indicate whose it is:

>> **o dinheiro dela** (ooh jing-*yay*-roh *deh*-lah) (*her money*)

>> **a comida deles** (ah koh-*mee*-dah *deh*-leez) (*their food* — for a group of males or a group that includes at least one male)

>> **as roupas delas** (ahz *hoh*-pahz *deh*-lahz) (*their clothes* — for a group of females)

Using a specific name is the easiest way to make this concept clear. Just say the name of the thing plus **de** plus the person's name:

>> **o carro de Mário** (ooh *kah*-hoh jee *mah*-ree-oh) (*Mario's car*)

>> **o cabelo de Ana Cristina** (ooh kah-*beh*-loh jee *ah*-nah krees-*schee*-nah) (*Ana Cristina's hair*)

SOUND NATIVE

In some parts of Brazil, an **o** or an **a** comes before a person's name (depending on whether the person is male or female); when combined with **de**, these words become **do** or **da**. When you want to say *Lucia's house*, you say **a casa da Lucia** (ah *kah*-zah dah loo-*see*-ah), which literally means *the house of Lucia.*

Check out some other examples:

>> **as empresas da Petrobrás** (ahz em-*preh*-zahz dah peh-troh-*brah*-eez) (*Petrobras' companies* — Petrobrás is Brazil's largest oil company)

>> **as praias do Pará** (ahz *prah*-ee-ahz doo pah-*rah*) (*Pará state's beaches*)

FUN & GAMES

Choosing when you're going to travel is the first step in planning a fun trip to Brazil. Unscramble the names of the 12 months in Portuguese. Then assign each month to a season. Is the month part of Brazil's spring, summer, winter, or fall? (Remember, the seasons in the Southern Hemisphere are opposite of those in the Northern Hemisphere).

Illustrations by Elizabeth Kurtzman

1. zdeobmer
2. liabr
3. otsmbeer
4. ieajnor
5. oima
6. vfeeiorre
7. çomar
8. goatso
9. lhjuo
10. vnoembor
11. ojnhu
12. tbuouro

Flip to Appendix C for the answers.

Chapter **14**

Money, Money, Money

Dinheiro (jing-*yay*-roh) (*money*) — like **o amor** (ooh ah-*moh*) (*love*) — is a universal language. Yet travelers need to understand the particulars of the money system of the countries they visit in order to pay for food, supplies, services, and activities.

In this chapter, I describe Brazilian **moeda** (moh-*eh*-dah) (*currency*). So you've come to the right place to find out what kind of money is circulating in Brazil, how to access your money from a bank or ATM in Brazil, and how to exchange your moolah for the Brazilian kind. I even give you Portuguese words and phrases so you can talk about money — and spend it!

Introducing Brazilian Reais and Centavos

The **moeda** (moh-*eh*-dah) (*currency*) in Brazil is called **real** (ooh hay-*ah*-ooh) (*the real*); the plural form is **reais** (hay-*ahys*) (*reais*). **Um real** (oong hay-*ah*-ooh) (*one real*) is worth around $0.20 (five reais per one U.S. dollar) as of 2022.

Brazilian **reais** come in several **notas** (*noh*-tahs) (*bills*), each with its own color and Brazilian animal on the back. The bills are as follows: R$1 (green/hummingbird), R$2 (blue/tortoise), R$5 (purple and blue/heron), R$10 (red/parrot), R$20 (yellow/golden-faced lion monkey), R$50 (brown/jaguar), R$100 (blue/grouper fish) and R$200 (gray/maned wolf).

Coins come in R$1, R$0.50, R$0.25, R$0.10, R$0.05 and R$0.01. The **um centavo** (*oong* sen-*tah*-voh) (*one-cent*) coin is tiny and hardly worth anything. Stores usually let you get away with paying to within R$0.05 of the price to avoid having the one-cent pieces around, which are worth 1/100 of one real, or less than half of a U.S. penny.

SOUND NATIVE

Brazilian slang for **dinheiro** (jing-*yay*-roh) (*money*) is **grana** (*grah*-nah). **Estou sem grana** (eh-*stoh* sang *grah*-nah) means *I don't have any dough*.

Getting Ahold of Brazilian Currency

Luckily, Brazil isn't one of those countries where the **taxa de câmbio** (*tah*-shah jee *kahm*-bee-oh) (*exchange rate*) is confusing and you need to keep a **calculador** (kah-ooh-koo-lah-*doh*) (*calculator*) on hand all the time. As of 2022, the **taxa de câmbio** between the Brazilian **real** (hay-*ah*-ooh) and the U.S. dollar was roughly five to one. So if something costs 100 **reais**, (hay-*ahys*) that's about 20 U.S. dollars. Just divide the Brazilian price by 5. Pretty easy!

In Brazil, your best bet for getting **dinheiro** (jing-*yay*-roh) (*cash*) is by making sure to pack your **cartão de débito** (kah-*tah*-ooh jee *deh*-bee-toh) (*debit card*). The **taxa de câmbio** is generally good at ATMs. Of course, you can always ask whether a vender accepts Apple Pay/Google Pay, in which case, you can just pay using your **celular** (sel-ooh-*lah*) (*cellphone*). You can ask, **Posso pagar com Apple Pay/Google Pay?** (*poh*-soo pah-*gah* koh-oong ah-*poo* peh-ee/*goo*-goh peh-ee) (*Can I use Apple/Google Pay?*) You'll likely need cash to pay vendors at markets and small stores outside big cities.

TIP

As of press time, if you want to **trocar** (troh-*kah*) (*exchange*) U.S. **dólares** (doh-lah-reez) (*dollars*) or some other **moeda** (moh-*eh*-dah) (*currency*) to **reais,** you're likely to find the best rates at an **agência de viagens** (ah-*zhang*-see-ah jee vee-ah-zhangz) (*travel agency*) that has special permission to change money. Conversely, **aeroportos** (ah-eh-roh-*poh*-tooz) (*airports*) generally charge high commission fees; avoid **casas de câmbio** (kah-zahs jee *kahm*-bee-ooh) (*currency exchange bureaus*) there.

Brick-and-mortar **agências de viagens** (ah-*zhang*-see-ahz jee vee-*ah*-zhangz) (*travel agencies*) are getting increasingly hard to find, because most people book vacations online. **Bancos** (*bahn*-kohs) (*banks*) are usually easy to find in big cities and touristy areas. At either a **banco** or an **agência de viagens**, you can ask these questions when you want to change money:

Vocês trocam dólares por reais? (voh-*sehz troh*-kah-ooh *doh*-lah-reez poh hay-*ahys?*) (*Do you change dollars for reais?*)

A quanto está o dólar? (ah *kwahn*-toh eh-*stah* ooh *doh*-lah?) (*What's the rate for the dollar?*)

Vocês cobram taxa de comissão? (voh-*sehz koh*-brah-ooh *tah*-shah jee koh-mee-*sah*-ooh?) (*Do you charge a commission fee?*)

TIP

Of course, the value of your money in Brazil depends on the **taxa de câmbio**. Do yourself a favor by checking the **taxa de câmbio** before planning a visit to Brazil.

Talkin' the Talk

AUDIO ONLINE

We are traveling to the future. **Silvio** (*see*-ooh-vee-ooh) just got back from a trip to New York and needs to change US $100 to **reais**. He goes to a travel agency to exchange his dollars for **reais**. The exchange rate is about 2.3 **reais** to each dollar.

Silvio: **Por favor, vocês trocam dólares por reais aqui?**

poh fah-*voh*, voh-*sehz troh*-kah-ooh *doh*-lah-reez poh hay-*ahys* ah-*kee?*

Excuse me, do you change dollars for reais here?

Worker: **Trocamos.**

troh-*kah*-mooz.

Yes, we do (Literally: *We change*).

Silvio: **Vocês cobram taxa de comissão?**

voh-*sehz koh*-brah-ooh *tah*-shah jee koh-mee-*sah*-ooh?

Do you charge a fee?

Worker: **Sim, é de dois por cento. Quanto quer trocar?**

sing, eh jee *doh*-eez poh-*sen*-toh. *kwahn*-toh keh troh-*kah?*

Yes, it's 2 percent. How much do you want to change?

Silvio: **Cem dólares. A quanto está o dólar?**

sang *doh*-lah-reez. ah *kwahn*-toh eh-*stah* ooh *doh*-lah?

One hundred dollars. What's the rate for the dollar?

Worker:	**Está a dois reais e trinta e quatro.**
	eh-*stah* ah *doh*-eez hay-*ahys* ee treen-tah ee *kwah*-troh.
	It's at 2.34 reais.
Silvio:	**Tá bom. Me dá em notas de dez?**
	tah *boh*-oong. mee *dah* ang *noh*-tahz jee *dez*?
	That's fine. Can you give it to me in bills of 10?
Worker:	**Tudo bem. Não tem problema.**
	too-doh *bang*. *nah*-ooh *tang* proh-*bleh*-mah.
	Okay. No problem.

WORDS TO KNOW

Me dá. . . ?	mee <u>dah</u>. . . ?	Can you give me. . . ?
notas	<u>noh</u>-tahz	bills
não tem problema	<u>nah</u>-ooh <u>tang</u> proh-<u>bleh</u>-mah	no problem

Using Brazilian Banks and ATMs

Most towns in Brazil have a **banco** (*bahn*-koh) (*bank*) and a **caixa eletrônico** (*kah-ee*-shah eh-leh-*troh*-nee-koh) (*ATM*) that takes **cartões internacionais** (*kah-toh*-eez *een*-teh-nah-see-ooh-*nah*-eez) (*international cards*). Chances are, your ATM/debit card from home will work in Brazil. Check with your credit card company before traveling to Brazil to find out whether you can use it to withdraw local currency as well as pay for food and buy things from shops. Generally speaking, international **cartões de débito** (kah-*toh*-ees jee *deh*-bee-toh) can be used to withdraw money at **bancos,** but will be declined in **lojas** (*loh*-zhahs) stores, unless you specify the clerk to choose **crédito** (*kreh*-jee-toh) (*credit*) instead of **débito** during the sales transaction.

TIP

Citibank and HSBC are good cards to use because they're international banks. Both have several branches in **Rio** (*hee*-ooh) and **São Paulo** (sah-ooh *pah*-oo-loh). Be sure to check with your bank to find out how much the service charge is per international transaction. Also, many banks only allow you to withdraw a certain maximum amount of cash per day — about $300 a day or so. You will be out of luck if you want to make a large cash purchase in Brazil and assume you can withdraw $800 in a single ATM visit, for example.

Many of the small beach towns, especially in the north and northeast parts of Brazil, don't have any bank access, which means you need to **tirar** (chee-*rah*) (*withdraw*) as much **dinheiro** (jing-*yay*-roh) (*money*) as you think you'll need before you get there. You might get lucky and find vendors that accept Apple or Google Pay, but there's no guarantee. Also keep in mind that smaller branches of Brazilian banks probably aren't connected to the international system. So your best bet is to withdraw at least a few days' worth of money from your **conta bancária** (*kohn*-tah bahn-*kah*-ree-ah) (*bank account*) when you're in one of Brazil's larger cities.

CULTURAL WISDOM

Brazilian vendors always seem to be out of **trocado** (troh-*kah*-doh) (*change*). Getting large bills changed into smaller bills at the **banco**, right after you get it out of the **caixa eletrônico**, is best. Vendors often ask **Tem trocado?** (*tang* troh-*kah*-doh?) (*Do you have change?*) when you pay, meaning *Do you have exact change? That would help me out.*

To ask where the nearest **banco** or **caixa eletrônico** is, use these questions:

> **Por favor, sabe onde tem um caixa eletrônico?** (poh fah-*voh, sah*-bee ohn-jee *tang* oong *kah*-ee-shah eh-leh-*troh*-nee-koh?) (*Excuse me, do you know where there's an ATM?*)

> **Por favor, tem um banco perto daqui?** (poh fah-*voh, tang* oong *bahn*-koh *peh*-toh dah-*kee?*) (*Excuse me, is there a bank near here?*)

Follow up by asking whether the area in which the bank or ATM is located is reasonably **seguro** (seh-*goo*-roh) (*safe*). Say **O local é seguro?** (ooh loh-*kah*-ooh eh seh-*goo*-roh?) (*Is the area safe?*). In any case, if you avoid withdrawing money at night, and if you make sure you're withdrawing from a machine located inside a building, rather than on the street, you should be fine.

O REAL IS BORN

O real (ooh hay-*ah*-ooh) (*the real*) was created in 1994, after several years of financial instability in Brazil. During the 20 preceding years, Brazil changed **moedas** (moh-*eh*-dahs) (*currencies*) several times. **A piada** (ah pee-*ah*-dah) (*the joke*) was that as soon as you got paid, you had to do your grocery shopping because inflation was so quick that food was cheaper in the morning than in the afternoon.

Checking Prices and Making Purchases

Talking about **preço** (ooh *preh–soo*) (*the price*) of **coisas** (ahz *koy–zahz*) (*things*) in Brazil is easy. To find the **preço**, just look on the price tag if you're in a store. If you're at an informal outdoor market, you'll probably need to ask the vendor for the **preço**.

Here are common ways of asking how much an item is:

> **Quanto custa?** (*kwahn*-toh *koo*-stah?) (*How much does it cost?*)

> **Quanto é?** (*kwahn*-toh eh?) (*How much is it?*)

Here's how the vendor usually answers — three common responses that all mean the same thing. (For a review of numbers in Portuguese, see Chapter 4.)

> **Vale . . . reais.** (*vah*-lee . . . hay-*ahys.*) (*It's worth [number] reais.*)

> **Custa . . . reais.** (*koos*-tah . . . hay-*ahys.*) (*It costs [number] reais.*)

> **São . . . reais.** (*sah*-ooh . . . hay-*ahys.*) (*They're [number] reais.*)

To say a **preço**, use the following formula: the number of **reais**, plus **e** (ee) (*and*) plus the number of **centavos** (sen-*tah*-vohz) (*cents*):

>> **R$12,30**

>> **doze reais e trinta centavos** (doh-zee hay-*ahys* ee *treen*-tah sen-*tah*-vohz) (*twelve reais and thirty cents*)

>> **R$4,60**

>> **quatro reais e sessenta centavos** (*kwah*-troh hay-*ahys* ee seh-*sen*-tah sen-*tah*-vohz) (*four reais and sixty cents*)

>> **R$2,85**

>> **dois reais e oitenta e cinco centavos** (*doh*-eez hay-*ahys* ee oh-ee-*tehn*-tah ee *sing*-koh sen-*tah*-vohz) (*two reais and eighty-five cents*)

For bargaining tips, see Chapter 8.

REMEMBER

Did you notice that instead of decimal points, Brazilians use commas (like in many other parts of the world)? The decimal point is reserved in Portuguese for numbers beginning with one thousand, which looks like 1.000. So R$2.440 is *two thousand, four hundred and forty reais*. The rule is easy: Just use commas where in English the period is used, and vice-versa.

The paying verb: Pagar

Luckily, when you **paga** (pah-*gah*) (*pay*), visible **números** (noo-meh-rohz) (*numbers*) are often involved, which makes communication easier. At a nice shop or supermarket, you see the number pop up on a cash register.

TIP

If you have a problem communicating at an informal outdoor market, you can always pull out your phone and show a number on your calculator or ask the vendor to type in the number.

Here's how to conjugate **pagar**:

Conjugation	Pronunciation
eu pago	*eh*-ooh *pah*-goh
você paga	voh-*seh pah*-gah
ele/ela paga	*eh*-lee/*eh*-lah *pah*-gah
nós pagamos	*nohz* pah-*gah*-mohz
eles/elas pagam	*eh*-leez/*eh*-lahz *pah*-gah-ooh
vocês pagam	voh-*sehz pah*-gah-ooh

This is what **pagar** looks like in the past tense (for a review of the past tense, see Chapter 6):

Conjugation	Pronunciation
eu paguei	*eh*-ooh pah-*gay*
você pagou	voh-*seh* pah-*goh*
ele/ela pagou	*eh*-lee/*eh*-lah pah-*goh*
nós pagamos	*nohz* pah-*gah*-mohz
eles/elas pagaram	*eh*-leez/*eh*-lahz pah-*gah*-rah-oong
vocês pagaram	voh-*sehz* pah-*gah*-rah-oong

Here are some uses of **pagar**:

> **Quer pagar agora, ou depois?** (*keh* pah-*gah* ah-*goh*-rah, ooh deh-*poh*-eez?) (*Do you want to pay now or later?*)

> **Já pagou?** (zhah pah-*goh*?) (*Did you pay already?*)

Paguei vinte reais. (pah-*gay* veen-chee hay-*ahys*.) (*I paid 20 reais.*)

Essa empresa paga bem. (*eh*-sah em-*preh*-zah pah-gah bang.) (*This company pays well.*)

Vão pagar a conta. (*vah*-ooh pah-*gah* ah *kohn*-tah.) (*They will pay the bill.*)

Paying for items and services

You can relax when you're at a Brazilian cash register. The process for paying is similar to what you're used to. That is, you can pay with cash, a **cartão de crédito** (kah-*tah*-ooh jee *kreh*-jee-toh) (*credit card*) and maybe even Apple Pay. Just remember to bring along a form of I.D. because you may need to present it if you pay by **cartão de crédito**.

Recibos (heh-*see*-boos) (*receipts*) are easy to get in an established store, and even vendors at informal markets can sometimes give you an official handwritten receipt.

These phrases may come in handy when you're at the **caixa** (kah-ee-shah) (*register*):

Tem desconto para estudantes/idosos? (*tang* des-*kohn*-toh *pah*-rah eh-stoo-*dahn*-cheez/ee-*doh*-zoos?) (*Do you have a student/senior discount?*)

Você tem uma caneta? (voh-*seh tang* ooh-mah kah-*neh*-tah?) (*Do you have a pen?*)

Me dá um recibo, por favor? (mee *dah* oong heh-*see*-boh, poh fah-*voh*?) (*Can you give me a receipt, please?*)

The vendor may ask you:

Tem algum documento? Um passaporte? (*tang* ah-ooh-*goong* doh-koo-*men*-toh? oong pah-sah-*poh*-chee?) (*Do you have some I.D.? A passport?*)

Qual é a validade do cartão? (*kwah*-ooh *eh* ah vah-lee-*dah*-jee doo kah-*tah*-ooh?) (*What's the expiration on the card?*)

Cual é o CVV/CVN? (*kwah*-ooh *eh* ooh seh-veh-*veh*/seh-veh-*eh*-nee) (*What's the CSV/security code?* In Brazil, the code is referred to as CVV or CVN)

Quer o CPF na nota? (*keh* ooh seh-peh-*eh*-fee nah *noh*-tah?) (*Do you want your national identity number* – the Brazilian equivalent of a Social Security number in the United States – *on the receipt?*)

For this final question, you can just say **Não, obrigado/a** (*nah*-ooh, oh-bree-*gah*-doo/dah – **obrigado** if you're male; **obrigada** if you're female – for non-binary people, see Chapter 2) (*No thanks*).

.... Talkin' the Talk ....

AUDIO ONLINE

Leila (*lay*-lah) is a Portuguese woman on vacation in the Brazilian state of **Minas Gerais** (*mee*-nahs zheh-*rah*-eez). She steps into a store to buy some beautiful stone sculptures.

Leila:	**Aceita cartão Visa?**
	ah-*say*-tah kah-*tah*-ooh *vee*-zah?
	Do you accept Visa?
Cashier:	**Aceitamos.**
	ah-say-*tah*-mooz.
	Yes (Literally: *We accept*).
Leila:	(Hands the cashier the credit card) **Aqui está.**
	ah-*kee* es-*tah.*
	Here you go.
Cashier:	**Tem algum documento? Um passaporte?**
	tang ah-ooh-*goong* doh-koo-*men*-toh? oong pah-sah-*poh*-chee?
	Do you have some I.D.? A passport?
Leila:	(Shows the cashier her passport) **Sim, tenho.**
	sing, tang-yoh.
	Yes (Literally: *Yes, I have*).
Cashier:	**OK, assine aqui, por favor.**
	oh-*keh*-ee, ah-*see*-nee ah-*kee, poh* fah-*voh.*
	Okay, sign here, please.
Leila:	**Me dá um recibo, por favor?**
	mee *dah* oong heh-*see*-boh, poh fah-*voh?*
	Can you give me a receipt, please?

Cashier: **Claro.**

eh klah-roo.

Of course.

● ●

WORDS TO KNOW

Aceita cartão?	ah-<u>say</u>-tah kah-<u>tah</u>-ooh?	Do you accept credit cards?
cartão Visa	kah-<u>tah</u>-ooh <u>vee</u>-zah	Visa
cartão American Express	kah-<u>tah</u>-ooh ah-<u>meh</u>-ree-ken eh-<u>sprez</u>	American Express
cartão Mastercard	kah-<u>tah</u>-ooh mahs-teh-<u>kah</u>-jee	Mastercard
cartão Discover	kah-<u>tah</u>-ooh jees-<u>koh</u>-veh	Discover
algum documento	ah-ooh-<u>goong</u> doh-koo-<u>men</u>-toh	some I.D.
um passaporte	oong pah-sah-<u>poh</u>-chee	a passport
Assine aqui, por favor	ah-<u>see</u>-nee ah-<u>kee</u>, poh fah-<u>voh</u>.	Sign here, please.
um recibo	oong heh-<u>see</u>-boh	a receipt

SOUND NATIVE

Brazilians often repeat a verb in response to a question they're being asked. With **Tem. . . ?** (*tang. . . ?*) (*Do you have. . . ?*), the answer is **Tenho** (*tang*-yoh) (*I have*) rather than just **Sim** (*sing*) (*Yes*). You may be asked, **Você é americano?** (*voh–seh* eh ah-meh-ree–*kah*-noh?*) (*Are you American?*). If you are, the answer is **Sou** (*soh*) (*I am*), not **Sim**.

FUN & GAMES

Imagine your friend Samantha has asked you to pick up a trendy Brazilian top for her while you're on vacation in Rio. She said she'll pay you back when you return. What do you do?

Fill in the blanks with the Portuguese translation of the English words in parentheses to find out.

First, you go to a local **1.** _____ (bank) to **2.** _____ (withdraw) **3.** _____ (money). Your **4.** _____ (account) has plenty of **5.** _____ (slang for money)! You punch into the **6.** _____ (ATM) that you want R$200. The machine dispenses **7.** _____ (two bills) of R$100 reais. Then, you head to the local mall, where you find the perfect top. It's colorful, and a couple of the saleswomen are wearing it. It only costs R$50 (you think, "What a bargain!"). You then **8.** _____ (pay) for it and ask for a **9.** _____ (receipt). Finally, you head to the beach, happy that you've gotten a practical matter out of the way and can relax for the rest of the day.

See Appendix C for the answers.

- » **Taking a bus or taxi**
- » **Checking out ride-hailing apps**
- » **Driving a rental car**
- » **Looking at verbs for arriving, leaving, and waiting**
- » **Following directions to your destination**

Chapter **15**

Getting Around: Planes, Buses, Taxis, and More

Brazil is a vast country — about the same size as the United States — and the best way to **viajar** (vee-ah-*zhah*) (*go;* Literally: *to voyage*) from place to far-away place is by **ônibus** (*oh*-nee-boos) (*bus*) or **avião** (ah-vee-*ah*-ooh) (*airplane*). You can also **alugar um carro** (ah-loo-*gah* oong *kah*-hoh) (*rent a car*). **Trens** (trangz) (*trains*) are seldom used in Brazil.

REMEMBER

In Brazil's two biggest cities, **Rio** (*hee*-ooh) and **São Paulo** (sah-ooh *pah*-ooh-loh), you can find a **metrô** (meh-*troh*) (*subway*). The subways are clean, punctual, and safe. **Táxis** (*talk*-seez) (*taxis*) are safe, too, and inexpensive. Ride-hailing apps are popular in Brazil, which you can use, including **Uber** (*ooh*-beh). City **ônibus** (this word means both *bus* and *buses*) can also take you anywhere you need to go. But be cautious, especially in Rio, where **ônibus** are sometimes robbed.

Near beach areas, you can take joyrides on **buggys** (*boo*-geez) (*sand dune buggies*) or on **jangadas** (zhan-*gah*-dahz) (*sailboats*). And **barcos** (*bah*-kooz) (*boats*) of all sizes are available to you for navigating in the **mar** (mah) (*ocean*) or down a **rio** (*hee*-ooh) (*river*). Boats are the main mode of **transporte** (trahn-*spoh*-chee) (*transport*) in the Amazon. Of course, you can always see the country by **bicicleta** (bee-see-*kleh*-tah) (*bicycle*) or **a pé** (ah *peh*) (*on foot*), too.

If you have cash to burn, you can also take a **helicóptero** (eh-lee-*kohp*-teh-roo) (*helicopter*) ride. This option is particularly popular in São Paulo, supposedly the city with the second-highest helicopter air **trânsito** (*trahn*-zee-toh) (*traffic*) in the world!

This chapter tells you how to talk about getting around — from accessing **táxi** services to discussing whether buses are on schedule. Here are a few quick transportation-related phrases:

>> **Vamos embora!** (*vah*-mooz em-*boh*-rah!) (*Let's go!*)

>> **Como se chega?** (*koh*-moo see *sheh*-gah?) (*How do you get there?*)

>> **Quanto tempo demora para chegar?** (*kwahn*-toh *tem*-poh deh-*moh*-rah pah-rah sheh-*gah?*) (*How long does it take to get there?*)

>> **Eu vou para . . .** (*eh*-ooh *voh* pah-rah . . .) (*I'm going to . . .*)

>> **Vamos para . . .** (*vah*-mohz pah-rah . . .) (*We're going to . . .*)

>> **Eu fui para . . .** (*eh*-ooh *fwee* pah-rah) (*I went to . . .*)

Making a Plane Reservation

Buying your **passagem de avião** (pah-*sah*-zhang jee ah-vee-*ah*-ooh) (*airplane ticket*) online is a great idea because you can often find the lowest fares for a given **voo** (*voh*-ooh) (*flight*) on websites. Even if your trip to Brazil is still a faraway dream, it's worth checking out these websites just for new vocabulary.

Here are some key terms that you may find on a Brazilian airline's website:

>> **voe** (*voh*-ee) (*fly*)

>> **ida e volta** (*ee*-dah ee *voh*-ooh-tah) (*round trip*)

>> **somente ida** (soh-*men*-chee *ee*-dah) (*one way*)

>> **de** (jee) (*from*)

>> **para** (*pah*-rah) (*to*)

>> **data da ida** (*dah*-tah dah *ee*-dah) (*departure date*)

>> **data da volta** (*dah*-tah dah *voh*-ooh-tah) (*return date*)

>> **horário dos voos** (ooh-*rah*-ree-ooh dooz voh-*ooz*) (*flight schedule*)

>> **formas de pagamento** (*foh*-mahz jee pah-gah-*men*-toh) (*method of payment*)

>> **cadastre-se** (kah-dah-*strah*-see) (*register*)

If you're in Brazil for more than a few days and prefer buying your **voo** or planning an entire **viagem** (vee-*ah*-zhang) (*trip*) through an **agência de viagens** (ah-*zhang*-see-ah jee vee-*ah*-zhangz) (*travel agency*), you're in luck. Major Brazilian cities and towns have a ton of **agências de viagens** to choose from, and often offer **pacotes** (pah-*koh*-chees) (*packaged deals*; Literally: *packets*) that combine your **voo** and a place to stay.

Expect to **fazer fila** (fah-*zeh fee*-lah) (*wait in line*) at the **agência de viagens.** You may even need to pick up a **ficha** (*fee*-shah) (*ticket*) with a number on it. After the **agente** (ah-*zhang*-chee) (*agent*) says **Olá, posso ajudar?** (oh-*lah* poh-soo ah-zhoo-*dah?*) (*Hello, can I help you?*), they may ask some of the following questions:

Qual é o destino? (*kwah*-ooh *eh* ooh des-*chee*-noo?) (*What is the destination?*)

Por quantos dias? (poh *kwahn*-tooz *jee*-ahz?) (*For how many days?*)

Quantos passageiros? (*kwahn*-tohz pah-sah-*zhay*-rooz?) (*How many passengers?*)

Importa o horário do dia? (eem-*poh*-tah ooh ooh-*rah*-ree-ooh doh *jee*-ah?) (*Does the time of day matter?*)

Quer reservar o voo? (*keh* heh-seh-*vah* ooh *voh?*) (*Do you want to reserve the flight?*)

Como vai pagar? (*koh*-moo *vah*-ee pah-*gah?*) (*How do you want to pay?*)

TIP

You may want to ask which flight is **mais barato** (*mah*-eez bah-*rah*-toh) (*cheaper*) or whether the agency can offer you a **pacote** that includes the hotel to get a better deal.

Talkin' the Talk

Daniela (dahn-ee-eh-lah) is from São Paulo and wants to visit her aunt in Rio for the weekend. The bus trip takes five hours. Not bad, but because Daniela only has a couple of days, she decides to book a flight.

Travel agent:	**Olá, posso ajudar?**
	oh-*lah*, *poh*-soo ah-zhoo-*dah*?
	Hello, can I help you?
Daniela:	**Queria fazer uma reserva para ir para o Rio.**
	kee-*ree*-ah fah-*zeh* ooh-mah heh-*zeh*-vah pah-rah *ee* pah-rah ooh *hee*-ooh.
	I'd like to make a reservation to go to Rio.
Travel agent:	**Que dia?**
	kee *jee*-ah?
	Which day?
Daniela:	**Na sexta, retornando no domingo.**
	nah *ses*-tah, heh-toh-*nahn*-doh noh doh-*ming*-goo.
	For Friday, coming back on Sunday.
Travel agent:	**Olha, não sei se tem vaga. Mas vou checar.**
	ohl-yah, nah-ooh *say* see tang *vah*-gah. mah-eez *voh* sheh-*kah*.
	Look, I don't know if there are any seats. But I'll check.
Daniela:	**Posso retornar também na segunda, de manhãzinha.**
	poh-soo heh-toh-*nah* tahm-*bang* nah seh-*goon*-dah, jee mahn-yah-*zing*-yah.
	I can also return on Monday, really early.
Travel agent:	**Aí vai ser mais fácil.**
	ah-*ee vah*-ee *seh* mah-eez *fah*-see-ooh.
	Now that will be easier.

Daniela:	**Fantástico.**
	fahn-*tahs*-chee-koh.
	Fantastic.
Travel agent:	**Tem duas opções — na Gol e na Tam.**
	tang *doo*-ahz ohp-*soh*-eez — nah *goh*-ooh ee nah *tahm*.
	You have two options — on Gol and on Tam.
Daniela:	**Ótimo.**
	oh-*chee*-moh.
	Great.

●●●

WORDS TO KNOW

retornando	heh-toh-<u>nahn</u>-doh	returning/coming back
olha	<u>ohl</u>-yah	look
vaga	<u>vah</u>-gah	seat/available spot
checar	sheh-<u>kah</u>	to check
retornar	heh-toh-<u>nah</u>	to return
de manhãzinha	jee mah-yah-<u>zing</u>-yah	really early in the morning
vai ser	<u>vah</u>-ee <u>seh</u>	it will be
opções	ohp-<u>soh</u>-eez	options

If you're successful in reserving **uma passagem de avião** (ooh-mah pah-*sah*-zhang jee ah-vee-*ah*-ooh) (*an airplane ticket*), you'll be assigned an **assento** (ah-*sen*-too) (*seat*). You may want to request an **assento** by a **janela** (zhah-*neh*-lah) (*window*) or by a **corredor** (koh-heh-*doh*) (*aisle*).

If you want to travel by **classe executiva** (*klah*-see eh-zek-ooh-*chee*-vah) (*business class*), ask, **Tem vaga em classe executiva?** (tang *vah*-gah ang *klah*-see eh-zek-ooh-*chee*-vah?) (*Do you have a seat in business class?*). Many domestic flights don't offer **classe executiva.** If you're like most people, you'll be traveling **classe econômica** (*klah*-see eh-koh-*noh*-mee-kah) (*economy class/coach*).

REMEMBER

Brazilian airlines usually charge a **taxa de embarque** (*tah*-shah jee em-*bah*-kee) (*boarding/airport tax*). It's only about US$8 for domestic flights, and $12 for international flights (as of press time). The **taxa** is included in the price quote you get for a flight, as is required by Brazilian law.

Here are some useful words and phrases you can use when you travel internationally to and from Brazil:

>> **comprar uma passagem de avião** (kohm-*prah* ooh-mah pah-*sah*-zhang jee ah-vee-*ah*-ooh) (*to buy an airline ticket*)

>> **levar o seu passaporte** (leh-*vah* ooh *seh*-ooh pah-sah-*poh*-chee) (*to bring your passport*)

>> **preencher os formulários** (pren-*sheh* ooz foh-moo-*lah*-ree-ooz) (*to fill out forms*)

>> **o visto** (ooh *vee*-stoh) (*the visa*)

>> **o consulado** (ooh kohn-soo-*lah*-doh) (*the consulate*)

>> **a embaixada** (ah em-bah-ee-*shah*-dah) (*the embassy*)

>> **o aeroporto** (ooh ah-*eh*-roh-*poh*-too) (*the airport*)

>> **duty-free** (*doo*-chee *free*) (*duty-free* — yes, Brazilians use the English term!)

REMEMBER

If you're coming to Brazil through another South American country, you'll probably be asked for proof of vaccination against **febre amarela** (*feh*-bree ah-mah-reh-lah) (*yellow fever*). Airport vaccination officials are quite strict, yet they often don't even alert your airline that you need it. I should know; I was stuck in Bolivia for a few days because Brazil wouldn't accept me without my vaccination papers! They were sitting in my apartment in São Paulo, but I had no idea I'd need them to reenter the country.

Taking Buses

I generally recommend taking an **ônibus** (*oh*-nee-boos) (*bus*) for traveling long distances in Brazil and a taxi or the subway to get around cities. Taxis are cheap, and **ônibus** travel within a city can **demorar** (deh-moh-*rah*) (*take a long time*).

The best way to get a **passagem de ônibus** (pah-*sah*-zhang jee *oh*-nee-boos) (*bus ticket*) is to go to the **rodoviária** (hoh-doh-vee-*ah*-ree-ah) (*central bus station*). These stations are gigantic in Brazil, and you have many **companhias** (kohm-pahn-*yee*-ahz) (*companies*) to choose from. The competing bus **companhias** have offices right next to each other at the **rodoviária**. A sign above the ticket window tells you the name of the company and to which **cidades** (see-*dah*-jeez) (*cities*) the buses travel.

Try to buy your bus ticket the day before you plan to leave to make sure you get a **poltrona** (pohl-*troh*-nah) (*seat*). And keep in mind that bus seating in Brazil is usually assigned — not first come, first served.

You can pay for your **passagem de ônibus** using **dinheiro** (jing-*yay*-roh) (*money/cash*) or a **cartão de crédito** (kah-*tah*-ooh jee *kreh*-jee-toh) (*credit card*). Brazilians do not use checks.

TIP

Bring your **passaporte** (pah-sah-*poh*-chee) (*passport*) when buying a **passagem de ônibus**, because the bus company needs to write down the number. Keep your passport handy as you get on the bus. You'll need to fill out a form with your **origem** (oh-*ree*-zhang) (*name of city you're traveling from/origin*) and **destino** (des-chee-noo) (*destination*) as well as your **nome** (noh-mee) (*name*), passport number, and the **data** (dah-tah) (*date*).

Brazilians use military time for bus tickets. Eight o'clock at night becomes **às vinte horas** (ahz *veen*-chee oh-rahz) (*at 8 p.m./at 20:00 hours*). See Chapter 4 for more on telling time.

CULTURAL WISDOM

Riding city buses in Brazil is a great way to see how polite Brazilians are with each other. The buses are often crowded, and the people sitting down regularly offer to hold bags for the people who have to stand; it's an optional act of courtesy. Brazilians are also very good about giving up seats to the **idosos** (ee-*doh*-zooz) (*elderly*), **deficientes** (deh-fee-see-*en*-cheez) (*disabled*), and **mulheres grávidas** (mool-*yeh*-reez grah-vee-dahz) (*pregnant women*).

If you plan to ride an **ônibus urbano** (oh-nee-boos ooh-*bah*-noh) (*city bus*), here are some phrases you can use to talk either with the **motorista** (moh-toh-*ree*-stah) (*driver*) or another **passageiro** (pah-sah-*zhay*-roo) (*passenger*):

>> **Vai para. . .?** (*vah*-ee *pah*-rah. . .?) (*Does [the bus] go to. . .?*)

>> **Pára na Rua. . .?** (*pah*-rah nah *hoo*-ah. . .?) (*Does [the bus] stop on . . . Street?*)

>> **Quanto (que) é?** (*kwahn*-toh kee *eh*?) (*How much?*)

Traveling by Taxi

Táxis (*talk*-seez) (*taxis*) are plentiful, but not so cheap in Brazil. **Uber** (*ooh*-beh) is more popular and cheaper (I cover Uber and other taxi apps in the very next section, "Using Ride-Hailing Apps"). You can flag one down in the street, just like you would in big cities in other countries. If you're having trouble finding one, ask someone whether a **ponto de táxi** (*pohn*-toh jee *talk*-see) (*place where taxis line up to wait for passengers*) is nearby.

CULTURAL
WISDOM

The **ponto de táxi** is basically a bunch of taxi drivers sitting on a bench, sometimes watching a **novela** (noh-*veh*-lah) (*soap opera*) or **jogo de futebol** (*zhoh*-goo jee foo-chee-*bah*-ooh) (*soccer match*) on a TV.

Here's some taxi talk:

Pára . . . por favor. (pah-rah . . . poh fah-*voh*.) (*To [destination], please.*)

Sabe como chegar em. . . ? (*sah*-bee *koh*-moo sheh-*gah* ang. . . ?) (*Do you know how to get to. . . ?*)

Quanto custaria? (*kwahn*-toh koos-tah-*ree*-ah?) (*How much would it cost?*)

É perto? (eh *peh*-too?) (*Is it close?*)

É longe? (eh *lohn*-zhee?) (*Is it far?*)

TIP

Be sure to have **dinheiro** (jing-*yay*-roh) (*money/cash*) on hand, because Brazilian **taxistas** (talk-*sees*-tahs) (*taxi drivers*) may or may not accept credit cards. Check with the driver before getting in the car: **Aceita cartão?** (ah-*say*-tah kah-*tah*-ooh) (*Do you accept cards?*) Locals generally do not offer a **gorjeta** (goh-*zheh*-tah) (*tip*).

Your **taxista** (tahk-*sees*-tah) (*taxi driver*) will undoubtedly have a cellphone and a GPS app on hand to get directions on navigating to your **destino** (des-*chee*-noo) (*destination*). To avoid confusion, you can just hold up your phone, with the **endereço** (en-deh-*reh*-soo) (*address*) clearly labeled on a **mapa** (*mah*-pah) (*map*).

Talkin' the Talk

AUDIO
ONLINE

Ricardo (hee-*kah*-doo) and Carolina (kah-roh-*lee*-nah) are visiting Rio for the first time. They're staying at a hotel near **Ipanema** (ee-pah-*neh*-mah) beach and are dying to see the city's world-famous soccer stadium **Maracanã** (mah-rah-kah-*nah*). They flag down a taxi.

Ricardo: **Olá, o Maracanã é longe?**

oh-*lah*, ooh mah-rah-kah-*nah* eh *lohn*-zhee?

Hi, is Maracanã Stadium far?

Taxi driver: **Não, é pertinho.**

nah-ooh, eh peh-*ching*-yoo.

No, it's really close.

Carolina:	**Quanto custaria?**
	kwahn-toh koos-tah-ree-ah?
	How much would it cost?
Taxi driver:	**Uns dez reais.**
	oonz dez hay-ahys.
	About 10 reais.
Ricardo:	**Tá bom.**
	tah boh-oong.
	Okay.
Taxi driver:	**É a sua primeira vez no Rio de Janeiro?**
	eh ah soo-ah pree-may-rah vez noh hee-ooh jee zhah-nay-roh?
	Is it your first time in Rio?
Ricardo:	**É. E nós estamos muito entusiasmados para ver o famoso Maracanã.**
	eh. ee nohz eh-stah-mooz moh-ee-toh en-too-zee-ahz-mah-dooz pah-rah veh ooh fah-moh-zoo mah-rah-kah-nah.
	Yeah. And we're really excited to see the famous Maracanã.
Taxi driver:	**Não tem jogo hoje.**
	nah-ooh tang zhoh-goo oh-zhee.
	There's no game today.
Carolina:	**Tudo bem, é só para ver.**
	tah boh-oong, eh soh pah-rah veh.
	That's okay, it's just to take a look.

• •

WORDS TO KNOW

pertinho	peh-ching-yoo	very close/close by
uns	oonz	about/some
vez	vez	time
entusiasmados	en-too-zee-ahz-mah-dooz	excited
famoso	fah-moh-zoo	famous

Using Ride-Hailing Apps

You can **baixar** (*bah-ee-shah*) (*download*) popular ride-hailing **apps** (ahps) (apps — yep, the same word as in English) in Brazil (such as Uber, 99 Taxi or Cabify, at press time) the same way you would download apps in English at home: by searching for the app in Google Play, the App Store on your iPhone, or wherever you normally find your apps.

Brazil is home to at least a couple of unique ride-hailing apps, in addition to the global apps such as Uber. If you're in Rio, try Taxi.Rio, a cheaper alternative to big-name apps that is run by the local government. If you're a woman visiting São Paulo, you may want to check out Lady Driver, an app created to help females safely arrive at destinations. The app connects female **motoristas** (moh-toh-rees-tuz) (*drivers*) with female **passageiras** (pah-sah-*zhay*-roos/rahs) (*female passengers*).

You can always ask a local for advice on the best local ride-hailing app to use: **Por favor, pode recomendar um app de taxi que é popular aqui?** (poh-fah-*vohr*, poh-jee heh-koh-men-*dah* oong *ahp* jee *tahk*-see kee *eh* poh-poo-*lah* ah-*kee*?) (*Would you please recommend a ride-hailing app that's popular here?*)

You, the **passageiro/a** (pah-sah-*zhay*-roh/rah) (*passenger*) can let the **motorista** (moh-toh-*rees*-tah) (*driver*) know your **destino** (des-*chee*-noo) (*destination*). Since many drivers in Brazil don't speak **inglês** (eeng-*glehs*) (*English*), you can hold your **telefone** (teh-leh-*foh*-nee) (*phone*) up to confirm to show the driver the exact address. Here are some useful terms to help navigate ride-hailing apps:

>> **uma viajem** (*oo*-mah vee-*ah*-zhang) (*a ride*)

>> **solicitar agora** (soh-lee-see-*tah* ah-*goh*-rah) (*request now*)

>> **local de partida** (loh-*kah*-ooh jee pah-*chee*-dah) (*starting point*)

>> **local de destino** (loh-*kah*-ooh jee des-*chee*-noo) (*ending point; destination*)

>> **agendar para mais tarde** (ah-zhen-*dah* pah-rah *my*-eez *tah*-jee) (*schedule for later*)

>> **cadastre-se** (kah-*dah*-streh-seh) (*register*)

Here are some phrases you can use with the **motorista** (*driver*):

Pode confirmar a taxa? (poh-jee kohn-feeh-*mah* ah *tah*-shah?) (*Can you confirm the rate/fee?*)

Pode me mostrar a taxa no seu telefone? (*poh*-jee mee moh-*strah* ah *tah*-shah noo *seh*-ooh teh-leh-*foh*-nee?) (*Can you show me the rate on your phone?*) (Use this phrase if you don't understand the numbers the driver is saying. The driver can simply write the numbers on their phone to prevent any misunderstandings).

Quanto tempo para chegar? (*kwahn*-too *tem*-poo pah-rah shay-*gah*) (*How long will the ride take?*)

Renting a Car

If you're the adventurous type, you may decide to **alugar um carro** (ah-loo-*gah* oong *kah*-hoh) (*rent a car*) from a **locadora de carros** (loh-kah-*doh*-rah jee *kah*-hohz) (*car rental agency*) in Brazil. Several international rental agencies, such as Hertz and Avis, operate in Brazil.

TIP

You can use your **carteira de habilitação** (kah-*tay*-rah jee ah-*bee*-lee-tah-*sah*-ooh) (*driver's license*) from home to drive in Brazil, although it's a good idea to get it translated by a **tradutor juramentado** (trah-doo-*toh* zhoo-rah-men-*tah*-doo) (*official translator*). The local consulate of your country or a local travel agency should be able to suggest where you can find a **tradutor juramentado**. Or, get an international driver's license.

Cars tend to be small in Brazil. Be sure to first ask what **modelos** (moh-*deh*-lohz) (*types of cars*) are available. The roads can get pretty bad, too, so ask about road conditions. Also, Brazil doesn't have nearly the number of **postos de gasolina** (*poh*-stooz jee gah-zoo-*lee*-nah) (*gas stations*) as North America, for example, so keep your **tanque de gasolina** (*tan*-kee jee gah-zoh-*lee*-nah) (*gas tank*) pretty full!

CULTURAL WISDOM

You may scratch your head when you first visit a **posto de gasolina**: In addition to **gasolina**, you sometimes have the option of choosing **álcool** (ah-ooh-kohl) (*ethanol*), a fuel made from **cana de açúcar** (*kah*-nah jee ah-*soo*-kah) (*sugarcane*) that's much cheaper than **gasolina**. A gallon of ethanol costs a little more than half the price of a gallon of gasoline. All cars made in Brazil in the last decade use technology that converts the ethanol to car fuel. So ask the rental car agent what type of fuel your rental can use.

People at the rental agency refer to the checking-out and checking-in of the car as the **retirada** (heh-chee-*rah*-dah) (*check-out*) and **devolução** (deh-voh-loo-*sah*-ooh) (*check-in*).

Here are some questions to ask at a **locadora**:

Tem um carro disponível para hoje? (*tang* oong *kah*-hoh jee-spoh-*nee*-veh-ooh pah-rah *oh*-zhee?) (*Do you have a car available for today?*)

Qual é a tarifa diária para esse modelo? (*kwah*-ooh *eh* ah tah-*ree*-fah jee-*ah*-ree-ah pah-rah *eh*-see moh-*deh*-loo?) (*What's the day rate for this [car] make?*)

Este carro usa álcool? (es-chee *kah*-hoo oo-zah *ah*-ooh-kohl?) (*Does this car take ethanol?*)

Oferecem quilometragem livre? (oh-feh-*reh*-sang kee-loo-meh-*trah*-zhang leev-ree?) (*Do you offer unlimited mileage?*)

Tem assistência vinte-quatro horas? (*tang* ah-see-*sten*-see-ah *ving*-chee kwah-troh *oh*-rahz?) (*Do you have 24-hour roadside assistance?*)

Tem alguma promoção? (*tang* ah-ooh-*goo*-mah proh-moh-*sah*-ooh?) (*Do you have any deals/promotions going on?*)

Oferece um plano de seguro? (oh-feh-*reh*-see oong *plah*-noh jee seh-*goo*-roh?) (*Do you offer an insurance plan?*)

Getting familiar with the Portuguese words for the parts of a car can help, especially if you notice a scratch, dent, or other problem at **retirada**. Here are the basics:

>> **freios** (*fray*-oohz) (*brakes*)

>> **motor** (moh-*toh*) (*engine*)

>> **pára brisa** (*pah*-rah *bree*-sah) (*windshield*)

>> **rodas** (*hoh*-dahz) (*wheels*)

>> **volante** (voh-*lahn*-chee) (*steering wheel*)

You may also need to ask about general driving in Brazil:

As estradas em . . . são boas ou ruins? (ahz eh-*strah*-dahz ang . . . *sah*-ooh *boh*-ahz oh hoo-*eenz*?) (*Are the roads in [insert location] good or bad?*)

Tem um mecânico por aqui? (*tang* oong meh-*kah*-nee-koh poh ah-*kee*?) (*Is there a mechanic around here?*)

Interpreting traffic signs

Brazil uses the international road sign system. The shapes and colors of **placas de trânsito** (*plah*-kahs jee *trahn*-zee-toh) (*road signs*) in Brazil are pretty much the same as they are in English-speaking countries. Most are easy to understand; you don't need to speak Portuguese to understand most **placas de trânsito**.

The only two **placas de trânsito** that use or reference Portuguese words are Stop signs, which say **Pare** (*pah*-ree) (*Stop*) and have eight sides like stop signs in most of the world, and No Parking signs, which show a capital **E with a line through it.** The **E** references the word **estacionamento** (eh-*stah*-see-oh-nah-*men*-toh) (*parking*).

Parking it

Parking your car in Brazil can be a hazard, particularly if you're in **São Paulo** (sah-ooh *pah*-ooh-loh) or **Rio** (*hee*-ooh), where **carros** (*kah*-hooz) (*cars*) are frequently broken into. You really don't need to have a car in these cities; it's safer to take the bus, taxi, or subway.

If you do have a car, many upscale restaurants, clubs, and other venues offer **serviço de valet** (seh-*vee*-soo jee vah-*leh*) (*valet service*), where a worker takes your car, parks it, and then brings it back to you at the end of the night. In these situations, you usually pay the valet fee with your bill inside the venue. A valet typically parks cars **na rua** (nah *hoo*-ah) (*on the street*), but if something happens to the car, you can sue.

TIP

At night, keep your **janelas** (zhah-*neh*-lahz) (*windows*) rolled up when driving to prevent an easy robbery at a **semáforo** (seh-*mah*-foh-roh) (*stoplight*). Some Brazilians even roll slowly forward at a red light, not even stopping, to prevent a robber with a weapon from approaching their car.

The best reason to **alugar** (ah-loo-*gah*) (*rent*) or **pedir emprestado** (peh-*jee* em-pres-*tah*-doo) (*borrow*) a car in Brazil is to get to a remote **praia** (*prah*-ee-ah) (*beach*), where buses don't go very often. Otherwise, you're more of a robbery target if you have a car.

If you do drive in Brazil, take note that you must be completely sober while driving. No amount of alcohol — not even a single glass of **cerveja** (seh-*veh*-zhah) (*beer*) — is allowed. Zero-tolerance laws on drunk driving are enforced with vigor in most large cities, especially during the weekend, with many checkpoints. If the breathalyzer detects any amount of alcohol, the legal consequences won't be mild. Better to be safe than sorry!

Talking About Coming and Going

When talking about transportation, timeliness is a fundamental issue. The main terms to know are **cedo** (*seh*-doo) (*early*) and **atrasado** (ah-trah-*zah*-doo) (*late*). **O atraso** (ooh ah-*trah*-zoo) refers to *the delay*.

Here are some sentences that include these terms:

O avião está atrasado. (ooh ah-vee-*ah*-ooh eh-*stah* ah-trah-*zah*-doo.) (*The plane is late.*)

O ônibus está atrasado? (ooh oh-nee-boos eh-*stah* ah-trah-*zah*-doo?) (*Is the bus late?*)

O metrô de São Paulo é muito pontual. (ooh meh-*troh* jee sah-ooh *pah*-ooh-loh eh moh-*ee*-toh pon-too-*ah*-ooh.) (*The São Paulo subway system is very punctual.*)

O atraso vai ser de uma hora. (ooh ah-*trah*-zoo *vah*-ee *seh* jee ooh-mah *oh*-rah.) (*The delay will be an hour.*)

In this section, I tell you how to use the verbs most associated with travel: *arriving, leaving,* and *waiting.*

Announcing an arrival

Chegar (sheh-*gah*) (*arriving/to arrive*) someplace is what you're ultimately trying to do when you enter an **avião** (ah-vee-*ah*-ooh) (*plane*), an **ônibus** (oh-nee-boos) (*bus*), or a **táxi** (*talk*-see) (*taxi*).

Chegar na hora (sheh-*gah* nah *oh*-rah) means *to arrive on time,* and **chegar a tempo** (sheh-*gah* ah tem-*poo*) means *to arrive in time.* **Pontual** (pon-too-*ah*-ooh) means *punctual.*

Here are the basic conjugations.

Conjugation	Pronunciation
eu chego	*eh*-ooh *sheh*-goh
você chega	voh-*seh sheh*-gah
ele/ela chega	*eh*-lee/*eh*-lah *sheh*-gah
nós chegamos	nohz sheh-*gah*-mooz
eles/elas chegam	*eh*-leez/*eh*-lahz sheh-*gah*-ooh
vocês chegam	voh-*sehz sheh*-gah-ooh

The past tense of **chegar** looks like this. (See Chapter 6 for more on forming the past tense.)

Conjugation	Pronunciation
eu cheguei	*eh*-ooh sheh-*gay*
você chegou	voh-*seh* sheh-*goh*
ele/ela chegou	*eh*-lee/*eh*-lah sheh-*goh*
nós chegamos	nohz sheh-*gah*-mooz
eles/elas chegaram	*eh*-leez/*eh*-lahz sheh-*gah*-rah-oong
vocês chegaram	voh-*sehz* sheh-*gah*-rah-oong

Here are some sentences that include the different tenses of **chegar**:

É sempre melhor chegar cedo. (eh *sem*-pree mel-*yoh* sheh-*gah* seh-doo.) (*It's always better to arrive early.*)

Acha que vamos poder chegar a tempo? (*ah*-shah kee *vah*-mooz poh-*deh* sheh-*gah* ah tem-poh?) (*Do you think we'll be able to arrive in time?*)

Vou chegar logo. (voh sheh-*gah* loh-goo.) (*I'm going to arrive soon.*)

Quase não chegamos a tempo. (*kwah*-zee *nah*-ooh sheh-*gah*-mohz ah *tem*-poh.) (*We almost didn't arrive in time.*)

SOUND NATIVE

Chega! (*sheh*-gah!) is a popular and useful expression that means *Stop it! Enough!*

Cheguei! (sheh-*gay!*) is what you say when you arrive someplace — *I'm here!*

Talking about leaving

Sair (sah-*ee*) (*to leave*) is a verb Brazilians use to talk about leaving. **Sair** also means *to go out*, as in *to go out and party.*

REMEMBER

Sair doesn't have that easy **-ar** ending that makes some verbs such a breeze to conjugate. Plus, it's a very short word so you have to conjugate based just on the root **sa.** But the normal rules apply to this conjugation. (See Chapter 2 for more on conjugation rules.)

Conjugation	Pronunciation
eu saio	*eh*-ooh *sah*-ee-oh
você sai	voh-*seh sah*-ee
ele/ela sai	*eh*-lee/*eh*-lah *sah*-ee
nós saimos	nohz sah-*ee*-mooz
eles/elas saem	*eh*-leez/*eh*-lahz *sah*-ang
vocês saem	voh-*sehz sah*-ang

And this is the past tense. (Find details on the past tense in Chapter 6.)

Conjugation	Pronunciation
eu saí	*eh*-ooh sah-*ee*
você saiu	voh-*seh* sah-ee-ooh
ele/ela saiu	*eh*-lee/*eh*-lah sah-ee-ooh
nós saímos	nohz sah-*ee*-mooz
eles/elas saíram	*eh*-leez/*eh*-lahz sah-*ee*-rah-ooh
vocês saíram	voh-*sehz* sah-*ee*-rah-ooh

Here are some handy phrases that include **sair**:

> **Ela já saiu.** (*eh*-lah *zhah* sah-ee-ooh.) (*She already left.*)

> **O ônibus sai às onze e quarenta.** (ooh *oh*-nee-boos *sah*-ee ahz *ohn*-zee ee kwah-*ren*-tah.) (*The bus leaves at 11:40.*)

> **A que horas sai o avião para Londres?** (ah *kee oh*-rahz *sah*-ee ooh ah-vee-*ah*-ooh pah-rah *lonh*-dreez?) (*What time does the plane leave for London?*)

Discussing the wait

Unfortunately, waiting is usually a big part of traveling. But don't think of waiting at a Brazilian **rodoviária** (hoh-doh-vee-*ah*-ree-ah) (*central bus station*) or **aeroporto** (ah-*eh*-roh-*poh*-too) (*airport*) as a pain. Instead, pick up a local **revista** (heh-*vee*-stah) (*magazine*) and soak up Brazilian culture, or observe and listen to the people around you!

First things first though: Conjugate **esperar** (eh–speh–*rah*) (*to wait/to wait for*) so you know how to talk about the stuff you hear and see while waiting around.

Conjugation	Pronunciation
eu espero	*eh*-ooh eh-*speh*-roo
você espera	voh-*seh* eh-*speh*-rah
ele/ela espera	*eh*-lee/*eh*-lah eh-*speh*-rah
nós esperamos	nohz eh-speh-*rah*-mooz
eles/elas esperam	*eh*-leez/*eh*-lahz eh-speh-*rah*-rah-ooh
vocês esperam	voh-*sehz* eh-speh-*rah*-rah-ooh

And here's the past tense. (See Chapter 6 for more on talking about the past.)

Conjugation	Pronunciation
eu esperei	*eh*-ooh eh-speh-*ray*
você esperou	voh-*seh* eh-speh-*roh*
ele/ela esperou	*eh*-lee/*eh*-lah eh-speh-*roh*
nós esperamos	nohz eh-speh-*rah*-mooz
eles/elas esperaram	*eh*-leez/*eh*-lahz eh-speh-*rah*-rah-ooh
vocês esperaram	voh-*sehz* eh-speh-*rah*–rah-ooh

Here are some example sentences:

Eu esperei duas horas. (*eh*-ooh eh-speh-*ray doo*-ahz oh-rahz.) (*I waited two hours.*)

Espere aqui, por favor. (eh-*speh*-ree ah-*kee*, poh fah-*voh*.) (*Wait here, please.*)

Onde se espera para o ônibus número 78? (ohn-jee see es-*peh*-rah pah-rah ooh *oh*-nee-boos noo-meh-roh seh-*ten*-tah ee *oh*-ee-toh?) (*Where do people wait for bus number 78?*)

Navigating Cityscapes

Some Brazilian cities are easier to figure out than others. **São Paulo** (sah-ooh *pah*-ooh-loh), for example, is very confusing, even for longtime residents. It's huge, yet it has a limited subway network that only covers about 10 percent of the city, making a car or taxi essential to getting around there. Brazil's largest city also doesn't have much of a real **centro da cidade** (*sen*-troh dah see-*dah*-jee) (*city center*) like other big cities in the world, so that makes orientation even more difficult.

Rio (*hee*-ooh) and **Brasília** (brah-*zee*-lee-ah), the capital of Brazil, are **fáceis** (*fah*-say-ees) (*easy*) and **divertidas** (*jee*-veh-*chee*-dahs) (*fun*) to figure out. They're relatively small cities, especially compared with São Paulo, and have just a few areas of major interest.

The two main touristic **regiões da cidade** (heh-zhee-*oh*-eez dah see-*dah*-jee) (*areas of the city*) in Rio to visit are **a zona sul** (ah soh-nah soo) (*the southern zone*), where the famous beaches **Copacabana** (koh-pah-kah-*bah*-nah) and **Ipanema** (ee-pah-*neh*-mah) are, and the **centro histórico** (*sen*-troh ee-*stoh*-ree-koh) (*historic center*), where you can find the **museus** (moo-zay-ooz) (*museums*) and **galerias de arte** (gah-leh-*ree*-ahz jee *ah*-chee) (*art galleries*).

Brasília is a very new **cidade** (see-*dah*-jee) (*city*). It was founded in 1960 and designed by Brazil's most famous architect, Oscar Niemeyer. The city is very well organized in large city **quarteirões** (kwah-tay-*roy*-eez) (*blocks*).

Here are some helpful terms for checking out a city:

>> **beira-mar** (bay-rah-*mah*) (*shoreline/seafront*)
>> **centro comercial** (*sen*-troh koh-meh-see-*ah*-ooh) (*shopping center*)
>> **igreja** (ee-*greh*-zhah) (*church*)
>> **jardim** (zhah-*jing*) (*garden*)
>> **mar** (mah) (*ocean*)
>> **morro** (*moh*-hoo) (*hill*)
>> **parque** (*pah*-kee) (*park*)
>> **ponte** (*pohn*-chee) (*bridge*)
>> **praça** (*prah*-sah) (*plaza*)
>> **rio** (*hee*-ooh) (*river*)
>> **rua** (*hoo*-ah) (*street*)

DISCOVERING SÃO PAULO

A great place to start your journey to explore São Paulo is **Avenida Paulista** (*ah*-veh-*nee*-dah pah-ooh-*lees*-tah) (*Paulista Avenue*), the most famous and busiest street in this giant city. Known mainly for the number of banks, **Avenida Paulista** also has at least four shopping centers with multiscreen cinema complexes, two music and arts centers, one of South America's most famous modern art museums (MASP), two of the city's largest hospitals, and at least five of the city's five-star hotels — all in a two-mile stretch.

Talking about distance

One question you may want to ask before hearing a complicated set of directions is **Fica longe?** (*fee*–kah *lohn*–zhee?) (*Is it far?*). Here are some handy words you can use for estimating distances:

» **longe** (*lohn*-zhee) (*far*)

» **perto** (*peh*-too) (*close*)

» **muito longe** (moh-*ee*-toh *lohn*-zhee) (*really far*)

» **muito perto** (moh-*ee*-toh *peh*-too) (*really close*)

» **pertinho** (peh-*cheen*-yoh) (slang for *really close*)

.... Talkin' the Talk ....

AUDIO ONLINE

Taís (tah-*eez*) is deciding how to spend her afternoon in **Vitória** (vee-*toh*-ree-ah), the capital of **Espírito Santo** (eh-*spee*-ree-toh *sahn*-too) state. Should she go to the shopping mall or beach or both? She asks the hotel concierge how far away each place is from the hotel.

Taís: **Por favor, qual fica mais perto, o shopping ou a praia?**

poh fah-*voh*, kwah-ooh *fee*-kah *mah*-eez *peh*-too, ooh *shoh*-ping ooh ah *prah*-ee-ah?

Excuse me, which is closer, the shopping mall or the beach?

Concierge:	**A praia é bem mais perto. Fica aqui do lado.**
	ah *prah*-ee-ah eh *bang* mah-eez *peh*-too. *fee*-kah ah-*kee* doo *lah*-doo.
	The beach is much closer. It's just on the other side of here.
Taís:	**E o shopping? Como se chega?**
	ee ooh *shoh*-ping? *koh*-moh see *sheh*-gah?
	And the mall? How do you get there?
Concierge:	**Olha, tem que pegar dois ônibus, ou pode ir de táxi.**
	ohl-yah, *tang* kee peh-*gah* doh-eez oh-nee-boos, oh *poh*-jee *eeh* jee *tahk*-see.
	Look, you have to take two buses, or you can take a taxi.
Taís:	**Tudo bem. O shopping parece longe demais para ir hoje.**
	too-doh *bang*. ooh *shoh*-ping pah-*reh*-see *lohn*-zhee jee-*mah*-eez pah-rah *eeh oh*-zhee.
	All right. The mall seems too far away for today.
Concierge:	**Melhor relaxar na praia.**
	mel-*yoh* heh-lah-*shah* nah *prah*-ee-ah.
	It's better to relax on the beach.

•••

WORDS TO KNOW

mais perto	<u>mah</u>-eez <u>peh</u>-too	closer
bem mais perto	<u>bang mah</u>-eez <u>peh</u>-too	a lot closer
tem que pegar . . .	<u>tang</u> kee peh-<u>gah</u> . . .	you have to take . . .
pode	<u>poh</u>-jee	you can
ir de táxi	<u>eeh</u> jee <u>tahk</u>-see	go by taxi
parece	pah-<u>reh</u>-see	it seems
longe demais	<u>lohn</u>-zhee jee-<u>mah</u>-eez	too far
relaxar	heh-lah-<u>shah</u>	to relax

Asking for directions

The word **onde** (*ohn*-jee) (*where*) can be your best friend as you navigate new places in Brazil. *Where is . . .* is expressed in two ways: **Onde é** (*ohn*-jee *eh*) and **Onde fica** (*ohn*-jee *fee*-kah).

REMEMBER

Onde é is used more for people and general locations, whereas **Onde fica** and **Onde está** are used to ask for the precise location of something. If someone asks, **Onde é Macau?** (*ohn*-jee *ee* mah-*kah*-ooh?) (*Where is Macau?*), they expect to hear an answer like "in Asia" — not the precise latitude and longitude of Macau. But if you ask, **Onde fica aquela loja?** (*ohn*-jee *fee*-kah ah-*keh*-lah *loh*-zhah?) (*Where is that store?*), you expect someone to tell you what street it's on, the cross street, and maybe the exact address so you can find it.

Generally speaking, **onde fica** is more commonly used than **onde está**.

Try out these phrases that use **onde**:

>> **Para onde. . . ?** (*pah*-rah *ohn*-jee. . . ?) (*To where. . . ?*)

>> **Onde é. . . ?** (*ohn*-jee *eh*. . . ?) (*Where is. . . ?*)

>> **Sabe onde fica. . . ?** (*sah*-bee *ohn*-jee *fee*-kah. . . ?) (*Do you know where . . . is located?*)

>> **Sabe onde tem. . . ?** (*sah*-bee *ohn*-jee *tang*. . . ?) (*Do you know where there's a. . . ?*)

>> **De onde. . . ?** (*jee ohn*-jee. . . ?) (*From where. . . ?*)

Here are some questions that use **onde**:

Onde é a Rua Pedralbes? (*ohn*-jee *eh* ah *hoo*-ah peh-*drah*-ooh-beez?) (*Where is Pedralbes Street?*)

Sabe onde fica o Citibank? (*sah*-bee *ohn*-jee *fee*-kah ooh *see*-chee-*bahn*-kee?) (*Do you know where the Citibank is located?*)

Sabe onde tem um supermercado? (*sah*-bee *ohn*-jee *tang* oong *soo*-peh-meh-*kah*-doh?) (*Do you know where there's a supermarket?*)

Another useful phrase is **Estou procurando . . .** (eh-*stoh* proh-koo-*rahn*-doh . . .) (*I'm looking for . . .*). The phrase uses the verb **procurar** (proh-koo-*rah*) (*to look/search for*). The verb is related to the old-fashioned word *procure* in English.

Talkin' the Talk

AUDIO ONLINE

Silvio (*see*-ooh-vee-ooh) is in Rio and wants to visit the nearby city of **Petrópolis** (peh-*troh*-poh-leez) for the weekend. He asks a passerby for directions.

Silvio:

Por favor, sabe onde passa o ônibus número sessenta e dois?

poh fah-*voh*, *sah*-bee *ohn*-jee *pah*-sah ooh *oh*-nee-boos *noo*-meh-roh seh-*sen*-tah ee *doh*-eez?

Excuse me, do you know where bus number 62 passes?

Passerby:

Para onde quer ir?

pah-rah *ohn*-jee *keh ee*?

Where would you like to go?

Silvio:

Quero ir para Petrópolis.

keh-roo *ee* pah-rah peh-*troh*-poh-leez.

I want to go to Petropolis.

Passerby:

Não conheço sessenta e dois, mas o quarenta e três vai para Petrópolis.

nah-ooh kohn-*yeh*-soo seh-*sen*-tah ee *doh*-eez, *mah*-eez ooh kwah-*ren*-tah ee *trehz vah*-ee pah-rah peh-*troh*-poh-leez.

I don't know the number 62, but the 43 goes to Petropolis.

Silvio:

Sabe onde tem uma parada do quarenta e três?

sah-bee *ohn*-jee *tang* ooh-mah pah-*rah*-dah doo kwah-*ren*-tah ee *trehz*?

Do you know where there's a bus stop for the 43?

Passerby:

Tem uma do lado do Pão de Açúcar. Sabe onde é?

tang ooh-mah doo *lah*-doo doo *pah*-ooh jee ah-*soo*-kah. *sah*-bee *ohn*-jee *eh*?

There's one next to the Pão de Açúcar (the name of a supermarket chain). Do you know where it is?

Silvio:	**Não, não sei.**
	nah-ooh, nah-ooh say.
	No, I don't.
Passerby:	(Points to a nearby corner) **Fica naquela esquina. Tá vendo?**
	fee-kah nah-keh-lah eh-skee-nah. tah ven-doh?
	It's on that corner. Do you see it?

WORDS TO KNOW

passa	pah-sah	passes
ônibus	oh-nee-boos	bus
número	noo-meh-roh	number
conheço	kohn-yeh-soo	I know/I'm familiar with
vai	vah-ee	goes
parada	pah-rah-dah	bus stop
do lado	doo lah-doo	next to
naquela	nah-keh-lah	on that
esquina	eh-skee-nah	street corner
Tá vendo?	tah ven-doh?	Do you see it?

Discussing how to get there

When Brazilians give directions, they use what grammar books call a *command* or *imperative*. It's what people use in English, too. The word *command* sounds authoritarian, but that's what you're asked to do — tell people where to go.

REMEMBER

In Portuguese, you can give commands to someone by using the **você** (voh–*seh*) (*you*) form of the verb. Simply use the **-e** ending for **-ar** verbs or the **-a** ending for **-er/-ir** verbs. The verb **ir** (ee) (*to go*), however, is irregular; it takes the form **vá** (vah) for commands. Just like in English, the subject of the sentence (*you*/**você**) is implied, so you can start the sentence with the verb: **Cruze a ponte** (*kroo*–zee ah *pohn*–chee) (*Cross the bridge*).

Here are some words you can use to give directions:

>> **vá** (*vah*) (*go*)

>> **cruze** (*kroo*-zee) (*cross*)

>> **olhe** (*ohl*-yee) (*look*)

>> **pegue** (*peh*-gee) (*take*)

>> **siga** (*see*-gah) (*follow*)

>> **suba** (*soo*-bah) (*go up*)

>> **desça** (*deh*-sah) (*go down*)

Getting directions straight is hard enough in English — let alone in Portuguese! And when spatial directions are thrown in on top of unfamiliar words and phrases, finding your way can be difficult. For instance, someone may explain that you can change your money at a travel agency that's **na frente** (nah *fren*–chee) (*in front of*) a certain large bank, or that the museum you're looking for is **do lado** (doo *lah*-doh) (*next to*) a subway station. Table 15-1 lists some common terms for explaining location.

TABLE 15-1 ## Words That Describe Locations

Term	Pronunciation	Translation
na frente	nah *fren*-chee	*in front of*
atrás	ah-*trah*-eez	*behind*
à direita	ah jee-*ray*-tah	*to the right*
à esquerda	ah es-*keh*-dah	*to the left*
abaixo/embaixo	ah-*bah*-ee-shoh/em-*bah*-ee-shoh	*below/underneath*
acima/em cima	ah-*see*-mah/*ang see*-mah	*above/on top of*
do/ao lado	doo/*ah*-ooh *lah*-doh	*next to*
dentro de	*den*-troh *jee*	*inside*
fora de	*foh*-rah *jee*	*outside*

Say these sentences that use directional words and phrases:

Fica na frente dos Correios. (*fee*-kah nah *fren*-chee dooz koh-*hay*-ohz.) (*It's in front of the post office.*)

Está atrás da igreja. (eh-*stah* ah-*trah*-eez dah ee-*greh*-zhah.) (*It's behind the church.*)

Vá para a direita. (*vah* pah-rah ah jee-*ray*-tah.) (*Go to the right.*)

Fica à esquerda da loja. (*fee*-kah ah es-*keh*-dah dah *loh*-zhah.) (*It's to the left of the store.*)

Pegue a segunda à direita. (*peh*-gee ah seh-*goon*-dah ah jee-*ray*-tah.) (*Take the second right.*)

O carro está fora da garagem. (ooh *kah*-hoh eh-*stah foh*-rah dah gah-*rah*-zhang.) (*The car's outside of the garage.*)

Straight ahead can be expressed a couple of ways: **direto** (jee-*ray*-too) (Literally: *direct*) or **reto** (*heh*-too) (Literally: *straight*). If you're driving, someone may give you one of these directions:

Pode ir reto. (*poh*-jee ee heh-too.) (*You can go straight.*)

Segue sempre direto. (*seh*-gee sem-pree jee-*reh*-too.) (*It's straight ahead, all the way*; Literally: *It's all straight.*)

Siga essa rua direto. (*see*-gah eh-sah *hoo*-ah jee-*reh*-toh.) (*Follow this road all the way.*)

Some of these connector words may come into play as well to communicate when to do something:

» **quando** (*kwahn*-doh) (*when*)

» **antes** (*ahn*-cheez) (*before*)

» **depois** (deh-*poh*-eez) (*after*)

» **logo** (*loh*-goo) (*as soon as*)

» **até** (ah-*teh*) (*until*)

Just for fun, here are two complicated sentences that show you how you can use those connector words:

Vá até a praça, e depois pegue a Rua Almirantes. (*vah* ah-*teh* ah *prah*-sah, ee deh-*poh*-eez *peh*-gee ah *hoo*-ah ah-ooh-mee-*rahn*-cheez.) (*Go until you reach the plaza, and then take Almirantes Street.*)

Suba a Faria Lima, e depois pegue a Bandeirantes quando chegar no posto de gasolina. (*soo*-bah ah fah-*ree*-ah *lee*-mah, ee deh-*poh*-eez *peh*-gee ah bahn-day-*rahn*-cheez kwahn-doh sheh-*gah* noo *poh*-stoo jee gah-zoh-*lee*-nah.) (*Go up Faria Lima, and then take Bandeirantes when you get to the gas station.*)

Over here, over there

Take a look at how you can say *here*, *there*, and *over there*. These words work in so many settings — when you're asking for directions, browsing in a shop, or pointing out a person on the street. These terms help you distinguish the physical position of the item or person in relation to your location.

» **aqui** (ah-*kee*) (*here*)

» **ali** (ah-*lee*) (*there*)

» **lá** (lah) (*over there*)

REMEMBER

In general, **lá** is reserved for places that are a few minutes' walk away or more. If you're talking about an office that's upstairs, use **ali**. If you're talking about your car parked on the other side of town, use **lá**. Also use **lá** to talk about stuff happening really far away, like in other countries.

Here are some examples:

Estamos aqui. (eh-*stah*-mohz ah-*kee*.) (*We're here.*)

Está ali, na mesa. (eh-*stah* ah-*lee*, nah *meh*-zah.) (*It's there, on the table.*)

Lá nos Estados Unidos, se come muita comida-rápida. (*lah* nohz eh-*stah*-dohz ooh-*nee*-dooz, see *koh*-mee moh-*ee*-tah koh-*mee*-dah *hah*-pee-dah.) (*Over there in the United States, they eat a lot of fast food.*)

Vá lá. (*vah* lah.) (*Go over there.*)

SOUND NATIVE

If you're in a taxi and you realize you've reached your destination — perhaps a bit earlier than you previously explained to the driver — say *Let me off right here* with **Aqui-ó!** (ah-*kee*-*ah*!) (*Right here!*) to sound like a native Brazilian.

The one time you won't use **aqui** when you mean *here* is with the expression *Come here*, where **cá** replaces **aqui**: **Vem cá!** (vang *kah*!) (*Come here!*).

FUN & GAMES

You've decided to do a heptathlon (you know, like a triathlon, except with seven types of activities) in Brazil. Okay, you'll just be sitting and enjoying the ride in most cases — not exerting your physical strength — but it'll be a challenge, nonetheless.

Match the drawing of each of the modes of transportation you plan to use to its Portuguese equivalent.

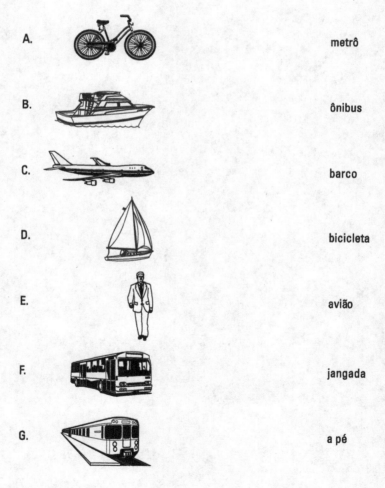

A. metrô

B. ônibus

C. barco

D. bicicleta

E. avião

F. jangada

G. a pé

Flip to Appendix C to check your answers.

Chapter **16**
Going to Sporting Events

Brazil has definitely proven that it has international sporting chops; it hosted the 2014 **Copa do Mundo** (*koh*-pah doh *moon*-doh) (*World Cup*) and the 2016 **Jogos Olímpicos de Verão** (*zhoh*-gooz oh-*leem*-pee-kohs jee veh-*rah*-ooh) (*Summer Olympic Games*).

Whether you plan to attend a high-profile sporting event in Brazil or you just want to watch a classic **jogo de futebol** (*zhoh*-goo jee foo-chee-*bah*-ooh) (*soccer game*) while visiting the country or hanging with your Brazilian friend at a bar in your neighborhood, this chapter offers some tips for talking about the games in Portuguese.

If you happen to be a **torcedor de futebol** (toh-seh-*doh* jee foo-chee-*bah*-ooh) (*soccer fan*), definitely try to see one of Brazil's famous soccer teams play in a live match. Try getting tickets to see **Corinthians** (koh-*reen*-chee-unz) in **São Paulo** (sah-ooh *pah*-ooh-loh) or **Flamengo** (flah-*mang*-goh) in **Rio** (hee-ooh). You'll make friends fast if you wear a home-team **camisa** (kah-*mee*-zah) (*sports jersey*).

CULTURAL WISDOM

It used to be illegal to consume **cerveja** (seh-*veh*-zhah) (*beer*) or any other type of **bebida alcoólica** (beh-*bee*-dah ah-ooh-*koh*-lee-kah) (*alcoholic drink*) at major Brazilian soccer stadiums because of potential fan violence. Thanks to pressure from FIFA, Brazil lifted the beer ban in 2014 when it hosted the World Cup. Today, some stadiums allow low-alcohol beer, and some still ban it. Don't be surprised to see police with guns at a Brazilian **estádio** (es-*tah*-jee-oh) (*stadium*). They're there to keep the peace among passionate fans.

Getting Hip to Soccer — Brazil's National Pastime

As may be the case for some of my fellow Americans, **futebol** (foo-chee-*bah*-ooh) (*soccer*) brings back memories of third-grade after-school sports. In my case, thinking of the **esporte** (eh-*spoh*-chee) (*sport*) conjures a memory of my adrenaline rush to the goal post that was quickly followed by a realization that I'd made the **gol** (*goh*-oo) (*goal*) for the wrong **time** (*chee*-mee) (*team*).

Within a few months in Brazil, though, I knew the names of several regional soccer **times** (*chee*-meez) (*teams* — **times** is a Brazilian translation of the English word *teams*) and how to associate specific friends with specific teams. People get upset if you peg them as a **torcedor** (toh-seh-*doh*) (*fan*) of the wrong team.

CULTURAL WISDOM

If you catch my drift, soccer is a very important topic in Brazil — maybe even more important than **religião** (heh-lee-zhee-*ah*-ooh) (*religion*). So the fastest way to make an **amigo** (ah-*mee*-goo) (*friend*) may be to share the same favorite Brazilian soccer team.

Most of Brazil's famous soccer teams are in **Rio** (*hee*-ooh) or **São Paulo** (sah-ooh *pah*-oo-loh). Here's a quick rundown of teams by area:

>> **Flamengo** (flah-*mang*-goh): City of Rio

>> **Botafogo** (boh-tah-*foh*-goh): City of Rio

>> **São Paulo** (sah-ooh *pah*-oo-loh): City of São Paulo

>> **Corinthians** (koh-*reen*-chee-unz): City of São Paulo

>> **Santos** (*sahn*-tohz): Coastal city in São Paulo state

> *Note:* Santos was Pelé's first professional team. **Pelé** (peh-*leh*), if you haven't heard of him, is known as one of the greatest soccer players in the world of all time. He played during the 1960s and 1970s.

So what do the millions of Brazilians do who don't live in São Paulo or Rio? They either root for the best team near them, or, in some cases, they just pick either Flamengo or Corinthians as their favorite team. These two teams always seem to have it out for each other.

REMEMBER

Brazilians also like to play **futebol!** You're more likely to see casual games on Brazil's **nordeste** (noh-*des*-chee) (*northeast*) beaches than on beaches in Rio or São Paulo state. That's because the farther south you go, the wealthier Brazil gets. And the richer a community is, the more money it has to build **campos de futebol** (*kahm*-pooz jee foo-chee-*bah*-ooh) (*soccer fields*).

Check out some basic soccer terms:

- **atacante** (ah-tah-*kahn*-chee) (*striker*)
- **avante** (ah-*vahn*-chee) (*forward*)
- **bola** (*boh*-lah) (*ball*)
- **campo de futebol** (*kahm*-poh jee foo-chee-*bah*-ooh) (*soccer field*)
- **goleiro** (goh-*lay*-roh) (*goalie*)
- **jogadores** (zhoh-gah-*doh*-reez) (*players*)
- **meia** (*may*-ah) (*midfielder*)
- **técnico** (*tek*-nee-koh) (*coach*)
- **volante** (voh-*lahn*-chee) (*defensive midfielder*)
- **zagueiro** (zah-*gway*-roh) (*center-back*)

Buying Tickets

If you want to **comprar** (kohm-*prah*) (*buy*) an **ingresso** (eeng-*greh*-soh) (*ticket*) to a **jogo** (*zhoh*-goo) (*game*), you don't need to physically go to the **bilheteria** (beel-yeh-teh-*ree*-ah) (*ticket office*) at the **estádio** (es-*tah*-jee-oh) (*stadium*) to get the goods; you can do it online. But if the site doesn't offer an English translation and you don't feel comfortable enough with your level of Portuguese to close the deal, then **fazer fila** (fah-*zeh fee*-lah) (*waiting in line*) at the **bilheteria** is still an option.

You may need to use these words when buying an **ingresso**:

- **data** (*dah*-tah) (*date*)
- **hora** (*oh*-rah) (*time*)
- **local do jogo** (loh-*kah*-ooh doo *zhoh*-goo) (*location of match*)
- **quantidade de ingressos** (kwan-tee-*dah*-jee jee een-*greh*-sooz) (*quantity of tickets*)
- **preço** (*preh*-soo) (*price*)
- **número da cadeira** (*noo*-meh-roh dah kah-*day*-rah) (*seat number*)
- **camarote** (kah-mah-*roh*-chee) (*box seat*)

>> **portão** (pohr-*tah*-ooh) (*entrance gate;* Literally: *big door*)

Note: **Porta** means *door;* add the **-ão** ending to indicate *big* for any object or thing.

The *main entrance* to any **estádio** is known as the **portão principal** (pohr-*tah*-ooh preen-see-*pah*-ooh) (Literally: *principal big door*).

··········· Talkin' the Talk ··············

AUDIO ONLINE

Hélio (*eh*-lee-oh) and **José** (zhoh-*zeh*) are standing in line outside the famous **Maracanã** (*mah*-rah-kah-*nah*) stadium in Rio to get tickets to see the Flamengo soccer team play.

Hélio: **Qual dia queremos?**

kwah-ooh *jee*-ah keh-*reh*-mooz?

Which day do we want?

José: **23 de janeiro, é um sábado?**

veen-chee *trehs* jee zhah-*nay*-roh, eh oong sah-bah-doh?

January 23, is that a Saturday?

Hélio: **Sim, é. Tá bom.**

sing, eh. tah *boh*-oong.

Yes, it is. Good.

José: **Compramos os ingressos mais baratos?**

kohm-*prah*-mooz oohz eeng-*greh*-sooz *mah*-eez bah-*rah*-tooz?

Should we buy the cheapest tickets?

Hélio: **Com certeza.**

koh-oong seh-*teh*-zah.

Of course.

José:	**Nós não somos gente de camarote, infelizmente.**
	nohz nah-ooh soh-mooz zhang-chee jee kah-mah-roh-chee, een-feh-leez-men-chee.
	We're not box-seat folks, unfortunately.
Hélio:	**Mas qualquer cadeira é melhor que assistir pela tevê!**
	mah-eez kwah-ooh-keh kah-day-rah eh mel-yoh kee ah-sees-chee peh-lah teh-veh!
	But any seat is better than watching on TV!

•••

WORDS TO KNOW

qual	kwah-ooh	which
tá bom	tah boh-oong	okay
baratos	bah-rah-tooz	cheap (plural)
com certeza	koh-oong seh-teh-zah	of course
gente	zhang-chee	people
infelizmente	een-feh-leez-men-chee	unfortunately
mas	mah-eez	but
qualquer	kwah-ooh-keh	any
melhor	mel-yoh	better

Finding Your Seat

In the days before Brazil secured its place as host for the World Cup in 2014 and Summer Olympics in 2016, Brazilian stadiums could be an uncomfortable experience. Fans in the nosebleed sections sat wherever they could find a place on concrete steps. Closer to the field were actual **cadeiras** (kay-*day*-rahs) (*seats*), but those tickets were more expensive than for those seats found higher up. And the priciest tickets were, and still are, for **camarotes** (kah-mah-*roh*-cheez) (*box seats*).

Now, after renovations, all tickets are for **cadeiras numeradas** (kah-*day*-rahs noo-meh-*rah*-dahs) (*numbered seats*), which makes it easier to figure out where to sit.

TIP

As in most sporting and entertainment venues, the easy way to quickly find your spot is to show an attendant your **ingresso** (een-*greh*-soo) (*ticket*) and ask, **Por favor, onde fica a minha cadeira?** (poh fah-*voh*, ohn-jee *fee*-kah ah *meen*-yah kah-*day*-rah?) (*Where is my seat, please?*). Flip to Chapter 15 to find the Portuguese words for directions.

For now, these are some words you may hear from the attendant as they motion with their arm:

>> **aqui** (ah-*kee*) (*here*)

>> **ali** (ah-*lee*) (*there*)

>> **lá** (lah) (*over there, farther away*)

Try to look at a **mapa** (*mah*-pah) (*map*) of the **estádio** (es-*tah*-jee-oh) (*stadium*) before heading inside. That way, you can at least see which numbered or lettered **portão** (pohr-*tah*-ooh) (*gate*) you should enter from the outside to get close to your **cadeira**.

Ordering Brazilian Concessions

It may be difficult to get **cerveja** (seh-*veh*-zhah) (*beer*) at your soccer stadium, depending on which stadium you're in and what the state laws are, but getting **comida** (koh-*mee*-dah) (*food*) is **fácil** (*fah*-see-ooh) (*easy*)! Here are some items you're likely to find for sale inside a Brazilian **estádio** (es-*tah*-jee-oh) (*stadium*) at a **quiosque** (kee-*ah*-skee) (*concession stand*):

>> **amendoim** (ah-men-doh-*eem*) (*peanuts*)

>> **cachorro quente** (kah-*sho*-hoh *kang*-chee) (*hot dog*)

>> **coxinha** (koh-*sheen*-yah), a fried ball of flour dough filled with shredded chicken or ground beef

>> **espetinho de carne** (es-peh-*cheen*-yoh jee *kah*-nee) (*beef shish kabob*)

>> **milho cozido** (*meel*-yoh koh-*zee*-doo) (*a boiled ear of corn*)

>> **pipoca** (pee-*poh*-kah) (*popcorn*)

>> **prato feito** (prah-toh *fay*-toh), complete meals that typically include rice, beans, meat, and salad

>> **sanduíches** (sahn-*dwee*-sheez) (*sandwiches*)

>> **sorvete** (soh-*veh*-chee) (*ice cream*)

> **Note:** This word sounds a little like *sorbet*.

When ordering, figure out how many items you want. Is **um/uma** (oong/*ooh*-mah) (*one*; masculine/feminine) enough? Or do you need **dois/duas** (doh-eez/*doo*-ahz) (*two*; masculine/feminine) or **três** (trehs) (*three*; no gender here)? (For the skinny on numbers, see Chapter 4.)

Check out these examples:

>> **uma coxinha** (*ooh*-mah koh-*sheen*-yah) (*one coxinha*)

>> **dois sanduíches** (*doh*-eez sahn-*dwee*-sheez) (*two sandwiches*)

>> **três pipocas** (trehs pee-*poh*-kuz) (*three popcorns*)

TIP

Use this formula to order: **Eu quero** (eh-ooh *keh*-roo) (*I want*) plus the quantity plus the name of what you want plus **por favor** (poh fah-*voh*) (*please*).

Practice these example orders:

> **Eu quero um sorvete, por favor.** (eh-ooh *keh*-roo oong soh-*veh*-chee, poh fah-*voh*.) (*I want one ice cream, please.*)

> **Eu quero dois cachorros quentes, por favor.** (eh-ooh *keh*-roo doh-eez kah-*shoh*-hooz *kang*-cheez, poh fah-*voh*.) (*I want two hot dogs, please.*)

To sound extra polite, you can try it this way instead: **Eu gostaria** (eh-ooh goh-stah-*ree*-ah) (*I'd like*) plus the quantity plus the name of what you want plus **por gentileza** (poh *zhang*-chee-lay-zah) (*if you would be so kind*).

Depending on the situation — ordering at a restaurant, buying a drink at a bar, getting tickets for an event, or another scenario — pick the most appropriate formula to place your order.

Making Sense of Yelling Fans

CULTURAL WISDOM

Brazilian **torcedores** (toh-seh-*doh*-reez) (*fans*) are a spirited bunch! Get ready for a **barulhento** (*bah*-rool-*yen*-too) (*noisy*) crowd who let loose their **paixão** (pah-eeh-*shah*-ooh) (*passion*) in the stands. **Cerveja** (seh-*veh*-zhah) (*beer*) may not be allowed at some stadiums, but good clean **rivalidade** (hee-vahl-ee-*dah*-jee) (*rivalry*) is allowed, of course, and often on full display!

CHEERING FOR CORÍNTHIANS

Here's the cheer for Corínthians, São Paulo's most popular soccer team:

Aqui tem um bando de louco (ah-*kee tang* oong *bahn*-doh jee *loh*-koo) (*Here is a group of crazy people*)

Louco por ti, Corínthians (*loh*-koo poh *chee*, koh-*reen*-chee-unz) (*Crazy for you, Corinthians*)

Aqueles que acham que é pouco (ah-*keh*-leez kee *ah*-shah-ooh kee eh *poh*-koo) (*Some who think it's not enough*)

Eu vivo por ti Corínthians (eh-ooh *vee*-voh poh *chee* koh-*reen*-chee-unz) (*I live for you Corinthians*)

Eu canto até ficar rouço (eh-ooh *kahn*-toh ah-*teh* fee-*kah* hoh-soo) (*I sing until I'm hoarse*)

Eu canto para te empurrar (eh-ooh *kahn*-toh pah-rah *chee* em-poo-*hah*) (*I sing to push you*)

Vamos, vamos, meu timão (*vah*-mooz, *vah*-mooz, *meh*-ooh chee-*mah*-ooh) (*Let's go, let's go, my great team*)

Vamos meu timão (*vah*-mooz *meh*-ooh *chee*-mah-ooh) (*Let's go, my great team*)

Não pára de lutar (nah-ooh *pah*-rah jee loo-*tah*) (*Don't stop fighting*)

If you're interested in hearing what this cheer sounds like or to hear the cheer for Rio's top team, Flamengo, try an online search by entering the name of the team and **"canto de torcida"** (*kahn*-toh jee toh-*see*-dah) (*fans' chant*).

Here are the most common **gritos** (*gree*-tooz) (*shouts*) from people in the stands during a Brazilian sporting event:

» **Vai, vai, vai!** (*vah*-ee, *vah*-ee, *vah*-ee!) (*Go, go, go!*)

» **Gooooool!** (gooooooohl!) (*Goal!* [for soccer only])

The latter is accompanied by either a comical expression of delight or disgust, depending on how the **time** (*chee*-mee) (*team*) of the **torcedor** (toh-seh-*doh*) (*fan*) is doing.

Some vulgar expressions circulate in the stands, too, but I don't include those here.

At Brazilian soccer matches, people wave lots of colorful **bandeiras** (ban-*day*-rahs) (*flags*) and sing cheers. Each **torcida** (toh-*see*-dah) (*group of fans for a particular team*) has its own cheer. See the nearby sidebar "Cheering for Corínthians" to learn the **São Paulo** (sah-ooh *pah*-ooh-loh) team cheer.

Talking about Sports

When you're talking about **esportes** (es-*poh*-cheez) (*sports*), you probably need to use the verbs **jogar** (zhoh-*gah*) (*to play sports*), **praticar** (prah-chee-*kah*) (*to practice*), and **preferir** (preh-feh-*reeh*) (*to prefer*). Lucky for you, this is exactly where you can find out how to use these sport-talk verbs.

Using the verb jogar, to play

Jogo (*zhoh*-goo) means *game* or *match* in Portuguese. Similarly, the verb **jogar** means *to play*, as in *to play sports*.

Take a look at the present tense conjugations for **jogar**.

Conjugation	Pronunciation
eu jogo	*eh*-ooh *zhoh*-goo
você joga	voh-*seh zhoh*-gah
ele/ela joga	*eh*-lee/*eh*-lah *zhoh*-gah
nós jogamos	nohz zhoh-*gah*-mooz

Conjugation	Pronunciation
eles/elas jogam	*eh*-leez/*eh*-lahz *zhoh*-gah-ooh
vocês jogam	voh-*sehz zhoh*–gah-ooh

Here are some sentences that include **jogar**:

Eu jogo futebol. (*eh*-ooh *zhoh*-goo foo-chee-*bah*-ooh.) (*I play football.*)

Você sabe jogar vôleibol? (voh-*seh* sah-bee zhoh-*gah* voh-lay-*bohl?*) (*Do you know how to play volleyball?*)

O time joga basquete muito bem! (ooh *chee*-mee *zhoh*-gah bah-*skeh*-chee moh-*ee*-toh *bang!*) (*The team plays basketball very well!*)

SOUND NATIVE

If you want to talk about *playing* as in *having fun*, then use the verb **brincar** (bring–*kah*):

>> **As crianças brincam.** (ahz kree-*ahn*-sahz *bring*-kah-ooh.) (*The children play.*)

>> **Eu só estou brincando.** (eu-ooh *soh* es-*toh* bring-*kahn*-doh.) (*I'm just joking.*)

Playing an instrument is expressed with the verb **tocar**. (Read more about how to use **tocar** and see plenty of examples in Chapter 9.)

Considering practice

Before any **jogo,** you can bet a **time** (*chee*-mee) (*team*), especially a pro team, has done a lot of practicing. **Praticar** sounds like *practice* in English, and it's an **–ar** verb, so this one is pretty simple. (Find more about verb conjugation in Chapter 2).

REMEMBER

You can use **praticar** to talk about practicing anything; **praticar** also means to *do* a sport.

Here are the present tense conjugations for **praticar**.

Conjugation	Pronunciation
eu pratico	*eh*-ooh prah-*chee*-koo
você pratica	voh-*seh* prah-*chee*-kah
ele/ela pratica	*eh*-lee/*eh*-lah prah-*chee*-kah

Conjugation	Pronunciation
nós praticamos	nohz prah-chee-*kah*-mooz
eles/elas praticam	*eh*-leez/*eh*-lahz prah-*chee*-kah-ooh
vocês praticam	voh-sehz prah-*chee*-kah-ooh

Here are some sample sentences using **praticar**:

O time pratica pouco. (ooh *chee*-mee prah-*chee*-kah *poh*-ooh-koh.) (*The team doesn't practice a lot;* Literally: *The team practices little*.)

Eu pratico capoeira. (eh-ooh prah-*chee*-koo kah-poh-*ey*-rah.) (*I do capoeira — a Brazilian martial arts form.*)

Você pratica violão muito? (voh-*seh* prah-*chee*-kah vee-oh-*lah*-ooh moh-*ee*-toh?) (*Do you practice the guitar a lot?*)

Elas praticam futebol todos os dias. (*eh*-luz prah-*chee*-kah-ooh foo-chee-*bah*-ooh *toh*-dooz ooz *jee*-ahz.) (*They practice soccer every day.*)

Expressing preferences

Preferir (preh–feh–*reeh*) (*to prefer*) is a versatile verb you can use to talk about all the different sports and your preferences for all kinds of things: foods, movies, vacation spots, tomorrow's plans, and so on.

Vamos lá (*vah*–mooz lah) (*let's start*) by seeing how to conjugate **preferir**. It's an –**ir** verb (more on these in Chapter 2), so the endings are a little different from **jogar** and **praticar**.

Conjugation	Pronunciation
eu prefiro	*eh*-ooh preh-*fee*-roh
você prefere	voh-*seh* preh-*feh*-ree
ele/ela prefere	*eh*-lee/*eh*-lah preh-*feh*-ree
nós preferimos	nohz preh-feh-*ree*-mooz
eles/elas preferem	*eh*-leez/*eh*-lahz preh-*feh*-rang
vocês preferem	voh-*sez* preh-*feh*-rang

Practice using **preferir** with these sample sentences:

Qual você prefere: correr ou caminhar? (*kwah*-ooh voh-*seh* preh-*feh*-ree: koh-*heh* oh kah-meen-*yah?*) (*Which do you prefer: running or walking?*)

Eu prefiro assistir jogos de futebol locais. (*eh*-ooh preh-*fee*-roh ah-sees-*chee zhoh*-gooz jee foo-chee-*bah*-ooh loh-*kah*-eez.) (*I prefer to watch local soccer games.*)

Eles preferem viajar durante o inverno. (*eh*-leez preh-*feh*-rang vee-ah-*zhah* doo-*rahn*-chee ooh een-*veh*-noo.) (*They prefer to travel during the winter.*)

Você prefere as loiras? (voh-*seh* preh-*feh*-ree ahz *loy*-rahs?) (*You prefer blondes?*)

Winning and losing

To talk about who's winning and losing a sports game or any other kind of **competição** (kohm-peh-chee-*sah*-ooh) (*competition*), use the verbs **ganhar** (gahn-*yah*) (*to win*) and **perder** (pehr-*dehr*) (*to lose*).

These sample sentences include **ganhar** and **perder**:

Quem vai ganhar? (*kang* vah-ee gahn-*yah?*) (*Who will win?*)

Eu perdi a aposta. (*eh*-ooh pehr-*jee* ah ah-*poh*-stah.) (*I lost the bet.*)

O meu time ganhou! (ooh *meh*-ooh *chee*-mee gahn-*yoh!*) (*My team won!*)

O Corínthians perdeu hoje. (ooh koh-*reen*-chee-unz pehr-*deh*-ooh *oh*-zhee.) (*The Corinthians [a São Paulo soccer team] lost today.*)

Nós ganhamos! (nohz gahn-*yah*-mooz!) (*We won!*)

Searching the Place

In the context of sporting events, you do a lot of *searching* and *looking for* things. First, you **procura** (proh-*koo*-rah) (*look for*) a game you want to see, and then you **procura** your seat after you walk into the arena. You probably need to **procurar** the **banheiro** (bahn-*yay*-roh) (*bathroom*) and the **quiosque** (kee-*ah*-skee) (*concession stand*) during the game, too.

Here are the present tense conjugations for **procurar**.

Conjugation	Pronunciation
eu procuro	*eh*-ooh proh-*koo*-roh
você procura	voh-*seh* proh-*koo*-rah
ele/ela procura	*eh*-lee/*eh*-lah proh-*koo*-rah
nós procuramos	nohz proh-koo-*rah*-mooz
eles/elas procuram	*eh*-leez/*eh*-lahz proh-*koo*-rah-oong
vocês procuram	voh-*sehz* proh-*koo*-rah-oong

The gerund (or –*ing* form) of **procurar**, is used a lot in the context of *searching* or *looking for*:

> **Eu estou procurando meu irmão. Você viu ele?** (*eh*-ooh es-*toh* proh-koo-*rahn*-doh *meh*-ooh eeh-*mah*-ooh. voh-*seh* vee-ooh *eh*-lee?) (*I'm searching for my brother. Have you seen him?*)

> **Eu estou procurando um bom restaurante. Você conhece um?** (*eh*-ooh es-*toh* proh-koo-*rahn*-doh oong *boh*-oong heh-stah-ooh-*rahn*-chee. voh-*seh* kohn-*yeh*-see oong?) (*I'm looking for a good restaurant. Know any?*)

REMEMBER

To translate sentences like these to Portuguese, use the form **estar** (*to be*) plus **procurando** (proh–koo–*rahn*–doh) (*searching/looking for*).

Here are a few other sentences that include **procurar**:

> **O que você procura?** (ooh *kee* voh-*seh* proh-*koo*-rah?) (*What are you looking for?*)

> **Ele procura a saída.** (eh-lee proh-*koo*-rah ah sah-*ee*-dah) (*He looks for the exit.*)

> **Nós procuramos nosso carro, mas não achamos.** (nohz proh-koo-*rah*-mooz noh-soo *kah*-hoh, mah-eez *nah*-ooh ah-*shah*-mooz.) (*We looked for our car, but we didn't find it.*) **Note:** This sentence uses the past tense. For more on the past tense, see Chapter 6.

> **Eu estou procurando o meu sapato.** (*eu*-ooh es-*toh* proh-koo-*rahn*-doh ooh *meh*-ooh sah-*pah*-toh.) (*I'm searching for my shoe.*)

> **Eles estão procurando o caminho certo.** (*eh*-leez eh-*stah*-ooh proh-koo-*rahn*-doh ooh kah-*meen*-yoh *seh*-toh.) (*They're looking for the right road.*)

Talkin' the Talk

AUDIO ONLINE

Celso (*sel*-soh) and his friend **Kátia** (*kah*-chee-ah) are on vacation in Rio. They're looking for a great restaurant and talking about what type of place they want. Listen for the verb **preferir** as well as **procurar**.

Celso: **Vamos procurar um bom restaurante?**

vah-mooz proh-koo-*rah* oong *boh*-oong heh-stah-ooh-*rahn*-chee?

Let's look for a good restaurant?

Kátia: **Vamos. Você prefere italiano ou japonês?**

vah-mooz. voh-*seh* preh-*feh*-ree ee-tah-lee-*ah*-noh oh zhah-poh-*nay-eez?*

Let's (do it). Do you prefer Italian or Japanese?

Celso: **Eu prefiro japonês.**

eh-ooh preh-*fee*-roh zhah-poh-*nay-eez.*

I prefer Japonese.

Kátia: **Eu adoro sushi!**

eh-ooh ah-*doh*-roo soo-*shee.*

I love sushi!

Celso: **Perfeito.**

per-*fay*-toh.

Perfect.

Kátia: **Vamos!**

vah-mooz!

Let's go!

WORDS TO KNOW

vamos	vah-mooz	let's (do it)
italiano	ee-tah-lee-ah-noh	Italian
japonês	zhah-poh-nay-eez	Japanese
perfeito	per-fay-toh	perfect
Vamos!	vah-mooz!	Let's go!

FUN & GAMES

You're at a soccer game in Rio. Identify the names of things you're likely to find:

Illustration by Elizabeth Kurtzman

(A) _____

(B) _____

(C) _____

(D) _____

(E) _____

(F) _____

Flip to Appendix C to check your answers!

IN THIS CHAPTER

» Discovering and celebrating Carnaval in Brazil

» Dancing in the streets: Getting your samba groove on

Chapter **17**

O Carnaval!

Brazil is world-famous for its **Carnaval** (kah-nah-*vah*-ooh) (*Carnival*). The festivities take place in **fevereiro** (feh-veh-*ray*-roh) (*February*) or **março** (*mah*-soo) (*March*), when the weather is hot in Brazil, during the four days preceding **Quarta-feira de Cinzas** (kwah-tah-*fay*-rah jee *seen*-zuz) (Ash Wednesday). In Brazil, **Carnaval** is a national, four-day holiday.

Other places that are famous for putting on a grand **carnaval** include Venice, New Orleans, and Trinidad and Tobago. The tradition dates back to the Middle Ages, and each place celebrates the days of revelry a bit differently.

In this chapter, I describe Brazil's three main **Carnaval** celebrations — parties in Rio, Salvador, and the Recife/Olinda area — and offer a bit of how-to on the famous Brazilian dance: **samba** (*sahm*-bah)!

REMEMBER

If you can't get to Brazil during **Carnaval** — **voos** (*vohz*) (*flights*) and **hotéis** (oh-*tay*-eez) (*hotels*) tend to be expensive — it doesn't mean you need to miss out on the fun. Brazilians hold unofficial **festas de Carnaval** (*fes*-tuz de kah-nah-*vah*-ooh) (*parties*) year-round.

The most famous of these **carnavais fora de época** (kah-nah-*vah*-eez *foh*-rah jee eh-*poh*-kah) (*out-of-season carnivals*) is **Fortal** (foh-*tah*-ooh), which takes place in the large northeastern city of Fortaleza in August. The name **Fortal** simply combines the words **Fortaleza** and **Carnaval**.

Exploring Carnaval in Brazil

Preparations for **Carnaval** — especially in **Rio de Janeiro** (*hee*-ooh jee zhah-*nay*-roh), where a ton of money is poured into the party — continue year-round. But a surprising thing about **Carnaval** in Brazil is that Rio's celebration isn't necessarily the best. Rio certainly has the best **desfile** (des-*fee*-lee) (*parade*) over the four-day period, in terms of gargantuan floats and dancers in flashy outfits, but its **carnaval de rua** (kah-nah-*vah*-ooh jee *hoo*-ah) (*street carnival*) activity is not as famous as it is in other places.

Two less-publicized but equally fantastic **Carnavais** (kah-nah-*vah*-eez) (*Carnavals*) — each unique in its own way — are those of **Salvador** (sah-ooh-vah-*doh*) and the towns of **Recife** (heh-*see*-fee) and **Olinda** (oh-*leen*-dah). These last two towns are located adjacent to each other, so it's easy to experience both.

TIP

In general, it's best to pick one of the three **Carnaval** locations to spend the entire four days of Carnaval; choose either Rio, Recife/Olinda, or Salvador. If you try to see all three in four days (or even two of the three), you'll spend at least a full day on some mode of transportation and miss the fun!

Every Brazilian has a different opinion on which **Carnaval** is best. And there are even people who don't like all the fuss of any of the celebrations; they prefer to use their two vacation days (Monday and Tuesday before Ash Wednesday) to head to a secluded **praia** (*prah*-ee-ah) (*beach*).

Here are some questions you can ask a Brazilian to help you decide which **Carnaval** is right for you:

Qual Carnaval no Brasil você acha melhor? (*kwah*-ooh kah-nah-*vah*-ooh noh brah-*zee*-ooh voh-*seh* ah-shah mel-*yoh*?) (*Which Carnaval in Brazil do you think is best?*)

Qual é o mais divertido? (*kwah*-ooh eh ooh *mah*-eez jee-veh-*chee*-doo?) (*Which one is the most fun?*)

Qual Carnaval tem o melhor show? (*kwah*-ooh kah-nah-*vah*-ooh *tang* ooh mel-*yoh shoh*?) (*Which Carnaval has the best show?*)

Qual cidade tem o melhor carnaval de rua? (*kwah*-ooh see-*dah*-jee *tang* ooh mel-*yoh* kah-nah-*vah*-ooh jee *hoo*-ah?) (*Which city has the best street carnival?*)

Já esteve no Carnaval de. . . ? (*zhah* eh-*steh*-vee noo kah-nah-*vah*-ooh jee. . . ?) (*Have you been to the Carnaval in. . . ?*)

Rio's Carnaval

The **Carnaval** in Rio is the one to attend if you want to see a huge **espetáculo** (eh-speh-*tah*-koo-loo) (*spectacle*). It's basically a major **competição** (kohm-peh-chee-*sah*-ooh) (*competition*) of pageantry.

During the four days of **Carnaval,** each of the city's **escolas de samba** (eh-*skoh*-luz jee *sahm*-bah) (*samba groups;* Literally: *samba schools*) has just one chance to move it, shake it, and show off its artistic talents and magnificently decorated floats. On Tuesday night (the eve of Ash Wednesday), **os juízes** (ooz zhoo-*ee*-zeez) (*the judges*) decide who performed best.

People from different **escolas de samba** make the **fantasias** (fahn-tah-*zee*-uz) (*costumes*) months ahead of time. The **compositor** (kom-poh-zee-*toh*) (*composer*) of the official song of a specific **escola de samba** starts humming ditties to themself for next year's hit as soon as the previous year's **Carnaval** ends.

Each **escola** has many **carros alegóricos** (*kah*-hohs ah-leh-*goh*-ree-kohs) (*floats*) decorated with the school's theme, and these floats take months to make. They are indeed works of art. And topping the floats are the famous samba-dancing babes with spectacular bodies, little clothing, and high heels. These women often wear impressive, feathery headdresses. On the ground, in front of and behind the float, are hundreds more **dançarinas** (dahn-sah-*ree*-nuz) (*dancers*), all in costume. The parading of a single **escola** takes about an hour during the actual competition.

In terms of music, the most important part of any **escola** is the **batucada** (bah-too-*kah*-dah) (*drumming*). Up to 200 drummers are in each **escola**. The sound of the drums is deafening, but the energy is contagious.

TIP

Tourists (Brazilian and foreign) can actually parade with an **escola de samba**. Participation costs anywhere from US$60 to $500, and you don't have to know how to **sambar** (sahm-*bah*) (*dance samba*) to get involved. Have your travel agent or someone at a local tourist bureau make calls for you to figure out which **escolas** offer this experience. You can really impress friends back at home with the photos. And don't worry; the **fantasias** for females generally aren't skimpy.

The entire four-day event takes place in Rio's **sambódromo** (sahm-*boh*-droh-moo) (*sambodrome*), an open-air venue with bleachers that looks like an oblong sports stadium. The space is longer than it is wide because a **desfile** goes through it.

Why is it called a *sambodrome*? Because people dance an extra-fast **samba** (*sahm*-bah) as they parade their way through. **Samba** is the most famous dance from Brazil. It's a three-beat step repeated over and over again. It can be fast- or medium-speed; but during **Carnaval**, it's very **rápido** (*hah*-pee-doh) (*fast*). Check out the section "Dancing the Samba!" for details.

ESCOLA DE SAMBA: CARNAVAL AS COMPETITION

I used to think that **uma escola de samba** (*ooh*-mah eh-*skoh*-lah jee *sahm*-bah) (*a samba school*) was a place where people learned **samba**. But they're not schools at all! **Escolas de samba** are places where a group of people who want to compete in **Carnaval** meet up to plan and practice the moves and anthem they'll use that year. These groups include the **músicos** (*moo*-zee-kooz) (*musicians*), **passistas** (pah-*see*-stuz) (*men and women in costume who parade with the school*), and people who make the **fantasias** (fahn-tah-*zee*-uz) (*costumes*). People who live nearby and want to come and dance to the music also join in. Because many **escolas de samba** in Rio are named after and originate in a specific **bairro/comunidade** (*bah*-ee-hoo/koh-moon-ee-*dah*-jee) (*neighborhood/community*), the feel of an **escola** is similar to an urban community center in the United States. People of all ages are there enjoying themselves.

Each **escola** has a new anthem every year. Anthem **letras** (*leh*-truz) (*lyrics*) often have socially progressive **temas** (*teh*-mahz) (*themes*), like calling for an end to racism or even encouraging water conservation. For one **Carnaval,** I saw people dressed like water faucets! The **fantasias** match the theme. What doesn't change from year to year are a school's two official **cores** (*koh*-reez) (*colors*).

Historically, the most famous **escolas de samba** in Rio are **Mangueira** (mahn-*gay*-rah), which means *mango tree;* **Salgueiro** (sah-ooh-*gay*-roh), a last name; and **Beija-Flor** (bay-zhah *floh*), which means *hummingbird*. One of these three schools (named for the neighborhood in which they're located) usually wins first or second place each year.

You can check out the websites for these **samba** schools to see their colors and get a real feel for Brazilian **Carnaval: Mangueira** (mangueira.com.br/site/), **Salgueiro** (www.salgueiro.com.br/), and **Beija-Flor** (www.beija-flor.com.br/). You can also find information about **ensaios** (en-*sah*-ee-ooz) (*rehearsals*) on the sites. These can be great fun. Attending **ensaios** is a way to hear the **escola's** band practice and see some of its dancers in costume. And of course, you're allowed to **dançar** (dahn-*sah*) (*dance*) with them! The entrance fee is about **40 reais** (around US$10).

Rio's **Carnaval** can be **caro** (kah-roo) (*expensive*). Prices for a single night's show range from about US$20 for a seat way back and up high in the bleachers, to up to US$1,000 for a box seat. You can get a good bleacher seat for around US$250.

TIP

In recent years, Rio's **carnaval de rua** (kah-nah-*vah*-ooh jee *hoo*-ah) (*street carnival*) has gotten much better, which means you may prefer to forego the expensive tickets for seats and just walk around the city, seeing people in their **fantasias**.

Many **bares** (*bah*–reez) (*bars*) and **botecos** (boh–*teh*–koos) (*informal restaurants*) throughout the city have a TV on during **Carnaval** showing the main event in the **sambódromo**, so that's an inexpensive option for watching it, too!

·················· Talkin' the Talk ··················

AUDIO
ONLINE

Susana (soo-*zah*-nah) and her friend **Lu** (*loo*) have finally decided to go for it. They want to join a **samba** school for the Rio **Carnaval,** so Lu talks to her friend **Clara** (*klah*-rah), who did it last year.

Clara:	**Vocês estão pensando em desfilar?**
	voh-*say*-eez eh-*stah*-ooh pen-*sahn*-doh ang des-fee-*lah?*
	You guys are thinking about parading?
Lu:	**Sim, é divertido?**
	sing, eh jee-veh-*chee*-doo?
	Yeah, is it fun?
Clara:	**É demais . . .**
	eh jee-*mah*-eez . . .
	It's fabulous . . . (Literally: *It's too much*)
Lu:	**Você desfilou com que escola?**
	voh-*seh* des-fee-*loh* koh-oong *kee* eh-*skoh*-lah?
	You paraded with which school?
Clara:	**Com o Salgueiro.**
	koh-oong ooh sah-ooh-*gay*-roh.
	With Salgueiro.
Lu:	**Custou caro?**
	koos-*toh kah*-roh?
	Was it expensive?
Clara:	**Bom, duzentos reais. Mas valeu a pena.**
	boh-oong, dooz-*en*-tooz hay-*ahys. mah*-eez vah-*leh*-ooh ah *peh*-nah.
	Well, 200 reais. But it was worth it.

WORDS TO KNOW

estão pensando	eh-<u>stah</u>-ooh pen-<u>sahn</u>-doh	are thinking
desfilar	des-fee-<u>lah</u>	to parade during Carnaval
é demais	eh jee-<u>mah</u>-eez	It's fabulous/great (Literally: It's too much)
desfilou	des-fee-<u>loh</u>	you paraded
custou	koos-<u>toh</u>	it cost
valeu a pena	vah-<u>leh</u>-ooh ah <u>peh</u>-nah	it was worth it

Carnaval in Salvador

Salvador's **Carnaval** is completely different from Rio's. Bleachers are set up in Salvador, but they're on the **rua** (*hoo*-ah) (*street*) and there's no **sambódromo**. Instead, a several-miles-long parade route winds its way through parts of the city. The parade starts at Salvador's most famous landmark, **o farol** (ooh fah-*roh*-ooh) (*the lighthouse*) — right on the beach. There's also a downtown route which is the oldest and most traditional (but less popular).

REMEMBER

Another major difference between the **Carnaval** in Rio and Salvador is that instead of **escolas de samba**, Salvador is best known for what are called **blocos** (*bloh*-kooz) (Literally: *blocks*). A **bloco** (*bloh*-koh) is a group of people all wearing the same T-shirt that follow different live bands atop a **trio elétrico** (*tree*-ooh eh-*leh*-tree-koo) (*motorized truck*) with a platform on top, where people dance and a singer sings.

In Salvador, the band is often famous nationwide. In Rio, the featured musicians aren't famous pop stars, though the traditional **samba** music composers often are some of the most famous in Brazil. If you want to hear some of Brazil's most famed and beloved stars and musicians playing live during **Carnaval**, Salvador is the place to go.

People who've paid to be part of a specific **bloco** dance on the ground and move forward slowly with the truck, in front of and behind it. About 40 different main **blocos** are involved in Salvador's **Carnaval**, and it's very common for tourists to pay money to join one of the **blocos**.

To separate the **bloco** from the crowd watching the parade, a group of people are paid to surround each **bloco** with a **corda** (*koh*-dah) (*rope*). They form a rectangle around each **bloco**, with the **trio elétrico** in the center. These paid sort-of security guards walk along slowly, while the people inside the **corda** jump and dance like crazy to the music. Though the music is fast-paced, the parade isn't.

Each **bloco** parades for about six hours a day. If you get tired, you can duck under the rope to escape. My friends and I had a lot of fun but decided before the end of the parade to leave our **bloco** and just walk around the city.

If you're not in a **bloco,** you can either watch the parade from the sidelines or just roam around Salvador. Areas near the parade route are filled with people, generally laughing and just hanging out. Some bars and restaurants remain open, but others close for the festivities.

On the streets of Salvador, stands that sell all kinds of tropical cocktail drinks with festive names are set up. But these are generally the only vendors you'll find along the parade route, because the parade is the main focus.

Salvador's **Carnaval** is hectic and crowded. It is in fact the "largest street carnival" in the world, according to *The Guinness Book of World Records.* Salvador's Carnaval can be music to your ears if you're the adventurous, fun-loving type, or it can sound like a gigantic **dor de cabeça** (*doh* jee kah-*beh*-sah) (*headache*) if you prefer low-key events. If you're the latter type, you may prefer **Carnaval** in Recife/Olinda rather than Salvador. I cover **Carnaval** in that locale later in this chapter.

Wearing abadás

Most Brazilians and tourists who go to Salvador for **Carnaval** buy a T-shirt or tank top called an **abadá** (ah-bah-*dah*) for a particular **bloco** months in advance.

Abadás can be expensive; they usually cost more than US$60. The price goes up for each of the four days you participate in **Carnaval.** For each day you pay for, you get a different T-shirt or tank top with a new design so you can prove you paid to be in the **bloco** for that specific day. Generally, you have to pick up the **abadás** from each **bloco's** headquarters. You may find street vendors with **abadás** to buy at the last minute, but beware, they could be stolen or fake.

You can buy an **abadá** online on a few websites. Generally, for foreign tourists the online price — anywhere between $60 and $500 — includes delivery of the **abadá** to the hotel or place you're staying at a prearranged date and time. If you're interested in participating in a **bloco,** search online for the terms "**Carnaval,**" "**blocos,**" "**Brasil,**" and "**comprar abadá**" (kohm-*prah* ah-bah-*dah*) (*buy abadá*)" to find out what's available and how you may be able to participate.

Unlike in Rio, if you choose to buy an **abadá** and participate in Salvador's **Carnaval,** no practicing is involved. You can just show up, pick up your shirt, and meet your **bloco** at its scheduled time to begin the parade route.

Guys usually wear an **abadá,** shorts, socks, and tennis shoes to attend a Carnaval **bloco.** Most women from Salvador take their **abadás** to a tailor months in advance. The tailors fashion the **abadás** into unique tops for each **garota** (gah-*roh*-tah) (*girl*) parading in Salvador's **Carnaval.** Those people in the huge crowd on the sidelines wear whatever they feel like wearing. It's advisable to wear light clothing, cover your feet (if you wear flip-flops, it will hurt if you get stepped on), and keep jewelry at home.

After you buy a top with the name of your **bloco,** you can travel along the parade route with that **bloco,** participating — not spectating! If you prefer not to dance along the parade route but still want a hard-partying atmosphere, you can try buying a ticket that gives access to one of many **camarotes** (kah-mah-*roh*-cheez) along the parade route, which are two-story open-air temporary structures with standing-room only. Any website that sells an **abadá** also sells **camarote** tickets.

Finally, if you don't want to pay a **centavo** (sen-*tah*-voh) (*Brazilian cent*) to experience **Carnaval** in Salvador, you can just roam the streets and watch the parade from the sidelines for free. Just beware that the crowd is thick.

Making music

A couple of the popular bands and singers that perform every year at **Carnaval** in Salvador are **Timbalada** (cheem-bah-*lah*-dah) and **Olodum** (oh-loh-*doong*).

Then there's a special treat: the world-famous Brazilian singers **Gilberto Gil** (zhee-ooh-*beh*-too *zhee*-ooh) and **Caetano Veloso** (kah-eh-*tah*-noo veh-*loh*-zoo) usually make an appearance every year at Salvador's **Carnaval.** However, as of press time (2022), both of these great musicians were 79 years old, so they may not be performing in the years to come.

The music of **Carnaval** in Salvador is different from what you hear in Rio, where the fast, chorus-based **samba** rules the sound waves. In Salvador, music known as **axé** (ah-*sheh*), which has just one singer, is more common. **Axé** sounds more contemporary than **samba.** The most unusual groups you'll see during **Carnaval** in Salvador in terms of Brazilian costume are **afoxés** (ah-foh-*shez*), Afro-Brazilian religious groups that parade during **Carnaval.** One **afoxé** (ah-foh-*sheh*) that dates back to 1949 is called **os Filhos de Ghandi** (ooz *feel*-yooz jee gahn-*dee*) (*Sons of Ghandi*). They wear white turbans.

There are various **afoxés** that participate in Salvador's **Carnaval**, and all play music that use rhythms based in the Afro-Brazilian religion of **candomblé** (kahn-dohm-*bleh*).

CULTURAL WISDOM

As for dancing, it's mostly jumping around — no special moves are required, though you will see that some of the most popular songs of the year have choreographed moves that a minority of people (who learned them from watching TV) will do in the street. **Carnaval** is so important in Brazil that there's even a verb that means *enjoying Carnaval*. It's **pular** (poo-*lah*), which also means *to jump*.

Talkin' the Talk

Zezé (zeh-*zeh*) is a tourist from Rio who's at the Salvador **Carnaval** for the first time. He strikes up a conversation with **Teresa** (teh-*reh*-zah), a woman in his **bloco**.

Zézé: **Oi, está gostando da festa?**

oh-ee, eh-*stah* goh-*stahn*-doh dah *feh*-stah?

Hi, are you enjoying the party?

Teresa: **Estou pulando muito.**

eh-*stoh* poo-*lahn*-doh moh-*ee*-toh.

I'm really enjoying myself.

Zezé: **Não tem tempo para a praia!**

nah-ooh *tang* tehm-poo pah-rah ah *prah*-ee-ah!

There's no time for the beach!

Teresa: **Não, é só festa!**

nah-ooh, eh *soh feh*-stah!

No, it's all partying!

Zézé: **Você é da onde? Veio no ano passado?**

voh-*seh* eh dah *ohn*-jee? *vay*-oh noo *ah*-noo pah-*sah*-doo?

Where are you from? Did you come last year?

Teresa:	**Sou de Minas. É a minha primeira vez no Carnaval de Salvador.**
	soh jee *mee*-nahz. *eh* ah ming-yah pree-*may*-rah *vez* noo kah-nah-*vah*-ooh jee sah-ooh-vah-*doh*.
	I'm from Minas (Minas Gerais state). It's my first time at the Salvador Carnaval.
Zezé:	**É o melhor do Brasil, com certeza.**
	eh ooh mel-*yoh* doo brah-*zee*-ooh, koh-oong seh-*teh*-zah.
	It's the best in Brazil, for sure.
Teresa:	**Eu concordo!**
	eh-ooh kohn-*koh*-doo!
	I agree!

●●

WORDS TO KNOW

estou pulando	eh-stoh poo-lahn-doh	I'm enjoying myself (at Carnaval)
não tem tempo	nah-ooh tang tehm-poo	there's no time
veio	vay-oh	did you come/you came
no ano passado	noo ah-noo pah-sah-doo	last year
com certeza	koh-oong seh-teh-zah	for sure
eu condordo	eh-ooh kohn-koh-doo	I agree

Carnaval in Recife/Olinda

Recife and Olinda are two beachside cities in the northeastern state of **Pernambuco** (*peh*-nahm-*boo*-koh). They're right next to each other, with less than a mile separating them. The cities are close enough that you can spend time in both places in a single day.

Recife, the state capital, is a large city with a population of about 4 million. Olinda is one of Brazil's most beautiful old colonial towns. It's very small, with narrow, winding streets, pastel-colored houses, and breathtaking views of the city and the ocean. Olinda is also home to many artists. The name of the town comes from **O, linda!** (*Oh, beautiful!*) — a Portuguese sailor was apparently smitten with the location.

REMEMBER

This area is where you can see a bit more of a historic type of Brazilian **Carnaval**, and for me, it's the most **mágico** (*mah*-zhee-koo) (*magical*). The vibe is more artistic than party-town. **Carnaval** here feels less official than the ones in Rio and Salvador; there are no fees to pay (except for the hotels, which may be hard to book at this time) and no T-shirts with logos.

The **Carnaval** celebrations take place in the old section of Recife — **Recife antigo** (heh-*see*-fee ahn-*chee*-goo) (*old Recife*) — and throughout Olinda. Between the two, Recife is a little more **tranquilo** (trahn-*kwee*-loo) (*low-key*) than Olinda, where parties are more energetic and narrow streets make for a close-together crowd that's difficult to walk through.

In both places, the **carnaval de rua** is the most colorful in Brazil. Most visitors don't wear a **fantasia** (fahn-tah-*zee*-uh), but some do, and you certainly can. Just keep in mind that costumes are flashy, colorful clothing or generally festive outfits — not like Halloween costumes.

People just mill about on the streets, **bebidas** (beh-*bee*-duz) (*drinks*) in hand, and stop to watch impromptu **blocos** parade by. The "parade" in Recife is pretty disorganized, although there seems to be more timing involved there than in Olinda. Both places feature **blocos** of all sorts. In either place, a **bloco** can simply be a group of co-workers who pick a theme for themselves, dress accordingly, and beat some makeshift percussion instruments.

Little about the **Carnaval** in either city feels "official," but the parading/roaming the streets lasts all day. You can buy food on the street or find a plaza where you can hang out in the open air and eat a more substantial meal while you hear drumbeats in the distance (or parading by you).

Parading giant dolls

REMEMBER

What's famous and incredible about **Carnaval** in this area are the **bonecos gigantes** (boo-*neh*-kooz zhee-*gahn*-cheez) (*gigantic dolls*). They're handmade figures that stand about 20 feet tall — which is great, because they're visible no matter where you are in the crowd. The **bonecos** are sometimes of famous Brazilian people, such as the 20th-century writer **Jorge Amado** (zhoh-zhee ah-*mah*-doo).

The most famous **bonecos** are the **Homem da Meia-Noite** (*oh*-mang dah *may*-ah-*noh*-ee-chee) (*Midnight Man*) in Olinda and the **Galo da Madrugada** (*gah*-loo dah mah-droo-*gah*-dah) (*Sunrise Rooster*) in Recife. Parading of the rooster kicks off the whole **Carnaval** in Recife on the first day, and the **bonecos** are paraded through the **ruas,** along with informal **blocos.**

Checking out local music

The traditional **Carnaval** music in Recife/Olinda is **o frevo** (ooh *freh*-voo) and **o maracatu** (ooh mah-rah-kah-*too*). **Frevo** music traditionally features a brass band (and no singer) playing a fast beat, and the dancing that goes with it is indeed intriguing when you first see it. Usually a small child or a man in a colorful, clownish outfit dances with a **guarda-chuva** (*gwah*-dah-*shoo*-vah) (*umbrella*). The name **frevo** comes from the verb **ferver** (feh-*veh*) (*to boil*) — the dancing and footwork are so fast, the dancer seems to be boiling.

Maracatu has a fast, distinctive beat that really shows off Brazilians' talent for drumming. The drummers wear huge, shaggy, sparkling headdresses. The tradition was brought to Brazil by African slaves, who used the music and dancing rituals for coronation ceremonies celebrating African royalty.

Dancing the Samba!

If you visit Brazil for **Carnaval** (kah-nah-*vah*-ooh) (*Carnival*), you can hear **samba** (*sahm*-bah) music and see people dancing **samba** regardless of where you go. So how is the famous **dança** (*dahn*-sah) (*dance*) performed?

There are two basic **tipos** (*chee*-pooz) (*types*) of samba. One is the step that the women **sambistas** (sahm-*bee*-stuz) (*samba dancers*) perform during Rio's **Carnaval** while wearing high heels on top of a float; the other is what everyone else does. High heels make the dance much more **difícil** (jee-*fee*-see-ooh) (*difficult*). I suggest that you leave those moves to the talented women who remain a tantalizing **mistério** (mee-*steh*-ree-ooh) (*mystery*) to dazzled spectators.

It took me a good three years to **aprender** (ah-pren-*deh*) (*learn*) to dance **samba,** and I still don't do it very well. The step is simple, but I'm convinced that you need to have Brazilian **sangue** (*sahn*-gee) (*blood*) in your veins to do it **muito bem** (moh-*ee*-toh bang) (*very well*). Nonetheless, for my fellow non-Brazilians, here's what to do:

1. Loosen your **joelhos** (zhoh-*el*-yooz) (*knees*); **relaxe** (heh-*lah*-shee) (*relax*) and bend them a little bit.

   Samba isn't danced with the **corpo** (*koh*-poo) (*body*) straight up but rather like you're going to sit down.

2. Now, put your feet together. Shift your weight onto your **pé direito** (*peh jee-ray*-too) (*right foot*), and then shift the weight to your **pé esquerdo** (*peh eh-skeh*-doo) (*left foot*).

   As you do this, fling your **pé direito** to the front, with your heel sliding on the ground, as if your heel is scuffing the floor; then, fling your heel up, just slightly, off the floor.

   As you do the scuff, point the toes of your right foot slightly to the right, as if you're just starting to make an arc with the right foot. Your body faces forward the whole time, and your upper body moves as little as possible. Arms should be bent at the elbows, as if to balance yourself.

3. Now, bring that **pé direito** back to where it was and step on it.

   You're just moving in place — shifting your weight back to your right foot.

4. Next, do the same thing, starting with the **pé esquerdo!**

   It's a three-beat move, and the dance is subtle, not showy.

If you feel awkward trying the **samba**, don't worry. I'll tell you a huge **segredo** (seh–*greh*–doo) (*secret*): Many Brazilians can't **samba**. So either try it again or just sit down, have a drink, and enjoy yourself. That's all that matters, anyway!

FUN & GAMES

You have a friend who's thinking about going to Brazil for **Carnaval.** You — now an expert on the topic — explain the three main options. Identify the city that's best known for the **Carnaval** celebration pictured.

Illustrations by Elizabeth Kurtzman

Match each term with the **Carnaval** it best describes — Rio, Salvador, or Recife/Olinda.

1. frevo

2. sambódromo

3. abadá

4. samba

5. bonecos

6. farol

7. trio elétrico

8. maracatu

9. axé

See Appendix C for the answers.

Chapter **18**

Socorro! Help! Handling Emergencies

Emergências (eh-meh-*zhang*-see-ahs) (*emergencies*) can happen anywhere, and you can best manage them if you're prepared. This chapter helps you with words and phrases to know when dealing with life's not-so-fun unexpected adventures.

Despite what you may have read or heard, Brazil is pretty **tranquilo** (trahn-*kwee*-loh) (*calm*) for visitors in terms of **roubos** (hoh-booz) (*robberies*). If you use **bom senso** (boh-oong *sen*-soo) (*common sense*), you'll most likely be fine. The **polícia** (poh-*lee*-see-ah) (*police*), especially in Rio, which attracts so many tourists, are helpful and trustworthy to foreigners, though they're famous for mistreating the city's poor who live in **favelas** (fah-*veh*-lahs) (*shantytowns*).

If you get hurt in the country, you may be glad to know that there are state-of-the-art **hospitais** (oh-spee-*tah*-eez) (*hospitals*) and **médicos** (*meh*-jee-kooz) (*doctors*) in most parts of Brazil, especially in major urban areas. But before you begin your trip, you may want to consider buying a **seguro de saúde** (seh-*goo*-roh jee sah-*ooh*-jee) (*health insurance plan*) specifically for travelers.

Finally, it's always best to stay out of a foreign country's **sistema legal** (sees-*teh*-mah lay-*gah*-ooh) (*legal system*) if you can because laws and **processos** (proh-*seh*-sohs) (*procedures*) can be so different from what you're used to. In Brazil, there's a lot of **corrupção** (koh-hoop-*sah*-ooh) (*corruption*), and the system often works **devagar** (deh-vah-*gah*) (*slowly*).

In this chapter, I offer advice for responding to a robbery, finding and receiving medical help, and managing a legal problem in Brazil.

Here are some basic emergency terms that are good to know:

>> **Cuidado!** (kwee-*dah*-doh!) (*Watch out!*)

>> **Fogo!** (*foh*-goo!) (*Fire!*)

>> **Me ajuda!** (mee ah-*zhoo*-dah!) (*Help me!*)

>> **Rápido!** (*hah*-pee-doh!) (*Quick!*)

>> **Vamos!** (*vah*-mooz!) (*Let's go!*)

Stick 'em Up: What to Say (and Do) if You're Robbed

The places where you're most likely to have a bad experience in Brazil are the most touristy parts of the country — the cities of **Rio** (*hee*-ooh) and **Salvador** (sah-ooh-vah-*doh*). They can be lots of fun but also **perigosas** (peh-ree-*goh*-zahs) (*dangerous*). Small towns and beach towns in Brazil tend to be **seguras** (seh-*goo*-rahs) (*safe*).

When visiting Brazil, use the same precautions you'd use in any **lugar que não conhece** (loo-*gah* kee *nah*-ooh kohn-*yeh*-see) (*place you don't know*): Avoid being out in the street late at night, don't wear expensive jewelry or watches, and ask locals which areas you should avoid.

TIP

Be extra careful during festivals like **Carnaval** (kah-nah-*vah*-ooh). Consider sticking your **dinheiro** (jing-*yay*-roh) (*money*) in your **sapatos** (sah-*pah*-tohz) (*shoes*). Also consider buying a money belt you can wear close to your belly, under your clothes. The good news is that you don't need much **dinheiro** to enjoy yourself during the festivities.

Pegar táxi (peh-*gah* talk-see) (*taking taxis*) is fine; Brazilian taxicab drivers don't rob the passengers like drivers do in some other countries.

KEEPING THINGS IN PERSPECTIVE AFTER A ROBBERY

During my three years in Brazil, I was robbed only **uma vez** (*ooh*-mah *vehz*) (*once*), and it happened in front of my apartment building in **São Paulo** (*sah*-ooh *pah*-ooh-loh). It was very late at night. I was upset at first but then realized that losing a little **dinheiro** (jing-*yay*-roh) (*money*) isn't that big of a deal and that reordering credit cards is just a small annoyance. But I was much more careful walking around **de noite** (jee *noh*-ee-chee) (*at night*) after that, for sure!

You may want to remember that **ladrões** (lah-*droh*-eez) (*robbers/pickpockets*) in Brazil are sometimes just very poor people who need to feed their children. My Spanish friend Mario once resisted a **ladrão** at the back of a bus in Rio. The next day, he ran into the **ladrão** at a bus stop. They recognized each other, and the guy ended up explaining his sad life story to Mario!

Brazil is actually much less **seguro** for locals, especially **os ricos** (oohz *hee*-kooz) (*the rich ones*) with nice **carros** (*kah*-hooz) (*cars*). These people are often **preocupadas** (preh-oh-koo-*pah*-dahs) (*worried*) about **sequestros** (seh-*kwehs*-trooz) (*kidnappings*), in which the **sequestradores** (seh-*kweh*-strah-*doh*-reez) (*kidnappers*) demand **dinheiro** from the **família** (fah-*mee*-lee-ah) (*family*) of the **vítima** (*vee*-chee-mah) (*victim*).

A more recent **problema** (proh-*bleh*-mah) (*problem*) is **sequestros relâmpagos** (seh-*kweh*-stros heh-*lahm*-pah-gohz) (*lightning-speed kidnappings*). In this situation, the **criminosos** (kree-mee-*noh*-zoos) (*criminals*) usually kidnap a driver in their car, take the victim to an ATM, and ask that person to withdraw a wad of cash. Then the criminal typically leaves. At most, the person is held captive overnight.

CULTURAL WISDOM

Having a car in Brazil makes you more likely to be a robbery target. People sometimes rob drivers at stoplights, which is why a lot of drivers go through red lights late at night.

Don't panic!

So what should you do if you're being robbed? The local refrain is **Não reaja** (*nah*-ooh hee-*ah*-zhah) (*Don't react*). Don't shout, don't try to get away, and don't punch the **ladrão** (lah-*drah*-ooh) (*robber/pickpocket*).

Just hand over your **carteira** (kah-*tay*-rah) (*wallet*), **relógio** (heh-*loh*-zhee-ooh) (*watch*), or **bolsa** (boh-ooh-sah) (*purse*) — whatever the assailant wants. Your stuff is less important than your safety.

It's a good rule of thumb to never carry your **pasaporte** (pah-sah-*poh*-chee) (*passport*) around with you, unless you have no choice. Also, leave at least one **cartão de crédito** (kah-*tah*-ooh jee *kreh*-jee-toh) (*credit card*) at home, which you can use in case you get robbed or lose your wallet or purse. And the smartest travelers hide **dinheiro** and cards in a safe pocket in clothes or a bag. Some people even use fake wallets, which they leave in a more obvious place, like a back pocket!

Saying nothing during a robbery is generally best, but here are some classic phrases you may want to know:

> **Não tenho dinheiro.** (*nah*-ooh *tang*-yoh jeen-*yay*-roh.) (*I don't have any money.*)
>
> **Não tenho nada.** (*nah*-ooh *tang*-yoh *nah*-dah.) (*I don't have anything.*)
>
> **Socorro!** (soh-*koh*-hoo!) (*Help!*)
>
> **Me ajuda!** (mee ah-*zhoo*-dah!) (*Help me!*)
>
> **É ladrão!** (eh lah-*drah*-ooh!) (*He's a robber/pickpocket!*)

It's also helpful to know these calls for help in case you hear them from a Brazilian visitor who may need assistance in your hometown.

REMEMBER

You want to avoid having any problems in Brazil, so be sure to take the same safety precautions you take at home and ask locals whether a certain area is safe:

> **Essa região é segura?** (*eh*-sah heh-zhee-*ah*-ooh eh seh-*goo*-rah?) (*Is this area safe?*)
>
> **Quais os bairros que são perigosos?** (*kwah*-eez oohz *bah*-ee-hooz kee *sah*-ooh peh-ree-*goh*-zooz?) (*Which neighborhoods are dangerous?*)

Asking for and receiving help

Say you've just been robbed. You had only a little money on you, and the robber didn't get anything else. You now need to get back home or to your hotel. In this situation, or any other time you need help for something that's not a major emergency, you can use these phrases when asking a Brazilian to help you:

> **Por favor, poderia me ajudar?** (poh fah-*voh*, poh-deh-*ree*-ah mee ah-zhoo-*dah*?) (*Excuse me, can you help me?*)
>
> **Eu preciso de ajuda, por favor.** (*eh*-ooh preh-*see*-zoo jee ah-*zhoo*-dah, poh fah-*voh*.) (*I need help, please.*)

If a Brazilian offers you **ajuda** (ah–*zhoo*–dah) (*help*), consider using one of these responses:

Obrigado/a, sim, eu preciso de ajuda. (oh-bree-*gah*-doh/dah, sing, *eh*-ooh preh-*see*-zoo jee ah-*zhoo*-dah.) (*Thanks, yes, I need help.*)

Estou bem, obrigado/a. (eh-*stoh* bang, oh-bree-*gah*-doh/dah.) (*I'm fine, thanks.*)

Não preciso de ajuda, obrigado/a. (*nah*-ooh preh-*see*-zoo jee ah-*zhoo*-dah, oh-bree-*gah*-doo/dah.) (*I don't need any help, thanks.*)

Eu prefiro ficar sozinho/a. (*eh*-ooh preh-*fee*-roo fee-*kah* soh-*zeen*-yoh/yah.) (*I prefer to be alone.*)

Reporting a problem to the police

Most Brazilians say they fear **a polícia** (ah poh–*lee*–see–ah) (*the police*) more than they trust them, but police officers in Brazil are generally fine with tourists, and they're good for filing insurance forms if you get robbed, especially in Rio, a city that relies economically on tourism.

Here's what you can tell the Brazilian **polícia** if you want to report a robbery:

Fui roubado/a. (*fwee* hoh-*bah*-doh/dah.) (*I've been robbed.*)

Eu preciso fazer um boletim de ocorrência. (*eh*-ooh preh-*see*-zoo fah-*zeh* oong boh-leh-*ching* jee oh-koo-*hen*-see-ah.) (*I need to report a robbery.*)

É para a minha companhia de seguros. (*eh pah*-rah ah *ming*-yah kom-pahn-*yee*-ah jee seh-*goo*-rohz.) (*It's for my insurance company.*)

The **polícia** may ask you some of the following questions:

Quando aconteceu? (*kwahn*-doh ah-kohn-teh-*seh*-ooh?) (*When did it happen?*)

Onde aconteceu? (*ohn*-jee ah-kohn-teh-*seh*-ooh?) (*Where did it happen?*)

O que que foi roubado? (ooh *kee* kee *foh*-ee hoh-*bah*-doh?) (*What was stolen?*)

Você viu o assaltante? (voh-*seh* vee-ooh ooh ah-sah-ooh-*tahn*-chee?) (*Did you see the assailant?*)

Ele usou uma arma? (eh-lee ooh-*zoh* ooh-mah *ah*-mah?) (*Did he use a weapon?*)

And here are some example answers to these questions:

Aconteceu no centro, perto dos arcos da Lapa, às 9 da noite, mais ou menos. (ah-kohn-teh-*seh*-ooh noo *sen*-troh, *peh*-too dooz *ah*-koos dah *lah*-pah, ahz *noh*-vee dah *noh*-ee-chee, *mah*-eez ooh *meh*-nooz.) (*It happened in the city center, near the Lapa Arches, at 9 o'clock at night, more or less.*)

O ladrão levou a minha carteira. (ooh lah-*drah*-ooh leh-*voh* ah meen-yah kahr-*tay*-rah.) (*The thief took my wallet*).

Ele usou uma faca. (eh-lee ooh-*zoh* ooh-mah *fah*-kah.) (*He used a knife.*)

The **polícia** will probably ask you the regular questions, like **Qual é seu nome?** (*kwah*-ooh *eh* seh-ooh *noh*-mee?) (*What's your name?*) and **Você é de que país?** (voh-*seh eh* jee *kee* pah-*eez*?) (*What country are you from?*). (See Chapter 3 for help with answering these questions.)

Handling Health Emergencies

In this section, I give you tips on what to do if you're injured or become ill in Brazil. Seeking medical treatment in another country can be scary, and it's never fun. Whether you scrape yourself badly at the beach, injure yourself while hiking, or come down with strange symptoms you need help interpreting, knowing a few phrases that can help you communicate is bound to calm you down a bit.

Heading off illnesses with vaccines

Possibly the best way to avoid a health issue while traveling is to think about your **saúde** (sah-*ooh*-jee) (*health*) before you begin your trip. You need certain vaccinations before you're even allowed to enter the country, and other vaccinations are highly recommended. I remember getting a ten-year shot for Hepatitis A as well as a shot for **febre amarela** (*feh*-bree ah-mah-*reh*-lah) (*yellow fever*).

If you've been in countries with a **febre amarela** alert within three months of your entry into Brazil, the Brazilian government will not let you in the country without a yellow fever proof-of-vaccination card. When planning your vaccination in terms of your travel dates, keep in mind that a **febre amarela** vaccination takes ten days to become effective.

You also may want to consider what part of the country you'll be visiting. If you're planning to spend time in the Amazon, ask a doctor whether you should take preventative medicine for **malária** (mah-*lah*-ree-ah) (*malaria*).

TIP

For information about recommended vaccinations, you have a variety of options:

>> In the United States, the Centers for Disease Control and Prevention (www. cdc.gov/) has good information, particularly about malaria.

>> Contact your national health agency or a Brazilian consulate.

If you're still concerned about getting sick in Brazil after getting the proper vaccinations, you can buy travel health insurance; rates are often more reasonable than you might expect. Also be sure to talk with your doctor or get travel tips from a local health clinic before you take off for Brazil. Most doctors' offices and hospitals have pamphlets and information sheets on disease prevention for international travelers.

Watching out for tropical illnesses

The most common tropical illness among locals and tourists in Brazil is one you may have never heard of — **dengue** (*dehn*-gee) (*dengue fever*). City subways in Brazil have ads to warn the public about dengue fever. Risk usually comes with stagnant water — a breeding ground for **mosquitos** (moh-*skee*-tohz) (*mosquitos*) that carry the sickness. Having dengue usually just means you have a stomachache and what feels like a **gripe** (ah gree-pee) (*the flu*) for a few days.

REMEMBER

Dengue also has a much more serious variant called *hemorrhagic dengue,* which can be **mortal** (mohr-*tah*-ooh) (*fatal*) if untreated. If your flu-like **sintomas** (*seen*-toh-mahs) (*symptoms*) worsen and you begin to suffer from **vômitos intensos** (*voh*-mee-tohs een-*ten*-sohs) (*intense vomiting*), **perda de conciência** (*peh*-dah jee kohn-see-*en*-see-ah) (*loss of consciousness/fainting*), or **boca seca** (*boh*-kah *seh*-kah) (*dry mouth*), get medical help right away. **Dengue** is caused by one of four viruses, and your chances of getting hemorrhagic dengue increase if you've had a different strain of **dengue** before.

One way to reduce your risk of contracting **dengue** is to always wear **repelente** (heh-peh-*len*-chee) (*insect repellent*) while you're in Brazil. Mosquitos are thick in the Amazon, but the worst bites I ever got were in **São Paulo** (*sah*-ooh pah-*ooh*-loh)! The climate in most of Brazil is humid at some point in the year, and mosquitoes love it. If you do end up in the Amazon, it's worth knowing that there are two major rivers that flow through the region, the **Rio Negro** (hee-ooh *neh*-groh) and the **Rio Amazonas** (*hee*-ooh ah-mah-*soh*-nus). The **Rio Negro** is mosquito-free, due to the unique acidity of the river's water. You can find hotels that advertise that they are mosquito-free along the Rio Negro!

Becoming ill from contaminated water is also a problem in Brazil. Avoid drinking **água da torneira** (*ah*-gwah dah tohr-*nay*-rah) (*tap water*) during your visit; even

Brazilians don't drink tap water, nor do they drink anything with **gelo** (*zheh*–loh) (*ice*), since the **gelo** was likely made using tap water. Also stay away from **verduras cruas** (veh–*doo*–rahs *kroos*) (*raw vegetables*) and **frutas não descascadas** (*froo*–tahs *nah*–ooh des–kahs–*skah*–dahs) (*unpeeled fruit*) and avoid consuming room–temperature sauces to reduce your chances of suffering from **diarréia** (jee–ah–*hay*–ah) (*diarrhea*) when visiting Brazil. Boiled, baked, or peeled foods are the safest.

TIP

Taking a small dose of bismuth subsalicylate (like Pepto–Bismol) every day — provided your trip is less than ten days — can also help to prevent **diarréia**. Talk to your doctor about this and other preventative measures that can make your travel as pleasant as possible.

Expressing pandemic-related needs

As long as COVID–19 is still a global pandemic, you'll probably want to learn some specialized words to take care of your health while visiting Brazil. Luckily, many Covid–related words in Portuguese look almost identical to English. Can you find some below? (I know you're not *really* a dummy, but you might appreciate easy answers: *Covid, test, PCR, positive/negative, vaccine, facial* are all words that look the same or almost the same in Portuguese.)

Here are some useful phrases to talk about Covid:

Onde posso comprar um teste rápido para Covid? (*ohn*–jee poh–soo kom–*prah* oong *tes*–chee *hah*–pee–doh pah–rah *koh*–vee–jee?) (*Where can I buy a rapid Covid test?*)

Onde posso fazer um teste PCR para Covid? (*ohn*–jee poh–soo fah–*zeh* oong *tes*–chee peh–seh–*eh*–hee pah–rah *koh*–vee–jee) (*Where can I get a Covid PCR test done?*)

Eu preciso fazer teste para Covid. (eh–ooh preh–*see*–zoo fah–*zeh tes*–chee pah–rah *koh*–vee–jee.) (*I need to get tested for Covid.*)

Onde posso comprar máscara facial para Covid? (*ohn*–jee poh–soo kom–*prah mah*–skah–rah fah–see–*ah*–ooh pah–rah *koh*–vee–jee?) (*Where can I buy a facemask for Covid?*)

Vocês têm desinfetante para as mãos? (voh–*say*–eez *tang* des–een–feh–*tahn*–chee pah–rah ahz *mah*–ooz?) (*Do you have hand sanitizer?*)

Eu estou vacinado/a para Covid. (eh–ooh eh–*stoh* vah–see–*nah*–doh/dah pah–rah *koh*–vee–jee.) (*I'm vaccinated for Covid.*)

Você está vacinado/a para Covid? (voh–*seh* es–*tah* vah–see–*nah*–doh/dah pah–rah *koh*–vee–jee?) (*Are you vaccinated for Covid?*)

Eu não estou vacinado/a para Covid. (*eh*-ooh *nah*-ooh eh-*stoh* vah-see-*nah*-doh/dah pah-rah *koh*-vee-jee.) (*I'm not vaccinated for Covid.*)

Onde posso tomar uma vacina para Covid? (*ohn*-jee poh-soo toh-*mah* ooh-mah vah-*see*-nah pah-rah *koh*-vee-jee?) (*Where can I get a Covid vaccine?*)

And here are some useful Covid terms:

>> **positivo** (poh-zee-*chee*-voo) (*positive*)

>> **negativo** (neh-gah-*chee*-voo) (*negative*)

>> **dose de reforço** (*doh*-zee jee heh-*foh*-soo) (*booster shot*)

>> **antígeno** (ahn-*chee*-zhen-oh) (*antigen*)

>> **gratuita** (grah-too-*ee*-tah) (*free — as in no cost*)

>> **duas doses** (*doo*-ahs *doh*-zeez) (*two doses*)

>> **marcar uma consulta** (mahr-*kah* ooh-mah kohn-*sool*-tah) (*make an appointment with a doctor*)

Dealing with your normal illnesses

In addition to tropical diseases and Covid, you can develop the run-of-the-mill sicknesses that plague you anywhere, like a **resfriado** (hes-free-*ah*-doo) (*cold*), **dor** (doh) (*pain*), or even a **ressaca** (heh-*sah*-kah) (*hangover*)! Brazil has plenty of **farmácias** (fah-mah-see-ahz) (*drugstores*) around, so getting the **remédio** (heh-meh-jee-ooh) (*medicine*) you need isn't hard.

Here are some helpful phrases to use, including how to describe common bodily **sintomas** (seen-toh-mahs) (*symptoms*), whether you're at the **médico** (meh-jee-koo) (*doctor*) or the **farmácia**:

Estou com dor de cabeça. (eh-*stoh* koh-oong *doh* jee kah-*beh*-sah.) (*I have a headache.*)

Estou congestionado/a. (eh-*stoh* kohn-zhes-chee-ooh-*nah*-doo/dah) (*I'm congested.*)

Estou com muita dor. (eh-*stoh* koh-oong moh-*ee*-tah *doh*.) (*I'm in a lot of pain.*)

Tenho dores no corpo. (*tang*-yoh *doh*-reez noh *koh*-poo.) (*I have body aches.*)

Tenho tosse. (*tang*-yoh *toh*-see.) (*I have a cough.*)

Sou diabético. (soh jee-ah-*beh*-chee-koh.) (*I'm diabetic.*)

Tenho alergias. (*tang*-yoh ah-*lehr*-zhee-ahs.) (*I have allergies.*)

Tenho asma. (*tang*-yoh *ahz*-mah.) (*I have asthma.*)

Tem band-aids? (*tang* bahn-*day*-ee-jeez?) (*Do you have Band-Aids?*)

Tem aspirina? (*tang* ah-spee-*ree*-nah?) (*Do you have aspirin?*)

Tem algo para diarréia? (*tang* ah-ooh-goh *pah*-rah ah jee-ah-*hay*-ah?) (*Do you have something for diarrhea?*)

Here are some questions the pharmacist or doctor may ask you:

Dói? (*doh*-ee?) (*Does it hurt?*)

Onde dói? (ohn-jee *doh*-ee?) (*Where does it hurt?*)

Tem febre? (*tang* feh-bree?) (*Do you have a fever?*)

Tem náuseas? (*tang* nah-ooh-zee-ahz?) (*Are you nauseous?*)

É alérgico? (eh ah-*leh*-zhee-koh?) (*Are you allergic?*)

Tem pressão alta? (tang preh-*sah*-ooh ah-ooh-tah?) (*Do you have high blood pressure?*)

Já foi operado? (*zhah foh*-ee oh-peh-*rah*-doh?) (*Have you ever had surgery?*)

Abra a boca, por favor. (*ah*-brah ah *boh*-kah, poh fah-*voh*.) (*Open your mouth, please.*)

Tome esses comprimidos. (*toh*-mee *eh*-seez kohm-pree-*mee*-dooz.) (*Take these pills.*)

Handling injuries

Dealing with the misfortune of breaking a bone or suffering a medical emergency in Brazil works much like it probably does in your home country. You can take a taxi to a local **emergência** (eh-meh-*zhang*-see-ah) (*emergency room*), or you can call a three-digit number and request that an **ambulância** (ahm-boo-*lahn*-see-ah) (*ambulance*) be sent to pick you up. The emergency number in Brazil is 190.

Brazil's large cities have some very good **hospitais** (oh-spee-*tah*-eez) (*hospitals*). You can get the same good care there that you'd get in the best **hospitais** in the world. The **emergência** can no doubt be a little scary in small towns, especially the rural ones, but rest assured: You'll get the basic medical care you need.

CULTURAL WISDOM

If you're concerned about the risk of contracting AIDS, keep in mind that Brazilian medical **pesquisas** (pes–*kee*–zahs) (*research*) and **a política** (ah poh–*lee*–chee–kah) (*politics*) regarding AIDS medicine is world–famous — in a good way. The AIDS rate in Brazil is much lower than in other developing countries, thanks to effective local campaigns to encourage the use of condoms. Also, local **cientistas** (see–en–*chees*–tahs) (*scientists*) figured out how to make patented AIDS–related drugs and began offering them despite protests from multinational **empresas farmacêuticas** (em–*preh*–zahs fahr–mah–*seh*–ooh–chee–kahs) (*pharmaceutical companies*).

Talking about your health problem

Whether you have a stomach virus or a broken leg, knowing what certain parts of the body are called in Portuguese is useful so you can more easily communicate with doctors in Brazil. I start with **a cabeça** (ah kah–*beh*–sah) (*the head*) and work my way down **o corpo** (ooh *koh*–poo) (*the body*):

- » **cabelo** (kah–*beh*–loo) (*hair*)
- » **sobrancelha** (soh–bran–*sel*–yah) (*eyebrow*)
- » **olho** (*ohl*–yoh) (*eye*)
- » **nariz** (nah–*reez*) (*nose*)
- » **boca** (*boh*–kah) (*mouth*)
- » **língua** (*ling*–gwah) (*tongue*)
- » **dente** (*dang*–chee) (*tooth*)
- » **orelha** (oh–*rel*–yah) (*ear*)
- » **rosto** (*hoh*–stoo) (*face*)
- » **pescoço** (peh–*skoh*–soo) (*neck*)
- » **ombro** (*ohm*–broh) (*shoulder*)
- » **costas** (*koh*–stahz) (*back*)
- » **peito** (*pay*–too) (*chest*)
- » **braço** (*brah*–soo) (*arm*)
- » **pulso** (*pool*–soh) (*wrist*)
- » **dedo** (*deh*–doo) (*finger*)
- » **polegar** (poh–leh–*gah*) (*thumb*)
- » **mão** (*mah*–ooh) (*hand*)

- » **barriga** (bah-*hee*-gah) (*belly*)
- » **quadril** (kwah-*dreel*) (*hip*)
- » **nádega** (*nah*-deh-gah) (*bottom/cheek*)
- » **perna** (*peh*-nah) (*leg*)
- » **coxa** (*koh*-shah) (*thigh*)
- » **joelho** (zhoh-*el*-yoh) (*knee*)
- » **batata da perna** (bah-*tah*-tah dah *peh*-nah) (*calf - Literally, "leg potato," because the calf muscle looks a bit like the shape of a* **batata**, *or "potato"!*)
- » **tornozelo** (toh-noh-*zeh*-loo) (*ankle*)
- » **pé** (peh) (*foot*)
- » **dedo do pé** (*deh*-doo doo peh) (*toe*)

And here are the Portuguese words for some internal organs:

- » **coração** (koh-rah-*sah*-ooh) (*heart*)
- » **fígado** (*fee*-gah-doo) (*liver*)
- » **intestinos** (een-tehs-*chee*-nooz) (*intestines*)
- » **pulmões** (pool-*moh*-eez) (*lungs*)
- » **sangue** (*sahn*-gee) (*blood*)
- » **estômago** (es-*toh*-mah-goh) (stomach)

·············· **Talkin' the Talk** ··············

AUDIO
ONLINE

João (zhoh-*ah*-ooh) hurt his leg playing soccer. Here's the conversation he has with his doctor.

Doctor: **Tem dores na perna?**

tang *doh*-reez nah *peh*-nah?

Your leg hurts?

João: **Sim, dói muito.**

sing, *doh*-ee moh-*ee*-toh.

Yes, it hurts a lot.

Doctor:	**Vamos fazer uma radiografia.**
	vah-mohz fah-*zeh* ooh-mah hah-jee-ooh-grah-*fee*-ah.
	We're going to do an X-ray.
João:	**Acha que está quebrada?**
	ah-shah kee eh-*stah* keh-*brah*-dah?
	Do you think it's broken?
Doctor:	**Não sei ainda.**
	nah-ooh say ah-*een*-dah.
	I don't know yet.
João:	**Vai ter que dar anestesia?**
	vah-ee teh kee *dah* ah-neh-*steh*-zee-ah?
	Are you going to have to give me anesthesia?
Doctor:	**Não, não é preciso.**
	nah-ooh, *nah*-ooh eh preh-*see*-zoo.
	No, that's not necessary.

WORDS TO KNOW

uma radiografia	ooh-mah hah-jee-ooh-grah-<u>fee</u>-ah	X-ray
quebrada	keh-<u>brah</u>-dah	broken
ainda	ah-<u>een</u>-dah	yet/still
Vai ter que. . .?	<u>vah</u>-ee <u>teh</u> kee. . .?	Will you have to. . .?
dar	dah	to give
anestesia	ah-neh-<u>steh</u>-zee-ah	anesthesia
Não é preciso	<u>nah</u>-ooh eh preh-<u>see</u>-zoo	That's not necessary

CULTURAL WISDOM

Brazil is supposedly the number-two country in the world, after the United States, for **cirurgia plástica** (see-rooh-*zhee*-ah *plahs*-chee-kah) (*plastic surgery*). And Brazil's **cirurgiões** (see-rooh-*zhoh*-eez) (*surgeons*) are among the world's best. Because the cost per operation is comparatively low, some people say there's a significant plastic surgery tourism trade in Brazil.

Discussing Legal Problems

Most types of **atividades ilegais** (ah-*chee*-vee-*dah*-jeez ee-lay-*gah*-eez) (*illegal activities*) in Brazil are also illegal in other Western countries. But the enforcement and consequences of breaking **a lei** (ah *lay*) (*the law*) can differ. For instance, in Brazil, possession of marijuana is treated much more seriously than it is in much of the West. Cultural norms are at play, too. For example, it's more normal for lawbreakers to pay off a police officer or customs agent in Brazil than in North America or Western Europe.

REMEMBER

It's best to leave any borderline illegal activities — even speeding in your rental car — for when you're at home, where you understand the language perfectly and have familiar **recursos legais** (heh-*koo*-sohz leh-*gah*-eez) (*legal resources*) at hand.

Misunderstandings with the police can occur. If a situation is at all **séria** (*seh*-ree-ah) (*serious*), the first thing to do is contact the nearest consulate for your country. You may also need to contact an **advogado** (*ahj*-voh-*gah*-doo) (*lawyer*). In that case, be sure to ask for one who speaks English:

> **Tem um advogado que fala inglês?** (*tang* oong ahj-voh-*gah*-doh kee *fah*-lah een-*glehz?*) (*Is there a lawyer who speaks English?*)

> **Aqui tem um consulado americano?** (ah-*kee tang* oong kohn-soo-*lah*-doh ah-meh-ree-*kah*-noh?) (*Is there an American consulate here?*) **Note:** If you need to ask for another consulate, see Chapter 6 for a list of nationalities.

Hopefully, you won't ever have to say or hear these phrases:

> **Quero fazer uma queixa.** (*keh*-roo fah-*zeh* ooh-mah *kay*-shah.) (*I want to register a complaint.*)

> **Vamos ter que dar uma multa.** (*vah*-mohz *teh* kee *dah* ooh-mah *mool*-tah.) (*We're going to have to give you a ticket.*)

> **Vamos te levar para a delegacia de polícia.** (*vah*-mohz chee leh-*vah pah*-rah ah *deh*-leh-gah-*see*-ah jee poh-*lee*-see-ah.) (*We're going to take you to the police station.*)

TIP

You want to **evitar** (eh-vee-*tah*) (*avoid*) a visit to **a cadeia** (ah kah-*day*-ah) (*jail*) at all costs — jails in Brazil are notoriously overcrowded, scary places.

FUN & GAMES

Your Brazilian friend **Caio** (*kah*-ee-oh) is such a flirt! He recently took up surfing to impress his new girlfriend. The thing is, Caio is going to wipe out just hours from now, and you'll accompany him to the doctor to explain what happened. Try to identify the Portuguese words for Caio's body parts that get injured in his surfing accident.

Illustration by Elizabeth Kurtzman

Flip to Appendix C for the answers. Don't worry, Caio's going to be fine; his ego took the hardest hit!

4

The Part of Tens

Grasp Brazilian Portuguese quickly.

Master Brazilian Portuguese slang.

Sound fluent (even when you aren't).

IN THIS CHAPTER

» **Practicing Portuguese in Brazil**

» **Meeting Brazilians in your hometown**

» **Going online for real-world exposure to Brazilian Portuguese**

» **Checking out Brazilian media and entertainment**

» **Taking a language class and practicing aloud**

Chapter **19**

Ten Ways to Pick Up Brazilian Portuguese Quickly

The real fun of learning Portuguese comes when you put down this book and listen to some Brazilians talk. Even if you can't find any Brazilians or other Portuguese-speaking people near you, you have options for immersing yourself in this language. Here are some ideas.

Go to Brazil!

The absolute best way to learn Portuguese, or any language, is to spend time in a country where the people speak it. Brazil is a particularly great place to learn a new language because locals are unbelievably friendly. Another bonus is the fact that most Brazilians don't speak English fluently, which means you'll be immersed in Portuguese.

You can practice what you've learned with waiters, people in shops, and new friends. They'll probably speak a little English, and you'll speak a little Portuguese. That's the perfect language-learning situation — you can both have fun teaching each other some words.

Find Brazilians (Or Other Portuguese Speakers) Near You

To find out whether you're in a Brazilian-immigration hot spot, look online for authentic Brazilian restaurants, Brazilian shops, or Brazilian live music in your area. If you get a hit, check it out. Ask one of the Brazilian workers (using a few Portuguese words if you can) where Brazilians in your area hang out. Or just make friends at the restaurant or venue.

Many Brazilians in the United States live on the East Coast — in Miami, New York City, New Jersey, and near Boston. San Francisco also has a sizeable Brazilian community. You're in luck if you live near one of these places, but don't worry if you don't. There are plenty of other ways to meet Brazilians.

TIP

If you're a sporty person, consider trying to meet people at a **capoeira** (kah-poh-*ey*-rah) (*Brazilian martial art/dance form*) class. It's very trendy at the moment, and most major U.S. cities have classes.

You can also investigate whether your area is home to a Portuguese-speaking community from Portugal. A few notable, large Portuguese-speaking communities, home to people whose families emigrated from Portugal, include Newark's Ironbound District in New Jersey, Fall River, Massachusetts and New Bedford, Massachusetts. The accent is different, but any exposure to the Portuguese language helps. Besides, written Portuguese (think restaurant menus) in Portugal and Brazil is nearly the same.

Date a Brazilian

This option isn't for everyone, of course. But if you do find a place where Brazilians hang out in your hometown and you're single, it's not a bad idea at all! Brazilians are a very affectionate and fun-to-date bunch. Plus, a sweetheart is sure to be more patient with your choppy sentences and questions about Portuguese than any formal teacher.

In major cities, you can join online communities to make friends, such as various groups on Facebook, InterNations (connects "global-minded" people and expats in various countries) or CouchSurfing (host Brazilians traveling to your city in your home — for the younger crowd). Face-to-face meetings can happen after you get acquainted with the members.

Read the News in Portuguese

Your brain is constantly absorbing new information in ways that you don't even realize. By reading news in Portuguese, you can familiarize yourself with the way Portuguese looks and the patterns its words make.

If you enjoy reading, consider browsing the day's top news online. First read a story in an English-language newspaper to get the facts. Then log on to a Brazilian newspaper's website and read the same story in Portuguese. It'll be easier to follow if you already know the context and most of the details, and it's okay if you don't recognize many of the words. I guarantee you'll notice a few words that look like English, and you may understand a few more given the context. Hopefully, you'll recognize other words that you pick up from this book.

The biggest newspapers in Brazil are *O Globo* (www.globo.com/) in Rio, the politically left-leaning *Folha de São Paulo*, known as *Folha* (www.folha.uol.com.br/), and the politically right-leaning *O Estado de São Paulo*, known as *Estadão* (www.estadao.com.br/). You can also check out *BBC Brasil* (www.bbc.com/portuguese), a service of the British Broadcasting Corporation.

Check Out Brazilian Websites

To research any topic in Brazilian Portuguese, go to Google Brazil (www.google.com.br/). **Pesquisa** (pes-*kee*-zah) means *Search*. The button next to **Pesquisa Google** — **Estou com sorte** — means *I'm feeling lucky*. If you choose that, the search engine automatically takes you to the first page your search hits.

Enter search terms on Brazilian Google in Portuguese. Consider using words related to a hobby, such as NASCAR or knitting. If an English-language site comes up, ignore it and find one in Portuguese. Use an online dictionary to look up how to say gardening, for example. You'll find that it's **jardinagem** (zhah-jee-*nah*-zhang) in Portuguese. Don't stress out when you see a ton of words you don't know when the results show up. Your curiosity is your best learning aid. As you expose yourself to Portuguese, you're taking steps toward improved understanding.

Here are some of Brazil's most popular sites and stores. Visit them to find out about Brazilian culture and pick up a few new words:

>> **Amazon Brasil** (www.Amazon.com.br) Shopping for just about anything you can think of

>> **Pão de Açúcar** (www.paodeacucar.com/): Supermarket goods

>> **Submarino** (www.submarino.com.br/): Shopping (wide range of categories)

Listen to Brazilian Music

Absorb the sound of Brazilian Portuguese through music. Take a look at the lyrics, too, if they're available online.

Brazil has many musical genres. The most famous are **Bossa Nova** (*boh*-sah *noh*-vah), lyrical music set to a moderate tempo from the 1960s; **Música Popular Brasileira (MPB)** (*moo*-zee-kah poh-poo-*lah* brah-zee-*lay*-rah [*eh*-mee *peh beh*]), which is mostly acoustic guitar and singing; **pagode** (pah-*goh*-jee), a fun genre with a light beat; **samba** (*sahm*-bah), call-and-response music with a medium beat; **chorinho** (shoh-*ring*-yoh), the precursor to **samba**, from the 1920s; **sertanejo** (sehr-tah-*neh*-zhoh) (country); and **axé** (ah-*sheh*), ultra-fast music that's typical of **Carnaval** (kah-nah-*vah*-ooh) in **Salvador** (sah-ooh-vah-*doh*). Of course, Brazil also has great musicians from genres that are popular worldwide such as **pop** (poh-pee) (*pop*) and **rock** (hoh-kee) (*rock*).

Here are some popular Brazilian musical artists:

>> Anitta (pop)

>> Bebel Gilberto (Bossa Nova/MPB)

>> Caetano Veloso (MPB)

>> DJ Patife (electronic)

>> Elis Regina (Bossa Nova/MPB)

>> Gal Costa (MPB)

>> Gilberto Gil (MPB)

- >> Ivete Sangalo (axé)

- >> João Gilberto (Bossa Nova/Samba/Latin Jazz)

- >> Jorge Ben Jor (MPB/funk)

- >> Marcelo D2 (rap)

- >> Marília Mendonça (sertanejo — she belonged to a sub-genre called Feminejo, or country music from a female perspective)

- >> Marisa Monte (MPB)

- >> Milton Nascimento (MPB, pop rock, rock, jazz)

- >> Os Mutantes (classic rock)

- >> Pabllo Vittar (pop)

- >> Revelação (pagode)

- >> Tim Maia (funk)

- >> Vinicius de Moraes (Bossa Nova)

- >> Zeca Pagodinho (samba/pagode)

Watch a Brazilian Movie

Watching a Brazilian movie is a great way to learn about Brazilian culture and pick up some new words at the same time. Pick a movie with English subtitles so you can absorb the new sounds as you read the translation in English.

Here are some famous Brazilian movies:

- >> *Bingo: The King of the Mornings,* 2017

- >> *Bye, Bye Brasil* (*Bye Bye Brazil*), 1979

- >> *Carandirú* (*Carandiru*), 2003

- >> *Central do Brasil* (*Central Station*), 1998

- >> *Cidade de Deus* (*City of God*), 2002

- >> *Deus É Brasileiro* (*God is Brazilian*), 2003

- >> *Dona Flor e Seus Dois Maridos* (*Mrs. Flor and Her Two Husbands*), 1976

- >> *Elite Squad,* 2007

- >> *Eu, Tu, Eles* (*Me, You, Them*), 2000

- >> *Linha de Passe* (*Pass Line*), 2008

- >> *Ônibus 174* (*Bus 174*), 2002

- >> *Orfeu Negro* (*Black Orpheus*), 1959

- >> *Pixote* (the movie has the same title in English), 1981

Watch Globo

Order **Rede Globo** (*heh-jee gloh-*boo) (*Globo Network*), Brazil's best-known TV station, and check out Brazilian **novelas** (noh-*veh-*lahs) (*soap operas*). This is an excellent way to learn about Brazilian culture! Simply sign up to its on-demand streaming service, Globoplay, on any smart device.

Take a Portuguese Language Class

If you can't make it to Brazil, the next best thing may be to take a Portuguese class near you or online. Make sure the teacher is a Brazilian if you're serious about learning Portuguese from Brazil and not Portuguese from Portugal. The accent and many common words are different.

"Say It Again, João!"

Talk to yourself on the street. If people think you're crazy, that's okay. Repetition is the only way to get new words to stick in your brain. Repeat words from this book and say them out loud whenever you feel like it.

I talked to myself on the streets of Brazil, attempting to get that nasal sound so I could fake being a real Brazilian for a minute while I was alone. I found practicing my accent easier that way because I'd get embarrassed trying to replicate all the new sounds in front of other people.

Chapter 20

Ten Common Brazilian Portuguese Slang Words

B razilians use the words in this chapter on a day-to-day basis. It's okay if you don't feel comfortable talking in slang yet; just being able to recognize **gíria** (*zhee-ree-ah*) (*slang*) when you hear it is enough fun.

Brega/Cafona

Maybe it's just me, but when I first got to Brazil, I found myself wanting to say *cheesy* in Portuguese. I discovered that Brazilians use two different words to express the concept. **Brega** (*breh*-gah) tends to mean *cheesy*, while **cafona** (kah-*foh*-nah) is more like *tacky*:

> **Essa música é muito brega.** (eh-sah *moo*-zee-kah eh moh-*ee*-toh *breh*-gah.) (*This music is really cheesy.*)

> **Viu o vestido dela? Que cafona!** (*vee*-ooh ooh ves-*chee*-doo *deh*-lah? kee kah-*foh*-nah!) (*Did you see her dress? How tacky!*)

Cara

Cara (*kah*-rah) means *guy*. Practice using this word with these examples:

Quem é aquele cara? (*kang* eh ah-*keh*-lee *kah*-rah?) (*Who is that guy?*)

Lembra daquele cara? (*lehm*-brah dah-*keh*-lee *kah*-rah?) (*Do you remember that guy?*)

Chato

This word is my personal favorite. What's interesting about **chato** (*shah*-toh) is that it doesn't have a precise translation in English. It means *boring, annoying,* or *lame,* depending on the context. Here are some examples of how to use this great word:

Aquele filme é muito chato. (ah-*keh*-lee *fee*-ooh-mee *eh moh*-ee-toh *shah*-toh.) (*That movie is really boring.*)

Que chato! (kee *shah*-toh!) (*How lame!*)

Chique

Chique (*shee*-kee) is a fun word. It's the Brazilianized version of the French word *chic.* You can use **chique** in place of the words **sofisticado** (soh–fees–chee–*kah*–doh) (*sophisticated*) and **glamuroso** (glah–moo–*roh*–zoo) (*glamorous*). Here are two examples:

Que chique! (kee *shee*-kee!) (*How glamorous!*)

O restaurante é muito chique. (ooh heh-stah-ooh-*rahn*-chee eh moh-*ee*-toh *shee*-kee.) (*It's a really nice restaurant.*)

Esperto

Esperto (eh-*speh*-too) is a funny word because it looks like the word *expert* in English, and its meaning in Portuguese is very similar. Brazilians use it to say that a person (or even an animal) is smart or street smart.

REMEMBER

When used to refer to a person, **esperto** can sometimes have a negative connotation, like trickster or even dishonest.

Here's how it's used in conversation:

> **Ele é muito esperto.** (*eh*-lee eh moh-*ee*-toh eh-*speh*-too.) (*He's really smart/street smart.*)

> **Os golfinhos são muito espertos.** (oohz goh-ooh-*feen*-yohz *sah*-ooh moh-*ee*-toh eh-*speh*-tooz.) (*Dolphins are really smart.*)

> **A bebé já diz dez palavras. Que experta!** (ah beh-*beh zhah jees* des pah-*lahv*-rus, kee eh-*epeh*-tah!) (*The baby already says 10 words. So smart!*)

Gato and Gata

If a man is good-looking, Brazilians call him a gato (*gah*-toh). A gata (*gah*-tah) is the Brazilian reference to a beautiful woman. **Gato** and **gata** literally mean *cat*. Both words also mean *sexy*. You may hear these words used as follows:

> **Ele é um gato.** (*eh*-lee *eh* oong *gah*-toh.) (*He's gorgeous.*)

> **Que gata!** (kee *gah*-tah!) (*What a sexy woman!*)

Grana

Grana (*grah*-nah) is slang for *money*. It's like saying *dough* in English. Here are some common ways to use the word:

> **Eu estou sem grana.** (*eh*-ooh eh-*stoh* sang *grah*-nah.) (*I don't have any money.*)

> **Tem grana para me emprestar?** (tang *grah*-nah *pah*-rah mee em-preh-*stah?*) (*Do you have some money you can lend me?*)

The real word for *money* in Portuguese is **dinheiro** (jing-*yay*-roh).

Legal

Legal (lay-*gow*) is a super-useful word. It's the equivalent of the English slang term *cool*. **Legal** actually translates to *legal* in English, as in *following the law*. Imagine shouting "Legal!" in English instead of saying "Cool!" Here are a couple of examples of how you're likely to hear the expression in Portuguese:

> **Que legal!** (kee lay-*gow!*) (*How cool!*)
>
> **Muito legal!** (moh-*ee*-toh lay-*gow!*) (*Very cool!*)

Pinga

Pinga (*ping*-gah) is slang for **cachaça** (kah-*shah*-sah) — Brazil's most famous alcoholic spirit. It's made from sugar cane and tastes like tequila. Some of the best **pinga** is made in the state of Minas Gerais. **Pinga** is also used to make **caipirinhas** (*kah*-ee-pee-*reen*-yahs), Brazil's national drink, which is made by grinding lime and sugar in a mortar and pestle and then pouring the mixture over ice and **pinga**.

Here are some sentences using **pinga**:

> **Um copinho de pinga, por favor.** (oong koh-*ping*-yoh jee *ping*-gah, poh-fah-*voh*.) (*A small glass of cachaça, please.*)
>
> **Que marcas de pinga tem aí?** (kee *mah*-kahz jee *ping*-gah tang ah-*ee?*) (*What brands of cachaça do you have?*)

Pinga com mel (*ping*-gah koh-oong *meh*-ooh) (*pinga with honey*) is very popular. In some places, you can also find **pinga** that has been distilled with figs and other fruits.

Valeu

Valeu (vah-*leh*-ooh) is an informal way of saying *Thanks* — instead of saying **obrigado** (oh-bree-*gah*-doh) if you're a guy or **obrigada** (oh-bree-*gah*-dah) if you're a woman. It's like saying *Thanks, man* in English.

Valeu is most often used alone, but it can be part of a sentence:

> **Valeu pela dica!** (vah-*leh*-ooh peh-lah *jee*-kah!) (*Thanks for the information/tip!*)
>
> **Valeu pela carona!** (vah-*leh*-ooh peh-lah kah-*roh*-nah!) (*Thanks for the ride!*)

Chapter **21**

Ten (Plus One) Brazilian Portuguese Terms That Make You Sound Fluent

People often say that Brazilian Portuguese is lyrical. The words in this chapter show you some of the nuts and bolts that give this language its sound. Some are filler words — comparable to the English "like," when it adds no meaning to the sentence (So, *like*, you remember when we went to the beach that one time. . . ?). Others are the shortened versions of words that Brazilians use.

No need to get worked up about this stuff. It's just here to help you recognize the words when you hear them. And if you're feeling spry, use them to sound fluent in Brazilian Portuguese.

Né?

Brazilians probably say **Né?** (neh?) more often than any other word. It means *Right?* They stick it at the end of sentences all the time:

   Você vai para o aeroporto amanhã, né? (voh-*seh vah*-ee pah-rah ooh ah-eh-roh-*poh*-too ah-mahn-*yah*, neh?) (*You're going to the airport tomorrow, right?*)

You may also hear **né** in the middle of sentences, where it doesn't really have any particular meaning:

Eu vi o meu amigo, né, e depois não lembro mais nada. (*eh*-ooh *vee* ooh *meh*-ooh ah-*mee*-goh, *neh*, ee deh-*poh*-eez *nah*-ooh *lem*-broh *mah*-eez *nah*-dah.) (*I saw my friend, right, and then I don't remember anything else.*)

Né is the short way of saying **não é?** (*nah*-ooh *eh?*) (Literally: *Is it not?*).

Tá

You know when you're listening to someone talking on the phone, and you hear them say *Oh . . . Yeah . . . Right . . . Uh-huh . . . ?* Well, **tá** (tah) is the Brazilian equivalent of these words. If someone's giving you directions on how to get somewhere, for example, you can repeat **Tá . . . Tá . . . Tá . . .** to indicate that you're understanding what they're saying.

Tá is the short way of saying **Está** (eh-*stah*) (*It is*).

Ah é?

Ah é? (ah *eh?*) is one of a few ways to say *Really?* It's also another of those phone conversation fillers. You can use it to say *Really?* to convey interest in what someone is saying or as a way to let your friend know that you haven't fallen asleep.

My friend Jenny, an American who lived in Bahia state, said **Ah é?** was one of the first phrases she learned to say in Brazil.

Então

Então (en-*tah*-ooh) (*so/then*) is a major conversation filler in Brazil. People often say **então** to change the subject to something more interesting when there's a lull in a conversation. It also can be used to simply say *so* or *then*.

Sabe?

Here's a case in which the use of a word in Portuguese is exactly the same as in English. A Brazilian saying **Sabe?** (*sah*-bee?) is the equivalent of weaving in the phrase *You know?* throughout a conversation.

Imagine two people talking on the phone. Person A is telling a story to Person B. Person A says **Sabe?** about every 20 seconds as they talk. What does Person B say? (See previous entries for clues): **Tá** . . . **Ah é?** . . . **Tá** . . . and so on.

Meio

Meio (*may*-o) (*sort of*) is an easy term for you to practice and use to wow native speakers. Just remember that the pronunciation sounds like *mayo* in English. Yes, the short way of saying *mayonnaise*.

Use **meio** when you'd say *sort of*:

Ele é meio alto. (*eh*-lee *eh may*-oh *ah*-ooh-*toh*-ooh.) (*He's sort of tall.*)

Estou meio cansada (es-*toh may*-oh kahn-*sah*-dah) (*I'm sort of tired.*) (Unrelated note on basic Portuguese grammar: The speaker is female here, because **cansada** ends in **–a** and not **–o**.)

Meio literally means *half*.

Ou seja

This phrase is pure conversation filler. **Ou seja** (ooh *seh*-zhah) means *in other words* but is often used to gain a few seconds to gather thoughts.

Cê Instead of Você

Here's an important one. People often shorten **você** (voh-*seh*) (*you*) to what sounds like **cê** (seh) when they speak. Instead of **Você entendeu? Você vai agora?** or **Você é da onde?** they say the following:

>> **Cê entendeu?** (seh en-ten-*deh*-ooh?) (*Did you understand?*)

>> **Cê vai agora?** (seh *vah*-ee ah-*goh*-rah?) (*Are you leaving now?*)

>> **Cê é da onde?** (seh *eh* dah *ohn*-jee?) (*Where are you from?*)

A gente

It's common for people to say **a gente** (ah *jang*-chee) instead of **nós** (nohz) to mean *we* or *us*. **A gente** literally means *the people*. At first, I felt strange calling myself and my friends *the people* — as if I were talking about a group of people I didn't know — but I got used to it.

REMEMBER

A gente is singular, so it's conjugated like **ele/ela** (*eh*-lee/*eh*-lah) (*he/she*) instead of like **nós**:

> **A gente não é daqui.** (ah *jang*-chee *nah*-ooh *eh* dah-*kee*.) (*We're not from around here.*)

> **A gente trabalha muito.** (ah *jang*-chee trah-*bahl*-yah moh-*ee*-toh.) (*We work a lot.*)

For more on verb conjugations, see Chapter 2.

Pra

Para (*pah*-rah) means *for* or *in order to*. Sometimes Brazilians pronounce **para** as **pra** (prah):

> **Vai pra praia?** (*vah*-ee *prah* prah-eeh-ah?) (*Are you going to the beach?*)

> **Pra fazer o que?** (prah fah-zeh ooh *keh?*) (*To do what?*)

Tô

Estou (eh-*stoh*) (*I am*) is often shortened to **tô**, both in speech and emails. Following are a couple of examples:

> **Tô com fome.** (*toh* koh-oong *foh*-mee.) (*I'm hungry.*)

> **Hoje tô feliz.** (*oh*-zhee toh feh-*leez*.) (*Today I'm happy.*)

5 Appendixes

IN THIS PART . . .

Verb tables

Mini-Dictionaries (Portuguese/English, English/
Portuguese)

Answer Key

Appendix A

Verb Tables

Portuguese Verbs

Regular Verbs Ending with -ar

For example: morar (to live)

	Present	Past	Future
eu (I)	moro	morei	vou morar
você (you)	mora	morou	vai morar
ele/ela (he/she)	mora	morou	vai morar
nós (we)	moramos	moramos	vamos morar
eles/elas (they)	moram	moraram	vão morar
vocês (you plural)	moram	moraram	vão morar

Regular Verbs Ending with -er

For example: comer (to eat)

	Present	Past	Future
eu (I)	como	comi	vou comer
você (you)	come	comeu	vai comer
ele/ela (he/she)	come	comeu	vai comer
nós (we)	comemos	comemos	vamos comer
eles/elas (they)	comem	comeram	vão comer
vocês (you plural)	comem	comeram	vão comer

Regular Verbs Ending with -ir

For example: abrir (to open)

	Present	Past	Future
eu (I)	abro	abri	vou abrir
você (you)	abre	abriu	vai abrir
ele/ela (he/she)	abre	abriu	vai abrir
nós (we)	abrimos	abrimos	vamos abrir
eles/elas (they)	abrem	abriram	vão abrir
vocês (you plural)	abrem	abriram	vão abrir

Regular Portuguese Verbs

		Present	Past	Future
achar	*eu*	acho	achei	vou achar
to find	*você*	acha	achou	vai achar
	ele/ela	acha	achou	vai achar
	nós	achamos	achamos	vamos achar
	eles/elas	acham	acharam	vão achar
	vocês	acham	acharam	vão achar

		Present	Past	Future
começar	*eu*	começo	comecei	vou começar
to start	*você*	começa	começou	vai começar
	ele/ela	começa	começou	vai começar
	nós	começamos	começamos	vamos começar
	eles/elas	começam	começaram	vão começar
	vocês	começam	começaram	vão começar

		Present	Past	Future
comprar	*eu*	compro	comprei	vou comprar
to buy	*você*	compra	comprou	vai comprar
	ele/ela	compra	comprou	vai comprar
	nós	compramos	compramos	vamos comprar
	eles/elas	compram	compraram	vão comprar
	vocês	compram	compraram	vão comprar

		Present	Past	Future
conhecer	*eu*	conheço	conheci	vou conhecer
to know	*você*	conhece	conheceu	vai conhecer
someone	*ele/ela*	conhece	conheceu	vai conhecer
	nós	conhecemos	conhecemos	vamos conhecer
	eles/elas	conhecem	conheceram	vão conhecer
	vocês	conhecem	conheceram	vão conhecer

		Present	Past	Future
escutar	*eu*	escuto	escutei	vou escutar
to listen	*você*	escuta	escutou	vai escutar
	ele/ela	escuta	escutou	vai escutar
	nós	escutamos	escutamos	vamos escutar
	eles/elas	escutam	escutaram	vão escutar
	vocês	escutam	escutaram	vão escutar

		Present	Past	Future
falar	*eu*	falo	falei	vou falar
to speak	*você*	fala	falou	vai falar
	ele/ela	fala	falou	vai falar
	nós	falamos	falamos	vamos falar
	eles/elas	falam	falaram	vão falar
	você	falam	falaram	vão falar

		Present	Past	Future
fechar	*eu*	fecho	fechei	vou fechar
to close	*você*	fecha	fechou	vai fechar
	ele/ela	fecha	fechou	vai fechar
	nós	fechamos	fechamos	vamos fechar
	eles/elas	fecham	fecharam	vão fechar
	vocês	fecham	fecharam	vão fechar

		Present	Past	Future
gostar	*eu*	gosto	gostei	vou gostar
to like	*você*	gosta	gostou	vai gostar
	ele/ela	gosta	gostou	vai gostar
	nós	gostamos	gostamos	vamos gostar
	eles/elas	gostam	gostaram	vão gostar
	vocês	gostam	gostaram	vão gostar

		Present	Past	Future
voltar	*eu*	volto	voltei	vou voltar
to come back	*você*	volta	voltou	vai voltar
	ele/ela	volta	voltou	vai voltar

		Present	Past	Future
	nós	voltamos	voltamos	vamos voltar
	eles/elas	voltam	voltaram	vão voltar
	vocês	voltam	voltaram	vão voltar

Irregular Portuguese Verbs

		Present	Past	Future
colocar	*eu*	coloco	coloquei	vou colocar
to put	*você*	coloca	colocou	vai colocar
	ele/ela	coloca	colocou	vai colocar
	nós	colocamos	colocamos	vamos colocar
	eles/elas	colocam	colocaram	vão colocar
	vocês	colocam	colocaram	vão colocar

		Present	Past	Future
dar	*eu*	dou	dei	vou dar
to give	*você*	dá	deu	vai dar
	ele/ela	dá	deu	vai dar
	nós	damos	demos	vamos dar
	eles/elas	dão	deram	vão dar
	vocês	dão	deram	vão dar

		Present	**Past**	**Future**
estar	*eu*	estou	estive	vou estar
to be	*você*	está	esteve	vai estar
(temporarily)	*ele/ela*	está	esteve	vai estar
	nós	estamos	estivemos	vamos estar
	eles/elas	estão	estiveram	vão estar
	vocês	estão	estiveram	vão estar

		Present	**Past**	**Future**
fazer	*eu*	faço	fiz	vou fazer
to make/do	*você*	faz	fez	vai fazer
	ele/ela	faz	fez	vai fazer
	nós	fazemos	fizemos	vamos fazer
	eles/elas	fazem	fizeram	vão fazer
	vocês	fazem	fizeram	vão fazer

		Present	**Past**	**Future**
ir	*eu*	vou	fui	vou
to go	*você*	vai	foi	vai
	ele/ela	vai	foi	vai
	nós	vamos	fomos	vamos
	eles/elas	vão	foram	vão
	vocês	vão	foram	vão

		Present	**Past**	**Future**
perder	*eu*	perco	perdi	vou perder
to lose	*você*	perde	perdeu	vai perder
	ele/ela	perde	perdeu	vai perder

		Present	Past	Future
	nós	perdemos	perdemos	vamos perder
	eles/elas	perdem	perderam	vão perder
	vocês	perdem	perderam	vão perder

		Present	Past	Future
pedir	*eu*	peço	pedi	vou pedir
to ask for	*você*	pede	pediu	vai pedir
	ele/ela	pede	pediu	vai pedir
	nós	pedimos	pedimos	vamos pedir
	eles/elas	pedem	pediram	vão pedir
	vocês	pedem	pediram	vão pedir

		Present	Past	Future
poder	*eu*	posso	pude	vou poder
to be able to	*você*	pode	pôde	vai poder
	ele/ela	pode	pôde	vai poder
	nós	podemos	pudemos	vamos poder
	eles/elas	podem	puderam	vão poder
	vocês	podem	puderam	vão poder

		Present	Past	Future
querer	*eu*	quero	quis	vou querer
to want	*você*	quer	quis	vai querer
	ele/ela	quer	quis	vai querer
	nós	queremos	quisemos	vamos querer
	eles/elas	querem	quiseram	vão querer
	vocês	querem	quiseram	vão querer

		Present	Past	Future
saber	*eu*	sei	soube	vou saber
to know/	*você*	sabe	soube	vai saber
understand	*ele/ela*	sabe	soube	vai saber
	nós	sabemos	soubemos	vamos saber
	eles/elas	sabem	souberam	vão saber
	vocês	sabem	souberam	vão saber

		Present	Past	Future
sair	*eu*	saio	saí	vou sair
to leave/go out	*você*	sai	saiu	vai sair
	ele/ela	sai	saiu	vai sair
	nós	saímos	saímos	vamos sair
	eles/elas	saem	saíram	vão sair
	vocês	saem	saíram	vão sair

		Present	Past	Future
ser	*eu*	sou	fui	vou ser
to be	*você*	é	foi	vai ser
(permanently)	*ele/ela*	é	foi	vai ser
	nós	somos	fomos	vamos ser
	eles/elas	são	foram	vão ser
	vocês	são	foram	vão ser

		Present	**Past**	**Future**
ter	*eu*	tenho	tive	vou ter
to have	*você*	tem	teve	vai ter
	ele/ela	tem	teve	vai ter
	nós	temos	tivemos	vamos ter
	eles/elas	têm	tiveram	vão ter
	vocês	têm	tiveram	vão ter

		Present	**Past**	**Future**
ver	*eu*	vejo	vi	vou ver
to see	*você*	vê	viu	vai ver
	ele/ela	vê	viu	vai ver
	nós	vemos	vimos	vamos ver
	eles/elas	veem	viram	vão ver
	vocês	veêm	viram	vão ver

		Present	**Past**	**Future**
vir	*eu*	venho	vim	vou vir
to come	*você*	vem	veio	vai vir
	ele/ela	vem	veio	vai vir
	nós	vimos	viemos	vamos vir
	eles/elas	vêm	vieram	vão vir
	vocês	vêm	vieram	vão vir

Appendix B

Portuguese-English Mini-Dictionary

A

a pé (ah *peh*): by foot

abacate (ah-bah-*koch*) m: avocado

abacaxi (ah-bah-kah-*shee*) m: pineapple

abadá (ah-bah-*dah*) m: shirt for a Carnival group performance

abraço (ah-*brah*-soo) m: hug

abril (ah-*bree*-ooh) April

abrir (ah-*bree*): to open

ação (ah-*sah*-ooh) m: share (as in a share of stock)

advogada (ahj-voh-*gah*-dah) f: lawyer (female)

advogado (ahj-voh-*gah*-doo) m: lawyer (male)

agência (ah-*zhang*-see-ah) f: agency

agora (ah-*goh*-rah): now

agosto (ah-*goh*-stoo): August

água (*ah*-gwah) f: water

água de coco (*ah*-gwah jee *koh*-koh) f: coconut water

ajuda (ah-zhoo-*dah*) f: help

alface (ah-ooh-*fah*-see) m: lettuce

algum (ah-ooh-*goong*): some

alho (*ahl*-yoh) m: garlic

almoço (ah-ooh-*moh*-soo) m: lunch

alto (*ah*-ooh-too): tall

amanhã (ah-mahng-*yah*): tomorrow

amarelo (ah-mah-*reh*-loo): yellow

andar (ahn-*dah*) m: floor (of a building); to walk

antigo (ahn-*chee*-goo): old

apimentado (ah-pee-men-*tah*-doo): spicy

app (ahp) m: app (as in app on your phone)

areia (ah-*ray*-ah) f: sand

arroz (ah-*hohz*) m: rice

árvore (*ah*-voh-ree) f: tree

ator (ah-*toh*) m: actor

avenida (ah-veh-*nee*-dah) f: avenue

avião (ah-vee-*ah*-ooh) m: airplane

avô (ah-*vah*) m: grandpa

avó (ah-*voh*) f: grandma

axé (ah-*sheh*): type of music

azul (ah-*zoo*): blue

B

bairro (*bah*-ee-hoo) m: neighborhood

baixar (bah-ee-*shah*): to download

banana (bah-*nah*-nah) f: banana

banco (*bahn*-koo) m: bank

banheiro (bahn-*yay*-roh) m: bathroom

barato (bah-*rah*-too): cheap

barco (*bah*-koo) m: boat

barriga (bah-*hee*-gah) f: belly

bastante (bah-*stahn*-chee): a lot

beijo (*bay*-zhoo) m: kiss

bicicleta (bee-see-*kleh*-tah) f: bicycle

bilhete (beel-*yeh*-chee) m: ticket (as in theater/lottery)

bilheteria (beel-yeh-teh-*ree*-ah) f: ticket office

biquini (bee-*kee*-nee) m: bikini

blusa (*bloo*-zah) f: shirt (female)

boate (boh-*ah*-chee) f: nightclub

boca (*boh*-kah) f: mouth

bom (bohng): good

bonecos (boo-*neh*-kooz) m: dolls

braço (*brah*-soo) m: arm

branco (*brahn*-koh): white

C

cabeça (kah-*beh*-sah) f: head

cabelo (kah-*beh*-loo) m: hair

cadeira (kah-*day*-rah) f: chair

cadeira de praia (kah-*day*-rah jee *prah*-ee-ah) f: beach lounge chair

café (kah-*feh*) m: coffee or a café

café da manhã (kah-*feh* dah mahn-*yah*) m: breakfast

caixa automático (*kah*-ee-shah ah-ooh-toh-*mah*-chee-koo) m: ATM

calças (*kah*-ooh-sahz) f: pants

cama (*kah*-mah) f: bed

camarão (kah-mah-*rah*-ooh) m: shrimp

câmera (*kah*-meh-rah) f: camera

caminho (kah-*meen*-yoo) m: road/path

camisa (kah-*mee*-zah): f: shirt (for a male)

camiseta (kah-mee-*zeh*-tah) f: T-shirt

canção (kahn-*sah*-ooh) f: song

cancelar (kahn-seh-*lah*): to cancel

carne (*kah*-nee) f: beef

caro (*kah*-roo): expensive

carro (*kah*-hoo) m: car

casa (*kah*-zah) f: house

casaco (kah-*zah*-koo) m: jacket

cebola (seh-*boh*-lah) f: onion

celular (sel-ooh-*lahr*) m: cellphone

cem (sang): one hundred

cerveja (seh-*veh*-zhah) f: beer

chapéu (shah-*peh*-ooh) m: hat

chinelos (shee-*neh*-lohs) m: flip-flops

chocolate (shoh-koh-*lah*-chee) m: chocolate

chuva (*shoo*-vah) f: rain

cidade (see-*dah*-jee) f: city

cinco (*sing*-koh): five

cinema (see-*neh*-mah) m: movie theater

claro (*klah*-roo): light (in color); the expression "of course"

coco (*koh*-koh) m: coconut

coisa (*koy*-zah) f: thing

colher (kool-*yeh*) m: spoon

com (kohng): with

comida (koh-*mee*-dah) f: food

computador (kohm-poo-tah-*doh*) m: computer

conta (*kohn*-tah) f: bill (at a restaurant); bank account

contente (kohn-*ten*-chee): happy

copo (*koh*-poo) m: glass (cup)

cozinha (koh-*zeen*-yah) f: kitchen

custar (koo-*stah*): to cost

D

data (*dah*-tah) f: date

dedo (*deh*-doo) m: finger

dedo do pé (*deh*-doo doo *peh*) m: toe

dela (*deh*-lah): her

dele (*deh*-lee): his

deles (*deh*-leez): their

dente (*den*-chee) m: tooth

dentista (den-*chee*-stah) m/f: dentist (male or female)

desempenho (des-em-*pen*-yoh) m: performance (of a company)

devagar (deh-vah-*gah*): slowly

dez (dez): ten

dezembro (deh-*zem*-broo): December

dia (*jee*-ah) m: day

difícil (jee-*fee*-see-ooh): difficult

dinheiro (jing-*yay*-roo) m: money

direção (jee-reh-*sah*-ooh) f: direction

direita (jee-*ray*-tah): right (as in physical location, such as "to the right")

divertido (jee-veh-*chee*-doo): fun

dividendo (dee-vee-*den*-doh) m: dividend

doce (*doh*-see): sweet

dois (*doh*-eez): two

domingo (doo-*ming*-goo) m: Sunday

dor (doh) f: pain

E

e (ee): and

email (ee-*may*-oh) m: email

encontrar (en-kohn-*trah*): to find; to meet

escuro (eh-*skoo*-roo): dark

escutar (es-koo-*tah*): to listen

especial (eh-speh-see-*ah*-ooh): special

espinafre (es-pee-*nah*-free) m: spinach

esquerda (es-*keh*-dah): left

esquina (es-*kee*-nah) f: corner

estação (es-tah-*sah*-ooh) f: station

estado (eh-*stah*-doo) m: state

estádio (es-*stah*-jee-oh) m: stadium

estar (es-*stah*): to be (temporary state)

experimentar (eh-*speh*-ree-men-*tah*): to try

exposição de arte (eks-poh-zee-*sah*-ooh jee *ah*-chee) f: art exhibition

F

faca (*fah*-kah) f: knife

fácil (*fah*-see-ooh): easy

falar (fah-*lah*): to speak

farmácia (fah-*mah*-see-ah) f: drugstore

farol (fah-*roh*-ooh) m: lighthouse

febre (*feh*-bree) f: fever

fechar (feh-*shah*): to close

feijão (fay-*zhah*-ooh) m: beans

feio (*fay*-ooh): ugly

feliz (feh-*lees*): happy

festa (*fehs*-tah) f: party

fevereiro (feh-veh-*ray*-roh): February

filha (*feel*-yah) f: daughter

filho (*feel*-yoo) m: son

flor (floh) f: flower

fome (*foh*-mee) f: hunger

foto (*foh*-too) f: photo

frango (*frahn*-goo) m: chicken

frevo (*freh*-voo) m: type of music

fruta (*froo*-tah) f: fruit

G

garota (gah-*roh*-tah) f: girl

garoto (gah-*roh*-too) m: boy

gato (*gah*-too) m: cat

gerente (zheh-*rang*-chee) m/f: manager

goiaba (goy-*ah*-bah) f: guava

gostar (goh-*stah*): to like

grana (*grah*-nah) f: money (slang)

grande (*grahn*-jee): big

guia (*gee*-ah) m/f: guide

H

hoje (*oh*-zhee): today

homem (*oh*-mang) m: man

hora (*oh*-rah) f: hour

I

identificação (ee-den-chee-fee-kah-*sah*-ooh) f: identification

idioma (ee-jee-*oh*-mah) m: language

ilha (*eel*-yah) f: island

imigração (ee-mee-grah-*sah*-ooh) f: immigration

impostos (eem-*pohs*-tohs) m: taxes

imprimir (eem-pree-*meeh*): to print out

inteligente (een-tehl-ee-*zhang*-chee): intelligent (male or female)

iPhone (*ah*-ee-fohn) m: iPhone

irmã (ee-*mah*) f: sister

irmão (ee-*mah*-ooh) m: brother

J

janeiro (zhah-*nay*-roo): January

jangada (zhan-*gah*-dah) f: sailboat

jantar (zhahn-*tah*) m: dinner/to have dinner

jardim (zhah-*jing*) m: garden

joelho (zhoh-*el*-yoh) m: knee

jovem (*zhoh*-vang): young

julho (*zhool*-yoh): July

junho (*zhoon*-yoh): June

L

legal (lay-*gow*): cool (excellent)/legal

leite (*lay*-chee) m: milk

leste (*les*-chee): east

ligar (lee-*gah*): to call

limão (lee-*mah*-ooh) m: lime

limpar (leem-*pah*): to clean

lindo (*leen*-doh) handsome/beautiful

língua (*ling*-gwah) f: language or tongue

livro (*leev*-roo) m: book

longe (*lohn*-zhee): far away

lua (*loo*-ah) f: moon

lucro (*loo*-kroh) m: profit

M

maçã (mah-*sah*) f: apple

mãe (*mah*-ee) f: mother

maio (*my*-oh): May

mais (*mah*-eez): more

manga (*mahn*-gah) f: mango; sleeve

manhã (mahn-*yah*) f: morning

mão (*mah*-ooh) f: hand

mapa (*mah*-pah) m: map

mar (mah) m: ocean

maracatu (mah-rah-kah-*too*) f: type of music

março (*mah*-soo): March

mariscos (mah-*rees*-kooz) m: shellfish

marróm (mah-*hohng*): brown

médica (*meh*-jee-kah) f: doctor (female)

médico (*meh*-jee-koo) m: doctor (male)

melhor (mel-*yoh*): better

menina (meh-*nee*-nah) f: girl

menino (meh-*nee*-noo) m: boy

menos (*meh*-nooz): less

mesa (*meh*-zah) f: table

metrô (meh-*troh*) m: subway

minuto (mee-*noo*-too) m: minute

moeda (moh-*eh*-dah) f: coin

morar (moh-*rah*): to live

muito (moh-*ee*-toh): a lot

mulher (mool-*yeh*) f: woman

museu (moo-*zeh*-ooh) m: museum

música (*moo*-zee-kah) f: music

N

não (*nah*-ooh): no

nariz (nah-*reez*) m: nose

neta (*neh*-tah) f: granddaughter

neto (*neh*-too) m: grandson

noite (*noh*-ee-chee) f: night

norte (*noh*-chee) m: north

nota (*noh*-tah) f: bill (as in dollar)

nove (*noh*-vee): nine

novela (noh-*veh*-lah) f: soap opera

novembro (noo-*vem*-broo): November

número (*noo*-meh-roh) m: number

O

óculos de sol (*oh*-koo-lohs jee *soh*-ooh) m: sunglasses

oeste (oh-*es*-chee) m: west

oi (*oh*-ee): hello

oito (*oh*-ee-toh): eight

olho (*ohl*-yoo) m: eye

ombro (*ohm*-broh) m: shoulder

ônibus (*oh*-nee-boos) m: bus

orelha (oh-*rel*-yah) f: ear

organizado (ohr-gahn-ee-*zah*-doh) organized

ou (ooh): or

ouro (*oh*-roo) m: gold

outro (*oh*-trooh): another

outubro (ooh-*too*-broo): October

ovo (*oh*-voo) m: egg

P

pagar (pah-*gah*): to pay

pai (*pah*-ee) m: father

país (pah-*eez*) m: country

pão (*pah*-ooh) m: bread

para (*pah*-rah): for/in order to

passaporte (pah-sah-*poh*-chee) m: passport

pé (peh) m: foot

peito (*pay*-too) m: chest; breast

peixe (*pay*-shee) m: fish

pequeno (peh-*keh*-noo): small

perguntar (peh-goon-*tah*): to ask

perna (*peh*-nah) f: leg

perto (*peh*-too): near

pescoço (pes-*koh*-soo) m: neck

pessoa (peh-*soh*-ah) f: person

pior (pee-*oh*): worse

pipoca (pee-*poh*-kah) f: popcorn

piscina (pee-*see*-nah) f: pool

polegar (poh-leh-*gah*) m: thumb

porta (*poh*-tah) f: door

portão (pohr-*tah*-ooh) m: entrance gate (to a stadium)

pouco (*poh*-koo): little

praça (*prah*-sah) f: plaza/square

praia (*prah*-ee-ah) f: beach

preço (*preh*-soo) m: price

preto (*preh*-too): black

prima (*pree*-mah) f: female cousin

primeiro (pree-*may*-doo): first

primo (*pree*-moo) m: male cousin

protetor solar (proh-teh-*toh* soh-*lah*) m: sunscreen

pulso (*pool*-soh) m: wrist

Q

quadril (kwah-*dreel*) m: hip

quando (*kwahn*-doo): when

quanto (*kwahn*-too): how much

quarta-feira (*kwah*-tah *fay*-rah) f: Wednesday

quarto (*kwah*-toh) m: room or bedroom

quatro (*kwah*-troo): four

que (kee): what

quem (kang): who

quinta-feira (*keen*-tah *fay*-rah) f: Thursday

quiosque (kee-*ah*-skee) m: concession stand

R

rápido (*hah*-pee-doo): fast

receita (heh-*say*-tah) f: revenue; recipe

recibo (heh-*see*-boo) m: receipt

rede (*heh*-jee) f: network

relógio smartwatch (heh-*loh*-zhee-ooh smaht-*wah*-chee) m: smartwatch

remédio (heh-*meh*-jee-oh) m: medicine

reservar (heh-seh-*vah*): to reserve

restaurante (heh-stah-ooh-*rahn*-chee) m: restaurant

retirar (heh-chee-*rah*): to withdraw (money)

reunião (hay-ooh-nee-*ah*-ooh) f: meeting

rio (*hee*-ooh) m: river

rosa (*hoh*-zah): pink

rosto (*hoh*-stroo) m: face

rua (*hoo*-ah) f: street

ruim (hoo-*eeng*): bad

S

sábado (*sah*-bah-doo) m: Saturday

saia (*sah*-ee-ah) f: skirt

sala de estar (*sah*-lah jee eh-*stah*) f: living room

sala de jantar (*sah*-lah jee zhahn-*tah*) f: dining room

salada (sah-*lah*-dah) f: salad

samba (*sahm*-bah) m: type of dance

sambódromo (sahm-*boh*-droh-moo) m: sambodrome

sangue (*sahn*-gee) m: blood

sapatos (sah-*pah*-tohs) m: shoes

segunda-feira (seh-*goon*-dah *fay*-rah) f: Monday

seis (*say*-eez): six

semana (seh-*mah*-nah) f: week

senha (*sen*-yah) f: password

senhor (seen-*yoh*) m: Mr./older man

senhora (seen-*yoh*-rah) f: Mrs./older woman

ser (sehr): to be (permanent state)

sete (*seh*-chee): seven

setembro (seh-*tem*-broo): September

sexta-feira (*ses*-tah *fay*-rah) f: Friday

simpático (seem-*pah*-chee-koh) nice (as in a "nice person")

sobremesa (soh-bree-*meh*-zah) f: dessert

sobrenome (soh-bree-*noh*-mee) m: last name/surname

sol (*soh*-ooh) m: sun

subir (sooh-*beeh*): to go up

sul (soo) m: south

surfista (soo-*fees*-tah) m/f: surfer

T

tamanho (tah-*mahn*-yoo) m: size

tarde (*tah*-jee): late

taxa de câmbio (*tah*-sha jee *kahm*-bee-oh) f: exchange rate

teatro (chee-*ah*-troo) m: theater

tela (*teh*-lah) f: screen

terça-feira (*teh*-sah *fay*-rah) f: Tuesday

tia (*chee*-ah) f: aunt

time (*chee*-mee) m: team

tio (*chee*-ooh) m: uncle

toalha (toe-*ahl*-yah) f: towel

torcedor (toh-seh-*doh*) m: fan (of a sport)

tornozelo (toh-noh-*zeh*-loo) m: ankle

trabalho (trah-*bahl*-yoh) m: job

tranquilo (trahn-*kwee*-loo): calm or relaxed

trânsito (*trahn*-zee-too) m: traffic

três (trehz): three

trio elétrico (*tree*-ooh eh-*leh*-tree-koo) m: motorized truck

U

um (oong): one

V

velho (*vel*-yoo): old

verde (*veh*-jee): green

vermelho (veh-*mel*-yoo) m: red

viagem (vee-*ah*-zhang) f: trip

vida (*vee*-dah) f: life

vinho (*veen*-yoo) m: wine

violão (vee-ooh-*lah*-ooh) m: guitar

vitamina (vee-tah-*mee*-nah) f: milkshake/vitamin

English-Portuguese Mini-Dictionary

A

a lot: **muito** (moh-*ee*-toh)

actor: **ator** (ah-*toh*) m

agency: **agência** (ah-*zhang*-see-ah) f

airplane: **avião** (ah-vee-*ah*-ooh) m

and: **e** (ee)

ankle: **tornozelo** (toh-noh-*zeh*-loo) m

another: **outro** (*oh*-trooh) m

app: **app** (ahp) m

apple: **maçã** (mah-*sah*) f

April: **abril** (ah-*bree*-ooh)

arm: **braço** (*brah*-soo) m

art exhibition: **exposição de arte** (eks-poh-zee-*sah*-ooh jee *ah*-chee) f

to ask: **perguntar** (peh-goon-*tah*)

ATM: **caixa automático** (*kah*-ee-shah ah-ooh-toh-*mah*-chee-koo) m

August: **agosto** (ah-*goh*-stoo)

aunt: **tia** (*chee*-ah) f

avenue: **avenida** (ah-veh-*nee*-dah) f

avocado: **abacate** (ah-bah-*koch*) m

B

bad: **ruim** (hoo-*eeng*)

banana: **banana** (bah-*nah*-nah) f

bank: **banco** (*bahn*-koh) m

bank account: **conta** (*kohn*-tah) f

bathroom: **banheiro** (bahn-*yay*-roh) m

to be (temporary state): **estar** (es-*stah*)

to be (permanent state): **ser** (sehr)

beach: **praia** (*prah*-ee-ah) f

beach lounge chair: **cadeira de praia** (kah-*day*-rah jee *prah*-ee-ah) f

beans: **feijão** (fay-*zhah*-ooh) m

bed: **cama** (*kah*-mah) f

beef: **carne** (*kah*-nee) f

beer: **cerveja** (seh-*veh*-zhah) f

belly: **barriga** (bah-*hee*-gah) f

better: **melhor** (mel-*yoh*)

bicycle: **bicicleta** (*bee*-see-*kleh*-tah) f

big: **grande** (*grahn*-jee)

bikini: **biquini** (bee-*kee*-nee) m

bill (as in dollar): **nota** (*noh*-tah) f

bill (at a restaurant): **conta** (*kohn*-tah) f

black: **preto** (*preh*-too) m

blood: **sangue** (*sahn*-gee) m

blue: **azul** (ah-*zoo*)

boat: **barco** (*bah*-koo) m

book: **livro** (*leev*-roo) m

boy: **menino** (meh-*nee*-noo) m or **garoto** (gah-*roh*-too) m

bread: **pão** (*pah*-ooh) m

breakfast: **café da manhã** (kah-*feh* dah mahn-*yah*) m

brother: **irmão** (eeh-*mah*-ooh) m

brown: **marróm** (mah-*hohng*)

bus: **ônibus** (*oh*-nee-boos) m

C

to call: **ligar** (lee-*gah*)

calm, relaxed: **tranquilo** (trahn-*kwee*-loo)

camera: **câmera** (*kah*-meh-rah) f

to cancel: **cancelar** (kahn-seh-*lah*)

car: **carro** (*kah*-hoo) m

cat: **gato** (*gah*-too) m

cellphone: **celular** (sel-ooh-*lahr*) m

chair: **cadeira** (kah-*day*-rah) f

cheap: **barato** (bah-*rah*-too)

chest: **peito** (*pay*-too) m

chicken: **frango** (*frahn*-goo) m

chocolate: **chocolate** (shoh-koh-*lah*-chee) m

city: **cidade** (see-*dah*-jee) f

to clean: **limpar** (leem-*pah*)

to close: **fechar** (feh-*shah*)

coconut: **coco** (*koh*-koh) m

coconut water: **água de coco** (*ah*-gwah jee *koh*-koh) f

coffee: **café** (kah-*feh*) m

coin: **moeda** (moh-*eh*-dah) f

computer: **computador** (kohm-poo-tah-*doh*) m

concession stand: **quiosque** (kee-*ah*-skee) m

cool (excellent): **legal** (lay-*gow*)

corner: **esquina** (es-*kee*-nah) f

cost: **custar** (koo-*stah*)

country: **país** (pah-*eez*) m

cousin: **primo** (*pree*-moo) m or **prima** (*pree*-mah) f

D

dark: **escuro** (eh-*skoo*-roo) m

date: **data** (*dah*-tah) f

daughter: **filha** (*feel*-yah) f

day: **dia** (*jee*-ah) m

December: **dezembro** (deh-*zem*-broo)

dentist: **dentista** (den-*chee*-stah) (male or female)

dessert: **sobremesa** (soh-bree-*meh*-zah) f

difficult: **difícil** (jee-*fee*-see-ooh)

dining room: **sala de jantar** (*sah*-lah jee zhahn-*tah*) f

dinner/to have dinner: **jantar** (zhahn-*tah*) m

direction: **direção** (jee-reh-*sah*-ooh) f

dividend: **dividendo** (dee-vee-*den*-doh) m

doctor: **médica** (*meh*-jee-kah) (female)

doctor: **médico** (*meh*-jee-koo) (male)

dolls: **bonecos** (boo-*neh*-kooz) m

door: **porta** (*poh*-tah) f

download: **baixar** (bah-ee-*shah*)

drugstore: **farmácia** (fah-*mah*-see-ah) f

E

ear: **orelha** (oh-*rel*-yah) f

east: **leste** (*les*-chee) m

easy: **fácil** (*fah*-see-ooh)

egg: **ovo** (*oh*-voo) m

eight: **oito** (*oh*-ee-toh)

email: **email** (ee-*may*-oh) m

entrance gate (to a stadium): **portão** (pohr-*tah*-ooh) m

exchange rate: **taxa de câmbio** (*tah*-sha jee *kahm*-bee-oh) f

expensive: **caro** (*kah*-roo)

eye: **olho** (*ohl*-yoo) m

F

face: **rosto** (*hoh*-stroo) m

fan (of a sport): **torcedor** (toh-seh-*doh*) m

far away: **longe** (*lohn*-zhee)

fast: **rápido** (*hah*-pee-doo)

father: **pai** (*pah*-ee) m

February: **fevereiro** (feh-veh-*day*-roo)

fever: **febre** (*feh*-bree) f

to find: **encontrar** (en-kohn-*trah*)

finger: **dedo** (*deh*-doo) m

first: **primeiro** (pree-*may*-roo) m

first name: **nome** (*noh*-mee) m

fish: **peixe** (*pay*-shee) m

five: **cinco** (*sing*-koh)

flip-flops: **chinelos** (shee-*neh*-lohs) m

floor (of a building): **andar** (ahn-*dah*) m

flower: **flor** (floh) f

food: **comida** (koh-*mee*-dah) f

foot: **pé** (peh) m

for/in order to: **para** (*pah*-rah)

four: **quatro** (*kwah*-troo)

Friday: **sexta-feira** (*ses*-tah *fay*-rah) f

fruit: **fruta** (*froo*-tah) f

fun: **divertido** (jee-veh-*chee*-doo)

G

garden: **jardim** (zhah-*jing*) m

garlic: **alho** (*ahl*-yoh) m

girl: **menina** (meh-*nee*-nah) f or **garota** (gah-*roh*-tah) f

glass (cup): **copo** (*koh*-poo) m

to go up: **subir** (sooh-*beeh*)

gold: **ouro** (*oh*-roo) m

good: **bom** (bohng) m

granddaughter: **neta** (*neh*-tah) f

grandma: **avó** (ah-*voh*) f

grandpa: **avô** (ah-*vah*) m

grandson: **neto** (*neh*-too) m

green: **verde** (*veh*-jee)

guava: **goiaba** (goy-*ah*-bah) f

guide: **guia** (*gee*-ah) (male or female)

guitar: **violão** (vee-ooh-*lah*-ooh) m

H

hair: **cabelo** (kah-*beh*-loo) m

hand: **mão** (*mah*-ooh) f

handsome/beautiful: **lindo** (*leen*-doh) m

happy: **feliz** (feh-*lees*) or **contente** (kohn-*ten*-chee)

hat: **chapéu** (shah-*peh*-ooh) m

head: **cabeça** (kah-*beh*-sah) f

hello: **oi** (*oh*-ee)

help: **ajuda** (ah-zhoo-*dah*) f

her: **dela** (*deh*-lah) f

hip: **quadril** (kwah-*dreel*) m

his: **dele** (*deh*-lee) m

hour: **hora** (*oh*-rah) f

house: **casa** (*kah*-zah) f

how much: **quanto** (*kwahn*-too)

hug: **abraço** (ah-*brah*-soo) m

hunger: **fome** (*foh*-mee) f

I

identification: **identificação** (ee-den-chee-fee-kah-*sah*-ooh) f

immigration: **imigração** (ee-mee-grah-*sah*-ooh) f

intelligent: **inteligente** (een-tehl-ee-*zhang*-chee) m/f

iPhone: **iPhone** (*ah*-ee-fohn) m

island: **ilha** (*eel*-yah) f

J

jacket: **casaco** (kah-*zah*-koo) m

January: **janeiro** (zhah-*nay*-roo)

job: **trabalho** (trah-*bahl*-yoh) m

July: **julho** (*zhool*-yoh)

June: **junho** (zhoon-yoh)

K

kiss: **beijo** (*bay*-zhoo) m

kitchen: **cozinha** (koh-*zeen*-yah) f

knee: **joelho** (zhoh-*el*-yoh) m

knife: **faca** (*fah*-kah) f

L

language: **língua** (*ling*-gwah) f

last name: **sobrenome** (soh-bree-*noh*-mee) m

late: **tarde** (*tah*-jee)

lawyer: **advogada** (ahj-voh-*gah*-dah) f or **advogado** (ahj-voh-*gah*-doo) m

left: **esquerda** (es-*keh*-dah) f

leg: **perna** (*peh*-nah) f

less: **menos** (*meh*-nooz)

lettuce: **alface** (ah-ooh-*fah*-see) f

life: **vida** (*vee*-dah) f

light (in color): **claro** (*klah*-roo) m

lighthouse: **farol** (fah-*roh*-ooh) m

to like: **gostar** (goh-*stah*)

lime: **limão** (lee-*mah*-ooh) m

to listen: **escutar** (es-koo-*tah*)

little: **pouco** (*poh*-koo)

to live: **morar** (moh-*rah*)

living room: **sala de estar** (*sah*-lah jee eh-*stah*) f

lunch: **almoço** (ah-ooh-*moh*-soo) m

M

man: **homem** (*oh*-mang) m

manager: **gerente** (zheh-*rang*-chee) m/f

mango: **manga** (*mahn*-gah) f

map: **mapa** (*mah*-pah) m

March: **março** (*mah*-soo)

May: **maio** (*my*-oh)

medicine: **remédio** (heh-*meh*-jee-ooh) m

meeting: **reunião** (hay-ooh-nee-*ah*-ooh) f

milk: **leite** (*lay*-chee) m

milkshake: **vitamina** (vee-tah-*mee*-nah) f

minute: **minuto** (mee-*noo*-too) m

Monday: **segunda-feira** (seh-*goon*-dah *fay*-rah) f

money: **dinheiro** (jing-*yay*-roo) m; **grana** (*grah*-nah) f (slang)

moon: **lua** (*loo*-ah) f

more: **mais** (*mah*-eez)

morning: **manhã** (mahn-*yah*) f

mother: **mãe** (*mah*-ee) f

motorized truck: **trio elétrico** (*tree*-ooh eh-*leh*-tree-koo) m

mouth: **boca** (*boh*-kah) f

movie theater: **cinema** (see-*neh*-mah) m

Mr./older man : **senhor** (seen-*yoh*) m

Mrs./older woman: **senhora** (seen-*yoh*-rah) f

museum: **museu** (moo-*zeh*-ooh) m

music: **música** (*moo*-zee-kah) f (Popular types of Brazilian music include **axé, frevo,** and **maracuta.**)

N

near: **perto** (*peh*-too)

neck: **pescoço** (pes-*koh*-soo) m

neighborhood: **bairro** (*bah*-ee-hoo) m

network: **rede** (*heh*-jee) f

nice (as in a "nice person"): **simpático** (seem-*pah*-chee-koh) m night: **noite** (*noh*-ee-chee) f

nightclub: **boate** (boh-*ah*-chee) f

nine: **nove** (*noh*-vee)

no: **não** (*nah*-ooh)

north: **norte** (*noh*-chee) m

nose: **nariz** (nah-*reez*) m

November: **novembro** (noo-*vem*-broo)

now: **agora** (ah-*goh*-rah)

number: **número** (*noo*-meh-roh) m

O

ocean: **mar** (mah) m

October: **outubro** (ooh-*too*-broo)

old: **velho** (*vel*-yoo) m

on foot: **a pé** (ah *peh*)

one: **um** (oong)

one hundred: **cem** (sang)

onion: **cebola** (seh-*boh*-lah) f

to open: **abrir** (ah-*breeh*)

or: **ou** (ooh)

organized: **organizado** (ohr-gahn-ee-*zah*-doh)

P

pain: **dor** (doh) f

pants: **calças** (*kah*-ooh-sahz) f

party: **festa** (*fehs*-tah) f

passport: **passaporte** (pah-sah-*poh*-chee) m

password: **senha** (*sen*-yah) f

to pay: **pagar** (pah-*gah*)

performance (of a company): **desempenho** (des-em-*pen*-yoh) m

person: **pessoa** (peh-*soh*-ah) f

photo: **foto** (*foh*-too) f

pineapple: **abacaxi** (ah-bah-kah-*shee*) m

pink: **rosa** (*hoh*-zah)

plaza: **praça** (*prah*-sah) f

pool: **piscina** (pee-*see*-nah) f

popcorn: **pipoca** (pee-*poh*-kah) f

price: **preço** (*preh*-soo) m

to print out: **imprimir** (eem-pree-*meeh*)

profit: **lucro** (*loo*-kroh) m

R

rain: **chuva** (*shoo*-vah) f

receipt: **recibo** (heh-*see*-boo) m

red: **vermelho** (veh-*mel*-yoo)

to reserve: **reservar** (heh-seh-*vah*)

restaurant: **restaurante** (heh-stah-ooh-*rahn*-chee) m

revenue: **receita** (heh-*say*-tah) f

rice: **arroz** (ah-*hohz*) m

right (as in direction/location): **direita** (jee-*ray*-tah) f

river: **rio** (*hee*-ooh) m

road: **caminho** (kah-*meen*-yoo) m

room or bedroom: **quarto** (*kwah*-toh) m

S

sailboat: **jangada** (zhan-*gah*-dah) f

salad: **salada** (sah-*lah*-dah) f

samba: **samba** (*sahm*-bah) m (a type of dance)

sambodrome: **sambódromo** (sahm-*boh*-droh-moo) m

sand: **areia** (ah-*ray*-ah) f

Saturday: **sábado** (*sah*-bah-doo) m

screen: **tela** (*teh*-lah) f

September: **setembro** (seh-*tem*-broo)

seven: **sete** (*seh*-chee)

share (as in a share of stock): **ação** (ah-*sah*-ooh) m

shellfish: **mariscos** (mah-*rees*-kooz) m

shirt (female): **blusa** (*bloo*-zah) f

shirt (male): **camisa** (kah-*mee*-zah) f; **abadá** (ah-bah-*dah*) m (shirt for a Carnival group performance)

shoes: **sapatos** (sah-*pah*-tohs) m

shoulder: **ombro** (*ohm*-broh) m

shrimp: **camarão** (kah-mah-*rah*-ooh) m

sister: **irmã** (ee-*mah*) f

six: **seis** (*say*-eez)

size: **tamanho** (tah-*mahn*-yoo) m

skirt: **saia** (*sah*-ee-ah) f

slowly: **devagar** (deh-vah-*gah*)

small: **pequeno** (peh-*keh*-noo) m

smartwatch: **relógio smartwatch** (heh-*loh*-zhee-ooh smaht-*wah*-chee) m

soap opera: **novela** (noh-*veh*-lah) f

some: **algum** (ah-ooh-*goong*)

son: **filho** (*feel*-yoo) m

song: **canção** (kahn-*sah*-ooh) f

south: **sul** (soo) m

to speak: **falar** (fah-*lah*)

special: **especial** (eh-speh-see-*ah*-ooh)

spicy: **apimentado**
(ah-pee-men-*tah*-doo)

spinach: **espinafre** (es-pee-*nah*-free) m

spoon: **colher** (kool-*yeh*) f

stadium: **estádio** (es-*stah*-jee-oh) m

state: **estado** (eh-*stah*-doo) m

station: **estação** (es-tah-*sah*-ooh) f

street: **rua** (*hoo*-ah) f

subway: **metrô** (meh-*troh*) m

sun: **sol** (*soh*-ooh) m

Sunday: **domingo** (doo-*ming*-goo) m

sunglasses: **óculos de sol** (*oh*-koo-lohs
jee *soh*-ooh) m

sunscreen: **protetor solar** (proh-teh-*toh*
soh-*lah*) m

surfer: **surfista** (soo-*fees*-tah) m/f

sweet: **doce** (*doh*-see)

T

table: **mesa** (*meh*-zah) f

tall: **alto** (*ah*-ooh-too)

taxes: **impostos** (eem-*pohs*-tohs) m

team: **time** (*chee*-mee) m

ten: **dez** (dez)

theater: **teatro** (chee-*ah*-troo) m

theirs: **deles** (*deh*-leez) m

thing: **coisa** (*koy*-zah) f

to think: **achar** (ah-*shah*)

three: **três** (trehz)

thumb: **polegar** (poh-leh-*gah*) m

Thursday: **quinta-feira** (*keen*-tah *fay*-
rah) f

ticket: **bilhete** (beel-*yeh*-chee) m: ticket
(as in theater/lottery)

ticket office: **bilheteria** (beel-yeh-teh-
ree-ah) f

today: **hoje** (*oh*-zhee)

toe: **dedo do pé** (*deh*-doo doo *peh*) m

tomorrow: **amanhã** (ah-mahng-*yah*)

tongue: **língua** (*ling*-gwah) f

tooth: **dente** (*den*-chee) m

towel: **toalha** (toe-*ahl*-yah) f

traffic: **trânsito** (*trahn*-zee-too) m

tree: **árvore** (*ah*-voh-ree) f

trip: **viagem** (vee-*ah*-zhang) f

to try: **experimentar**
(eh-*speh*-ree-men-*tah*)

T-shirt: **camiseta** (kah-mee-*zeh*-tah) f

Tuesday: **terça-feira** (*teh*-sah *fay*-rah) f

two: **dois** (*doh*-eez)

U

ugly: **feio** (*fay*-ooh)

uncle: **tio** (*chee*-ooh) m

W

water: **água** (*ah*-gwah) f

Wednesday: **quarta-feira** (*kwah*-tah *fay*-rah) f

week: **semana** (seh-*mah*-nah) f

west: **oeste** (oh-*es*-chee) m

what: **que** (kee)

when: **quando** (*kwahn*-doo)

white: **branco** (*brahn*-koh)

who: **quem** (kang)

wine: **vinho** (*ving*-yoo) m

with: **com** (kohng)

to withdraw (money): **retirar** (heh-chee-*rah*)

woman: **mulher** (mool-*yeh*) f

wood: **madeira** (mah-*day*-rah) f

worse: **pior** (pee-*oh*)

wrist: **pulso** (*pool*-soh) m

Y

yellow: **amarelo** (ah-mah-*reh*-loo)

young: **jovem** (*zhoh*-vang)

Appendix C

Answer Key

Chapter 1: You Already Know Some Portuguese!

1. e; 2. c; 3. b; 4. a; 5. d

Chapter 2: The Nitty-Gritty: Basic Portuguese Grammar

1. **inteligente** (him, her)
2. **simpático** (him)
3. **tranquila** (her)
4. **linda** (her)
5. **alto** (him)
6. **jovem** (him, her)
7. **médico** (him, her)
8. **organizado** (him)

Chapter 3: Oi! Hello! Greetings and Introductions

1. across: **senhor;**
2. down: **estar;**
3. down: **oi;**
4. down: **falar;**
5. across: **alto;**
6. down: **nome**

Chapter 4: Getting Your Numbers, Times, and Measurements Straight

1. b; 2. c; 3. a; 4. d

Chapter 5: Speaking Portuguese at Home

A. o banheiro; **B.** o quarto; **C.** a sala de jantar;

D. a cozinha; **E.** a sala de estar

Chapter 6: Getting To Know You: Small Talk

A. o meu pai; **B.** a sua mãe; **C.** o irmão dele;

D. a irmã deles; **E.** a nossa avó

Chapter 7: Dining Out and Going to the Market

A. arroz e feijão; **B.** salada; **C.** peixe;

D. carne; **E.** frango

Chapter 8: Shopping

1. *green*/**verde**; **2.** *white*/**branco**; **3.** *red*/**vermelho**;

4. *blue*/**azul**; **5.** *pink*/**rosa**; **6.** *brown*/**marróm**

A. blusa; **B.** saia; **C.** sapatos; **D.** gravata;

E. chapéu; **F.** casaco; **G.** calças

Chapter 9: Going Out on the Town

1. d; **2.** e; **3.** b; **4.** a; **5.** c

Chapter 10: Using Technology to Keep in Touch

1. c; **2.** h; **3.** a; **4.** f; **5.** b; **6.** g; **7.** d; **8.** e

Chapter 11: Chatting About Business

1. g; **2.** i; **3.** c; **4.** f; **5.** d; **6.** b; **7.** h; **8.** e; **9.** a; **10.** j

Chapter 12: Recreation and the Outdoors

A. óculos de sol; **B.** areia; **C.** cadeiras de praia; **D.** surfistas; **E.** biquini; **F.** toalha; **G.** água de coco; **H.** protetor solar; **I.** chinelos

Chapter 13: Planning a Trip

A. junho (11), julho (9), agosto (8)

B. dezembro (1), janeiro (4), fevereiro (6)

C. setembro (3), outubro (12), novembro (10)

D. março (7), abril (2), maio (5)

Chapter 14: Money, Money, Money

1. banco; **2.** retirar; **3.** dinheiro; **4.** conta; **5.** grana; **6.** caixa eletrônico; **7.** duas notas; **8.** pagar; **9.** recibo

Chapter 15: Getting Around: Planes, Buses, Taxis, and More

A. bicicleta; **B.** barco; **C.** avião; **D.** jangada;
E. a pé; **F.** ônibus; **G.** metrô

Chapter 16: Going to Sporting Events

A. portão; **B.** estádio; **C.** pipoca (at the) quiosque;
D. torcedor; **E.** bilheteria; **F.** time

Chapter 17: O Carnaval!

A. Salvador: 3, 6, 7, 9
B. Rio: 2, 4
C. Recife/Olinda: 1, 5, 8

Chapter 18: Socorro! Help! Handling Emergencies

A. olho; **B.** nariz; **C.** dente or boca; **D.** ombro;
E. peito; **F.** pulso; **G.** dedo; **H.** barriga;
I. joelho; **J.** tornozelo; **K.** dedo do pé; **L.** pé;
M. batata da perna; **N.** braço; **O.** polegar;
P. quadril; **Q.** pescoço; **R.** orelha;
S. cabelo; **T.** rosto

Index

A

ã, 19
a (letter), 12, 18–19
a gente, 159, 356
a gente se vê, 58
a senhora, 29, 43–44, 46
a/as (articles), 27–28
abadás, 315–316
abraço, 94, 174, 186–187
abrir, 360
açaí na tigela com granola, 122
acarajé, 122
accent marks, 11
accents, 11, 97, 118, 177
accommodations, 245–248
 amenities, 247
 registration, 246–247
 reservations, 245–246
 types of, 245
achar, 360
acordar, 83
adjectives, 26–27
 Fun & Games activities, 38
 gender, 26–27
 placement, 26
 plural, 27
adorar, 32, 221
afoxés, 316–317
agora mesmo, 179
Ah é? 354
air travel, 266–270
 airlines, 234
 phrases and terms, 266–267, 269–270
 reserving flights, 267, 269–270
 Talkin' the Talk dialogues, 268–269
 taxes, 270
 travel agencies, 267
almoço, 86–87

alô, 93, 174
alphabet, 11–13
 consonants, 13–18
 Fun & Games activities, 23
 pronouncing names of letters, 12–13
 vowels, 18–20
alugar, 81, 275–276
Amazon Brasil, 346
Amazonas (state), 235
Amazônia, 209, 216–218
andares, 66, 80
Angola, 10
-ão, 14, 19
apelidos, 42
Apple Pay, 254, 257, 260
-ar verbs, 31–32. *See also specific -ar verbs*
 commands, 287
 future tense, 359
 past tense, 112–113, 359
 present tense, 32, 359
áreas de serviço, 79
art, 164–165
 phrases and terms, 164–165
 venues, 164
artesanato, 151
articles, 27–28
 gender, 27–28
 plural, 28
até, 57–58
Até logo, 57–58, 93, 174, 182, 203
atendentes, 142, 144
ATMs, 254, 256–257
atrasado, 203, 278
atraso, 278
Avis, 275
axé, 316, 346
azeite de dendê, 87, 122–123
Azul airline, 234

B

b, 12

Bahia
  beaches, 214
  food, 122–123
  music, 151
  regional accent, 21
  visiting, 235
bahianos/as, 105
banheiro, 78, 84, 89
banks, 254–257
bargaining, 153
Barra da Tijuca, 210
bars, 82, 132, 160
bathroom, 78, 84, 89
BBC Brasil, 345
beach chairs, 212
beach umbrellas, 212
beaches, 210–216
  attire and accessories, 210–211
  describing, 214–215
  food vendors, 212
  Fun & Games activities, 223–224
  recommended, 210, 214–215
  Talkin' the Talk dialogues, 213–216
  transportation, 265
beber, 134–135
  present tense, 134
  usage examples, 135
bebidas, 131–132
beer, 132, 293
Beija-Flor, 312
beijo, 94, 174, 186–187
Belém, 236
bem-vindo, 81
berimbaus, 151, 162
bermudas, 211
bijouteria, 152
bikinis, 210
biodiversity, 217–218
  plant life, 218
  wildlife, 218–219, 235–236
Blumenau, 132
Boa noite, 40, 82

Boa tarde, 40
body parts, 335–336, 339
Bolsa de Valores de São Paulo, 195
Bom dia, 40
bonecos gigantes, 319–320
Bonito, 236
bossa nova, 91, 346
botecos, 123, 313
Brasília
  art, 164
  getting around, 282
  visiting, 236
Brazilian Portuguese
  accent marks, 11
  alphabet, 11–13
    consonants, 13–18
    pronouncing names of letters,
      12–13
    vowels, 18–20
  business, 195–208
    appointments, 203
    economy, 195
    fazer, 197–198
    formal letters, 201–202
    home office, 205–207
    meetings, 203–205
    professions and positions,
      196–197
    stock market, 195
    telephone, 202–203
    trabalhar, 199
Carnaval, 309–323
  crime, 326
  out of season, 309
  Recife/Olinda, 318–320
  Rio de Janeiro, 310–313
  Salvador, 314–317
  samba, 320–321
dates
  specifying, 71–72
  years, 64
days of the week, 61, 68–69
dictionary
  English to Portuguese, 379–388
  Portuguese to English, 369–378

dining, 121–135
  bars, 132
  beach food vendors, 212
  breakfast, 85–86
  churrascarias, 132–133
  dinner, 87–88
  drinks, 131–132
  expressions, 128
  extras to ask for, 127
  foods, 121–131
  ingredients, 127–128
  lunch, 86–87
  ordering and eating meals,
    126–127
  sporting event concessions, 298–299
  tipping, 129
  utensils and place-settings, 88–89
  vegetarians, 125, 133
  verbs, 133–135
emergencies, 309–323, 325–339
  basic terms, 326
  crime, 326–330
  health emergencies, 330–337
  legal problems, 338
English words used in, 11, 13
European Portuguese vs., 9–10, 22
grammar, 25–38
  adjectives, 26–27
  articles, 27–28
  commands, 287–288
  connector words, 289
  contractions, 35–37
  indirect objects, 37
  nouns, 26–27
  possessives, 36, 108–111, 248–250
  pronouns, 28–30
  sentence construction, 30–31
  verb conjugation, 31–35
  verbs, 30–35
greetings and introductions, 39–59
  formal vs. informal, 43–44, 46
  making introductions, 41
  names, 42–43
  saying good-bye, 57–58
  saying hello, 40–41

home, 77–100
  bathroom, 84
  city life, 80–81
  cleaning, 89
  food, 84–89
  guests, 99
  living-space words, 78–79
  neighborhood, 90–91
  renting, 81
  sleep and waking up, 82–83
  telephone, 92–98
Internet, 186–192
  e-mail, 187–188
  social media, 190–193
  tablets, 191–192
learning quickly, 343–348
  dating, 344–345
  language classes, 348
  movies, 347–348
  music, 346–347
  news, 345
  speaking to Brazilians near home, 344
  talking to yourself, 348
  travel, 343–344
  TV, 348
  websites, 345
Metric system, 72–73
money, 253–263
  ATMs, 254, 256–257
  banks, 254–257
  currency denominations and values, 253–254
  decimal points and commas, 258
  exact change, 257
  exchange rate, 254
  exchanging, 254
  pagar, 259–260
  prices, 258
  purchases, 258–260
  withdrawal limits, 256–257
names
  de, 42
  first names, 42
  last names, 42
  making introductions, 41
  nicknames, 42–43

Brazilian Portuguese *(continued)*
  names of other languages in, 54
  number who speak Portuguese, 1
  numbers, 62–66
    1-10, 62
    11-19, 62–63
    20-100, 63
    101–199, 63
    201–999, 63
    floor levels, 66
    higher numbers, 64
    ordinal numbers, 65–66
    years, 64
  permanent qualities, 46–51
  reasons to learn, 1
  recreation and the outdoors, 209–223
    asking people what they like to do, 219–221
    beaches, 210–216
    biodiversity, 217–218
    rainforest, 216–217
    sports, 219–220
  regional differences, 9, 21–22
  roots of, 10–11
  shopping, 140
    clothing, 142–143
    clothing sizes, 143
    colors, 144
    comparisons, 148–149
    experimentar, 145–146
    expressing opinions, 144, 148–149
    levar, 146–147
    making purchases, 260
    negotiating, 153
    outdoor markets, 136–137
    prices, 258
    receipts, 260
    salespeople, 142, 144
    souvenirs, 151–153
    supermarkets, 135–136
    types of venues, 141–142
  sightseeing and going out, 157–172
    art, 164–165
    cover charges, 160
    dating, 168–169
      invitations, 158–159
      movies, 165–166, 168, 347–348
      music, 160–164, 346–347
      planning, 157–160
      questions and answers, 159–160
  slang, 22, 97, 180, 254, 283, 349–352
  small talk, 103–120
    connector words, 117–118
    contact information, 118–119
    family connections, 107–108
    past tense, 112–116
    place of origin, 103–107
    possessives, 108–111
    "save me!" phrases, 118
    who, what, and where, 111–112
  sporting events, 293–308
    ganhar, 304
    jogar, 301–302
    perder, 304
    praticar, 302–303
    preferir, 303–304
    procurar, 304–305
    soccer, 293–301
  telephone, 92–98, 172–186
    business calls, 202–203
    communication apps, 184–186
    emojis, 194
    getting used to language, 97–98, 177
    international calls, 93, 175
    leaving messages, 181–182
    ligar, 96–97, 179–180
    making arrangements, 183
    making calls, 92–94, 173–174
    telling someone to call you, 180–181
    texting, 184–185
  temporary qualities, 51–53
  time, 66–67, 71–72
  transportation, 265–291
    buses, 270–271
    car rentals, 275–277
    cities, 281–290
    modes of, 265–266
    phrases and terms, 265–266, 278–283, 285
    planes, 266–270

ride-hailing apps, 274–275
taxis, 271–273
trip planning, 227–252
accommodations, 245–248
customs, 244
health concerns, 232–233
ir, 241–242
map, 229
packing, 233–234
passports, 232
place to go, 234–239
possessives, 248–250
timing, 228
visas, 232
weather, 227–229
words that resemble English, 11
written, 9
breakfast, 85–86, 247
brega, 349
brincar, 162, 302
Bündchen, Gisele, 47, 51
bus transportation, 270–271
buying tickets, 270–271
manners, 271
business, 195–208
appointments, 203
economy, 195
fazer, 197–198
formal letters, 201–202
home office, 205–207
meetings, 203–205
professions and positions, 196–197
stock market, 195
Talkin' the Talk dialogues, 98–99, 178
telephone, 202–203
trabalhar, 199
Búzios, 237

C

c, 12–14
ç, 14
Cabify, 274
cabines telefônicas (orelhões), 94, 175
Cabo Verde, 10

Cabral, Pedro Álvares, 10
cachaça, 45, 352
cadeiras de praia, 212
café da manhã, 85–86, 247
cafezinho, 129
cafona, 349
caipifrutas, 132
caipirinhas, 45, 73, 132, 352
caipiroskas, 132
camelôs, 211
Campo Grande, 236
cangas, 211
cantar, 163–164
present tense, 164
usage examples, 164
capitalization, 54, 104, 229
capivaras, 218–219
capoeira, 162, 235, 303, 344
cara, 350
Cardoso, Fernando Henrique, 42–43
cariocas, 21, 105
Carnaval, 245, 309–323
crime, 326
Fun & Games activities, 322–323
out of season, 309
Recife/Olinda, 318–320
Rio de Janeiro, 310–313
Salvador, 314–317
samba, 320–321
Talkin' the Talk dialogues, 313, 317–318
cars, 275–277
crime, 327
drinking and driving, 277
gasoline, 275
parking, 277
renting, 275–277
traffic signs, 277
cavaquinhos, 162
cê, 355–356
Ceará, 214, 236
cedilha, 14
cedo, 278
centavos, 254, 258
Centers for Disease Control and Prevention, 331
CEP (Código de Endereçamento Postal), 201

cerveja, 132, 293

Chapada Diamantina, 235

chato, 350

chegar, 278–279
  past tense, 279
  present tense, 278
  usage examples, 279

chique, 350

chorinho, 162, 188–189, 346

churrascarias, 105–106, 132–133, 238

churrasco, 84, 105, 122, 238

circumflex, 20

Citibank, 256

cities. See also names of specific cities
  getting around, 281–283
  life in, 80–81

cleaning, 89

clothing, 142–146
  colors, 144
  experimentar, 145–146
  expressing opinions, 144
  Fun & Games activities, 154–155
  packing, 233–234
  shopping for, 142–143
  sizes, 143

coco, 122

Código de Endereçamento Postal (CEP), 201

colocar, 363

colors, 144

comandas, 160

combinar, 69, 183

começar, 32, 360

comer, 133–134
  future tense, 359
  past tense, 359
  present tense, 134, 359
  usage examples, 134

commands, 287–288

communication apps, 184–186

como, 111–112, 118

comprar, 361

comunidades, 77, 80

conhecer, 361

conjunctions, 117–118

connector words, 117–118, 289

contact information, 118–119

contractions, 35–37
  with de, 36
  with em, 35–36
  né, 51
  with por, 36
  possesives, 36

convidar, 158–159

Copacabana, 91, 210, 282

CouchSurfing, 345

cover charges, 160

COVID-19, 124, 332–333

coxinhas, 123

cozinha, 84

cozinhar, 84

CPF, 260–261

credit cards, 256, 260, 271–272, 327–328

crime, 326–330
  asking for help, 328–329
  how to react, 327–328
  perspective, 327
  police, 329–330

Cristo Redentor, 91, 237

cuícas, 162

cupuaçu, 131

currency denominations and values, 253–254

customs, 244

D

d, 12, 14

da Silva, Luiz Inácio Lula, 42–43

da Silva surname, 42

dançar, 163

dancing, 163. See also Carnaval; names of specific dances

dar, 363

dates
  months, 229–230
  seasons, 228
  specifying, 71–72
  years, 64

dating, 168–169
  boyfriend/girlfriend, 168
  flirting, 169

learning language quickly, 344–345

novelas, 168

romantic phrases, 168–169

sweet nothings, 169

Talkin' the Talk dialogues, 200–201

days of the week, 61, 68–69

de, 42, 110, 250

decimal points, 258

deixar, 113

dele/dela/deles/delas, 36, 110, 249–250

demais, 144–145

devagar, 93, 118, 174

diaristas, 89

digitar, 184

dining, 121–135

bars, 132

beach food vendors, 212

breakfast, 85–86

churrascarias, 132–133

classic foods, 121–123

desserts, 128–129

dinner, 87–88

drinks, 131–132

expressions, 128

extras to ask for, 127

ingredients, 127–128

lunch, 86–87

menus, 124–126

ordering and eating meals, 126–127

ordering and enjoying meals, 126–128

sporting event concessions, 298–299

Talkin' the Talk dialogues, 105–106, 129–130, 306

tipping, 129

types of eateries, 123–124

utensils and place-settings, 88–89

vegetarians, 125, 133

verbs, 133–135

virus precautions, 124

dinner, 87–88

directions, 285–289

direto, 289

do/da/dos/das, 36, 110

dormir com os anjinhos, 83

drinks, 131–132

driving and, 277

sporting events, 293

driving, 275–277

car rentals, 275–277

drinking and, 277

gasoline, 275

parking, 277

traffic signs, 277

E

é, 30

ê, 19

e (letter), 12, 19

eating. See dining; food

electrical adaptors, 234

ele/ela/eles/elas, 27, 29

elu, 29

em, 230

e-mail, 187–188

embassies, 232

emergencies, 325–339

basic terms, 326

crime, 326–330

asking for help, 328–329

how to react, 327–328

perspective, 327

police, 329–330

health emergencies, 330–337

legal problems, 338

emojis, 194

encontrar, 113

então, 354

-er verbs, 31, 34–35. See also specific -er verbs

commands, 287

future tense, 359

past tense, 359

present tense, 34, 359

escolas de samba, 311–312

escutar, 114, 361

esperar, 281

esperto, 350–351

estar, 51–53
  conjugation chart, 51
  future tense, 364
  past tense, 364
  present tense, 364
  ser vs., 46
  temporary qualities, 51–52
  usage examples, 52–53
eu, 28
European Portuguese, 9–10, 22
exaggerations, 149
experimentar, 145–146
  clothing, 145–146
  present tense, 145
  usage examples, 146

F

f, 12
Face (Facebook), 190–191, 345
Fala inglês? 97, 177
falar, 53–56
  future tense, 362
  past tense, 114, 362
  present tense, 53, 362
  usage examples, 54–55
family connections, 107–108
farinha, 133
farofa, 123
favelas, 77, 325
fazer, 197–198
  future tense, 364
  past tense, 197–198, 364
  present tense, 197, 364
  usage examples, 198
fechar, 32, 114, 362
feiras
  food items, 136–137
  negotiating, 153
  souvenirs, 141–142
Fernando de Noronha, 215
Filhos de Ghandi, 316
films, 165–166
  learning language quickly,
    347–348

questions, 168
  translated titles, 168
fio dental, 211
first names, 42
fitas do Bonfim, 151
fixe, 22
flirting, 169–171
floor levels, 66
Florianópolis, 214, 239
Folha de São Paulo, 345
food, 84–89
  bars, 132
  beach food vendors, 212
  breakfast, 85–86
  dinner, 87–88
  expressions, 128
  extras to ask for, 127
  Fun & Games activities, 140
  ingredients, 127–128
  lunch, 86–87
  market, 135–139
  ordering and eating meals, 126–127
  sporting event concessions, 298–299
  tipping, 129
  utensils and place-settings, 88–89
  vegetarians, 125, 133
forró, 162–163
Fortal, 309
Fortaleza
  out-of-season carnaval, 309
  regional accent, 21
Foz do Iguaçu, 239
frescobol, 213
frevo, 320
Fun & Games activities
  adjectives, 38
  alphabet, 23
  beach, 223–224
  body parts, 339
  Carnaval, 322–323
  clothing, 154–155
  emojis, 194
  food, 140
  going out, 172
  greetings and introductions, 59

home, 100
meetings, 208
money, 263
months, 251–252
overview, 3
possessives, 120
soccer, 308
time, 75
transportation, 291

G

g, 12, 14–15
Galo da Madrugada, 319
ganhar, 304
gasoline, 275
gato/a, 351
gaúchos/as, 22, 105
gente boa, 48, 105
Gil, Gilberto, 316
"Girl from Ipanema," 42, 91–92
Gol airline, 234
Google Brazil, 345
Google Pay, 254, 257
gorjetas
    restaurants, 129
    taxis, 272
gostar
    asking people what they like to do, 220–221
    de, 148
    future tense, 362
    past tense, 362
    present tense, 362
    Talkin' the Talk dialogues, 115–116
Gramado, 20, 238
grammar, 25–38
    adjectives, 26–27
    articles, 27–28
    commands, 287–288
    conjunctions, 117–118
    connector words, 117–118, 289
    contractions, 35–37
    indirect objects, 37
    nouns, 26–27
    possessives, 36, 108–111, 248–250

prepositions, 117–118
pronouns, 28–30
sentence construction, 30–31
verb conjugation, 31–35
verbs, 30–35
grana, 254, 351
greetings and introductions, 39–59
    formal vs. informal, 43–44, 46
    Fun & Games activities, 59
    making introductions, 41
    names, 42–43
    saying good-bye, 57–58
    saying hello, 40–41
Guaraná Antártica, 131–132
guests, 99
Guiné-Bissau, 10

H

h, 12, 15
hammocks, 142, 151
handmade items, 153
Havaianas, 90, 151, 211
health concerns, 330–337
    body parts, 335–336
    COVID-19, 124, 332–333
    emergencies, 330–337
    injuries, 334–335
    normal illnesses, 333–334
    risks, 233
    Talkin' the Talk dialogues, 336–337
    tropical illnesses, 331–332
    vaccination, 124, 232–233, 270, 330–331
Hertz, 275
home, 77–100
    bathroom, 84
    city life, 80–81
    cleaning, 89
    food, 84–89
    Fun & Games activities, 100
    guests, 99
    home office, 205–207
    living-space words, 78–79
    neighborhood, 90–91
    renting, 81

home *(continued)*
  sleep and waking up, 82–83
  telephone, 92–98
home offices, 205–207
  advantages of, 205
  phrases and terms, 206
Homem da Meia-Noite, 319
hotels, 245–248
  amenities, 247
  pousadas vs., 245
  registration, 246–247
  reservations, 245–246
  Talkin' the Talk dialogues, 70–71
HSBC, 256

I

i, 12, 20
ile, 29
Ilha Grande, 237
Índice Bovespa, 195
indirect objects, 37
injuries, 334–335
Insta (Instagram), 190
international calls, 93, 175
InterNations, 345
Internet, 186–192. *See also* telephone
  e-mail, 187–188
  social media, 190–193
  tablets, 191–192
introductions. *See* greetings and introductions
invitations, 158–159
Ipanema, 90–91, 210, 220, 282
ir, 241–242
  future tense, 241–242, 364
  past tense, 114–115, 364
  present tense, 241, 364
  Talkin' the Talk dialogues, 115–116, 243–244
  usage examples, 241–242
-ir verbs, 31, 34–35. *See also specific -ir verbs*
  commands, 287
  future tense, 360
  past tense, 360
  present tense, 34, 360
Itacaré, 235

J

j, 12, 15
jantar, 87–89, 99
jewelry, 152
Jobim, Antônio Carlos, 91
jogar, 162, 301–302
  present tense, 301–302
  usage examples, 302
juice bars, 131

K

k, 12
kidnappings, 327
knickknacks, 152

L

l, 12, 15–16
Lady Driver, 274
lanchonetes, 123, 125
last names, 42
LATAM Brazil, 234
legal, 22, 105, 352
legal problems, 338
leite de coco, 123
Lençóis Maranhenses, 236
levar, 146–147
  present tense, 146
  usage examples, 146–147
lh, 15
ligar, 96–97, 179–180
  past tense, 113
  present tense, 96, 179
  usage examples, 96, 180–181
living-space words, 78–79
lunch, 86–87

M

m, 12, 16
mail
  business letters, 201–202
  e-mail, 187–188
  polite terms, 202

Manaus, 217, 235
mandioca frita, 122
Mangueira, 312
máquinas de lavar, 89
maracatu, 320
Maranhão, 236
markets, 135–139
  outdoor markets, 73–74, 136–139, 141–142, 153
  practical items, 136
  produce, 136–137
  supermarkets, 135–136
Mato Grosso do Sul, 218, 236
me, 37
meetings, 203–205
  business terms, 204
  company performance, 204
  Fun & Games activities, 208
  goals and plans, 205
  setting up, 203
  virtual, 206–207
meia-noite, 67
meio, 355
meio-dia, 40, 67
melhor, 149
Metric system, 72–73
meu/meus, 108–111, 119, 249
Minas Gerais, 105
  artesanato, 142
  food and drink, 123, 352
  regional accent, 21
  visiting, 238
mineiros/as, 105
minha/minhas, 108–110
Moçambique, 10
money, 253–263. See also shopping
  ATMs, 254, 256–257
  banks, 254–257
  currency denominations and values, 253–254
  decimal points and commas, 258
  exact change, 257
  exchange rate, 254
  exchanging, 254
  Fun & Games activities, 263
  pagar, 259–260
  prices, 258

  purchases, 258–260
  Talkin' the Talk dialogues, 255–256
  withdrawal limits, 256–257
months, 229–230, 251–252
moqueca, 87, 123
Moraes, Vinícius de, 42, 91
morar, 359
Morro de São Paulo, 235
Morro Dois Irmãos, 91
mosquitos, 217, 331
movies, 165–166
  learning language quickly, 347–348
  questions, 168
  Talkin' the Talk dialogues, 166–167
  translated titles, 168
MPB (Música Popular Brasileira), 346
music, 160–164. See also names of specific types of music
  artists, 346–347
  cantar, 163–164
  dançar, 163
  instruments, 161–162
  learning language quickly, 346–347
  Talkin' the Talk dialogues, 188–189
  tocar, 161–162
  top hits, 161
Música Popular Brasileira (MPB), 346

N

n, 12, 16
names
  de, 42
  first names, 42
  last names, 42
  making introductions, 41
  nicknames, 42–43
namorar, 168
Natal, 21
nationalities, 104
né, 51, 353–354
negotiating prices, 153
neighborhood, 90–91
nh, 15
nicknames, 42–43

Niemeyer, Oscar, 80, 282
99 Taxi, 274
no momento, 179
nomes, 42–43
no/na/nos/nas, 35–36, 68–69, 72
non-profits, 196
nós, 29, 159
Nossa senhora! 215
nossa/nossas, 109–110, 249
nosso/nossos, 109–111, 249
nouns, 26–27
  defined, 26
  gender, 26
  plural, 27
novelas, 87, 168, 348
numbers, 62–66
  1-10, 62
  11-19, 62–63
  20-100, 63
  101–199, 63
  201–999, 63
  floor levels, 66
  higher numbers, 64
  ordinal numbers, 65–66
  years, 64

O

ô, 20
o (letter), 20
o Copan, 80
O Estado de São Paulo, 345
O Globo, 345
o que, 111–112
o senhor, 29, 43–44, 46
Obama, Barack, 43
obrigado/a, 99
oi, 40–41, 93, 174, 181
olá, 40–41, 181
Olinda
  Carnaval, 310, 315, 318–320
  music, 320
  pousadas, 245
  visiting, 236

Olympic Games, 91, 293, 297
onde, 111–112, 285
online resources
  audio files (companion to book), 3, 6
  Cheat Sheet (companion to book), 6
  escolas de samba, 312
  Google Brazil, 345
  newspapers, 345
  shopping, 136, 346
o/os (articles), 27–28
orelhãos (cabines telefônicas), 94, 175
ou seja, 355
Ouro Preto, 238
outdoor markets
  food items, 136–137
  negotiating, 153
  souvenirs, 141–142
  Talkin' the Talk dialogues, 73–74, 138–139

P

p, 12
packing, 233–234
padarias, 123
pagar, 259–260
  past tense, 259
  present tense, 259
  usage examples, 259–260
pagode, 346
pandeiros, 162
Pantanal
  biodiversity, 209, 218
  visiting, 236
Pão de Açúcar (mountain), 91, 237
Pão de Açúcar (supermarket), 135, 346
pão de queijo, 123
pão francês, 122
paquerar, 169
Pará, 235
para, 96, 241
Paraná, 239
Paraty, 237
Parintins, 235

passports
  bus transportation, 271
  crime, 328
  obtaining, 232
past tense, 112–116
paulistanos/as, 80, 105
paulistas, 105
paxixis, 162
pedir, 365
Pelé, 43
"Pelo Telefone," 93, 174
pelo/pela/pelos/pelas, 36
Pelourinho, 235
perder
  future tense, 364–365
  past tense, 364–365
  present tense, 364–365
  usage examples, 304
Pernambuco
  artesanato, 142
  Carnaval, 318
  visiting, 236
Petrópolis, 237
photography, 185, 190, 234
pickpockets, 210, 327–328
pimenta, 122
pinga, 352
Pinto, Heloísa Eneida de Menezes Paes, 91
Pipa, 236
place of origin, 103–107
place-settings, 88–89
planes, 266–270
  airlines, 234
  phrases and terms, 266–267, 269–270
  reserving flights, 267, 269–270
  Talkin' the Talk dialogues, 268–269
  taxes, 270
  travel agencies, 267
plastic surgery, 337
poder, 365
police, 293, 325, 329–330, 338
por quê, 111–112
Porto Alegre, 238

Porto Seguro, 235
Portuguese. See Brazilian Portuguese
possessives, 36, 108–111, 120, 248–250
Posto 9, 210
pousadas, 245–248
  amenities, 247
  hotels vs., 245
  registration, 246–247
  reservations, 245–246
pra, 356
Praia do Forte, 235
praticar, 302–303
  present tense, 302–303
  usage examples, 303
preferir, 303–304
  present tense, 303
  Talkin' the Talk dialogues, 306
  usage examples, 304
prepositions, 117–118
procurar, 285, 304–305
  present tense, 305
  Talkin' the Talk dialogues, 306
  usage examples, 305
professions, 196–197
pronouns, 28–30
  gender, 27–29
  neutral, 29
  plural, 27, 29
  Talkin' the Talk dialogues, 45, 55–56
pular, 316

Q

q, 12
qual, 111–112
quando, 66, 111–112
quanto, 111–112
quem, 111–112
Quer? 126
querer
  future tense, 365
  past tense, 365
  present tense, 126, 365
  using in restaurants, 126–127

R

r, 12, 16–17
rainforest, 209, 216–218
  accessing, 216–217
  activities, 217
  biodiversity, 217–218
reáis, 62, 253, 257–258
recados, 181–182
Recife
  Carnaval, 310, 315, 318–320
  music, 320
  visiting, 236
recreation, 209–223
  art, 164–165
  asking people what they like to do, 219–221
  beaches, 210–216
  biodiversity, 217–218
  dating, 168–169
  invitations, 158–159
  movies, 165–166, 168
  music, 160–164
  planning, 157–160
  questions, 159–160
  rainforest, 216–217
  sightseeing and going out, 157–172
  sporting events, 293–308
  sports, 219–220
Rede Globo, 348
redes, 142, 151
regions, 235–239
  Central-West, 236
  North, 235
  Northeast, 235–236
  South, 238–239
  Southeast, 237–238
renting
  apartments, 81
  cars, 275–277
restaurantes à quilo, 86, 124
restaurants and eating out, 121–135
  bars, 132
  beach food vendors, 212
  breakfast, 85–86
  churrascarias, 132–133

classic foods, 121–123
desserts, 128–129
dinner, 87–88
drinks, 131–132
expressions, 128
extras to ask for, 127
ingredients, 127–128
lunch, 86–87
menus, 124–126
ordering and eating meals, 126–127
ordering and enjoying meals, 126–128
sporting event concessions, 298–299
Talkin' the Talk dialogues, 105–106, 129–130, 306
tipping, 129
types of eateries, 123–124
utensils and place-settings, 88–89
vegetarians, 125, 133
verbs, 133–135
virus precautions, 124
reto, 289
ride-hailing apps, 274–275
Rio Amazonas, 217, 235, 331
Rio de Janeiro. *See also names of specific sights in Rio*
  art, 164
  banks, 256
  beaches, 210, 213–214, 220
  business, 195
  Carnaval, 310–313
  crime, 210, 325–327
  getting around, 282
  juice bars, 131
  name of, 238
  newspapers, 345
  parking, 277
  police, 325, 329
  regional accent, 9, 21
  soccer, 294
  transportation, 265, 274
  visiting, 237–238
  weather, 228–229
Rio Grande do Norte, 214–215, 236
Rio Grande do Sul
  regional accent, 22
  visiting, 238
  weather, 228

Rio Negro
  tropical illnesses, 331
  visiting, 217
Rio Solimões, 217
Rio Tietê, 219
robbery, 326–330
  asking for help, 328–329
  how to react, 327–328
  perspective, 327
  police, 329–330
roots, 11
rr, 16

S

s, 12, 17
Sabe? 355
saber, 366
safety. *See* emergencies
sair, 279–280
  future tense, 366
  past tense, 280, 366
  present tense, 280, 366
  usage examples, 280
sala de estar, 78
sala de jantar, 85
salespeople, 142, 144, 147–148
Salgueiro, 312
Salvador, 9, 151
  Carnaval, 310, 314–317
  crime, 326
  music, 346
  visiting, 235
samba, 163, 311, 320–321, 346. *See also* Carnaval
sambódromos, 131, 311
sanduíches na chapa, 122
sanfonas, 162
Santa Catarina, 132, 214, 239
são, 30, 66–67
São Luis, 236
São Paulo (city), 9
  art, 164
  bars, 256
  beaches, 214

business, 195
city life, 80
crime, 327
food, 87
getting around, 265–266, 281–283
immigrants, 119, 125
mosquitos, 217, 331
newspapers, 345
parking, 277
soccer, 293–294, 300
transportation, 274
visiting, 237–238
weather, 228
São Paulo (state), 10
  beaches, 238
  regional accent, 21
  soccer, 294
  wildlife, 219
São Tomé das Letras, 238
São Tomé e Príncipe, 10
Saramago, José, 9
sarongs, 152, 211
se liga, 97, 180
seasons, 228
Senhor, 43–44
Senhora, 43–44
senhorita, 44
sentence construction, 30–31
ser, 46–51
  adjectives, 48–49
  estar vs., 46
  future tense, 366
  past tense, 366
  present tense, 3, 47, 366
  Talkin' the Talk dialogues, 49–50
  usage examples, 47–48
Serra Gaúcha, 238
sertanejo, 346
seu/seus, 108–111, 119
shopping, 141–142
  making purchases, 260
  markets, 135–139
    outdoor markets, 136–137, 141–142, 153
    practical items, 136

shopping *(continued)*
   produce, 136–137
   supermarkets, 135–136
  negotiating, 153
  prices, 258
  receipts, 260
  souvenirs, 151–153
  Talkin' the Talk dialogues, 73–74, 138–139, 147–148, 150, 261–262
sightseeing and going out, 157–172. *See also* recreation
  art, 164–165
  cover charges, 160
  dating, 168–169, 344–345
  Fun & Games activities, 172
  invitations, 158–159
  making arrangements over the phone, 183
  movies, 165–166, 168, 347–348
  music, 160–164, 346–347
  planning, 157–160
  questions, 159–160
sim, 93
singing, 163–164
slang, 22, 97, 180, 254, 283, 349–352
sleep and waking up, 82–83
small talk, 103–120
  connector words, 117–118
  contact information, 118–119
  family connections, 107–108
  past tense, 112–116
  place of origin, 103–107
  possessives, 108–111
  "save me!" phrases, 118
  who, what, and where, 111–112
sobremesas, 128–129
sobrenomes, 42–43
soccer, 293–301
  buying tickets, 295–296
  cheering, 300
  concessions, 298–299
  finding seats, 297–298
  Fun & Games activities, 308
  phrases and terms, 295
  Talkin' the Talk dialogues, 296–297
  teams, 294

social media, 190–193
  feelings, 192–193
  reactions, 193
sombrinhas, 212
sonhos, 83
sono, 83
sotaques, 11, 97, 118, 177
souvenirs, 151–153
sporting events, 293–308
  ganhar, 304
  jogar, 301–302
  perder, 304
  praticar, 302–303
  preferir, 303–304
  procurar, 304–305
  soccer, 293–301
   buying tickets, 295–296
   cheering, 300
   concessions, 298–299
   finding seats, 297–298
   phrases and terms, 295
   teams, 294
  sport-related words, 219–220
stock market, 195
stoves, 79
sua/suas, 108–110
Submarino, 346
suco, 131
sungas, 211, 233
sunscreen, 234
supermarkets, 135–136

T

t, 12, 17
tá, 354
tablets, 191–192
Talkin' the Talk dialogues
  air travel, 268–269
  asking people what they like to do, 33, 221–222
  back from vacation, 115–116
  beaches, 213–216
  business, 98–99, 178
  café, 49–50, 55–56
  Carnaval, 313, 317–318

churrascaria, 105–106
dating, 200–201
dining, 105–106, 129–130, 306
directions, 286–287
distance, 283–284
doctor, 336–337
events, 70–71
exchanging money, 255–256
flirting, 170–171
gostar, 115–116
hotel concierge, 70–71
ir, 115–116, 243–244
movies, 166–167
music, 188–189
outdoor market, 73–74, 138–139
overview, ser
preferir, 306
procurar, 306
pronouns, 45, 55–56
restaurant bill, 129–130
salespeople, 147–148
school, 243–244
ser, 49–50
shopping, 73–74, 138–139, 147–148, 150, 261–262
soccer, 296–297
taxis, 272–273
telephone, 94–95, 98–99, 175–176, 178
weather, 230–231, 239–240
tatus, 10
Taxi.Rio, 274
taxis, 271–273, 326
Tchau! 39, 57, 93
te, 37
telephone, 92–98, 172–186
  business calls, 202–203
  communication apps, 184–186
  emojis, 194
  getting used to language, 97–98, 177
  international calls, 93, 175
  leaving messages, 181–182
  ligar, 96–97, 179–180
  making arrangements, 183
  making calls, 92–94, 173–174
  Talkin' the Talk dialogues, 94–95, 98–99, 175–176, 178

telling someone to call you, 180–181
  texting, 184–185
Tem trocado? 257
ter, 125–126, 366
texting, 184–185
  abbreviations, 186
  checking in, 184
  Zap (WhatsApp), 185
tilde, 19
time
  dates, 71–72
  Fun & Games activities, 75
  past tense, 114
  telling time, 66–67
tipping
  restaurants, 129
  taxis, 272
tô, 356
toalete, 84
tocar, 161–162
  musical instruments, 162
  present tense, 161
todo mundo, 57
tomar
  breakfast, 85
  drinking, 135
trabalhar, 199
Trancoso, 235
transportation, 265–291
  buses, 270–271
  car rentals, 275–277
  chegar, 278–279
  cities, 281–290
  directions, 285–289
  distance, 283
  esperar, 281
  Fun & Games activities, 291
  here and there, 290
  locations, 288–289
  modes of, 265–266
  phrases and terms, 265–266, 278–281
  planes, 266–270
  ride-hailing apps, 274–275
  sair, 279–280
  taxis, 271–273

travel agencies, 254, 267, 275, 288, 311

tropical illnesses, 331–332

Tudo bem? 40–41

Tudo bom? 39–41

Tudo ótimo! 41

Tupi-Guarani, 10

Twitter, 190

U

u, 12, 20

Uba-Chuva, 10

Ubatuba, 10

Uber, 271, 274

um/uma/uns/umas, 28

utensils and place-settings, 88–89

V

v, 12

vaccination, 124, 232–233, 270, 330–331

vai, 30

valeu, 352

vatapá, 122

vegetarians, 125, 133

Veloso, Caetano, 316

ver, 366

verbs, 30–35. *See also specific verbs*

  -ar verbs, 31–32

    commands, 287

    future tense, 359

    past tense, 112–113, 359

    present tense, 32, 359

  conjugation, 31–35

  -er verbs, 31, 34–35

    commands, 287

    future tense, 359

    past tense, 359

    present tense, 34, 359

  -ir verbs, 31, 34–35

    commands, 287

    future tense, 360

    past tense, 360

    present tense, 34, 360

  irregular, 363–367

  order of in tables, 2–3

  repeating in answer to questions, 262

viajar, 242

vir, 366

visas, 232

vitaminas, 90, 112, 131

você/vocês, 28, 44, 355

voltar, 362–363

W

w, 13, 18

water, 79, 331–332

weather, 227–229

  Talkin' the Talk dialogues, 230–231, 239–240

what, 111–112

WhatsApp (Zap), 185

where, 111–112

who, 111–112

Words to Know blackboards, 3, 33, 46, 51, 57, 71, 74, 95, 99, 107, 116, 130–131, 139, 148, 151, 167, 170–171, 176, 178, 189, 201, 214, 216, 221–222, 231, 240, 244, 256, 262, 269, 274, 284, 287, 297, 307, 314, 318, 336–337

World Cup, 293, 297

X

x, 13, 18

Y

y, 13

Z

z, 13

Zap (WhatsApp), 185

Zona Sul, 210, 282

About the Author

Karen Jacobson-Sive (formerly Keller) is a journalist who lived and worked in São Paulo, Brazil, for three years as a business reporter. Before moving to Brazil, the California native, who has also lived in Spain, spent a couple of years teaching Spanish for a foreign language education website in New York City. Jacobson-Sive is a published Brazil travel guide writer. She spent many years working as a newspaper reporter for American newspapers in New Jersey and New York. She currently lives with her husband and two children in the Boston area, where she is a freelance journalist/writer. She holds a master's degree in Journalism from Columbia University's Graduate School of Journalism.

Dedication

To my dear non-Brazilian friends from the São Paulo days, for our chuckles over the **maravilha** that is Brazilian Portuguese

Author's Acknowledgments

I'd like to extend my profound thanks to the editors at Wiley who helped me through the writing process: Paul Levesque and Christy Pingleton. My gratitude also extends to my technical editor — Nola Senna (MA, MBA, Director, Portuguese Language and Brazilian Studies Program, University of Illinois at Urbana-Champaign) for ensuring that I don't accidentally steer people wrong with the information I provide in this book.

I must also thank my Columbia University Graduate School of Journalism professor Tim Harper for putting me in touch with my literary agent for the book, Jessica Faust. Jessica, thanks for putting good faith in me.

Next, my warmest gratitude goes out to my former boss in Brazil, Matthew Cowley. Your job offer made my Brazilian adventure possible, and you gave me my very first Portuguese lessons. I still remember sitting in my office in New York and talking with you in Brazil over the phone before we met. "Rodrigo has an 'h' sound at the beginning," you said. That was my first glimpse of the language that would soon mesmerize me.

Now for those non-Brazilian friends I dedicate this book to: Ivan, Mario, Ainhoa, Anna, Diego, Andrea, Juan, Sophia, and Marisol. The sharing of our perspectives on life in Brazil and on that **língua esquisita** is the stuff of my best memories. Thanks, too, to the Brazilian who always helped set us straight. Dayanne Mikevis, you became my closest Brazilian confidante.

Chloe, thanks for all the sensible advice you've ever given me and for inspiring my first trips abroad. Jenny, you're my linguistic soul mate and the best person ever for last-minute queries on Portuguese. **Yolanda, si no fuera por ti y tu obsesión sobre Brasil, jamás hubiera ido.**

Finally, to my family: I'm not that crazy, after all. After having melted away into the Southern Hemisphere, I came back. And Mom: My open mind, curiosity, and word-wonder all stem from you. Thank you, all!

Publisher's Acknowledgments

Acquisitions Editor: Kelsey Baird
Senior Project Editor: Paul Levesque
Copy Editor: Christy Pingleton
Tech Editor: Nola Senna

Production Editor: Pradesh Kumar
Cover Image: © Gonzalo Azumendi/Getty Images

Leverage the power

Dummies is the global leader in the reference category and one of the most trusted and highly regarded brands in the world. No longer just focused on books, customers now have access to the dummies content they need in the format they want. Together we'll craft a solution that engages your customers, stands out from the competition, and helps you meet your goals.

Advertising & Sponsorships

Connect with an engaged audience on a powerful multimedia site, and position your message alongside expert how-to content. Dummies.com is a one-stop shop for free, online information and know-how curated by a team of experts.

- Targeted ads
- Video
- Email Marketing
- Microsites
- Sweepstakes sponsorship

20 MILLION
PAGE VIEWS
EVERY SINGLE MONTH

15 MILLION
UNIQUE
VISITORS PER MONTH

43%
OF ALL VISITORS
ACCESS THE SITE
VIA THEIR MOBILE DEVICES

700,000 NEWSLETTER
SUBSCRIPTION
TO THE INBOXES OF
300,000 UNIQUE INDIVIDUALS EVERY WEEK

# of dummies

Custom Publishing

Reach a global audience in any language by creating a solution that will differentiate you from competitors, amplify your message, and encourage customers to make a buying decision.

- Apps
- Books
- eBooks
- Video
- Audio
- Webinars

Brand Licensing & Content

Leverage the strength of the world's most popular reference brand to reach new audiences and channels of distribution.

For more information, visit dummies.com/biz

ad

PERSONAL ENRICHMENT

9781119187790
USA $26.00
CAN $31.99
UK £19.99

9781119179030
USA $21.99
CAN $25.99
UK £16.99

9781119293354
USA $24.99
CAN $29.99
UK £17.99

9781119293347
USA $22.99
CAN $27.99
UK £16.99

9781119310068
USA $22.99
CAN $27.99
UK £16.99

9781119235606
USA $24.99
CAN $29.99
UK £17.99

9781119251163
USA $24.99
CAN $29.99
UK £17.99

9781119235491
USA $26.99
CAN $31.99
UK £19.99

9781119279952
USA $24.99
CAN $29.99
UK £17.99

9781119283133
USA $24.99
CAN $29.99
UK £17.99

9781119287117
USA $24.99
CAN $29.99
UK £16.99

9781119130246
USA $22.99
CAN $27.99
UK £16.99

PROFESSIONAL DEVELOPMENT

9781119311041
USA $24.99
CAN $29.99
UK £17.99

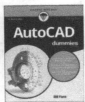
9781119255796
USA $39.99
CAN $47.99
UK £27.99

9781119293439
USA $26.99
CAN $31.99
UK £19.99

9781119281467
USA $26.99
CAN $31.99
UK £19.99

9781119280651
USA $29.99
CAN $35.99
UK £21.99

9781119251132
USA $24.99
CAN $29.99
UK £17.99

9781119310563
USA $34.00
CAN $41.99
UK £24.99

9781119181705
USA $29.99
CAN $35.99
UK £21.99

9781119263593
USA $26.99
CAN $31.99
UK £19.99

9781119257769
USA $29.99
CAN $35.99
UK £21.99

9781119293477
USA $26.99
CAN $31.99
UK £19.99

9781119265313
USA $24.99
CAN $29.99
UK £17.99

9781119239314
USA $29.99
CAN $35.99
UK £21.99

9781119293323
USA $29.99
CAN $35.99
UK £21.99

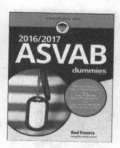

Small books for big imaginations

9781119177173
USA $9.99
CAN $9.99
UK £8.99

9781119177272
USA $9.99
CAN $9.99
UK £8.99

9781119177241
USA $9.99
CAN $9.99
UK £8.99

9781119177210
USA $9.99
CAN $9.99
UK £8.99

9781119262657
USA $9.99
CAN $9.99
UK £6.99

9781119291336
USA $9.99
CAN $9.99
UK £6.99

9781119233527
USA $9.99
CAN $9.99
UK £6.99

9781119291220
USA $9.99
CAN $9.99
UK £6.99

9781119177302
USA $9.99
CAN $9.99
UK £8.99

Unleash Their Creativity

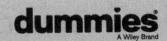